# THE ROMARE BEARDEN READER

ROBERT G. O'MEALLY / EDITOR

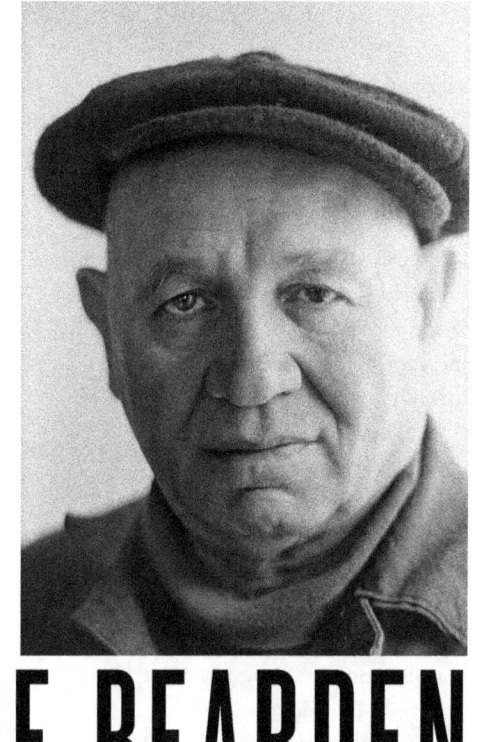

# THE
# ROMARE BEARDEN
# READER

*Duke University Press  Durham and London  2019*

Text designed by Mindy Hill. Cover designed by Courtney Leigh Baker
Typeset in Minion Pro by Westchester Publishing Services
Library of Congress Cataloging-in-Publication Data

Names: O'Meally, Robert G., [date] editor.
Title: The Romare Bearden reader / Robert G. O'Meally, editor.
Description: Durham : Duke University Press, 2018. |
Includes bibliographical references and index.
Identifiers: LCCN 2018047200 (print)
LCCN 2019000353 (ebook)
ISBN 9781478002260 (ebook)
ISBN 9781478000440 (hardcover)
ISBN 9781478000587 (pbk.)
Subjects: LCSH: Bearden, Romare, 1911–1988. |
Artists—United States—Biography. | African American
artists—Biography.
Classification: LCC N6537.B4 (ebook) | LCC N6537.B4 R665 2018  (print) |
DDC 709.2 [B]—dc23
LC record available at https://lccn.loc.gov/2018047200

FRONTISPIECE:  Romare Bearden. Photo by Frank Stewart

COVER ART:  *The Woodshed*, 1969. Romare Bearden. © VAGA at ARS, NY. Photograph © The Metropolitan Museum of Art. Courtesy of Art Resource, NY.

# CONTENTS

## PART III / REFLECTIONS ON A LAYERED LEGACY

# ACKNOWLEDGMENTS

No book is a solitary endeavor — thank goodness! This is particularly true of an anthology, with so many parts and pieces. Certainly this anthology has benefitted from the generosity of many persons, across several categories of expertise.

The Columbia University community has provided indispensable support. Warmest thanks to the many undergraduates and graduates whose questions and writings impacted me. Certain students and former students were exceptionally helpful: Nijah Cunningham, Claire Ittner, Elleza Kelley, Kaveh Landsverk, Aidan Levy, Emily J. Lordi, and Hiie Saumaa.

The Jazz Study Group at Columbia has been invaluable in this and all my intellectual pursuits: for this project I am especially grateful to Dwight Andrews, C. Daniel Dawson, Gerald Early, Brent Hayes Edwards, Krin Gabbard, Maxine Gordon, Farah Jasmine Griffin, Diedra Harris-Kelley, Vijay Iyer, Robin D. G. Kelley, George Lewis, Jason Moran, Fred C. Moten, Richard J. Powell, Helen Shannon, J. John Szwed, and Daniel Veneciano. All are present, here and there, in this work. So are Columbia colleagues and friends Marcellus Blount, Julie Davidson, Mary Gordon, Edward Mendelson, Richard Sacks, and George Stade, as well as colleagues and friends beyond Columbia: Joseph W. Reed, Phyllis Rose, Richard Slotkin, Alfred J. Smith, Edgar Sorrells-Adewale, Daniel Soutif, and Andrew Szegedy-Maszak.

Deep thanks to Columbia for granting leaves and sabbaticals over the years, and particularly for my current fellowship at the wonderful new Institute for Ideas and Imagination at Reid Hall, home of Columbia Global Center | Paris.

I am deeply indebted to the richly fertile Dorothy and Lewis B. Cullman Center of the New York Public Library, where I was a fellow in 2009–10. Special thanks to Akeel Bilgrami, Lauren Redniss, Jean Strouse, and Rosanna Warren.

Thanks to the Smithsonian Institution Traveling Exhibition Service, and particularly to Marquette Foley, for always supporting my work on Romare Bearden.

Thanks to all the contributors to this volume, especially to Toni Morrison, whose talk at Columbia University's Center for Jazz Studies conference on Romare Bearden in 2004 was generative for this volume.

Heartfelt thanks to the Romare Bearden Foundation, and especially to Diedra Harris-Kelley, for steadily supporting this project and for locating and granting use of so much Bearden material included here. Thanks to my friends at DC Moore Gallery, particularly to Bridget Moore, for steady guidance and support.

Particular thanks to John F. Callahan, literary executor of Ralph Ellison's estate, for permission to reprint the two Ellison pieces in this book. Thanks to Lewis P. Jones, literary executor of Albert Murray's estate, for his work in making available the essay included here, and to Paul Devlin for his guidance regarding the Murray material. I am appreciative of the permission granted by the estate of August Wilson to reprint his work in this volume, and of that granted by Elizabeth Alexander and Grant Hill for inclusion of her essay.

This book would not have been possible without the professionalism and patience of Livia Tenzer, to whom I will always be grateful. Particular thanks also to Yulanda McKenzie, my colleague at the Center for Jazz Studies at Columbia University.

Special thanks to my sons, Douglass and Gabriel Malone-O'Meally, and to Sylvie Fortin.

Robert G. O'Meally
December 2018
Paris

# "PRESSING ON LIFE UNTIL IT GAVE BACK SOMETHING IN KINSHIP"
## AN INTRODUCTORY ESSAY

*Robert G. O'Meally*

*As Bearden demonstrated here so powerfully, it is of the true artist's nature and mode of action to dominate all the world and time through technique and vision. His mission is to bring a new visual order into the world, and through his art he seeks to reset society's clock by imposing upon it his own method of defining the times.*
—Ralph Ellison, "The Art of Romare Bearden"

The modern black American artist Romare Bearden's most urgently pursued subject was that of first-person identity, or, one might say, first-person *identities*. What does it mean to be "modern"? "Black"? Or "American"? What does it mean to be an "artist"? *Who am I?* These were Bearden's touchstone questions. And then, across these and other categories: Who are *we?* And how, in this world where "trouble stretched above us, longer than the sky," as Bearden's friend the writer James Baldwin once put it, do we deploy our best talents?[1] To weigh these old/new line items, this introduction mines Bearden's own twice- and thrice-told tales—the ones he recounted most often in interviews and conversations—an abundance of which narrative gold is spun into this anthology's pages. Some of it I collected firsthand, as a witness to his story-telling sessions with friends and collaborators.[2] There's other precious metal in this book as well, collected by others and reflecting not only on who Bearden is, but also on who Americans are, and trying to establish new ways of seeing ourselves and defining our times.

Bearden's most profound terms for order reside, as we shall see, in the forms of his art itself, and particularly in the U.S. black/global elements of a Bearden collage—its cut and sometimes torn layers and fragments of history flitting and flashing and "pressing upon life until it gives back something in kinship."[3] We are a fractured and fragile people, we black and white Americans—and we humans—in search of ways to reassemble ourselves to be stronger and more beautiful than before. Seeking ways to heal ourselves and one another. To do more than merely survive and tolerate one another: to persevere together, to flourish as one people who, with all our differences, are more alike than unalike.

Who, then, was Romare Bearden, and how does he fit into the ongoing story of modern art history?[4] Born in Charlotte, North Carolina, in 1911, Howard Romare Bearden was a painter, collagist, and printmaker whose name itself hints at important parts of his story. He rarely used "Howard," which he inherited from his father, but introduced himself as Romy ("*ROH*-mee") or Romare ("*ROH*-mery")—the middle name coming from a family friend, Fred Romare. (The artist's wife, with Franco-Caribbean roots, sometimes called him "*Roh-MARR*," with the French *rr*'s rolling). Indeed the artist started and remained a "roaming" individual, physically speaking and in his imagination, body and soul. In 1914 he moved with his parents from Charlotte to Harlem, where he attended Public School 5. When Romare was seven he moved with his parents to Saskatchewan, Canada, where his father had found work on railroad lines connecting Alberta and Moose Jaw; from Canada it was back to Harlem, where the family settled permanently, with only-child Bearden spending extended periods of time with relatives in Pittsburgh, Pennsylvania; Lutherville, Maryland; and, most often, back and forth to Charlotte, North Carolina.

What this means is that Bearden was a person on the move who often told interviewers that he "liked journeying things." Birds, bridges, waterways, boats, and particularly trains figure throughout his oeuvre. He also frequently depicts shape-shifting spirit-travelers, most often women, posted at water- or forest-edge—crossroads between this and other worlds. Each of his childhood moves and stops contains a story of first artistic inspirations—the most persistent one, retold here by the artist and then re-retold in the shimmering fictional version by John Edgar Wideman (included in this volume), is of the summer in Pittsburgh when a neighborhood pal named Eugene Bailey taught twelve-year-old Romare how to draw the scenes Eugene secretly eyed through the floorboards of the whorehouse where his mom turned tricks.[5] Often when Bearden spoke of Eugene, who suffered from infantile paralysis, he would mention that the youngster inspired him and "might have been another Lautrec." Of course, it is Bearden himself whose many artistic representations of Harlem of the 1960s and 1970s reveal traces of the influence of Henri de Toulouse-Lautrec's racy Paris. But those drawings of little Eugene are part of Bearden's story, too.

It is significant that Bearden's first publicly presented works were humorous and political cartoons done for college magazines, followed by stark political satires drawn for such black publications as the *Crisis, Opportunity,* and the *Afro-American.* At its best, Bearden's mature painting retained the power of the expedient lines of the cartoon figure and scene (elsewhere, truth be told, this quick work could devolve into cartoon simplicity at its worst). Once he chooses painting (not cartooning) as a profession—sometime in the college years—influences from a global caravan of canonical painters abound.[6] His teacher at the Art Students League, the German-born New Objectivity artist George Grosz, was a profound influence on Bearden's earliest paintings and drawings. Another League teacher, Carl Holty, would collaborate with Bearden on one of the key books in Bearden studies, *The Painter's Mind: A Study of the Relations of Structure and Space in Painting* (1969). Inspired by both the Mexican and the WPA muralists of the 1930s and 1940s, Bearden extended the lessons of cartooning and of Grosz-style satire into frames of broader and broader implication. (See Bearden's public art works of the 1960s, 1970s, and 1980s commissioned by the cities of New York, Baltimore, Pittsburgh, and Berkeley, among others.[7]) From the beginning, this artist aimed to create works that had meaning at first sight.

The influence on Bearden of canonical European modernism, particularly the experiments of Picasso with Cubist shapes and spaces and of Matisse with color, is profound and enduring. Explorations into the Cubists' aesthetic sources and practices led him in many fruitful directions, most importantly, Chinese ink-wash painting and calligraphy for its particular styles of brushwork and its leaving "open corners" where the eye could rest and gain perspective, and where, Bearden said, the viewer could participate in the creation of meaning.[8] Bearden's early studies introduced him to certain Dutch Masters, whose windows, doors, and other interior boxes presented a lifetime of homework, as Bearden's journals and forthcoming *catalogue raisonné* clearly show. Moderns European and American (including African American), along with leading theorists of the Harlem Renaissance, also prompted Bearden's lifelong search for ways to incorporate African aesthetics into his work. (In this volume, see "Encounters with African Art" and the essay by Bearden and Harry Henderson on aspects of the Harlem Renaissance.) How might Bearden, particularly as an African American, seek the most profound revelations from that continent's art traditions without giving in to the "primitivist" uses of Africa as raw material (*sans histoire*) or as a simplified foil against which to regard Europe or the United States? How to see African art on its own terms, not just as geometry for Euro-modernization? And what would define a specifically *African American* aesthetic?

One may track Bearden's career from relatively realistic figurative painting of the 1930s to explicitly Picasso-like experiments in evocatively spare-line drawing and Cubistic design to his often maplike Abstract Expressionist canvases done from the early 1950s until about 1964. In the early 1960s Bearden's work underwent a sea change as he discovered and nurtured the media for which he now is best known: collage and printmaking.[9] During this last quadrant of his career (the final years, of mastery, are emphasized in Myron Schwartzman's essay for this volume), one sees the fullness of Bearden's achievement as an artist who loves bold color and layered mixes of media: cutout colored papers painted and affixed to other surfaces, also sometimes painted and overlain, added and torn away, one piece after another. At a Bearden retrospective show at the Whitney Museum in 2004, I asked the painter William T. Williams to help me see, in a Bearden collage, where the brushwork left off and the addition of colored papers and other materials began. We both stared at the work—layered, torn, painted over, cut. (A guard eyed us as we moved closer and closer to the collage.) Then Williams stepped back and looked at me. "Romy doesn't want us to know that," he said.

One common thread, from the cartoon work to the end, is Bearden's impulse to vivid statement—often with the richness of perspective by incongruity—in the form of narration. Taken as a whole, Bearden's works, even when "Untitled," have tales to tell, one work to another. Almost always Bearden's desire is to retell the epic story—possibly the world's best-known story of human struggle against injustice—of being black in the United States: to "[bring] his art to bear upon the task (never so urgent as now) of defining Negro American identity, of pressing its claims for recognition and for justice."[10] As these ringing words on Bearden by his friend the novelist Ralph Ellison (who is represented by two important essays in this volume) imply, Bearden's is the opposite of a local-color project. In his continuing engagement with the polis—with the broadest possible conception of the political/community sphere—Bearden hitched his artistic wagon to stories arching across the horizon. His aim was to frame the U.S. black story in terms of the Bible (a source throughout his career, in work after work), Homer's *Iliad* and then (years later) the *Odyssey*, Lorca's bullfight drama, Derek Walcott's Caribbean poetry, and the blues and jazz as tragicomic poetry. Telling his personal history in a series of collages done in response to Calvin Tomkins's superb *New Yorker* profile (included in this volume)—which as a nod to Tomkins the artist also called "Profiles" (part I and part II)—Bearden worked with the novelist Albert Murray, who helped with titles and with the sentence or two accompanying each work (see Plate 1, *Artist with Painting and Model*; also figs. 1–3, 21, 23, 34). (One may read Murray's fiction and monographs on the blues as indices to Bearden's picture narratives, especially after 1960.) He also created several illustrated books for children (see Robert B. Stepto's essay in this volume.) At times his oils and works on paper dance and swim with words, drawn in paint or assembled in letters cut out one by one: these images are rich with reference to the vast world of art and, as jazz musicians put it, were *sayin something!*

In fact, improvisation is another vital through-line in Bearden's oeuvre: one line, color, or shape leading, in sometimes quite surprising ways, to another, in the manner of a great jazz soloist like Charlie Parker, who improvised, said the writer Stanley Crouch, "at the tempo of emergency."[11] One feels in Bearden the fresh spirit of exploration and discovery à la Parker: the will to capture the zest of new invention, tone by tone, as the story unfolds.

Part I of the present volume offers an encounter with Bearden's life and times: the *New Yorker* profile by Tomkins and an extensive interview of Bearden for the Smithsonian's Archives of American Art. Part II is the first gathering of this artist's most significant statements about art: indispensable essays and book chapters, speeches, reviews, and journal entries. His most far-reaching and definitive essay, "Rectangular Structures in My Montage Paintings" (1969), composed with the assistance of Murray, is here.[12] So is his detailed discussion on how he takes the "pulses" of African art and learns to use African masking in particular—an important though little-known work ("Encounters with African Art"). Gathered together, this selection of Bearden's writing from the late 1930s through the late 1970s offers a set of autobiographical notes granting rare insight into the artist's aesthetic values and practices. The texts register the shifts, as well as the overlapping planes, from Bearden's Left political and humorous cartooning of the 1930s through his (still *engagé*) mid- to late-century works on canvas and mixed-media collages. Very alive on the page, these written and transcribed words by the artist have much to teach about how to read modern black American art, and indeed any art, in our time. And again: much to teach as well about who we are as members of a collage of a human family, what time it is, and what to do about it.

Part III gathers some of the strongest texts ever written *about* Bearden. These particular works were chosen because of their broad interdisciplinary thrust. Here you'll find essays by art historians systematically tracking Bearden's stylistic trajectory, particularly the development of his work through Cubism and

Abstract Expressionism—modes he never completely abandoned—toward his signature printmaking and collage. Yet most of the essays in this section are written by novelists and poets, lending this part of the book a bias that is unmistakably *literary*. How apt that in response to Bearden's paintings, where so often scenes and characters are drawn from literature, these writers return the favor in flying word-colors! What this means is that in their heft and quickness of signification, and in artistic qualities so difficult to put into words, these literary responses to Bearden stand up to his paintings. Note, for example, the sinewy language of playwright August Wilson, who recalls, in the essay included here, making his way to the artist's apartment on New York's Canal Street, but then failing to muster what it took to knock on the man's door—Bearden's art had been so profound a guide for him:

> I have never looked back from that moment when I first encountered his art. He showed me a doorway. A road marked with signposts, with sharp and sure direction, charting a path through what D. H. Lawrence called the "dark forest of the soul." I called to my courage and entered the world of Romare Bearden and found a world made in my image. A world of flesh and muscle and blood and bone and fire. A world made of scraps of paper, of line and mass and form and shape and color, and all the melding of grace and birds and trains and guitars and women bathing and men with huge hands and hearts, pressing on life until it gave back something in kinship.[13]

In several cases, these writers create a practical vocabulary to spell out ways of working that they share with Bearden and with visual artists in general, and perhaps with all artists. All require *structure, color, and rhythm*, says Toni Morrison.[14] Put her triad alongside Bearden's assertion that all painting is "putting something over something else."[15] Is not all art a matter of placing one thing over the other (in the case of the writer, placing many-storied words and storylines one over the other): of collage-like layering? Put this query alongside Bearden's declaration that he learned much about the art of painting from jazz musicians, improvising layer on layer of rhythm and tune over the chord changes of a blues melody or atop a popular song like Gershwin's "I Got Rhythm." Jazz musicians have coined a wonderful phrase for improvisations on this Gershwin standard: "playing the 'Rhythm changes.'" I like to think of Bearden, too, as playing "Rhythm changes." (See Albert Murray's essay on Bearden and jazz in this volume.)

This part of the book has something to do, as well, with questions of influence and translation, not only from painter to painter but from painter to writer, writer to painter, from painter and writer to musician—back and forth. One wonders if Brent Hayes Edwards is not right that *all* true works of art cry out for translation into other languages, including into the terms of other artistic forms.[16] Bearden belongs in the ranks of leading modern artists who translated literature and music into visual art. And how many writers, not just August Wilson, have taken Bearden and other painters as models for poetry and fiction?

Taking the advice of his friend Stuart Davis, whose jazz paintings Bearden much admired, Bearden studied masters of jazz whose additions, subtractions, and other rearrangements of received material, note-by-note and chord-by-chord, had made Davis think of painting as playing the intervals of a piano keyboard in the tradition of Earl Hines, in particular. "Interval" is a key word for Bearden studies: *the spaces between.* Miles Davis said, "It's not the notes you play, it's the notes you don't play.... Play what's not there." Bearden listened closely to what was there and not there in the work of jazz keyboardists as well as horn players and singers who could pronounce one note that implied several others; and who, in the cases of Louis Armstrong and Thelonious Monk, could make a single note *swing.* So many of Bearden's rhythmically placed images of singers and horn players, keyboardists and keyboards—some of them urban row-house keyboards—suggest jazz rhythms and layers: John Coltrane-like sheets of sound on canvas.[17]

By the early 1960s Bearden began to arrange his rectangular shapes in compositions that were strongly influenced by the Cubists and Dutch Masters Pieter de Hooch and Johannes Vermeer, in a way that gave his work more *movement*—the element he said was missing in the Europeans' paintings. As models for his jazz series, the Europeans offered "a classic quality to rival the Greeks," Bearden told an interviewer. But the jazz works forming in his mind could not be "as static as theirs." "I listened to jazz," Bearden continued, "and just drew. I did this for three months or so, just trying to pick up these rhythms.... By turning my rectangles from here to here, you make certain interval relationships which give a sense of movement."[18] Bearden's acute- and oblique-angle tilting of these rectangular boxes within his paintings gave them something of what the artist considered jazz's "speed." The Harlem painter did not want a Cubism that was too square!

This jazz analogy makes us wonder how August Wilson's plays or Ralph Ellison's fictions may also be jazzlike in their shapes, spaces, and colored improvisations—and what, as these influences circle around, Bearden learned from writers about jazz. How can literary works, which like paintings may be regarded as fixed on silent two-dimensional surfaces, nonetheless make a kind of music? (Ellison's phrase for his technique for writing across the art forms is "planned dislocation of the senses."[19] Toni Morrison says she takes pains to use language that makes her readers literally move their lips and sound out her words aloud while reading.[20]) How to make literature speak and move? How to give it an improvised musical quality? The jazz composer/reed master Henry Threadgill calls literally *all* art improvisatory.[21] When, he asks, are Beethoven's first drafts of a sonata's score not like Charlie Parker's first takes on an on-the-spot blues composition like "Parker's Mood"? When not like the successive canvases (or layers on canvas) of a painter? With such questions ringing in the air (coloring it and, to borrow a term from Thelonious Monk, "rhythm-a-ning" it), Part III explores what Morrison terms the "liquid" spaces where the art forms melt, meet, and flow together.[22] It was the search for better understanding of this liquid space that informed my choosing so many literary writers to comment on this highly literary and musical painter.

"*Improvisation*," said Bearden's friend Murray, "*is the ultimate (i.e., heroic) endowment*... even as flexibility or the ability to swing (or to perform with grace under pressure) is the key to that unique competence which generates the self-reliance and thus the charisma of the hero."[23] Consider how many of the most heroic characters in Bearden's paintings, figures male and female, from this or some other world, are improvisers of the first degree. Consider his many Billie Holidays, Louis Armstrongs, Duke Ellingtons, Charlie Parkers. Or his many drop-dead beautiful Circes, as well as conjure women, Obeah women, and other supernaturals—all gifted with the peculiar strength and skill of the improvising artist to turn the world around (see the essays herein by Rachel DeLue, Farah Jasmine Griffin, and Richard Powell). Routinely presenting such charismatic shape-shifters in his paintings, Bearden celebrated jazz as a model for the visual artist, while he developed ideas about improvisation required not only of Americans but also of citizens of the globe everywhere. What would it mean for the planet if more of us had the sense of self and community as one swinging band implied by the improvised music of top jazz musicians—whether in slow time or *at the tempo of emergency?*

Parts I and II of this anthology emphasize that for Bearden—as for many American artists black, white, brown, and beige—"the quest for identity" stands front and center. One is reminded of James Baldwin's definition of the layers of identity as loose robes "through which one's nakedness can always be felt."[24] Interview by interview, essay by essay, Bearden raises the question of what it means to "know thyself,"[25] to explore the planet from the hub of home and self. The question was connected directly with his art: "I didn't know what to paint," he says, over and over again, to his interlocutors.

Indeed, in public pronouncements, Bearden usually approached the question of identity in terms of finding his way as an *artist:* his search for subjects, perspectives, and techniques. His search, one might say, for artistic "ancestors."[26] But Bearden also would surprise listeners by broaching these big subjects from a side door with references to his career as a young *athlete*—an important aspect of the artist's identity that Bearden scholars almost never mention. In 1931–32 Bearden was the starting fullback on the football team at Boston University, where, during the spring seasons, he was also an ace pitcher on the freshman and later the varsity baseball teams. During those years, Bearden earned summer money on a professional baseball team called the Boston Colored Tigers, a Roxbury-based sandlot outfit that was good enough to challenge top-ranked Negro League teams when they passed through New England. Bearden smiled when telling about his close loss of a pitching duel against Satchel Paige, probably the Negro League's most famous star. An equally emphatic testimony of the artist's baseball prowess, and of the larger question of Bearden's layered identity, came in 1932 when Connie Mack, owner/manager of the Philadelphia Athletics (of the then whites-only Major Leagues), invited Bearden to join the team that had won World Series championships in 1929 and 1930 and the American League pennant in 1931. Coming fifteen years before Jackie Robinson's historical breakthrough of white baseball's color line in 1947, the only way to understand the offer by Mack, who even in 1947 was not a proponent of integrating pro baseball, is that Mack did not realize that Bearden, who was light-skinned, was African American. Seeing that he could join Mack's team only if he "passed for white," Bearden—whose family (his mother, the community leader Bessye J. Bearden, in particular) had been active in the black freedom movement all his life—declined. Who strove to add a complexly heroic (one might say a big league *athletic*) blackness to the modern project of painting? Bearden did. Who could have disappeared in the white world but *chose* to be African American? Bearden did.

Bearden frequently would speak of race and American identity by referring to such black ball-field practices as celebratory solo end-zone dances and high-fiving one's teammates—this latter black athlete's gesture of the 1950s and

1960s having become part of the lingua franca of contemporary athletes all over the world and nowadays of young people and even babies everywhere.[27] With their jagged changes of pace and dancelike running games, American sports themselves are "jazz-shaped," writes Ellison.[28] Above all it is Ellison who argues that if Americans could only become more conscious of their deeply shared national-family inheritances—many of them passed along via popular or vernacular culture—perhaps next (ethical/political) steps would follow: from consciousness to conscientiousness. Seeing the other in oneself, the self in the other.

These sports references shed new light on Bearden's paintings and his ways of making them. There's athleticism in Bearden's protagonists, male and female (and sometimes androgynous): the Lorca bullfighters and Homeric warriors but also the conjure women and Sirens, guitarists, and even Deep South gardeners—with their mighty hands. Those assisting the artist in the studio report that he would stick with a painting that was resisting him—Bearden often said that "the canvas was always saying no to me"—by insisting that he would "not let the painting win": *he* would win.[29] If in a given moment the color he wanted was not available, he would work with whatever color he had. Whether in visual art, sports, or music, "necessity," said the composer Muhal Richard Abrams, "is the mother of improvisation."[30] (The saxophonist Lester Young once revised the maxim to declare that "Necessity is a *mother*.")

Nor should we forget that Bearden was a child of the 1910s and 1920s, when as the Harlem Renaissance was taking shape every other black barbershop in the United States sported a famous photo of the black heavyweight champion Jack Johnson. Blacks who had never heard of Langston Hughes or W. E. B. Du Bois would know that a handsome, trash-talking black dandy named Johnson had knocked out one white man after another en route to world championship, the brown-skin southerner crossing the color line every time he stepped into a "white men only" boxing ring or even inside "the workout circle around the punching bag."[31] Level the playing fields, the example of black athletes proclaimed, and they could go toe-to-toe with anybody. Few athletes figure in Bearden's works (notable exceptions are his watercolor, gouache, and ink painting of boxers, circa 1952; a 1976 collage made for the Montreal Olympics; and a 1977 collage made for a *TV Guide* cover). But when he speaks about sports he knows what he's talking about, and very often the underlying subjects are the making of art and, yes, the complexities of *identity.* Like Jack Johnson, Bearden the former pitcher and fullback wanted to be the best at whatever he did; he wanted to win! Is not Bearden's highly competitive spirit akin to that of the contemporary African American artist Kerry James Marshall, who unabashedly compares his own desire and will to prepare to be the best with those of Muhammad Ali and Stephen Curry?[32]

Concerning identity, race, and American culture, Bearden routinely quoted the insights of Constance Rourke, the mid-century cultural historian also frequently cited by his close friends Ellison and Murray. To be an American, she argued, was to inherit three specific bundles of cultural traits: all Americans are part Yankee, part "Frontiersman" (including Native American), and part black.[33] With the blackness stirred into the American cultural mix (see Ellison's essay "What America Would Be Like Without Blacks"),[34] Americans at their best are not only masters of improvisation but also of masquerade, as well as the inheritors of other black practices and modes of self-presentation. Ironically it is the blacks, says Ellison, who serve as stubbornly undiscouragable guardians of the American Dream: who know the nation has not come close to living up to its promises, but who continue to challenge us all to make things right. You might say that among the many things blacks bring to American cultural life are the elusive qualities called (suggesting their own philosophical/political stances) *coolness* and *soul*. "The three figures [the Yankee, the Frontiersman, the African American] loomed large," says Rourke, "not because they represented any considerable numbers in the population, but because something in the nature of each induced an irresistible response. . . . Their comedy, their irreverent wisdom, their sudden changes and adroit adaptations, provided emblems for a pioneer people who required resilience as a prime trait. Comic triumph appeared in them all; the sense of triumph seemed a necessary mood in the new country." The spirit Rourke identifies as "comic" pervades American culture, including its literary culture. "Emerson had it in everything he wrote," she says. "Whitman had it, and was aware of the quality: it was that of improvisation. In one way or another every major American writer had shown its traces. . . . [Dickinson's poetry] has an abounding fresh intensity, a touch of conquering zeal, a true entrance into new provinces of verbal music."[35]

Bearden had it, too, this improviser's "abounding fresh intensity," an aspect of his Rourke/Ellison/Murray sense of American identity as substantially black. For all of them, Richard Wright's formula retained its measure of truth: "The Negro," wrote the author of *Native Son*, "is America's metaphor."[36]

Bearden expressed the mystery of a multicolored American/African American mix in painting after painting where the red-white-and-blue flies along-

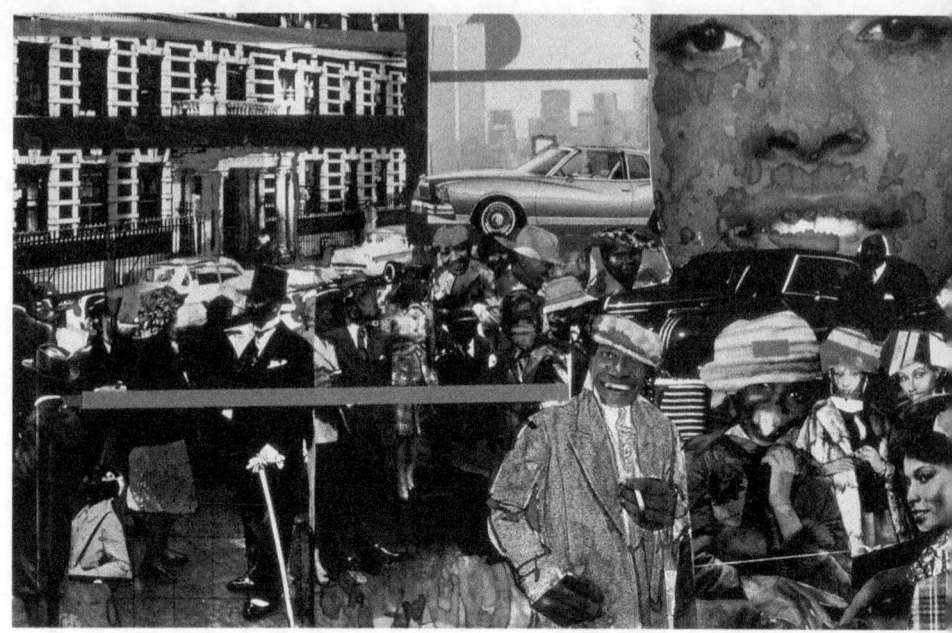

FIGURE 1 Romare Bearden, *Profile/Part II, The Thirties: I'm Slapping Seventh Avenue with the Sole of My Shoe*. Art © Romare Bearden Foundation/Licensed by VAGA, New York

side the red-black-and-green, neither set of colors eclipsing or contradicting the other. His Harlem collages expressed the excitement of that neighborhood when it was a cultural mecca (see fig. 1, *I'm Slapping Seventh Avenue with the Sole of My Shoe*) as well as the edginess of a neighborhood under siege: Harlem as metaphor, "the 'harlemness' of the national human predicament."[37] Turning the tables, Bearden also sought characters, scenes, and storylines from cultural storehouses marked "global" or "universal" to tell the broad story of black America. And so his Bible characters are black, brown, and beige. And so, in his *Odyssey* series, the hero's search for father, family, and home spell not only an ancient Greek quest but a contemporary black American one—the outcast group's search for an at-home feeling in the strangely hostile land of their birth. Accordingly, Bearden chose to make all the *Odyssey*'s characters, deadly temptresses and loyal wife along with monstrous killers and magical saviors, using the blackest bolts of paper he could find. How interesting, too, that in that series Bearden identifies most strongly not only with Circe the witch but also with others tempting and threatening Odysseus: the man-devouring Cyclops and even the vile killer Scylla. Bearden's quest for an American/African

American identity involves a robust quest for the other in the self, the self in the other, going beyond race, beyond even the human race, to include empathetic identification even with genuinely dangerous monsters.

Bearden sometimes explained the blackening of his Homeric characters in terms of audience: a black child in Alabama or Africa viewing his black translation of the work "might see the myth the way I did." Concerning his Africanizing the *Odyssey*, Bearden told an interviewer:

> After Odysseus leaves Circe, he has to go and see an old prophet in the netherworld who will tell him how to get back home. Circe had recommended that he see the prophet. So in that particular work I have Odysseus with a mask of a crocodile to protect him from the terror. He's going down into the land of the Shades. It would seem perfectly appropriate if this were down in Africa [that] he would have this kind of protection as a warrior. You say it's universal. It's universal to me in *this* way.[38]

In any case, "We all live in a mask," said Bearden. "We all have a hundred different identities. Sometimes a mask can be a truer indicator of a person than his true face."[39]

Before further exploring Bearden's long artistic range, let us unpack a few more of his anecdotes concerning the question of identity, these now with an emphasis not on sports but on self-discovery through the labor of making art—or trying to make art.[40] By far Bearden's most frequently told tale in this category is one set in the late 1930s.[41] He and his friend the writer Claude McKay were strolling through black Manhattan some time during the Great Depression. Like most people McKay had no money. Still, the novelist so valued his signed copy of George Grosz's volume of reproduced drawings and watercolors called *Ecce Homo* (a work that was also highly important to Bearden) that he (McKay) could not bear to sell the book. Walking near the Apollo Theater, Bearden and McKay heard the peremptory jangling of keys, the prostitute's signal of that era. "There she was," says Bearden, "the homeliest woman I ever saw in my life. 'Gentlemen, two dollars,' she said to us. And then 'A dollar' and then 'Fifty cents?' and then at last, *"Gentlemen please, just take me!"* Informing her that she was "in the wrong profession," Bearden directed the woman, whose name was Ida, to see his mother Bessye, whose community-mindedness and contacts extended all over Harlem, and beyond. Bessye Bearden did find Ida a job, and to thank Bearden and his mother, Ida cleaned his studio, which was upstairs in the Apollo, once a week.

During this period the brown paper on Bearden's easel remained blank week after week (as often happened in his artist-as-young-man stories). He was stuck for a subject to paint. "You told me *I* was in the wrong profession," said the woman, observing the blank paper. "Why don't you paint me?" She could tell by Bearden's expression what he was thinking. ("She was not exactly a beauty-contest winner" as he sometimes put it.) "I know what I am," she told him. "But when you can look at me and see something beautiful, maybe you'll be able to put something on that paper of yours." She stared at him. "That," says the artist, "was the most important lesson in art that I have ever received." In 1947 Bearden made this journal entry: "Rembrandt took beggars, draped them in exotic garments and painted them as kings. They were kings, but his greatness consists in the fact that you can see that they were also beggars."[42] The former streetwalker's challenge—one interpretation of which is that the true artist can see beauty and discern truths about the human family in absolutely anyone and everyone—"was a lesson I've never forgotten," said Bearden.

A related Bearden anecdote is set in 1950, when the artist was living in Paris.[43] At a Left Bank café across from Notre Dame, someone handed Bearden what he thought was a strong, bad-tasting French cigarette, hand-rolled. It turned out to be hashish. "I don't know how I got there," Bearden said, "but suddenly I found myself across the river, standing in front of the cathedral. And as I stood there I saw one of the angels step down from Notre Dame, and she began walking on the Seine, in the moonlight. And I thought, 'I'll paint that angel, walking on water.' Just then a lady of the evening appeared and said, 'Don't you want to come home with me?' And I said, 'No, I want to paint that angel on the water. I wonder what she's doing there.' And she said, 'You men are all alike. Those angels hold up that big church all day. Don't you think they get tired!? Don't you know she needs to take a rest!?' After that I never could paint that angel. The streetwalker had spoiled it for me!" Bearden said he never could paint at all while in Paris. There was just too much going on. But note that in this scene, frequently repeated by the artist, another workingwoman gives him a lesson that produces a kind of revelation. Whether in Paris or Harlem—America's "own homegrown version of Paris"[44]—great lessons in art could be taught not only by Picasso and Jacob Lawrence but by wise persons from all walks of life. One part of the lesson learned has to do with finding art-subjects in the world as it is, the world the artist knows best—all hashish-fueled fantasies notwithstanding!

Another story along these lines that Bearden liked to tell is set in the 1950s and features the artist and two box turtles called Abercrombie and Fitch, whose owner was leaving town and seeking new homes for his matching pets.[45] Abercrombie already had a new place to stay. "Well," said Bearden, "I thought, 'Maybe I'll paint the turtle,' so I took Fitch. Right away he disappeared. Turns out he bored into the mattress and hid there. I didn't want to paint him anyway!" Once again at a loss for a subject, Bearden had contemplated the turtle and recalled a conversation with the painter William Baziotes. "How do you decide what to paint?" Bearden had asked him. Baziotes said he'd had the same problem and solved it by asking himself what it was that he really liked. "I came up with goblets," he told Bearden, "wine goblets." He just loved their shape. "So he started painting them," said Bearden, "and everyone thought they were mountains and liked them very much. . . . I had run out of things to think about by this time, so I started to just paint remembrances of Charlotte, North Carolina, where I was born [see figs. 2, 3, *The Daybreak Express* and inscription]. When I finally did that, the turtle crawled out of the mattress, so I guess he must have liked what I was doing."[46] *What do you really like?* the artist asked himself.

Back in New York from his seven months in Paris, Bearden was still excited about his memories of the place, but confused about what to do next as an artist. He wanted to return to the City of Lights. How to get there? Bearden's studio had an old upright piano in the corner—maybe he could tap out a hit song that would buy him a ticket back to France. This effort produced modest success. His friend Billie Holiday was interested in one of his songs (evidently never recorded). Another, "Seabreeze," was recorded by Billy Eckstine and then picked up as an advertisement melody.[47] Still, one friend, Heinrich Blücher the philosopher/poet (then the husband of Hannah Arendt, also a friend of the artist), warned Bearden that he'd better get back to painting—that pursuing the secondary talent of songwriting could mean he'd "soon dissipate any meaningful ability I had and I'd never paint again."[48] It was during this period of straining to make song lyrics with a musician friend that Bearden became seriously ill. Sometime in 1953 he collapsed in the street and woke up in the psychiatric ward of Bellevue Hospital. "You blew a fuse," a doctor there told him.

Once the artist was pronounced fit to return home, his father came to pick him up. In interviews Bearden recalls walking down the hospital stairs and suddenly remembering that his old friend the Mexican artist Luis Arena had had a

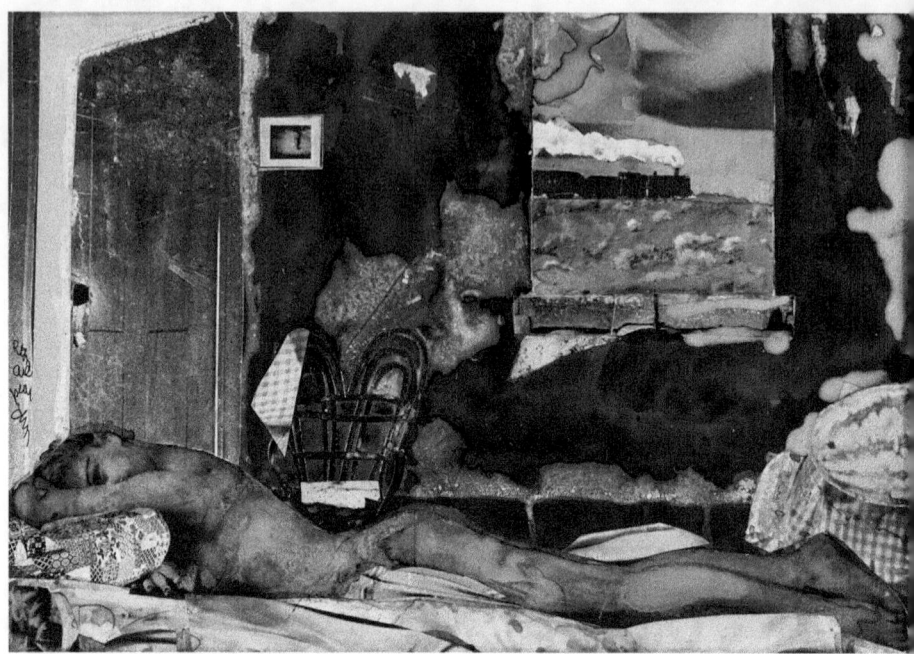

FIGURE 2 Romare Bearden, *Profile/Part I, The Twenties (Mecklenburg County): The Daybreak Express*, 1978. Collage on board, 10 1/4 × 14 7/8 in. (26 × 37.8 cm). Collection of Joseph McConnell. Art © Romare Bearden Foundation/Licensed by VAGA, New York

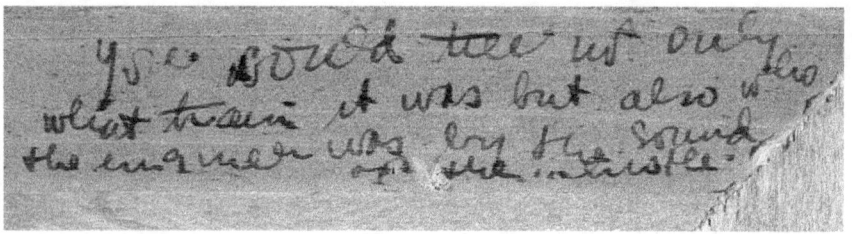

FIGURE 3 Romare Bearden, *The Daybreak Express*, inscription: You could tell not only what train it was but also who the engineer was by the sound of the whistle. © Romare Bearden Foundation/ Licensed by VAGA, New York

job with the WPA helping to create frescoes on that same hospital wall. "When you do a fresco you put wet plaster on the wall and you have to work into this wet plaster," said Bearden. "You can't let it dry. If you don't finish what the plasterer put down for the day, he has to knock all that down and put fresh plaster on because only in the drawing do the colors fuse and get into the wall." So the artist has to work with the plaster as it is put on, and as fast as possible. Bearden continued:

> Well, I came down and said to my father, "Gee, I was here before, in the 1930s. The fresco was over here. These people must have painted over it." I went to the wall and was trying to prove it to him by feeling for a seam. I was going along the wall with my hand, feeling like a blind person, and there happened to be a guard who was standing there looking at me. He called my father over and said, "Is that your son? I'm afraid that boy is not well. *He's coming back!*" We laugh at it now, but this is what the artist has to do. You have to take all of that and make it into your art, and then make it look like it's easy.[49]

Bearden's way of telling this incident recalled not only the difficult discipline, teamwork, and psychological support that it took to make art look easy; but also that despite its being plastered over and forgotten, the art could still be experienced—if not seen, literally *felt*. Somehow the art would not be denied. According to this important anecdote, then, Bearden's exit interview from the mental ward included his rediscovery of the power of art and the calling of the artist. Heroic through all of this was his wife, Nanette Rohan: Bearden often told the Bellevue story in her praise, remembering that once he was back home, she told him to throw away all the pills he had been given and get back to painting. "She saved my life," the artist often said.

In the *New Yorker* profile by Tomkins (and elsewhere) Bearden records a related, if earlier, story.[50] The date of the incident is not given, but evidently it was during the 1930s when Bearden was trying to find his artistic voice that a local gangster commissioned him to create a portrait of his beloved children. The man gave Bearden a photograph of the kids from which to work, a conventional black-and-white snapshot. Bearden wrestled in vain with the project—nothing seemed to work, not even trying a Degas-like treatment of the subject. And then he followed a friend's advice and took the photo downtown to have it blown up on sensitized canvas, and then to have someone touch up the enlarged photograph to give it color. The result was not at all good. "The kids looked like they were made up for Forest Lawn!" recalled Bearden, referencing one of New York's larger cemeteries. Shortly after, the gangster came by Bearden's studio with two bodyguards to check on the commissioned portrait's progress, and when he saw the garish blow-up he broke into tears of joy. "*My babies!*" the man said. He paid fifty dollars over the set price, at that time a big bonus, and insisted that Bearden sign the work. Not wanting to be embarrassed by it later, Romare spelled his name backwards as a *nom de plume*: "Eramor." "Eramor," the man said, "You're one helluva painter!"

Start looking for self-discovery stories in the Bearden file and they turn up everywhere. Their punchlines vary, but repeatedly the point is to resist the temptation to imagine drawing strength for artistic creation from some fanciful source, whether deep in the heart of nature, in Paris, in some magic imaginary realm or get-cash-quick scheme. Nor does the answer lie in traveling under false colors into the "big leagues," whether in sports or in the world of art, where one person's source of inspiration (touched-up photos or goblets or turtles or whatever) is probably not yours. Rather, the true source of originality lies in the raw fabric of one's own lived experience, in the creative processes of "re-membering" that experience (to paraphrase Toni Morrison),[51] and in the solitary study hall that jazz musicians call *the woodshed:* the hard place of self-investigation and practice-practice-practice.

The other side of this true-to-home-base aesthetic or "vernacular impera-tive" (Albert Murray's term) is that throughout his career Bearden took issue with those who advocated artistic inspiration all by itself, the *isolato's* inward-ness without outward study and responsibility to others, to the polis. That Bearden started his professional career as a satirical political cartoonist is a fact from which much may be learned: the sense of political urgency of those first cartoons remained in his work.[52] It is just as important that when telling of his early 1960s discovery of collage as a new path-finding ("Frontiersman's") way of working, Bearden typically points to the formation of the black artists' col-lective Spiral, convened at first in his Canal Street studio to consider how black artists might participate most meaningfully in the Civil Rights movement. (See Brent Hayes Edward's essay on Bearden's politics, in this volume.) "It was at this time," says art historian Lowery Sims, "that Bearden came up with the idea of organizing a group project that would express or symbolize some kind of con-sensus and unity, so he proposed that the group work on a communal collage."[53] By all reports no other Spiral members wanted to follow up on this suggestion. But Bearden started a first collage to show Spiral what he had in mind, and in so doing found himself hooked on the form. Given the backdrop of the Civil Rights movement, small wonder that Bearden's first series in this genre—the photomontages—have a jagged-edge in-your-face challenge quality: the star-ing Harlem eyes and hands "pressing on life." Not created for a commercial market but for his own purposes as woodshed practice pieces as he and Spi-ral were finding their way, these first montages were too direct and strong to sell to the public, Bearden felt. But indeed they did form an important gallery show—at precisely a point when the gallerist Arne Ekstrom was concerned that Bearden was experiencing a stylistic lull; and, as we know now, they were a key to Bearden's oeuvre going forward.[54] This Spiral narrative forms another landmark Beardenian sense-of-direction story: the beginning of his signature artistic mode as an act both of art and of politics.

Bearden's sense of the artist's task as more than loner's introspection is seconded by his reports on his artistic training beyond the early cartoon work. Art, he repeatedly said, comes not from sincere emotion or inspiration or "nature" alone. Not from overcooked technical tricks or mundane faithfulness to original scenes or sources, however beautiful, art comes from other art—from finding one's own artistic ways by studying the ways of other artists. So in making the transition from cartoonist to fine artist, Bearden enrolled in 1936 at the Art Students League, where Grosz, the German emigré artist, offered studio classes. Considering his piercing anti-Fascist paintings (some of which appear in the illustrated book treasured by Claude McKay), Grosz was an exceptionally apt mentor for Bearden. As a teacher his goal was to build upon Bearden's quick-draw cartoonist's skill: to create a more detail-oriented draftsman. "He taught the fundamentals of drawing," said Bearden. "He made me draw a hand, a foot, a face on a large sheet of paper—with very accurate attention to detail. He introduced me to the great draftsmen of the past—Holbein, Dürer and Ingres." Bearden could not wait to get into the classes with Grosz. "I studied from seven till ten at night drawing from the models. Every day I was learning something. . . . I hated to see ten o'clock come!"[55]

The young artist's education continued through the war years. By 1945, when his affiliation with the Samuel Kootz Gallery began, his horizons had expanded. He had known the black artists Aaron Douglas, Jacob Lawrence, and Charles Alston (Bearden's cousin), but the Kootz connection signaled a break in the pattern of New York's race-divided art world. "The great thing about being in a gallery was meeting the [other Kootz] artists, because I hadn't had that kind of exposure," Bearden told an interviewer. "And Kootz would have a meeting about every month; all the artists would be there and there would be exchanges of ideas which at that time meant a great deal to me. My work became more and more, you might say, non-representational."

Upon his return from his 1950 stay in Paris, Bearden continued to feel he had nowhere near enough formal training in art. Grosz had taught little about oil painting, for example. Then came the breakthrough that Bearden mentions in almost every interview: his discovery of the journals of the nineteenth-century French artist Eugène Delacroix. "I noted how Delacroix almost to the end of his life was always going to the Louvre and copying paintings," said Bearden. "I felt that I wanted to do the same thing, so I took perhaps two years and made a very systematic study of the old masters. Starting with Early Renaissance painters like Giotto, Duccio, I made copies of their work—right on down to the High Renaissance, men like Veronese."[56]

Realizing that doing this copy-work in the rooms of museums was not for him, instead Bearden would take his own photographs of paintings he admired to a friend who would print them on large sheets of paper. In his studio Bearden could create his own oil-on-canvas copies. Working from such blow-ups (how interesting it is that photography has so often been important to Bearden's processes of making art as well as learning about art), Bearden could study works from New York museums and from elsewhere. "I did very interesting and good copies of these paintings," says the artist:

> It taught me a lot about painting. . . . The copy that gave me the most difficulty was a Rembrandt, *Pilate Washing His Hands*, because, while it looks so easy, it looks so simple on the surface, you find it's so intricately involved. Because, if a painter has certain rhythms going and these things are all done right, say five or six rhythms that intertwine right, these things kind of expand even more. Even without the painter's intention, it becomes even more intricate.[57]

"An artist is an art lover who finds that in *all* the art that he sees, he sees something is missing," said Bearden. "And to touch at the core of what he feels is missing, what needs to be there, becomes the center of his life's work."[58] In an important interview he elaborated: "You go to see art in the museum, you know, all the paintings. You say, 'Well, this is fine; *there's only one thing missing.*'" In the monograph he co-authored with his teacher and friend Carl Holty, *The Painter's Mind*, this subject of the *something missing* is broached again and again. Throughout that book Bearden and Holty present reproductions of historically important paintings coupled with their own re-drawn images of them—their exploratory outlines of the pathways in and through the Manets, Monets, Picassos, and the Dutch Masters (including, prominently, Rembrandt) are particularly telling. These dramatic pairings uncover the originals' underlying strategies for using space and structure, as detected by these modernists in search of techniques they could use, as well as the "something" found missing in every case: something of their own.

Here again Ellison provides a helpful perspective. During Q-and-A after a 1990 public reading in New York, a young black woman asked what advice he might give her as an aspiring writer. "Read the Russians," Ellison said, chuckling as he stood to leave the stage. "Read the Russians!" No doubt he was thinking of Dostoyevsky and Tolstoy in particular, two of his indispensable models for *Invisible Man*. Maybe he was thinking of Turgenev or Chekov, other important models. But beyond such specifics, I think Ellison was advising the young woman to read widely, across all categories. He was advising that she choose her own artistic "ancestors" and do it boldly—without regard to color lines or any lines of "race," nationality, or gender.

In this spirit, Bearden's range of reference is global by design. Again and again, his paintings' lyrical horizon lines, their strings of stylized letters, their open corners—places for the viewer's eye to rest and to co-sign the creation of meaning—reflect Bearden's lifetime of studying Asian art, particularly the Chinese calligraphers. The references to Africa are just as explicit: not only to masks and textiles but also to the dance-beat rhythmical play of structural elements and the prevalence of troubled water, these last offering reflections on the Middle Passage and the many thousands gone, as well as black diasporic rituals of purification. Asia and Africa overlap the many European references—particularly to Manet, Picasso, Matisse, and the Dutch Masters. "I am a man concerned with truth, not flattery," says Bearden, "who shares a dual culture that is unwilling to deny the Harlem where I grew up or the Haarlem of the Dutch masters that contributed its element to my understanding of art."[59]

And so Bearden's *Two Women in a Harlem Courtyard* (1964) alludes specifically to Pieter De Hooch's *A Courtyard in Delft at Evening: A Woman Spinning* (1657) and, of course, to spaces in black Manhattan.[60] Most interesting of all are the works where a chorus of influences sounds off. Consider, for example, the collage *Return of Odysseus (Homage to Pinturicchio and Benin)*, from 1976, where Bearden repeats the figures and structures of the Italian Renaissance painter at the same time that he pays tribute to the classical bronzes of Benin. By the way, while Ulysses/Odysseus is Pinturicchio's protagonist, Bearden seemingly reduces him to a shadow, shifting the narrative to Penelope, who stands toe-to-toe with her African-masked counterpart, evidently one of the intruding suitors against whom she (and now Odysseus, ready to enter) must contend. Or, in this Beardenian reinvention, is the foregrounded male figure Odysseus himself, the old lion returning to a wrestling match with his wife (who in some versions of the folktale, not Homer's, has been consorting with various suitors) and to a hard-edged and dangerous home place, perhaps the best the world-full-of-blues has to offer? Improvisation and ambiguity—in this case, suggesting a turn of the tale in new directions—help provide Bearden's "missing piece."

In general, the missing part of the world of art that Bearden is adding is the African American piece, defined with extraordinary richness: an interpretation of the world's art traditions through a wide black American lens. See his classic genre images, blues figures, and highballing trains—hugely resonant black American tropes. See his many images of quilts and black women's quilting circles, so brilliantly outlined by Elizabeth Alexander in this volume. And see his repeated retellings of classic literary texts from a black American perspective. His Poseidon, for example, is not an arch-enemy but an African king who is furious about the way his son the Cyclops has been treated. His Sea-Goddess is a black woman savior, extending an African cloth as a sign of the way home—or is her ritual fabric a winding sheet for those black and unknown victims of the slave trade whose spirits haunt those waters? When finally Bearden's Odysseus does arrive at home to Ithaka, he meets his father there, beneath a structure showing the star and crescent of the Islamic faith.

So the "home" sought in Bearden's Homeric series (and throughout his oeuvre) is both local and global. For here the motive for the return journey is not a matter of nostalgia but of being at home everywhere, as global citizens who recognize kinship across lines of race, nation, gender, and continent—across Bearden's sparkling blue, instead of the Greek epic's "wine-dark," seas. For again, Bearden sees the human as not as homestead settler but instead as a man or woman *ever on the move.* Perhaps Bearden would agree with Edward Said's ambiguous "ideal" of being at home *nowhere*—that is, happy enough everywhere and anywhere, without sacrificing the impulse to question and push back intellectually, aesthetically, and politically against a planet out-of-joint.[61] Maybe above all Bearden's point here is that we are all one global family, saints and sinners, all a collage of a human race living in a monumentally unfair and often bleak world. Let us ever strive for greater and greater awareness of this global kinship and the mighty sense of responsibility it brings, not forgetting the joys: this seems to be the over-riding message of Romare Bearden's bright blue pieced-together pictures.

A few final words about collage. So many people writing about Bearden's collages emphasize their presentation of fragmented black selves and communities: the pulverizing effects of life under the long cannons of American racism. Those taking this approach to Bearden certainly are more than justified, lest any of us forget that injustice maims and kills, or that its hardiest survivors pay a terrible price for the ticket to stay alive. Before going on to praise the survival skills of these oppressed, may those Baldwin icily calls "the splendid ones" recall that by the cruelest turns of fate their heroic darker sisters and brothers remain endangered precisely for these very skills/cultural forms, for which they also are so eagerly praised and for which they are so universally imitated. These blues/jazz people and their offspring hip-hop stylists influence the globe's cultures, but, with obvious star exceptions, no one seems to want to hire them—much less to accept them as family. Who can wonder at the blunt-weapon lyrics and heavy beats of their musical forms (or at the let's-have-a-party-anyway spirit ironically going with them, as in the blues), any more than at the hard knife-cuts in Bearden's collages?

Still it is just as important to see that Toni Morrison and Elizabeth Alexander (and others in this volume) are right to regard Bearden's collages as indicating not only the fragmentation of black selves and communities but their complex *layeredness*, their refusal ever to be only one thing. This is a matter of black Americans' will to step out, as Édouard Glissant has said, from any single identity as they become citizens not only of a city or county or nation here or there but of the world in motion.[62] These Bearden banners reflect the many kinds of people who comprise black America as well as the ever-turning kaleidoscope of perspectives and personae that comprise each individual self. "Collage lets us think about identity as a spoked wheel," writes Alexander,

> or gyroscope on which its aspects spin and recombine. . . . In other words, the disparate aspects of personalities and of influence that might seem contradictory can actually coexist in a single personality, or a single identity. . . . Collage . . . is a continual cutting, pasting, and quoting of received information, much like jazz music, like the contemporary tradition of rapping, and indeed

like the process of reclaiming African-American history (or of any historiography). African-American culture from the Middle Passage forward is of course broadly characterized by fragmentation and reassemblage, sustaining what can be saved of history while making something new. Collage constructs wholes from fragments in a continual, referential dialogue between the seemingly disparate shards of various pasts and the current moment of the work itself, as well as the future the work might point toward.[63]

In an environment where simple racial stereotypes are easier to imagine than the truth of human selves in black skins, this fact of complex layered blackness, so magnificently articulated by Bearden, is most important to assert.

It is his proclaiming, through collage, the truth of both these perspectives, fragmentation and reassemblage, that may be Bearden's greatest achievement. For in his quiltlike and stained-glass-windowlike work, Bearden insists on a multiplicity of perspectives on the questions of identity that are central to his project as an artist. His "open corners" invite viewers to try to work with him to compose new answers-in-progress to the galaxy of problems that his paintings raise. Here is Bearden's most forceful gesture toward bringing "a new visual order into the world," as Ellison says, his best effort to "reset society's clock": not by replacing one meaning with another—not even with the highly oxygenated meanings of irony and ambiguity—but by his insistence on sharing the power to make meaning. Even more profound than his work's answer to the question repeated in this essay's paragraphs—Who am I?—is the set of answers to that other question implied everywhere in Bearden's oeuvre: Who are we? For starters, Bearden's pictures say, we are the collage people: individuals and communities with big hands and big hearts, scarred and battered but reassembled and layered. We are drawn together.

## NOTES

1. James Baldwin, "Sonny's Blues," in *Going to Meet the Man* (New York: Dial, 1965), 140. The full sentence is: "And I was yet aware that this was only a moment, that the world waited outside, as hungry as a tiger, and that trouble stretched above us, longer than the sky."

2. I was witness to Bearden's conversations with a number of his collaborators and friends, and heard many of his stories first-hand, beginning in 1979–80, when I met weekly with him and Albert Murray, initially in connection with my research on Ralph Ellison. Over the subsequent years, I visited Bearden's home on Canal Street on oc-

casion, and I attended all of his gallery openings, as well as performances by his wife Nanette Bearden's dance company and events involving Murray, where Bearden was a regular. I saw him off and on until he passed away, in 1988, and attended his funeral service at the Cathedral of St. John the Divine.

3. From the essay by August Wilson, in this volume.

4. Biographical data presented here is drawn from Myron Schwartzman, *Romare Bearden: His Life and Art* (New York: Abrams, 1990), and Ruth E. Fine et al., *The Art of Romare Bearden* (Washington, DC: National Gallery of Art, 2003). See in particular "Romare Bearden: A Chronology," by Rocío Aranda-Alvarado and Sarah Kennel with Carmenita Higginbotham, in the Fine volume.

5. Recounted in Calvin Tomkins's profile of the artist, in this volume, and reflected upon in the essay by John Edgar Wideman, also in this volume.

6. His friend the cartoonist Elmer Simms Campbell, also African American, urged Bearden to stick with cartooning, where he was more likely to earn a living than as a museum artist. See Schwartzman, *Romare Bearden: His Life and Art*, 73.

7. The Romare Bearden Foundation's website offers the most comprehensive list of these public works; https://beardenfoundation.org/public-art/.

8. On the influence of Chinese brushwork, see Tracy Fitzpatrick, *Romare Bearden: Abstraction* (Purchase, NY: Neuberger Museum of Art, 2017), pp. 13–38. On the "open corner" in Chinese landscape painting, see the Tomkins profile, in this volume, p. 31.

9. New scholarship has shown that Bearden's first experiments in collage came as early as the mid-1950s. See Fitzpatrick, *Romare Bearden: Abstraction*, pp. 48–52.

10. Ralph Ellison, "The Art of Romare Bearden" in *Going to the Territory* (New York: Random House, 1986), 231; for full text, see "The Art of Romare Bearden," pp. 196–203, in this volume.

11. Stanley Crouch, *Kansas City Lightning: The Rise and Times of Charlie Parker* (New York: Harper Collins, 2013), 19.

12. Calvin Tomkins, Papers, Museum of Modern Art Archives, New York.

13. See August Wilson, "Bearden: Black Life on Its Own Terms," pp. 175–77, in this volume.

14. From Morrison's talk on Bearden, transcribed for this volume.

15. From the Tomkins profile, in this volume.

16. Edwards made this point at a Bearden conference at Reid Hall, Columbia Global Centers, Paris, January 19, 2015.

17. Speaking of his painting called *The Block* (1971; Metropolitan Museum of Art, New York, 1978.61.1–6), Bearden compares his presentation of Harlem row houses to a piano keyboard; in *Bearden Plays Bearden* (1980, dir. Nelson Breen; 2012 DVD, Third World Cinema Production). See also Lawrence Toppman, "Romare Bearden: Painter of Memories" *Charlotte News* (October 4, 1980): 2C; and for the Coltrane example, see the *Charlotte Observer* (October 12, 1980): 11F.

18. Tomkins papers, MoMA Archives.

19. From John Hersey, "'A Completion of Personality': A Talk with Ralph Ellison" (1974), reprinted in *Conversations with Ralph Ellison*, ed. Maryemma Graham and Amritjit Singh (Jackson: University of Mississippi Press, 1995), 284.

20. From the transcribed talk by Morrison, in this volume, where she refers to her essay "Unspeakable Things Unspoken," presented as the Tanner Lecture on Human Value at the University of Michigan, October 7, 1988; see *The Norton Anthology of African American Literature*, 3rd ed., vol. 2, ed. Henry Louis Gates et al. (New York: Norton, 2014), 1099–1100.

21. Threadgill made this point at a conference of the Association for the Advancement of Creative Musicians at the University of Chicago campus in Paris, October 19, 2015.

22. From the transcribed talk by Morrison, in this volume.

23. Albert Murray, *The Hero and the Blues* (Columbia: University of Missouri Press, 1973), 107.

24. From *The Devil Finds Work*. (New York: Vintage, 1976), 80.

25. These words were inscribed on the gate of Apollo's temple at Delphi; see, for example, Plato, *Charmides*, 164e.

26. The "ancestors" reference comes from "The World and the Jug," in *The Collected Essays of Ralph Ellison*, ed. John F. Callahan (New York: Modern Library, 1995), 155–87, where Ellison argues that all artists are free to move beyond the tents of their immediate "family" to claim whatever artistic models and influences they choose.

27. See "The Black Artist in America: A Symposium," *Metropolitan Museum of Art Bulletin*, New Series, 27.5 (January 1969): 254.

28. See Ellison's "What America Would Be Like Without Blacks," in *Going to the Territory* (New York: Vintage, 1987), 110.

29. Paul Richard, "Romare Bearden's Blues," *The Washington Post* (March 14, 1988), https://www.washingtonpost.com/archive/lifestyle/1988/03/14/romare-beardens-blues/7fe69eaf-dc74-4ee4-8711-61cca7cc66c6/?utm_term=.55febee2a218;  Lawrence Toppman, "Romare Bearden: Painter of Memories," *Charlotte News* (October 4, 1980): 2C.

30. Abrams said this at a conference at Columbia University, May 2008.

31. From Albert Murray, *Train Whistle Guitar* (New York: McGraw-Hill, 1974), 33.

32. See the public interview with Marshall by William C. Rhoden at the Metropolitan Museum of Art, New York, December 15, 2016; https://www.metmuseum.org/metmedia/video/lectures/evening-with-kerry-james-marshall.

33. Constance Rourke, *American Humor: A Study of the American Character* (New York: Harcourt Brace, 1931). This formulation by Rourke was routinely cited by Bearden, who often would associate Rourke with Ellison and Murray.

34. Written for *Time* magazine (April 6, 1970); reprinted in *Going to the Territory*.

35. Rourke, *American Humor*, 86–101.

36. Richard Wright, *White Man, Listen!* (New York: Doubleday, 1957), 109; Wright's novel *Native Son* was published in 1940.

37. Ellison, "The Art of Romare Bearden," 232.

38. From Charles H. Rowell's interview with Bearden published as "Inscription at the City of Brass," *Callaloo* 36 (Summer 1988): 433–34.

39. Tomkins papers, MoMA Archives.

40. Most appear in printed interviews, including ones included in this volume; some are stories told directly to me in the late 1970s to early 1980s.

41. This version of the story was told directly to me—though it also appears in the Tomkins profile in this volume. Another version is recounted in Bearden's recorded museum talk of October 20, 1982; Archive, Office of Public Programs, Reynolda House Museum of American Art, Winston-Salem, North Carolina.

42. From "The Journal of Romare Bearden," in this volume.

43. This version of the tale was told directly to me. It can also be found in the Nelson Breen documentary *Bearden Plays Bearden* (1980), issued on DVD in 2012 with bonus material that includes, along with this anecdote, a version of the prostitute's jangling keys story.

44. This phrase by Ralph Ellison appears in his jacket blurb for Jervis Anderson's *This Was Harlem: A Cultural Portrait, 1900–1950* (New York: Farrar, Straus & Giroux, 1982).

45. This version of the tale is told by Guy Trebay, "Talking Heads: Romare Bearden's Way," *Village Voice* (October 14–20, 1981): 63. Bearden also tells it again on the bonus disk included with the 2012 DVD of the documentary *Bearden Plays Bearden* (1980).

46. Trebay, "Talking Heads," 63.

47. Eventually "Seabreeze" was also recorded by Dizzy Gillespie, Tito Puente, Oscar Pettiford, and Chick Corea, among others. Branford Marsalis recorded it as part of a Bearden tribute album, *Romare Bearden Revealed* (Marsalis Music, 2003).

48. Tomkins papers, MoMA Archives.

49. "Interview of Romare Bearden by Camille Billops and James V. Hatch," *Artist and Influence* 17 (1998): 36. (The interview was conducted on December 6, 1972.)

50. See Bearden's "The 1930s: An Art Reminiscence" in this volume.

51. Toni Morrison, "Memory, Creation, and Writing," *Thought* 59.4 (December 1984): 385.

52. It also is important to remember that before he could earn a living with his art, Bearden did so as a New York City social worker (Department of Welfare), from 1935 until 1969, when sales of his paintings finally permitted him to retire from this "day job." This was a job from which there was much to learn about people on the outskirts of official U.S. urban history. How significant that Bearden's assignment was to assist New York's Romani population, popularly (some would say offensively) called "Gypsies." See Aidan Levy, "The Quilt of Romare Bearden's Life," *The Nation* (July 13, 2018), https://www.thenation.com/article/the-quilt-of-romare-bearden-life/.

53. Sims, "The Unknown Romare Bearden," *ARTnews*, 85.8 (October 1986): 120

54. Sims, "The Unknown Romare Bearden," 120. Ekstrom and his French partner, Daniel Cordier, represented Bearden at Cordier & Ekstrom gallery from 1960 until Bearden's death.

55. From an undated article, evidently unpublished, commissioned by *Essence* magazine; Tomkins papers, MoMA Archives.

56. From the Tomkins profile, in this volume.

57. From the Tomkins profile, in this volume.

58. "Artist's General Remarks," undated, Tomkins papers, MoMA Archives.

59. Charles Childs, "Romare Bearden: Identification and Identity," *ARTnews* 63 (October 1964): 62.

60. Bearden's version is represented by *Two Women in a Harlem Courtyard*, photostat collage on fiberboard, 41 × 30 in., from an edition of 6 (unrealized), DC Moore Gallery, New York; De Hooch's oil painting belongs to the Royal Collection Trust, London, RCIN 405331.

61. See Edward Said, *Reflections on Exile and Other Essays* (Cambridge, MA: Harvard University Press, 2002).

62. See the documentary *Edouard Glissant: One World in Relation*, directed by Manthia Diawara (2010, Third World Newsreel).

63. From the essay by Elizabeth Alexander, in this volume.

PART I / LIFE AND TIMES

# PUTTING SOMETHING OVER SOMETHING ELSE

*Calvin Tomkins*

For the opening of a memorable Romare Bearden show at the Cordier & Ekstrom gallery in February 1975, Arne Ekstrom engaged Danny Moore's five-man jazz group and a fine blues singer, Denise Rogers, whose resonant, earthy voice delighted the predominantly but by no means exclusively black opening-night crowd. The show was called "Of the Blues," and the pictures all sang in tune: "Carolina Shout," "Storyville," "New Orleans Farewell," "At the Savoy," "Kansas City 4/4," and fifteen other collage paintings, richer in color than any of Bearden's previous work, more luminous, more complex. The series did not illustrate the blues or chart the history of the blues or anything like that; each painting had come out of Bearden's memory and experience.

Growing up in Harlem in the twenties, Bearden lived and breathed the music and came to know most of the great performers. Duke Ellington, Fats Waller, Billie Holiday, Louis Armstrong, and Jelly Roll Morton were his early masters (to be joined later on by Duccio, Vermeer, Delacroix, and Mondrian). Ekstrom had urged him to paint the blues series, and the two men agreed that it had been a fine idea. During a break between sets by the musicians, Bearden answered a friend's question about the paintings. "One of the things I did was listen to a lot of music," he explained. "I'd take a sheet of paper and just make lines while I listened to records — a kind of shorthand to pick up the rhythm and the intervals." When Bearden was starting to paint seriously, in the thirties, he got a lot of help and encouragement from Stuart Davis. Bearden would go downtown to see Davis, who lived in Greenwich Village, and would usually find him listening to Earl Hines records. Once, he asked Davis why he liked Hines so much, and Davis said, "For his wonderful sense of intervals." Hines made the pauses between notes into something important; the silences were as expressive as the sounds. In Bearden's painting, the separations between colors, or between different values of a color, are expressive in this way. Like Hines, Bearden is a virtuoso of the interval.

A heavyset man of sixty-three, with features that look more Russian than anything else, Romare (he pronounces it "Rome-ery") Bearden has the unusual ability to appear at all times both perfectly composed and entirely spontaneous. He is so light-skinned that most people meeting him for the first time assume he is white. At this particular juncture, we seem to be stuck with the term "black," however, and Bearden is generally referred to as America's leading black painter. His work is in the Museum of Modern Art, the Metropolitan, the Whitney, and other museums. The Modern gave him a retrospective exhibition in 1971; the show subsequently went on tour, and ended up in the Studio Museum in Harlem, around the corner from Bearden's old West 125th Street studio. He has been elected to the American Academy and Institute of Arts and Letters — the hallmark of acceptance by the cultural establishment — and he is a member of the board of the New York State Council on the Arts. His work is much in demand these days — a recent series of brilliant collage paintings on the theme of Homer's *Odyssey*, which he showed at Cordier & Ekstrom last spring, was so successful, aesthetically and otherwise, that he has already redone the series in watercolor — and while he and his wife, Nanette, continue to live very simply, in a fourth-floor walk-up apartment on Canal Street, they have built a vacation house and studio on some property owned by Nanette's family on the Caribbean island of St. Martin.

Most of Bearden's friends agree that he is painting better than ever. "His work has a kind of warmth and satisfaction that's new," according to Harry Henderson, a writer and editor with whom Bearden collaborated on *Six Black Masters of American Art*, a book for young readers. "His new paintings lack the harshness of some of the earlier ones; they seem to glow. It's something that's come out of Romie — his proud feeling about what black people have achieved."

# PITTSBURGH

Three boys, aged ten to twelve, are shooting marbles in the back yard of a boarding house in Pittsburgh, in the neighborhood known as Lawrenceville, one day in 1926. A strange kid with braces on both legs appears out of nowhere and stands watching them. "What the hell you looking at?" says Bearden's friend Dennis. Dennis is a pretty rough kid. The newcomer doesn't reply, just stands there, and after a while Dennis gets up and belts him one. Then Dennis and Bearden's cousin Charlie and Bearden all start beating on the stranger — who still doesn't say anything, or even cry — until Bearden's grandmother happens to look out the window and comes out wielding a broom. She picks up the strange kid and carries him into the house. His name is Eugene. "And then he got to be our friend," Bearden says, telling the story many years later. "He'd had infantile paralysis, and he couldn't run with us — he couldn't even eat very fast — but he was always around the house."

Although Bearden was born in Charlotte, North Carolina, where his father's family came from, his parents lived in Harlem, and Harlem is where he grew up. He used to visit his Charlotte relatives in the summer, and later he began spending summers in Pittsburgh, with his mother's mother. She lived near the steel mills and took in boarders, as many as twenty at a time. This was the period of the first great black migration from the rural South to the Northern industrial cities. Bearden remembers his grandmother's rubbing new boarders at night with cocoa butter. "They didn't realize, when they first started, the terrific heat from those furnaces," he says. "They'd strip to the waist, and when the furnace doors opened, the flames would lick out like evil tongues and scorch them. But they were making forty to fifty dollars a week, which was a tremendous wage in comparison with what they'd been getting. I loved it there. I found it fascinating looking at the mills. For a while, I spent my summers in Pittsburgh, and then, after my first year of high school, in Manhattan, I decided I preferred living in Pittsburgh, so I went to school there."

Bearden was twelve the summer he met Eugene. Nobody knew anything about Eugene at first — where he lived or who his parents were. One day, he showed Bearden some drawings he had done, on sheets of brown paper. Bearden was enthralled. "He'd done one drawing of a house of prostitution not far from where we lived, run by a woman named Sadie. We always liked to go there and try to sell newspapers, because the music was so interesting — that kind of rolling piano. Eugene had drawn Sadie's house with the façade cut off, so you could see in all the rooms. And somebody had shot off a pistol, and the bullet was going all through the house. Women were on top of men, and the bullet was going through them, into the next room and the next, until it came down through the ceiling into the front parlor, and Sadie had her pocketbook open, and the bullet had turned into coins and was dropping into her pocketbook. I said to Eugene, 'You did this? Can you teach me to do it?' He said, 'Sure.' So I started taking drawing lessons from Eugene.

"My grandmother set up a table in my room, and Eugene and I would go and draw every day. All his drawings were about what happened in Sadie's house, and I was just trying religiously to copy what he did. After a week or so, my grandmother came around wanting to see what he had done. She took one look, and she grabbed all those drawings and threw them into the furnace. She said, 'Eugene, where did you ever see anything like that?' Eugene said, 'My mother is a whore. She works over at Sadie's place.' My grandmother told him, 'Eugene, don't you go home tonight.' My grandmother finished making dinner for everybody, and then she got a big suitcase and all three of us went to Sadie's, and she knocked on the door. The music was going, and Sadie came to the door, and as soon as she saw my grandmother she knew what had happened. 'I didn't want this boy here,' she said. My grandmother said, 'I'm not coming in, but you let Eugene go up and get his clothes, because I'm taking him home to live with me.' So Eugene and I went up to where she lived, which was way up on the top floor; you could look down through the cracks in the floor into the room below. We brought Eugene back to live with us. His mother would come every Sunday to visit him. They'd sit in the front room, where there was an old German clock that had written on it 'Every Hour Wounds. The Last One Kills.' How I hated to look at that! Eugene never did any more drawings after he left Sadie's house. He died about a year later, and we went to his funeral. But I always thought that with his drawings he could have been another Lautrec. That was the first time I ever thought about drawing — and then for years I forgot about it."

## HARLEM

Bessye J. Bearden did not approve of her son's wanting to become an artist. This was the Depression, and people were starving. Bessye J. was an activist, a tremendously energetic and public-spirited woman — New York editor of the *Chicago Defender*, the widely read Negro weekly; chairman of her local school board (after having been the first woman appointed to a school board in New York City); national treasurer of the Council of Negro Women; a member of the executive board of the New York Urban League. She had dealt in real estate, and in 1935 she was appointed Deputy Collector for the Third New York Internal Revenue District. She was a political force in Harlem, having been the manager of several congressional campaigns, an organizer of the National Council of Negro Women, and the founder and first president of the Negro Women's Democratic Association — someone you came to see when you wanted to cut through red tape and get action. Everyone in Harlem knew Bessye J., and Bessye J. knew everyone: Eleanor Roosevelt and Mary Bethune, councilmen and judges, editors and mayors, not to mention all the musicians and singers and actors who played at Connie's Inn or the Lafayette Theatre, half a block from the Beardens' apartment, which was on the third floor at 154 West 131st Street. (From a front window you could see the Tree of Hope, the famous old elm at the corner of Seventh Avenue and 131st Street, where out-of-work actors used to gather and talk.) Duke Ellington was a friend of the family, and bought an oil from Bearden's first formal exhibition. Fats Waller and his lyricist, Andy Razaf, and Razaf's wife, the singer Minta Cato, used to drop in regularly. Bearden remembers his mother as someone who was constantly in movement and among people. "Once, I came into the house and found her crying," he recalls. "I asked if she was sick. She said, 'No I'm just by myself.' She had to be with people all the time." His father, Howard Bearden, worked for the New York City Department of Health as a sanitation inspector. He was an intelligent, sensitive man, and a drinker; he was very much in Bessye J.'s shadow.

Bessye Bearden had helped any number of young people get started in their careers — the actor Canada Lee, for one — and she and Howard felt that Romare, their only child, should stick to his original plan, which had been to become a doctor. After two years at Boston University, he transferred to New York University, where he majored in mathematics, with the idea of going on to medical school, but while he was at NYU he started drawing for the college humor magazine. He met E. Simms Campbell, the highly successful black cartoonist, who gave him advice and encouragement; he began contributing a weekly political cartoon to the nationally circulated *Afro-American*. Bearden was also being urged at this period to become a professional baseball player. He had been Boston University's star varsity pitcher, and for two summers while he was in college there he pitched for the Boston Tigers, a Negro team that often played exhibition games with semi-pro clubs. Bearden was told that if he wanted to "pass" he could easily play in the majors (this was before Jackie Robinson broke the color line), but he had no inclination to do that. His inclination, more and more, was to continue drawing.

It was the Depression, curiously, that gave many Negroes the chance to be artists. In 1935, Bearden went to a meeting of Harlem artists at the YMCA on 135th Street. He was amazed to find forty or fifty there — he had been told that there were very few Negro artists. This was the beginning of the Harlem Artists Guild, headed first by the painter and muralist Aaron Douglas and then by the sculptor Augusta Savage. Bearden himself was ineligible for the Works Progress Administration art program, because of his family's income, but the knowledge that other Negroes were devoting themselves seriously to painting and sculpture made a strong impression on him. "I found that the WPA, even at the worst time of the Depression, gave artists a salary and materials to work with," Bearden says. "It gave minority artists what they could never have afforded otherwise." In 1936, a year after he graduated from NYU with a bachelor's degree in science, he enrolled in the Art Students League, to study with the German expatriate George Grosz. Grosz's corrosive line drawings and watercolors of German society "made me realize the artistic possibilities of American Negro subject matter," Bearden once wrote. At first, he was still thinking mainly in terms of political cartooning, but Grosz changed his mind about that. It was Grosz, he said, who "led me to study composition, through the analysis of Bruegel and the great Dutch masters, and who in the process of refining my draftsmanship initiated me into the magic world of Ingres, Dürer, Holbein, and Poussin."

A year and a half at the League constituted Bearden's only formal training in art. In 1938, he took a job with the New York City Department of Welfare as a caseworker. He continued to live with his parents but as soon as he could manage it he rented a studio at 33 West 125th Street, which was then on the edge of Harlem; across Fifth Avenue, the neighborhood was all white. Jacob Lawrence, another young painter, had the studio on the floor beneath, and soon afterward the poet Claude McKay moved into the building. "Things were still very lively in Harlem then," Bearden recalls. "So much of the life in those days was lived out in the open, on the street. People were still coming in from the South, and you still had the house-rent parties — somebody would need to raise money to pay the rent, so they'd throw a party, pass out little cards on the street, and you'd come and pay a quarter for admission, and there would be plenty to eat and drink and usually some good music, and that way you got to meet all sorts of people."

The Harlem artists were a close-knit group in the late thirties. They met regularly at "306" — 306 West 141st Street, where Charles Alston and the sculptor Henry Bannarn lived, sharing a big studio that for a short time also doubled as a WPA-sponsored art school. Alston, an accomplished painter, who was related to Bearden by marriage, kept open house for all the creative talents of the day. "There was always a hot discussion going on at 306," according to Alston. "Langston Hughes would drop by, and Claude McKay, and sometimes William Saroyan and Bill Steig or Carl Van Vechten, from downtown. Musicians, too — Andy Razaf, and Sammy Stewart, and John Hammond, the jazz musicologist, and lots of others." When Bannarn moved out, Alston shared the place for a while with Ad Bates, who was a dancer with the Doris Humphrey/Charles Weidman troupe, and who also worked as an artists' model at the Art Students League. Bates organized several art exhibitions at 306, including Bearden's first one-man show in 1940 (mostly student work); later, he introduced Bearden to a number of white artists downtown, including Stuart Davis and Walter Quirt.

"There was a great interchange of people coming up to Harlem from all over," Bearden recalls. "You got to know all kinds of people — actors, musicians, underworld characters, intellectuals, society types. I met García Lorca once at a party. There was always a lot of movement from place to place, and it was so easy to know people." In those days, the center of Harlem was Seventh Avenue and 135th Street. Negroes had started to move to 135th Street about 1902. W. E. B. Du Bois, James Weldon Johnson, Augusta Savage, and other prominent people lived on 135th, although the really fashionable blocks were 138th and 139th between Seventh and Eighth, streets of handsome town houses, several of which were designed about the turn of the century by Stanford White for wealthy clients, and inhabited since the twenties by well-to-do black doctors, lawyers, and entertainers; they were known locally as Strivers' Row. The famous nightclubs were all within a few blocks of 135th and Seventh. Negro customers were not allowed in the Cotton Club or Connie's Inn (once a year, the Cotton Club revue would play at the Lafayette, so the Harlemites could see it), but Charles Buchanan, the manager of the Savoy Ballroom, used to let the Harlem artists in free to dance there, and Bearden and his friends went several times a week.

Bearden, Alston, Bannarn, Bates, Norman Lewis, Ernest Crichlow, Francisco Lord, Vertis Hayes, Jacob Lawrence, and the other artists had their own special gathering places. They would usually drop in every night at a place called Joe's, on Seventh Avenue at 137th Street, and later in the evening would go on to Mom Young's, on 132nd between Seventh and Lenox, where for a quarter you could get a coffee can full of beer and a steaming bowl of gumbo or chili or whatever Mom was making that day. "Of course, it wasn't all good times and laughter," Bearden points out. "This was still the Depression."

Bearden worked for the city from nine to five and painted for several hours in the evening. For a long time after his studies with Grosz, he had not been able to get started on his own. The same piece of brown paper, unmarked, had remained on his easel for weeks at a time. One evening, leaving the studio with Claude McKay, he heard the familiar sound of keys jangling — prostitutes jangled keys to attract business — and, turning around, saw what he describes as the smallest and homeliest woman he had ever seen. "She said, 'Two dollars, boys.' Then she said, 'A dollar?' Then, 'Fifty cents?' Then, 'A quarter?' Finally, she said, 'For God's sake, just take me.' She was so pathetic I told my mother about her, said she was in the wrong business, and my mother got a job for this woman — Ida. After that, Ida came every Saturday to clean my studio. And in the studio was my easel, with the piece of brown paper on it. When you're young, you have a lot of ideas and a lot of dreams, but you don't have the ability to realize them; I think that as you mature you don't have the same kind of ideas and dreams, because you let the work make its own fantasy. Anyway, Ida would come once a week to clean, and the brown paper was there on the easel, and one day she asked if it was the same piece of paper, and I told her that it was — that I didn't have my ideas together. She said, 'Why don't you paint me?' Well, the way I must have looked at her she could see what was going through my mind. 'I know what I look like,' she said. 'But when you can look and find what's beautiful in me, then you're going to be able to do something on that paper of yours.' That always sort of stuck with me, what she said."

When Bearden did find his way, it was with a series of paintings based on his childhood memories of the rural South. Painted in tempera on brown paper, they are characterized by strong, bright colors and stylized, highly formal composition. Most of the Harlem artists then were working in the predominating vein of social realism, influenced by Thomas Hart Benton and by the Mexican muralists. From the start, Bearden's paintings were more lyrical, and were concerned more with plastic values than with social themes. "Romie was never a poor kid," Charles Alston once said. "He was straight out of the middle class, and the urban middle class at that. Jake Lawrence grew up in the middle of real Harlem poverty, and there's always been something very simple and direct about his approach, but Romie's approach to art is more intellectual. He's read a great deal all his life, and he's been intensely curious about many different kinds of art."

Alston introduced Bearden to African sculpture, and Claude McKay took him to meet Charles Christopher Seifert, an elderly gentleman who had filled his comfortable Harlem home with books on African and Afro-American history. In 1935 Seifert took Bearden and a number of other young artists to see the first exhibition of African Negro art put on by the Museum of Modern Art. What Bearden got from this experience was not racial pride as much as a sense of the tremendous formal power and majesty of African art. Twenty years later, he used fragments of Benin heads and Dan masks in his own collage paintings.

The artist's life in Harlem had its bizarre aspects. Once, Bearden was commissioned to paint a portrait of an underworld figure's two children. Working from a photograph, he struggled nervously with the compositional problems, trying to make it look like a Degas. Then a friend of his came in and said he was going about it all wrong. Acting on his friend's advice (the promised completion date was fast approaching), he took the photograph downtown and had it blown up on photosensitized canvas; then he got a professional retoucher to put in the color until, he says, "the two kids looked as if they were made up for Forest Lawn." When the father came, with his bodyguard, to claim the picture, he was so moved that he broke into tears and insisted on paying fifty dollars more than the agreed-on price. "Eramor," he said (Bearden had signed it with his first name spelled backward) — "Eramor, you're one hell of a painter." Another time, Bearden invited an exotic dancer to spend the night in his studio. Unknown to Bearden, her luggage contained an eight-foot python (her working costume), which got loose during the night and entwined itself around his easel. "Some people have looked at my work and said it was Surrealism," he said recently. "But these things were all around me all the time. The things I saw every day — the people, the music, the dancing. My models were as great as Lautrec's."

"I think the artist has to be something like a whale," Bearden has said, "swimming with his mouth wide open, absorbing everything until he has what he really needs. When he finds that, he can start to make limitations. And then he really begins to grow."

## PARIS

Bearden lived in Paris for six months in 1950, and did not paint a single picture. He studied philosophy at the Sorbonne, under the GI Bill of Rights. He lived at 5 Rue des Feuillantines, near the Luxembourg Gardens, and spent a good part of his time just wandering around the city. Paris in the early fifties, he says, was very much like Harlem in the twenties. "There was that sense of something happening, and of life being lived out in the open, on the streets. Paris has never been a city for somebody who wants to find himself. It's too seductive. Of course, I thought I'd go right to the Louvre, but it got to be like something in Kafka's 'Castle.' I could never bring myself to go there. There was too much to see and do just walking the length and breadth of Paris."

By the time Bearden got to Paris, in early February of 1950, he was a fairly well-established artist, with half a dozen one-man shows to his credit. Caresse Crosby had seen his work in 1943, when she was trying to organize a group show of Negro artists, and decided on the spot to give him a solo show in her G Place Gallery, in Washington, D.C. Bearden was in the Army then; he served for three years with the 372nd Infantry, a Negro regiment, doing stateside duty in a number of different posts before his discharge, in 1945, with the rank of sergeant. Soon after a show of Bearden's "Ten Hierographic Paintings" in Washington, Caresse Crosby introduced him to the New York dealer Samuel Kootz, who represented Adolph Gottlieb, William Baziotes, Robert Motherwell, Carl Holty, and several other first-generation Abstract Expressionists. Kootz gave Bearden three one-man shows between 1945 and 1947, and during this period his work also appeared in a number of important group shows and museum exhibitions. His paintings of the forties are rather austere in color and are figurative, usually being related to literary or biblical themes. He painted a series called "The Passion of Christ," and other works were inspired by the Iliad, "Gargantua and Pantagruel," and García Lorca's "Lament for Ignacio Sánchez Mejías." Close friends of Bearden's say that his mother's death, in 1943 — she was in the hospital, recovering from an operation when she contracted pneumonia and died — was a profound shock to him, and that the change is evident in the somber, stained-glass quality of his "Passion of Christ" series. For Bearden, the biblical allusion was not religious but humanistic — an attempt to reach beyond personal experience to universal archetypes that would be communicable to others. Bearden's first show at Kootz — the "Passion of Christ" series — sold out, and a number of important collectors, among them Sam Lewisohn, became regular purchasers of his work.

Still, the art market in the forties was not what it became in the late fifties and sixties, and Bearden could not make a living from his picture sales. He went back to work for the Department of Welfare in 1946, and again painted in his spare time. His new studio was in the Apollo building, at 243 West 125th Street, between Seventh and Eighth Avenues. The Apollo Theater, next door, had succeeded the Lafayette as the leading Harlem showplace for big bands and headliners, and 125th Street, with the Theresa Hotel and the Harlem Opera House and the Apollo, had become the center of a rather different Harlem from the one in which Bearden grew up. There had been a race riot in Harlem in 1943, and during the war years the area was declared off limits to white servicemen. The atmosphere was less ebullient in the postwar years than it had been in the thirties. The Harlem Artists Guild was no longer active. Many of the artists had moved away, and Bearden's friendships with Baziotes, Holty, and others who showed at Kootz did not completely offset a feeling of loneliness and isolation. He had no particular interest in emulating the gestural Abstract Expressionist work of Jackson Pollock and Willem de Kooning, whose influence on New York artists was already immense; at the same time, he had not really found his own aesthetic alternative. He had heard a lot about Paris, of course, from Claude McKay and others, and late in 1949 he took a leave of absence from his job with the city and in 1950 went over to see it for himself.

Americans in Paris on the GI Bill used to congregate at the big cafes on the Boulevard du Montparnasse — the Coupole and the Sélect — or else at the ones around Saint-Germain-des-Prés. Albert Murray, a young black writer, who became one of Bearden's close friends, remembers meeting Bearden for the first time at the Coupole: "Romie was with Myron O'Higgins, the poet. I couldn't tell if he was a Russian or what — people used to say about Romie over there that, seeing him first, you thought it must be either Khrushchev or Jean Genet. But then he put his head back and laughed, and I thought, Nobody but a Negro man is going to laugh like that. Romie already knew everybody, it seemed. He was going to all the galleries, looking in all the shops, being part of Paris."

James Baldwin and Richard Wright were both in Paris then, and Baldwin read part of his first novel, Go Tell It on the Mountain, to Bearden and a few others one night in Bearden's room on the Rue des Feuillantines. Bearden also knew a number of French artists and intellectuals, many of whom he had met in the atelier of the painter Jean Hélion. Kootz had given Bearden letters of introduction to Picasso, Braque, and Brancusi. Picasso was on the Cote d'Azur, and anyway, Bearden said, meeting him would have been like shaking hands with the Eiffel Tower. He did call on Braque, who was polite but formal, and on Brancusi, who became a friend. "I went to see him often in his studio, in the Impasse Ronsin," he said. "He wasn't working anymore. I used to go shopping for groceries with him. In the markets, at noon and again in the late afternoon, they would ring a bell five minutes before closing time. The prices would drop a little after the bell, and Brancusi would always wait until the last minute to shop. He had that quality of a real peasant."

Although Bearden never met Matisse, he and his friends used to see him from time to time. "Once, I was sitting at the Dôme when Matisse walked by with a friend," Bearden said. "There was a rustle of excitement in the café, and all the waiters came out to see him, and as he passed they applauded. Matisse didn't notice at first, until his friend called his attention to it; then he turned and came back and shook hands with all the waiters, one by one. Oh, Paris was just wonderful for me. I liked everything about it. If you were an American, there was a way to get whiskey very cheap then and give parties for almost nothing. One night, a bunch of us were eating in a restaurant in Montparnasse, and we'd met some Russian musicians and asked them to come along to a party and play. On our way to the party, I heard jazz coming from an apartment, and it seemed to me that it didn't sound like French musicians playing, so I went up and knocked on the door, and there inside the room were Sidney Bechet and Roy Eldridge and Minta Cato, the singer who had been married to Andy Razaf, and a few others. I knew them! They were just having some fun by themselves. So I had them come along to the party. And it was a terrific party. Finally, at about three in the morning, they made us leave, and we ended up continuing the party out on the street — the music and the dancing.

"Another time, I was having dinner with Sam Menashe, the poet, and another poet named Sam Allen, a guy I'd known in the Army, at a little working-class restaurant called Signe de la Bonne Étoile. It was a misty March night, and after dinner Menashe said we should go and look at Notre Dame; it was a perfect night to see it. When we got to the *quai* on the Left Bank opposite the Ile de la Cité, Menashe took us down the steps to the cobblestone walk along the river, and we looked up at the cathedral from there. It was spotlighted, but in the mist the uppermost sections were barely visible, and the spires seemed to move end-lessly up into the sky. For the first time, I really had a feeling of the Gothic ca-thedral as the hand of God, with a finger pointing to Heaven. I'd never had such a feeling of extension and height. A few days later, I was in a place called Chez Inez, run by Inez Cavanaugh, an American jazz singer, who was married to the jazz impresario Timme Rosenkrantz. I met a Chinese guy there who offered me one of his cigarettes, and I didn't realize it was hashish. I smoked French Gauloises then, and this didn't taste much different. Anyway, I smoked two of his hashish cigarettes, and I was thinking about Notre Dame, about going there again. I don't know how I got there — it seemed like right after I had the thought

I was down there by the water looking at Notre Dame. And I thought I saw an angel walking across the Seine. It was late at night, and there was nobody around to talk to but a woman, a prostitute. I told her I'd just seen something amazing, an angel walking across the river. She said, 'Men are all alike.' I asked her what she meant. She said, 'Look up at Notre Dame. Don't you see all those angels holding up the whole goddam cathedral? Don't you think they get tired? And you're worried about one of them taking a little walk at night.' She said, 'Don't you want to come home with me?' I said no, I was going to go and paint a picture of that angel walking across the river. But, of course, I didn't do it. I couldn't *ever* do a painting in Paris."

Bearden went home in August of 1950. He had applied for a Fulbright grant, and had been told he must return to the United States in order to collect it. He expected the Fulbright to send him back to Paris right away; even so, it wasn't easy to leave. Albert Murray, who was staying another month before returning to a teaching job at Tuskegee, was with him the day before he left. "Romie spent the whole day buying paper," he recalls. "All kinds of drawing papers — rice papers, special sizes and surfaces, different colors. His eyes got more and more moist the later it got. 'This goddam Paris,' he kept saying."

## NEW YORK

Bearden did not get the Fulbright, and it was many years before he returned to Paris. He tried to get started painting again, with little success. Painting seemed enormously difficult. In his studio in the Apollo building, surrounded by musicians and rehearsal studios, he began to think that maybe the thing to do was to write a popular song that would make a lot of money and get back to Paris that way. Although he knew next to nothing about the technical aspects of music (he had taken violin lessons very briefly as a child, and hated them), Bearden had a lot of friends in the music business. Fred Norma and Larry Douglas, professional arrangers, helped him get started, and over the next couple of years Bearden, who seems to be one of those people who can do almost anything they set their minds to, achieved some success as a songwriter. About twenty of his songs were recorded, one of which, "Seabreeze," became a substantial hit. By the mid-fifties, Billy Eckstine, Oscar Pettiford, and others had recorded it, and Seagram Distillers had used the song to promote a mixed drink.

"I just turned away from painting," Bearden has said of this period. "And meanwhile the years were going by. One day, I went to see Hannah Arendt and her husband, the philosopher Heinrich Blücher, who were friends of mine. He said, 'You're wasting your life. In the first place, you don't even believe in what you're doing. Do you think Irving Berlin and Cole Porter could do what they do if they didn't believe in it?' Hannah said I was just going to wreck myself as a painter. I thought about that. But, you know, when you're serious about something, you don't really like doing it. Painting is so difficult; the canvas was always saying no to me. And all the time I was getting more and more nervous. One night, I thought I was going to die. I called my father and said I thought I must have cancer of the stomach. But when I went to the doctor he examined me and said nothing was wrong. A couple of weeks later, I felt sure I was going to have a heart attack. Then, one day, walking on the street, I suddenly felt I couldn't walk a step farther. The next thing I knew, I was in the hospital. I asked the nurse, 'Where am I?' She said I was in the psychiatric ward at Bellevue. A doctor came by, and I asked him what had happened to me. 'You blew a fuse,' he said. Just what Arendt and others had said was going to happen to me had happened."

Gradually his life came back together. "I just had to be a painter; that was it," he concluded. "Some people are like that. I've always thought Delacroix could easily have been a great writer, while a man like Courbet could only have been a painter." Bearden feels that his marriage, in 1954, was what really gave him the strength to return to painting. He met Nanette Rohan at a benefit party in Harlem to help the survivors of a West Indies hurricane; she herself had grown up on Staten Island, but her parents came from St. Martin. She and Bearden were married soon afterward. "I was on Miltown then," he recalls. "Nanette said if I was going to be a painter I couldn't be on pills, and she threw them all out. I never had any more nervousness after that."

One of the problems that Bearden felt most acutely was the meagerness of his formal art training. Reading in Delacroix's *Journal* that Delacroix had spent a lot of time copying the work of Old Masters, he decided that this would be a way he could learn more about painting. He was reluctant to go to a museum and copy there, in public, but he found he could take a reproduction of a painting to a photography studio and have it blown up in black and white and then copy that, substituting his own color scheme for the original. "I did that with Giotto, Duccio, Veronese, Rembrandt — right on up to Monet," he said. "I spent three years copying. The one I had the most trouble with was Rembrandt. It was that picture in the Metropolitan, *Pilate Washing His Hands*. There were so many subtle rhythms and carefully planned relationships that I finally had to give up on it."

Another problem was color. Bearden found that color as he had been using it in the past tended to break apart the forms that he was dealing with — to weaken the overall structure. He became interested in exploring color for its own sake, and this led him increasingly into abstraction. At about this time, in the late fifties, he met a Mr. Wu, a scholar in the fields of Chinese art and calligraphy. Bearden arranged to study with him informally. What he learned about Chinese landscape painting had to do mainly with pictorial space: the open corner, which allows the viewer's eye to enter the painting, and the areas left unfinished, so that the onlooker may complete them in his imagination; the contrast of masses and voids; the Chinese perspective, in which distant mountains bulk much larger than the shapes in the foreground. He began painting on rice paper (the paper he had bought in Paris), gluing it to the canvas and then tearing away sections, tearing them upward and across the picture plane until some motif engaged him, then adding more paper and painting in additional areas. By the late fifties, Bearden was painting in a totally nonrepresentational style, but one that had little in common with the work of Pollock or de Kooning. Some of his paintings of these years have the ancient, eroded look of rock faces or weathered walls. Others suggest the architectural solidity of Cézanne.

Occasional commissions and sales were not enough to let Bearden paint full time. In 1952, he had gone back to work for the Welfare Department and had been assigned to keep track of the city's fluctuating population of gypsies. "I wasn't enthusiastic about the idea at first, but eventually I hated to leave them," he has said. "I began to know so many families. They were truly a culture within a culture. They had such a strong sense of identity — anyone who wasn't a gypsy they used to call *gagco*. They came from India originally, and migrated into Persia and Europe. There seem to have always been gypsy tribes — Rumanian gypsies, Hungarian gypsies, Spanish gypsies — each with its own separate identity. They did certain kinds of traditional work. Relining copper pots and kettles was one of their specialties, and, of course, fortune-telling. We used to have an immigrant population coming in that believed in gypsy fortune-tellers, and a lot of gypsies lived down on the Lower East Side, around Orchard Street and the Bowery. But that faded out, and they moved to Queens and Coney Island. Their way of life was disintegrating. You don't have any longer the hundreds of small circuses and carnivals that they followed, and their old trades are no longer needed. Young people were marrying nongypsies, which had never happened before. The children were being forced to go to school."

Bearden's job was to keep an eye on the gypsies — their movements in and out of the city, their problems and needs. Few of them could read, and they had little interest in the laws of the *gagco*. When a gypsy got into a fight, or was arrested for stealing or for a con job, Bearden would go to police headquarters and do whatever he could. The gypsies had their own system of justice, he found. "They had trials, and they abided by the judgments. For example, a bridegroom found on his wedding night that his bride had been badly burned from her neck to her ankles as a child, so he took her back to her family and demanded his money back. It was an arranged marriage, and money had been paid. He lost the case, because sexually she was fine."

Not all the gypsies Bearden encountered were poor. "Once, I had to go and see a man in Brooklyn, a guy named Mike. He lived in a storefront, and his wife and children lived in another storefront nearby. He was a huge man, who must have weighed over three hundred pounds. He wore a white suit, like Mark Twain. And I made the mistake of asking him something about his job. He hit the ceiling. 'Look at my hands!' he yelled. 'I've never worked a day in my life!' His sons did repair work on milk-pasteurizing machines, and they supported him in style. He just sat there all day listening to music on his hi-fi, and every hour or so one of his daughters would come in with food — either Chinese food or barbecued spareribs. After he'd finished, he'd throw the ribs in the back room, where there were some of the biggest rats I've ever seen. He also had a rackful of guns, and now and then he'd take down a rifle and start shooting at the rats. Not at *them*, exactly; he'd wait until a rat got up on a piece of china — a cup or a plate — and then he'd try to shoot it out from under him."

Bearden worked with the gypsies off and on for fourteen years. Then, in 1966, his income from painting enabled him to leave the Welfare Department for good. The experience had always been interesting, but in the end it was rather saddening and it helped to strengthen Bearden's own feeling that the path of separatism within a culture is basically self-defeating. Like his friend Ralph Ellison, the writer, Bearden has tried to make art out of the totality of his experience as an American. "Al Murray says that when a person comes to America from some other country, he becomes four things," Bearden said not long ago. "Even though his ancestry may be Greek or French, if he becomes an American he becomes part Anglo-Saxon, part Indian, part frontiersman, and part black. Those are the main cultural roots that make the American character. You see the evidence all the time. Athletes slapping each other's hands instead of shaking them — that started with blacks. And jazz music. I don't think any critic has ever gone into it, but Abstract Expressionism is very close to the aesthetics of jazz. That's the feeling you get from it — involvement, personality, improvisation, rhythm, color. In the twenties, Benny Goodman used to come up to Harlem a lot. He was teaching himself about jazz the only way he could, and he had to become a little black to learn it. By the same token, when I started copying and learning from those pictures by Vermeer and Delacroix and the rest, in a sense I was joining the white world. It's all a little more complicated than some people try to make out."

## CANAL STREET

For the first two years of their married life, the Beardens lived on West 114th Street, in an apartment they shared with Bearden's father. They needed more space, and when a friend told them in 1956 of an artist's loft that was being vacated on Canal Street, they took it. The move to lower Manhattan in no way weakened Bearden's ties with the black community. In fact, it was in the Canal Street loft that the Spiral Group of black artists was formed, in 1963. The civil rights movement was in full swing then, and the original purpose of the meeting at Bearden's loft was to discuss going down as a group to that summer's March on Washington. They decided at that time to work together on the common problems of black artists. With the exceptions of Bearden and Jacob Lawrence (who was out of town at the time, and did not join the Spiral Group), very few black artists had been able to show at any of the rapidly proliferating New York galleries. Many competent black artists had difficulty exhibiting their work in New York, and the opportunities for younger artists seemed almost nonexistent. The Spiral Group — the name, contributed by Hale Woodruff, was intended to suggest a movement up and out — included Bearden, Alston, Woodruff, Calvin Douglass, Norman Lewis, Merton Simpson, Emma Amos, Perry Ferguson, Richard Mayhew, James Yeargans, Earl Miller, William Majors, Reginald Gammon, Al Hollingsworth, and Felrath Hines. They rented a small room on Christopher Street, in the Village, where they met once a week and eventually put on exhibitions of work by the members.

At one of the early Spiral meetings, the idea of a collaborative effort came up — a painting on which several artists could work together. Bearden thought about this afterward, wondering how it could be done. The solution that occurred to him was collage. He cut a lot of pictures out of the magazines that Nanette liked to read — *Life, Vogue, Harper's Bazaar, McCall's, Ebony* — and took

them to the next meeting, but nobody responded to his idea. Bearden, however, was sufficiently interested to try a few experiments on his own. He made
half a dozen small collages, pasting his cutouts to sheets of typewriter paper
and filling in with drawing and watercolor. He chose pictures that suggested to
him something out of his own experience — jazz musicians, landscapes, street
scenes, African sculpture, urban black faces. Reginald Gammon saw them and
suggested taking them to a photo shop to be photographed and blown up (as
Bearden had done earlier with reproductions of the Old Masters). Bearden did
this, but at first the results did not particularly interest him. The large photomontages were rolled up in a corner of the Canal Street loft when Arne Ekstrom
came there early in 1964 to discuss Bearden's next exhibition, scheduled for the
fall. Ekstrom had shown Bearden's abstract paintings in 1961, at what was then
the Cordier & Warren Gallery, on Madison Avenue. He looked at some new
abstract canvases that Bearden showed him. "I felt a lack of movement, a sort
of lost momentum," Ekstrom recalls. "I had just moved into a new gallery, in
the French & Company Building, and I was worried that the paintings wouldn't
hold up in the large space there." Then he noticed the rolled-up photomontages
in the corner, asked to see them, and said immediately, "That's your next show."

Bearden's "projections," as he and Ekstrom agreed to call them, were the
basis for everything he has done since 1964. When they were shown at the Cordier & Ekstrom gallery that fall, Bearden's old friend and fellow artist Ernest
Crichlow said, "Romie, it looks like you've come home," and most of the others
at the opening felt the same way. "It was not only an aesthetic but an emotional
breakthrough for Romie," Crichlow said later. "There was something entirely
fresh about them, about that vision." It was as though Bearden had reinvented
collage, which became in his hands the ideal medium for the transmission of all
he had learned as an artist and as a man.

The "projections," of course, were really prints. Each was issued in an edition
of six, and sales were very encouraging. But Bearden wanted to find a more
direct way of working in collage. He tried gluing his cutout photographs to canvas, but the glue made the canvas warp. It occurred to him that many of the Old
Master paintings he had copied in the fifties had been on wood panels, so he
did some research at the Metropolitan Museum, where a friend in the restoring
room let him examine the backs of some of the old panel paintings, and afterward he went to John Schindler, a commercial designer who was a former class-
mate at NYU, and Schindler helped him devise a Masonite panel with a special
wood backing that would not warp. Then he was free to develop and deepen his

new method, and also to work with color. All of Bearden's former discoveries seemed to come together in the new collage paintings: the shallow space of Byzantine mosaics, the strong forms of African sculpture, the spatial harmonies of Chinese landscapes, and, most significant of all, the carefully planned structure of Vermeer and the little Dutch masters. "Because many of the paintings I was doing were of interiors," he has said, "I began to look again at Vermeer and Pieter de Hooch and Jan Steen. I found that, especially with Vermeer and Steen, a lot of the work was controlled, like Mondrian's, by the use of rectangles over rectangles. I really think the art of painting is the art of putting something over something else, and in a way these new pictures of mine, while they used representational images, were more abstract than the work I'd been doing before. I would work with rectangular shapes that were in proportion to the overall rectangle of the whole painting. Delacroix said of the Dutch that in their purity and nobility of form they rival the Greeks. That was the quality I was trying to get. I wanted to make my formal language strict and classical, in the manner of the great Benin heads. But I also thought that by using photographs that way, almost cinematically, I could convey a sense of 'You are there' — a documentary feeling that would have something to do with the speed-fractured tempo of contemporary urban life."

The images that Bearden worked with were predominantly those of Negro life, but the way he fragmented and combined these images gave them another character and another dimension. Bearden felt that he did not have the right to use someone's photograph intact without permission. Superimposing the features of a Benin bronze on a contemporary black face, however, or giving someone grass for hair and corn for teeth, combining three or more photographs into a composite face whose features were jarringly out of scale changed more than the individual likeness. In Bearden's paintings, the Southern sharecropper's cabin and the Harlem street take on mythic overtones. This is quite deliberate on Bearden's part. A number of the paintings clearly echo major themes in Western art: the Annunciation, La Primavera, Susannah at the Bath. (Bearden's Susannah bathes alone in a cabin in the woods, watched only by a bird.) His *Woman in a Harlem Courtyard* alludes specifically to Pieter de Hooch's *The Spinner and the Housemaid*. The prevalence of ritual (as Albert Murray has phrased it) in American Negro life became the dominant theme of Bearden's mature work.

Certain images recur throughout his paintings of the sixties. Trains, for example, and birds — "journeying things," Bearden has called them. "Trains are so much a part of Negro life," he explains. "Negroes lived near the tracks, worked on the railroads, and trains carried them North during the migration." The "conjur woman," another recurring image, was a strong presence in the rural South of Bearden's boyhood, and a link to the ancient mysteries remembered from Africa; even in Pittsburgh, living in the house in back of his grandmother's, there was an old woman much feared for her power to put spells on people, and in Harlem as late as the thirties there were people like Black Hermann, a performing magician who also sold roots and strange potions in his drugstore on Lenox Avenue.

The blind guitarist of many Bearden paintings is a memory of a certain old Mr. Johnson, of Lutherville, Maryland. When Bearden was a boy, he sometimes visited his paternal grandmother, who after his grandfather's death had married a Methodist minister named Charles Cummings and moved from Charlotte to his parish in Maryland. A parishioner had a special cake she used to make, in several iron pans that had come down from the time of slavery; the cake looked like a watermelon, and had chocolate seeds, which she cut out and inserted by hand in the red batter. She would make a batch of watermelon cakes and get Romare to deliver them around town in a wagon he pulled. "Mr. Johnson, her husband, would always come along when I delivered those cakes," Bearden recalls. "He was blind, and he played the guitar. Whenever he heard somebody on the road, he'd ask who it was, and then he'd say, 'Get him over here. I had a dream about him last night, and he was laid out in his coffin so plain. . . .' Of course, everybody made tracks as soon as they saw us coming." Mr. Johnson is also Tiresias, the blind prophet of Greek drama, the man with inner sight.

Inevitably, perhaps in the emotional climate of the sixties, critics read social content into these powerful and evocative paintings. They saw "tormented faces," "vision of beauty and horror," and the travail and anguish of the Negro's existence; the work, as the *Times* noted, was "propagandist in the best sense." Bearden has made it plain that this was not part of his intention. "A lot of people see pain and anguish and tragedy in my work," he conceded a while ago. "It's not that I want to back away from this, or to say those things are not there. Naturally, I had strong feelings about the civil rights movement, and about what was happening in the sixties. But you saw that on television every night, you saw the actuality of it, and something was needed, I thought, other than to keep repeating it in art. I thought there were other means that would convey it better than painting."

Bearden believed, moreover, that the Negro was becoming something of an abstraction in the sixties, a sort of caricature of protest and injustice. For his own part, he wanted as he said in 1964, to "establish a world through art in which the validity of my Negro experience could live and make its own logic." Bearden was concerned with art, not propaganda. "I have not created protest images," he said. "The world within the collage, if it is authentic, retains the right to speak for itself."

Standing on the terrace of Albert Murray's apartment, on West 132nd Street, one day in 1971, looking across at the rows of four-story buildings that make up the block on Lenox Avenue between 132nd and 133rd, Bearden conceived the idea for his largest painting. *The Block* is actually six pictures joined together, making an eighteen-foot work. When it was shown at the Museum of Modern Art, in Bearden's 1971 retrospective exhibition there, it was supplemented by an audio collage of street sounds that had been tape-recorded, but Bearden now feels that this was not a good idea. The painting needs no accompaniment. It shows not only the street and the houses but also (shades of Eugene) the rooms behind the facades, where people are eating, bathing, making love, attending church (the block has two churches), getting their hair cut — just going about the ordinary business of life. The feeling conveyed is one of celebration.

When the Metropolitan Museum was planning its ill-fated "Harlem on My Mind" show, in 1968, Bearden was asked to be a consultant. He agreed at first, but when he saw how the plans were developing he withdrew. "They were giving it a sort of light, sensational treatment," he has explained. "I thought it deserved something more in-depth than that. I was so mad I never even went to see the exhibition."

Bearden has done as much as anyone to celebrate the achievements of black artists, both living and dead. In 1966, he organized a show called "Art of the American Negro" in a transformed basement on 125th Street — the first time since the nineteen-thirties that an exhibition of Negro artists of such scope had been seen in Harlem. The following year, Bearden and Carroll Greene, a collector of nineteenth-century black American paintings, put together a huge exhibition called "The Evolution of Afro-American Artists: 1800–1950" in the Great Hall of City College, with a hundred and fifty works by fifty-five artists. This was something of an eye-opener to a large number of people, blacks as well as whites, who had never before seen paintings by Joshua Johnston, Robert S. Duncanson, Henry Ossawa Tanner (the first black artist to win a prize at the Salon des Artistes Français), and other nearly forgotten talents. A great deal of research had gone into organizing the show, and Bearden became something of a scholar in the field. With Harry Henderson, he has recently completed a book on the history of Afro-American art, to be published by Doubleday in 1978.[1]

An increasing number of young blacks are studying art in school and college these days, and more and more have been deciding to make careers as artists. Although the odds are heavily against success for anyone in this line, it still seems harder for a young black than for a young white artist to find a gallery willing to show his work, and with this in mind Bearden, Ernest Crichlow, and Norman Lewis started the Cinque Gallery in 1969. The Cinque (named for the African prince who led a successful revolt aboard the slave ship *Amistad* in 1839) operates under a grant from the New York State Council on the Arts, which pays all its administrative costs; it is now at 2 Astor Place, around the corner from Joseph Papp's Public Theater, in space donated rent-free by Papp, and the artists who show there receive a hundred per cent of the proceeds of anything they sell. In its first years, the Cinque showed only young unknowns, but lately it has broadened its scope to exhibit older black and other minority artists who have been overlooked by the commercial galleries. Marcia DuVall, the administrative director, is besieged by artists who want to show there. Most of the younger artists who come in want to meet Bearden, she says. "I think Romie's success is maybe more of an influence than his work," says Chris Shelton, the Cinque's first administrative director. "They see one black man who's made it, and that makes them think they have a chance, too. Romie sees them all. When he gets home from his own studio at night, his phone never stops ringing. He spends most of his free time now helping other artists."

Sitting in Albert Murray's apartment not long ago, Bearden said he would feel better about the current crop of young artists if they showed more of an interest in aesthetic problems. "Most of the questions I hear now are about making it," he said. "I get very few who seem to have a real historical interest in the craft. Of course, this is a difficult time for artists. Valéry said that the invention of the machine destroyed man's patience. To sit down today and paint like van Eyck is impossible, or to do something like the Unicorn Tapestries, where, I'm told, there are more than a hundred different kinds of flowers and plants portrayed. Talent can even get in the way of an artist now, because every artist coming up must make a whole new tradition for himself. In the Renaissance, when there was such an explosion of skill, it was possible for men who were not great painters to paint great pictures just by leaning on the achievements of a Leonardo or a Raphael. That's not possible now. Only a great artist can make a great painting today. What's essential is that you make some statement, that you offer some vision of life. For example, Persia — Iran — seems to be largely a desert country. But in Persian miniatures I've never seen any desert. There's always the garden, which is in daylight, but at the top the stars are out. It's the vision of the oasis. Cézanne wasn't particularly talented, nor was van Gogh. It was only late in life that Cézanne got all he needed to do what he wanted to do, and when he confronted that mountain of Sainte-Victoire he had the means, he had his vision of the world. Now we seem to be at the end of an era, the romantic era. Even Mondrian was a kind of romantic with his idea that the world could be transformed through art. The notion that everyone is creative is all romanticism, and that seems to be ending, but it's not clear what will take its place. There is a kind of interregnum now."

Murray put an Earl Hines record on the record-player, and the two men listened to it intently. In addition to novels, Murray has written extensively about jazz — his magnum opus in this field, *Stomping the Blues*, came out last year. When the Hines record was over, he played some Fats Waller, and then some James P. Johnson, king of the old Harlem stride pianists. After that, he put on a very early side of Louis Armstrong, with a great, ringing Armstrong solo.

"One time, I was in Spain," Bearden said. "In Málaga. It was in 1950. For some reason, I went to a funeral. There was all that mournful music, and then, after the burial, somebody began to blow on a trumpet, another kind of sound entirely, and an Englishman who was standing next to me turned and said, 'You see, now life has taken over again.' I think that's what art is — it celebrates a victory. A blues singer up at the old Lafayette, she sings about waking up one morning, there's a letter from my man, he done left me, I'm going down to the river and God knows what I'll do — but then here comes Freddy Jenkins on the trumpet, playing with a mute in, and he does a funny kind of riff that turns what might have been tragic into something else, into farce, so you don't feel like going out and committing suicide after all. Life is going to triumph somehow."

## NOTE

From *The New Yorker*, November 28, 1977.

1. The book, *A History of African-American Artists: From 1792 to the Present* (New York: Pantheon Books, 1993), was not published until after Bearden's death; Henderson completed the manuscript. See "The Twenties and the Black Renaissance," in this volume, pp. 133–55.

# INTERVIEW WITH ROMARE BEARDEN

*Henri Ghent*

The following oral history transcript is the result of a tape-recorded interview with Romare Bearden on June 29, 1968. The interview was conducted by Henri Ghent for the Archives of American Art, Smithsonian Institution, Washington, D.C.

## INTERVIEW

HENRI GHENT: This is Henri Ghent interviewing Romare Bearden, painter. Mr. Bearden, where were you born?

ROMARE BEARDEN: I was born in Charlotte, North Carolina, September 2, 1914 [*sic*]. However, my mother and father were living in New York and I think they just went to Charlotte and returned shortly after I was born. I grew up mostly in New York and some time in Pittsburgh where I would to go see my grandmother. But I had very little interest in painting, or in art, I should say, as a young boy. It was only when I was about to graduate from high school that I began to become interested in art and in drawing cartoons at that time. I was then with my grandmother. The only time that I won any prizes was during this period of my last year in high school and I remember the first was a poster for a cleanup campaign. Another one had to do with a moving picture in Pittsburgh. With both of them my grandmother had me simplify what I had done. When

I went to college I thought that I was going to be a doctor and I majored in science and later in mathematics. But when I got out of college — I graduated from NYU — I decided that I wanted to study art. But I was still interested in cartoon. And I had met E. [Elmer] Simms Campbell who you know was a famous cartoonist, and I imagine the first Negro cartoonist to be shown in all the big magazines. He still draws for *Esquire*. In those days *Life*, and *Judge*, *College Humor*, *Collier's*, the *New Yorker*, these were the big markets for the cartoons. And, as a young student in college, I had cartoons in most of these magazines that I've mentioned. And I was often at Elmer's and he was very helpful to me. After I finished college I went to study with George Grosz at the Art Students League. Now you know Grosz was the great German artist who did the famous book *Ecce Homo* which has recently been republished. He was a marvelous draftsman. And when I started studying with Grosz, unlike the other students who usually were very tight, I would draw all over the paper. And Grosz said, "Now look, I want you to just draw the model's hand, or maybe just the face. Just use the whole paper and draw it here because I want you to really observe." And this is what I did. I spent a couple of years studying with Grosz. And then I did watercolors; I had never painted in oil. When I finished studying with Grosz I drew at home and I got a job as a political cartoonist with the *Afro-American* which was a well-known Negro newspaper published in Baltimore. For two or three years I did political cartoons. Grosz had introduced me to a number of the great draftsmen of the past like Ingres, Holbein, Dürer, and with my interest in cartooning I became intimate with Daumier and Forain and some of the other great satirical draftsmen. But then I become more and more interested in painting and gradually gave up my cartooning to concentrate mostly on painting because I felt that if I stayed too long in cartooning, you know, it would hurt my painting. And I got a studio. I ran into Jacob Lawrence on the street one day. He said he had a studio and there was one vacant above him. He was living at 33 West 125th Street. So I went and got this studio, my first studio. It was eight dollars a month including the electricity.

HENRI GHENT: It was cheap enough.

ROMARE BEARDEN: At first I had steam heat but later the landlord sold all the radiators for scrap iron. In those days before the war Japan was buying all the metal they could get. We had to heat with kerosene stoves after that. Besides Jake — I mean Jacob Lawrence — Claude McKay had a studio there, you know, the famous poet and writer. And then Bill Attaway stayed there for a while, another writer. In recent years he has done a number of things for Belafonte. I think he wrote one of Belafonte's last things on Negro comedy or humor. Then the late Allan Morrison who was one of the editors of *Ebony* had a place there.

Actually they — he and George Norfolk — formulated the idea for *Negro Digest* which later broadened into *Ebony*. So it was an interesting building. And there I was. When you're a young student you have a lot of ideas to express. And I was trying to be very precise in my drawing. One day later on, Bill Attaway said to me, "Why don't you draw — you know, just let yourself go and draw some of the things that you know about!" And I began at that time to do my Southern themes, the people that I'd seen as a young boy when I'd sometimes visit North Carolina where I was born. I did these on brown paper in a gouache tempera medium. I must have done about twenty of these paintings before World War II when I went into the Army. Just about the end of the war a painter came by my studio, William H. Johnson, who was very well-known at that time. Johnson had lived in Europe for many years and he came by with a woman named Caresse Crosby. Caresse was one of the well-known American expatriates of the '20s. And she had a press in Paris at one time, book publishing, with her husband Harry Crosby who was a well-known banker and writer and poet. He later committed suicide. And Caresse had opened a gallery in Washington called the "G" Place Gallery and she was thinking of doing a show of Negro artists. She came by with Johnson and she decided that she wanted to do a one-man show of my work. And that was really my first gallery show, at Caresse Crosby's gallery in 1945 in Washington, DC. Then I got out of the Army in a couple of months. The war was coming to an end, or was at an end. I met Caresse in New York and we went to the Samuel Kootz Gallery which Kootz was just then opening. He had been interested in art but I think was doing something else, writing advertising for a motion picture company. But his ambition was to open his own art gallery. His first idea I think was to have some of the leading modern American painters. And then, when Peggy Guggenheim closed her gallery, he turned his attention to the younger painters who were doing more abstract work. So he took me into the gallery. He had William Baziotes (who is dead now), Bob Motherwell. Later he had Hans Hofmann, Byron Browne (who is dead), Carl Holty, Adolph Gottlieb; most of these people who have become very well-known started showing either with Kootz or the gallery behind Kootz, the Betty Parsons Gallery where Rothko and Pollock, Stamos, and some of the other painters showed. I had my first New York show at the Samuel Kootz in 1945. He decided he wanted to show me right away.

And I had this show built around the Passion of Christ. It was a great success and the work was sold out in a couple of days. I thought that art would be like that for always. Also, the great thing about being in a gallery was meeting the artists because I hadn't had that kind of exposure. And Kootz would have a meeting about every month; all the artists would be there and there would be exchange of ideas which at that time meant a great deal to me. My work became more and more, you might say, non-representational. I had several shows with the Kootz Gallery.

Then, at a certain period, I felt that I really didn't know enough about painting, that I hadn't really gone to art school enough. My training with Grosz hadn't given me much training in oil painting. I had read Delacroix's *Journal* and I noted how Delacroix almost to the end of his life was always going to the Louvre and copying paintings. I felt that I wanted to do the same thing so I took perhaps two years and made a very systematic study of the Old Masters, starting with Early Renaissance painters like Giotto, Duccio — I made copies of their work — right on down to the High Renaissance. Men like Veronese. Usually my procedure would be to get a reproduction of the paintings of these masters and have them enlarged by photostat and copy the painting from the photostat instead of going to the museum. Of course a lot of the paintings were not in New York City. And I did very interesting and good copies of these paintings. It taught me a lot about painting. The copy that gave me the most difficulty was a Rembrandt, *Pilate Washing His Hands*, because, while it looks so easy, it looks so simple on the surface, you find it's so intricately involved. Because, if a painter has certain rhythms going and these things are all done right, say five or six rhythms that interwind right, these things kind of expand even more. Even without the painter's intention, it becomes even more intricate. I don't know if I'm making that clear.

HENRI GHENT: Yes.

ROMARE BEARDEN: You know what I mean. This was the case with Rembrandt, this marvelous *Pilate*. You always could find something new in it. I did the best that I could and I finally had to surrender without really completing this Rembrandt. It was at this time really too difficult for me. But after two years of this painting. . . . And I would get sometimes big sheets of paper and varnish them and just practice painting with a brush — then I felt I had some feeling for painting. I had been in the Army, as I've mentioned, and I still had the GI Bill of Rights which I hadn't used. And I decided to go to Paris. Some of my friends had gone. A very close friend who had been in the Army, Samuel Allen, who is a poet. So I went to Paris. Sam Kootz gave me a number of letters to Picasso, Braque, Brancusi, Hélion, and a number of other painters in Paris. Well, this was one of the great times of my life. Paris was just like a thing of dreams to me. It was about three months before I could get to the Louvre and I only got there by accident. I happened to be in that vicinity one day. This was the place that I mainly wanted to see but there was always something to do. I found that if you don't know exactly what you want to do, Paris was a bad place to go to discover yourself. Because you could easily get lost.

HENRI GHENT: Sidetracked.

ROMARE BEARDEN: Right. Because the land is so pleasant you could get sidetracked in Paris. But there I became very close to Brancusi and often visited him. That was another very meaningful period to me, those couple of years in Paris. And I didn't paint at all. I thought that I would like to but I was so absorbed in seeing and walking in Paris from one end of the city to the other that I could never get around to doing any painting. Then I came back. And the transition from there into my studio in Harlem on 125th Street took me a long time to get used to, to readjust. I decided that I'd live there after my GI Bill of Rights was used up. I thought, oh, I'll become a songwriter because I had a lot of friends who were writing songs. Somebody had left an old piano in this studio and I decided I'd learn this and I'd be a songwriter and make a lot of money and go back to Paris. Actually somehow I did write a number of songs. I got into ASCAP — I still get quarterly statements from ASCAP — and wrote one or two songs that kind of became hits. And I had a friend named Heinrich Blücher, the husband of Hannah Arendt, you know, both of them are famous philosophers. One day, Heinrich said, "Would you come over to my house, Ro- mare, I want to talk with you. You know, you're not painting. You're just wasting your time trying to be a songwriter and, if you keep on at this, you'll just go to pot and you'll never paint again." And I said, "You know, you're kind of right." I gradually got back to painting again.

And when I did I found I had very definite ideas about color. I began to just put color down in big marks and I found that using the color in this mosaic-like way destroyed the form, you know, opened up the form. So my color work be- came then increasingly non-representational as I allowed this color to give itself free rein. And I felt by using these tracks of color up and down and across the canvas, that I learned a great deal about the color's action. I had known Stuart Davis and Stuart, in a talk to me one time, said always remember about color that in a painting it has a position and a place, and it makes space. And thinking of color this way, not as a separate entity but color also as a form, as space, and not as decoration, taught me a great deal about space and color. Then I began to expand these paintings. I hadn't showed in some time. And then a woman became interested in my painting who had a gallery called the Barone Gallery. I had a one-man show there about 1955, my first show in New York since I went to Paris. I stayed with this gallery a couple of years and then I think she moved or went out of business. I kept expanding my ideas until I got with the gallery where I am presently, the Cordier & Ekstrom Gallery. I had a show there in 1960 and since 1960 I've had about four shows at Cordier & Ekstrom, the last being in October 1967. My last work has been kind of a reversion, you might say, back to my earliest work of the Negro subject matter: Negro genre, or Negro life, of whatever you might call it, that I first started with. So that is a kind of short summary of my painting career.

HENRI GHENT: Let's backtrack a bit. Would you like to tell me a little about your ethnic and spiritual background?

ROMARE BEARDEN: Well, in Pittsburgh I had the first consciousness of my spiritual background. The grandparents who had come from the South, that is my mother's father and mother, were of course Baptists. As Martin Luther King said, "If you weren't a Baptist you had escaped from the true religion." So my first recollections were of Shiloh Baptist Church. And of course I had to go to Sunday school or the other services, and my grandmother sometimes went on a Wednesday night, I think, the BYPU. And it was the church all around me, the Baptist church and Reverend Russell and, you know, you just can't forget these things. Now my mother and father were Episcopalians here in New York. They went to a church called St. Philip's Church in Harlem and later to St. Martin's Church. But, after a certain age, I would say 18 or 19, when I started college and I didn't have to go to church anymore, I just never went. I never had any interest.

HENRI GHENT: Would you say that remains until this day?

ROMARE BEARDEN: Yes. My wife is Episcopalian and she goes to church every Sunday and a few times I've gone with her. But I'm not myself what you'd call a churchgoing man, although I still have membership in St. Martin's.

HENRI GHENT: Tell me, do you have any recollection of sounds, tactile feelings, visual associations from your childhood?

ROMARE BEARDEN: Well, one of the things that I remember as a visual association that still remains with me somehow, and I certainly must have seen other things, was from Charlotte. I had gone . . . I must have been ten, nine or ten years old, and I was in Charlotte. And my great-grandfather had a garden in front of his house and there were flowers. And I was struck by this one flower because it was so beautiful to me; it seemed to me it was an unusual, beautiful flower. They told me it was a tiger lily. I would look at this lily every day when I was down there. And one day the lily was gone. And I couldn't understand it. There was nothing but a green stem, and this beautiful flower was gone. My grandfather had cut it to give to my great-grandmother to wear to church. And I still remember how I was so disheartened at seeing that flower gone. He told me, well, when you come back next summer it'll be here again. But I couldn't get that in my mind, you know, that that flower was gone would be there again. He said, you know, it's good earth here; it'll be here again. He said, you know, it will be. But I think that the things that make an artist paint, early recollections of things, or a sunset. . . . Malraux said that few artists are impelled to paint because of these early sensations. It's seeing finally the work of other artists that makes you want to paint rather than things from nature.

HENRI GHENT: What sort of reading habits did you have as a child?

ROMARE BEARDEN: Well, I liked adventure stories. Tom Sawyer, the Merriwell stories, baseball, sports. I remember other things that I read but I don't know if they made much impression on me, like *Don Quixote*. I must read that again. Or Herman Melville's *Moby Dick*. I'd skip a lot of it because I wanted to get to the adventure part. Or Robert Louis Stevenson's *Treasure Island*. Although it didn't mean too much. It was supposed to be for children but I preferred other things.

HENRI GHENT: Your early artistic leanings — can you pinpoint when they sort of evidenced themselves?

ROMARE BEARDEN: Well, as I explained earlier, when I was in the last year of high school I got interested in cartoons.

HENRI GHENT: Tell me some more about your school experiences.

ROMARE BEARDEN: Well, specifically as it relates to art it wasn't much until actually I had finished school and was in the Art Students League studying with George Grosz. After about six months he made me the monitor of the class so that I didn't have to pay any tuition. And I couldn't wait to get there. I studied from seven till ten at night drawing from the models. Every day I was learning something. It was such a great time for me. And when I look at some of the students now goofing off! I hated to see ten o'clock come. And I never will forget this. I made a book of all notes from the class, little drawings and things that

Grosz said. I loaned it to somebody; I don't know what happened to it. One of the terrible things that I lost. It would mean so much to have it now.

HENRI GHENT: Did you particularly like school as a child?

ROMARE BEARDEN: No.

HENRI GHENT: Were you considered a good student?

ROMARE BEARDEN: Well, I was considered a good student if I found a teacher who interested me. But I found that most teachers were dull, and not interested in their students. For instance, in mathematics, in the study of trigonometry most teachers, at least in that day, would just put certain angles on the board and you'd have to learn those formulas: O over H, A over H, and O over A. And you're lost when they say that. You say what the hell does it mean, unless you've got someone to give you the background of why this was important and really to relate mathematics to what was happening, you know, in the life around you. And when I had a teacher who did this I found a great interest in mathematics. Or anything. I was very poor in languages. I just didn't have the ear for it. I couldn't get any of them. I studied Latin, Greek, Spanish, and French and I was poor in all of them.

HENRI GHENT: You've told me that you were subjected to religious training as a child. Do you believe that your religious training had any influence on you as a person and as an artist today?

ROMARE BEARDEN: Well, I think so, especially the early religious experiences, I would say, rather than training, of seeing the baptisms. Because, as I said, I went to a Baptist church and sometimes in the summer they would have the baptisms in the river or little streams. And going south again and seeing this in Virginia or North Carolina, these baptisms as they did in the '20s, of maybe a mass baptism, 40 or 50 people at once. And I've tried to interpret some of this in my painting. This type of thing, of visual and emotional experiences and its effect on people, still interests me. Another thing that interests me is the message of some of the ministers and the way they say it. There was a tradition the way they did these things. And there was a famous minister of Norfolk, Virginia, I believe. I went with my grandparents one day to hear him. Each year he gave a famous sermon I think around the valley — "Passing through the Valley of Dry Bones." And he was so famous that a section of the church was set aside for white people. It was roped off and they came and sat in that section that day. I believe that these set sermons have been published. Reverend Jasper. And they were sensational thunderous sermons, you know. And his sentences and that whole thing if you could hear this, you know, it was tremendous. James Weldon Johnson in his *God's Trombones*, I think, tried to get the flavor of the Negro minister. So these are the types of things that I would say remain with me rather than any Christian doctrine.

HENRI GHENT: You were obviously impressed by this form of ritual?

ROMARE BEARDEN: Yes, I was impressed by the baptism. By those things, yes I was, because I looked at it as a continuity of what had happened earlier in many societies. Now that I look back I see that I had that interest in them.

HENRI GHENT: As a man and an artist have you any desire to escape from reality or tensions? Are you plagued by these two things?

ROMARE BEARDEN: I think the way to escape from reality is to get to the heart of it. Confronting it, moving toward the core, is the only way.

HENRI GHENT: As opposed to running away from it?

ROMARE BEARDEN: Yes, is the thing. Like a hurricane, you know, destroying everything around it — if you get to the eye of it there's a certain calm. And I think that this is something that the artist. . . . Proust said you never know from what direction talent may come, or you never know from what direction an artist may approach his subject. So I think this would be the way for me to move into that type of confrontation with reality. But this poses so many questions. What is reality? It has different meanings for different people.

HENRI GHENT: Are you plagued by tensions?

ROMARE BEARDEN: I think I am if I don't paint.

HENRI GHENT: To whom or what do you attribute your drive to communicate?

ROMARE BEARDEN: I don't know just how I could answer that. To whom I would attribute it I don't know, but I say any artist has this desire for a vision of the world and you have something. There's some painting someplace that's not in a museum and it's your idea as a painter to put that one thing that is missing there.

HENRI GHENT: If you had one particular aspect of communication to relate through your work, which would it be?

ROMARE BEARDEN: One particular aspect of communication to relate through my work? I wouldn't know because painting is the act of discovery and you're constantly enlarging your horizon or finding yourself every time you paint. I wouldn't want to say something now that I may change tomorrow, as I find something new. I don't think that a painter at this time is in a set tradition like the Renaissance where the aim was to perfect yourself in the particular tradition you were working in — Mannerism, Baroque, High Renaissance — that lasted one or two hundred years. The emphasis now is so on the individual and we're all in such a state of flux, constantly changing, that it's hard to say any one particular thing that motivates me.

HENRI GHENT: Is there any one person who helped to bring about your self-realization?

ROMARE BEARDEN: Well, I'd say there were several. Just in art alone there was Grosz who meant a great deal to me. And, as I said, there were these meetings of artists at the Kootz Gallery. I was particularly friendly with Carl Holty and Bill Baziotes and their friendship meant a great deal to me. When I first began to paint, as I mentioned, there was E. Simms Campbell and then there was Charles Alston who had been the early teacher of Robert Blackburn and Jacob Lawrence and was very helpful and encouraging when I first decided that I'd like to paint. There were a number . . . these are names that first come to my mind but all of them were very helpful.

HENRI GHENT: Now when you say "helpful," do you mean personally, artistically, or what? Give me a for instance.

ROMARE BEARDEN: Well, helpful in the sense of talking out my ideas to them. Alston showed me a lot of things about painting when I first began. Grosz introduced me to the requirements of good drawing. Holty into the ideas of abstract painting. Baziotes into certain ideas of feeling through painting. All of them in some way or other opened my eyes to things that I had never realized before.

HENRI GHENT: When and how did a personal identity apart from your family begin? When did you really begin to personally identify with your work?

ROMARE BEARDEN: Well, I think that after the war I began to arrive at some kind of personal identification, about 1945. And I hope that this identification has expanded throughout the years. As I said before, this is self-searching. I think that at about 1945 I had arrived at something that I could say — well, this has continuity to it, say ten or fifteen paintings had a resemblance to each other. You know, some type of a personal style had emerged at this time.

HENRI GHENT: Have you any impressions and experiences with boys and girls of your own age that you might like to recall?

ROMARE BEARDEN: Well, when I was with Kootz there were the meetings with the artists. And later, after 1945, a group of artists formed The Spiral. This was the time of the first March on Washington and we thought it might be interesting as a group of Negro artists maybe to hire a bus — a great number of people, as you know, were converging on Washington — and go down to represent the Negro artists. Then a number of the people who came to the first meetings when we were discussing this idea felt what we had was so important that we should continue. And finally we got our own studio and meeting place on Christopher Street. And these meetings and discussing the identity of the Negro, what a Negro artist is, or if there is such a thing, all of these pro and con discussions, meant a great deal to me especially in the formulation of my present ideas and way of painting.

HENRI GHENT: Let's talk about some of your friends and associates in the art world, early heroes and perhaps some of the painters that you most admire today.

ROMARE BEARDEN: Well, you see, my early heroes in the very beginning were all illustrators like Norman Rockwell, when I first became interested in painting. And I admired Daumier. And I liked the painter Pieter Bruegel so much when I was in art school that the fellows used to call me Pete for a nickname. I still have this affinity. You ask me who my heroes were and from what I learned something. They were the Dutch painters, Vermeer, ter Borch, Pieter de Hooch in particular. And from them and the drawings of Rembrandt I tried to incorporate the strength of the rectangle, of the breaking down of the picture in these rectangular relationships and moving out from there that gave certain solidity to the painting. This was a great influence. But early heroes — Zurbarán. As for painters I kind of favor the classic type of painter — Poussin, the Dutchmen that I mentioned, Mondrian, Picasso, Paul Klee. I am partial to all these painters. And the Sienese painter, Duccio. I like the structural things — the people who have concentrated on that.

HENRI GHENT: Who are some of your friends in the art world? And associates?

ROMARE BEARDEN: Well, any member. Norman Lewis is a close friend. I mentioned Carl Holty. There would be so many. The people that I see all the time that I'm close to: Alston, Hale Woodruff. These are the names that come to mind but I certainly know a great number of people in the art world.

HENRI GHENT: Do you have any feelings about bending or breaking conventions?

ROMARE BEARDEN: No. I don't set out to do that just for the sake of doing it. What I feel is what I mentioned to you: self-discovery will lead to something where you would have to break a convention, I certainly would. In the last works that I did, these Projections, so-called, collages, that I made small and had them blown up photographically was kind of a breaking. Using the photographic image in painting which I have done is a kind of breaking of convention. But it was particularly what I wanted to do. You asked me about my heroes. One of them is an artist whose art work doesn't influence me so much as his life and some of the things that he attempted to do — Courbet. I think there were painters in the last century who were greater than Courbet — although he was certainly a great painter. But the realism, this type of approach, his objectivity, interests me, too, in what I attempt to do.

HENRI GHENT: Let's talk about the Projections you mentioned. How were they received? I mean critically and from the standpoint of public reaction? Tell me something about them.

ROMARE BEARDEN: Well, the first exhibition I had of the Projections was in October 1964 at Cordier & Ekstrom Gallery. And I think that they were critically well-received. My idea in doing the Projections was . . . I mentioned Spiral, this group of Negro artists — we were talking one day about the possibility of a group of the artists working jointly on a picture and I was thinking of a possible way that this could be done. I thought that if we had photographs maybe we could each paste some down. And I mentioned this to several artists, one who was a landscape painter. I cut out some trees and I cut out some figures, and I said, maybe you could make a landscape and I could paste some of the figures on it and let's see what we can do. I worked on one or two alone just to try to get the idea myself to show the other artists. But they didn't seem to be too interested in it and I continued. I was talking to a painter and he suggested that I have these enlarged photostatically. He said he had a letter from a photostatic company saying they do large enlargements of art works. And I might take my things there and see what could be done. And I did. I did four or five. When Mr. Ekstrom came to my studio to talk about the possibility of a show in 1964, he asked me, "What are these things that are wrapped up?" I said, "It's something that wouldn't interest you." But I told him of this experiment I was doing and he said, "Oh, this is the very thing that I want for your next show." This was in late spring or early summer. He was going to Europe and he said when he came back he hoped that I'd have twenty or so done, enough for a show. He would open the gallery with a show of these. He called them "Projections," because they were large heads and they seemed to project themselves right out to the viewer.

HENRI GHENT: I've seen some of the Projections and was tremendously impressed, not only for the artistic originality but the stark reality of the Projections. Were other Negroes impressed?

ROMARE BEARDEN: Well, some were and some weren't. There's a lady whose husband is a physician and he had long been interested in my work. She came to the exhibit and she walked out; the work was disturbing to her.

HENRI GHENT: How so?

ROMARE BEARDEN: Well, she never stated just what was wrong. Another person did say that it showed the circumstances in which people were living, in which I showed people to be living, were a bit too stark; showed people in their worst or poorer circumstances. Art to her meant people living a little more elevated or what she considered more beautiful in costume or in manner. Because she had predicated, as most people do, the idea of beauty from the Greek ideal or the Hollywood ideal of the pretty girl. So that my work for people who think like that would be rather stark. And an interviewer for a magazine felt that it was a show of head-hunters.

HENRI GHENT: Of head-hunters?

ROMARE BEARDEN: Yes. Of head-hunters. Well, it was frightening to her. Here were Negroes with big heads and something within her reacted to this, you know. They were frightening; they were after her. I told her head-hunters are in the Solomon Islands and these are the people that you must deal with, that live in Harlem. You have to look at them a little longer.

HENRI GHENT: Well, tell me about some of the positive reactions from people.

ROMARE BEARDEN: Well, one of the most positive reactions was a review of the show. The show opened in 1964, as I told you, in New York at the Cordier & Ekstrom Gallery. And in October the following year I had a show of the same works at the Corcoran Gallery in Washington. And a review by Frank Getlein in a Washington newspaper was a very long and very fine and I thought a very substantive review. And there was a very good article on the work by a young Negro writer, Charles Childs, in the October 1964 ARTnews. And also one by Dore Ashton in Quadrum 17. Each of these three reviewers, each in his own way, saw qualities in it or brought something to it that I had not thought of myself.

HENRI GHENT: And you had a show last year, wasn't it?

ROMARE BEARDEN: In October, 1967.

HENRI GHENT: That was a phenomenal success, wasn't it?

ROMARE BEARDEN: Yes, that was very successful.

HENRI GHENT: Of the same medium?

ROMARE BEARDEN: No, I found that the Projections . . . I did small collages, say, about the size of a piece of typewriter paper, out of certain magazine photographs and colored material that I put together, and these were photostated and enlarged about to four by five feet and the photostats were then mounted onto masonite. Then they were taken to a framer. Going through all these steps is a very expensive process and, since they were considered as prints, they couldn't sell for too much, you know; it was a print. And the expense of making one of these was several hundred dollars just to have it blown up, mounted, and framed. So in the last show I did the same but, instead of doing the collage about the size of a sheet of typewriter paper, I did them large, four by five feet and colored and put them on a board myself. So that what was shown was the original. There were not prints made from it. It was original work.

HENRI GHENT: They also sold very well, too, didn't they?

ROMARE BEARDEN: Yes, the show was sold out.

HENRI GHENT: Can you recall any of the collectors?

ROMARE BEARDEN: Well, I know Senator Javits has one. Roy Neuberger. Howard University. And several other people I just can't recall now.

HENRI GHENT: Tell me, do you make a living now exclusively as an artist?

ROMARE BEARDEN: Yes.

HENRI GHENT: How long has it been so?

ROMARE BEARDEN: About two years.

HENRI GHENT: Have you found it necessary to supplement your income by working at other jobs?

ROMARE BEARDEN: Before I did, yes. I worked as an expert with the City on the gypsies. And sometimes I might do a book about that because this is also a very interesting culture. It was easy and I did have time to paint.

HENRI GHENT: Tell me some more about your work with the gypsies.

ROMARE BEARDEN: Well, what is interesting about the gypsies is that they came from India originally. I didn't know — did you know that?

HENRI GHENT: No.

ROMARE BEARDEN: The gypsies came from India. And from their language they've been traced almost to the exact place in the Himalayas where they came from. They're a wandering tribe in the Himalayas. And around the ninth or tenth century they left India. A number of them went to Persia, and a number of them embraced Zoroastrianism. I think around the eleventh century the first gypsies began to come to the European continent, into Greece and moving up into what is now Russia, Poland, and Bulgaria. These were the places where you have the largest enclaves of gypsies. In Victor Hugo's *The Hunchback of Notre Dame*, you know, a gypsy girl figures as one of the principal characters. So in the time that he was writing about, the 1400s, the gypsies had come to the Western part of Europe. And they were called gypsies because people thought they were from Egypt, you see. And with their boldness a lot of them had said, yes, we came from there, we're emissaries from the Pharaoh. And in some cases they were received as royal ambassadors. They've maintained their own particular culture down through the years. They had their own so-called kings, chiefs, trials, of their own. And in the present day, they conduct trials that ordinarily would go to a court — such as divorce. This the gypsies handle among themselves. Marriage ceremonies, things leading to monetary disputes between two people, are settled in a gypsy court. Usually they have a trusted person or two or three and they will hire a hall and, say, there's a dispute about a money matter. . . . I'll tell you about one trial that I attended once. It involved a young girl and a young fellow. They were married by gypsy custom which the fathers arranged. And the bride as a child had been badly burned. A kerosene stove or something had fallen on her. So her skin — with the long dresses that they wear it wasn't noticeable — but from her bust, let's say, down to her kneecaps her body had been very severely burned. On the wedding night the bridegroom wondered what he was touching — cellophane or what — and he called his mother and father and said, look, I don't want this; this is no bride. They bundled up the girl in the morning and took her back to her mother and father to whom they had paid ten thousand dollars for this beautiful girl. And the mother and father of the bride took her back in the house but they refused to give the money — ten thousand dollars — back to this man. They just said, "You married her, there she is, what's wrong with her? Here's the girl, take her." No, they didn't know that she was burned. This is the type of thing that might come up.

Another case was a fellow who had had tuberculosis and had been in a sanatorium. He called on a gypsy friend who refused to eat with him. Now when gypsies call on each other, you bring out food and drink, and to refuse to allow a man to eat and drink is the height of insult. The judge, very interestingly, consulted the hospital and found that this man did have tuberculosis, that it was arrested, and that if he had used any of the utensils it wouldn't have hurt any of the family. So he passed the word that if he visits he must be received. So the gypsies constitute culture right within ours. There's certain work that they do and certain things that they don't do. They don't want to go to school. They want to live entirely with their own customs and by themselves. I think the gypsies are going to disappear because the economic basis of gypsy life with the encroachment of many things of modern civilization is disappearing. They were coppersmiths and now we have stainless steel. They used to fix the fenders of cars. Now you need electric jackhammers to do it because the fenders don't come off the cars as they used to. Or their fortunetelling — people don't believe in it anymore. You see, there's no way for them to make a living as they used to. No, eventually they will disappear.

HENRI GHENT: Do you think in the process they will abandon their culture?

ROMARE BEARDEN: They'll abandon . . . usually they marry or stay within their tribes. The Russian gypsies will stay by themselves. The Russian gypsy man will do a certain kind of work that a Spanish gypsy wouldn't do. It's funny that the sociologists have never touched gypsy life or their customs and, before it all disappears, it certainly would make an interesting study. Somebody like Oscar Lewis who did things about the Mexican family should investigate the gypsies.

HENRI GHENT: Your own association with the gypsies here in New York has been in which capacity — sociological?

ROMARE BEARDEN: Yes. I was working for the Department of Social Services and that was my job — gypsies.

HENRI GHENT: Being as elusive as they would appear to be, have you formed any kind of working relationships or friendships with these people?

ROMARE BEARDEN: Oh, yes. I am going back in a few weeks to see some of my friends among the gypsies. A lot of them are good friends.

HENRI GHENT: You've mentioned that you lived and worked for a time in Paris. Have you done other travels as well?

ROMARE BEARDEN: Yes, our last trip was to the Caribbean last year. I went with my wife and Gippo to, oh, about fourteen different islands in the Caribbean. When I left for the islands, I hadn't thought that I would do any painting. But I did get a little sketchbook and did some little watercolors and sketches while I was down there. I think it would be a fascinating place to live and I certainly would like to live on one of the islands three or four months of the year. I enjoyed it so much down there.

HENRI GHENT: Any particular one of the islands?

ROMARE BEARDEN: Yes, I found Martinique extremely interesting. A few miles out of Fort-de-France, the capital of Martinique, you find things very much as they were when Gauguin was there. You know, before Gauguin went to Tahiti he stayed for some time in Martinique and did paintings there. Martinique is mountainous. And although they're not large, there are about ninety-six rivers in Martinique. Did you ever know that?

HENRI GHENT: Ninety-six?

ROMARE BEARDEN: Yes. They just come pouring out of the hills. And up in the hills there's a marvelous rainforest, something like in the Amazon or certain parts of Africa with marvelous woods, mahogany. And there's always this haze, or kind of a drizzle. It's just magnificent. I would just like to stay there for a while.

HENRI GHENT: Is it a humid drizzle or just . . . ?

ROMARE BEARDEN: It is humid. I imagine it could be very humid. But in other places up where you get out of the rainforest it is quite cool and nice. I found the weather very pleasant in Martinique. I hate to use the word "colorful" but some of the fishing villages. . . . It's too bad that the French government hasn't done more for Martinique and Guadaloupe because conditions are very primitive. Especially in the back country Martinique is very primitive — as are many of the West Indies islands. And I think it's going to be the next hotbed of social unrest, if it is not there already, because the disparity between the affluent and the poor is a tremendous gap; it's tremendous.

HENRI GHENT: Do you think this tropical surrounding would be particularly inspirational from an artistic viewpoint?

ROMARE BEARDEN: Definitely. Each place that you are in, I think, affects you in some way or another. And an island like Grenada would seem to be a perfect setting for Shakespeare's *The Tempest* — it's hard to differentiate what is sea and what is sky; they all seem to be blended together out of sea and air, this marvelous island. Certainly if I lived there for any length of time, I know it would affect the way I work.

HENRI GHENT: You mentioned that you were accompanied on this trip to the Caribbean by your wife and — was it Gippo?

ROMARE BEARDEN: Well, I have a cat — Gippo the cat. And we didn't know what to do with Gippo so we just took him.

HENRI GHENT: How old is Gippo?

ROMARE BEARDEN: Gippo will be six in August. When we got back Gippo was the official mascot of the ship. People loved Gippo and he loved the ship and he didn't want to leave because they fed him nearly a pound of calf's liver every day. He just loved it.

HENRI GHENT: Describe him.

ROMARE BEARDEN: Well, Gippo is I think a very handsome cat. He's perfectly symmetrically striped with gray and tan markings. We found him in the woods and he has a little wildcat in him and it took a long time, about six or eight months, when he was a young kitten, to get him trained. But now he's happy. The studio he feels is his. It's hard to keep a cat like that for any length of time in a cage at a veterinarian's. So we took him and it worked out quite all right. We couldn't take him to some of the islands, like Barbados, for instance, because of . . .

HENRI GHENT: The quarantine laws.

ROMARE BEARDEN: Yes, the quarantine laws.

HENRI GHENT: In researching some material on you I noticed that there was a cat in very many of the informal photographs. Was that Gippo?

ROMARE BEARDEN: That was Gippo, yes.

HENRI GHENT: He's quite a star in his own right then, isn't he?

ROMARE BEARDEN: Well, I keep telling my wife that she should have trained Gippo and used him for ads for cat food and those things because he's a natural ham. And he's such a handsome cat that he'd have been a perfect model.

HENRI GHENT: He loves to be photographed then?

ROMARE BEARDEN: Oh, he loves that attention.

HENRI GHENT: Tell me . . . let's talk a bit about Mrs. Bearden. What is her maiden name?

ROMARE BEARDEN: Nanette Rohan (R-o-h-a-n).

HENRI GHENT: Is she a New Yorker?

ROMARE BEARDEN: Nanette was born on Staten Island. Her mother and father came from the Caribbean — the island of St. Martin. And St. Martin is not a large island — but half of it is French and half of it is Dutch. Her mother came from the Dutch part of the island and her father from the French.

HENRI GHENT: Well, I know that Mrs. Bearden is extremely attractive. Tell me more about her. What does she do? Is she artistically inclined?

ROMARE BEARDEN: Yes. She doesn't paint; she is more interested in fashion design, you know, clothing, designing dresses. Actually she has taken some courses in this in a fashion training institute. She makes a number of her own clothes. And I think if she had persisted she might have gone into this field, which is a rather difficult field to break into from what I understand, that of dress design.

HENRI GHENT: How long have you been married?

ROMARE BEARDEN: Fifteen years.

HENRI GHENT: And you have no children?

ROMARE BEARDEN: No.

HENRI GHENT: Is she — or has she been rather an inspiration to you in your career?

ROMARE BEARDEN: Yes. And also she has a good eye for painting. When I begin to make things too complicated, she'll know often the right things to tell me. She has an extremely good eye and fine taste. I rely on her judgment a great deal in these things. And she's very objective — not like a lot of artists' wives who talk about "we." She can be very objective.

HENRI GHENT: I would think that she was terribly excited about the tremendous success of your last show.

ROMARE BEARDEN: Yes, she was.

HENRI GHENT: And the many things that followed?

ROMARE BEARDEN: Right.

HENRI GHENT: You've traveled extensively in this country, too, haven't you?

ROMARE BEARDEN: Yes. In the Army, going from camps, getting around the various parts of the United States I saw the East Coast, the Midwest, and something of the Far West.

HENRI GHENT: Have you been back to the South recently?

ROMARE BEARDEN: Well, my last trip south was in April of this year, 1968. I was at Spelman College. That's one of the five colleges of Atlanta University. Atlanta University is mostly a graduate school: Spelman, which is a school for women; Morehouse, where Martin Luther King went to school, is often referred to as the Negro Princeton; and Morris Brown, and Clark; the five colleges of Atlanta University.

HENRI GHENT: What were you doing in Atlanta?

ROMARE BEARDEN: Well, they have a Fine Arts building and quite an art program. I was looking at the students' work and giving a series of lectures on "Structure and Space."

HENRI GHENT: Do you enjoy teaching and lecturing?

ROMARE BEARDEN: Well, I have never taught. I have lectured at Hampton in February. I'm doing a book on Negro artists, and I lectured on nineteenth-century Negro artists at Hampton. I enjoyed that very much. And I enjoyed being on the campus in Atlanta very much.

HENRI GHENT: Tell me, what are your political affiliations, if any?

ROMARE BEARDEN: I have none.

HENRI GHENT: You abstain completely from politics?

ROMARE BEARDEN: No. I mean I've voted or registered as a Democrat. But I may have missed a few of the last elections — I don't have a great interest in that.

HENRI GHENT: How do you feel about the upcoming election?

ROMARE BEARDEN: Well, I was extremely interested until Senator Kennedy was shot. And — you know, if it's the same old tired fire horses that they are going to offer, I would be uninterested again. Not in the election but in the candidates.

HENRI GHENT: I take it that you felt he did indeed have something very meaningful to offer?

ROMARE BEARDEN: Oh, I think that he had . . . King was shot and now Kennedy. You know, a lot of the Negro people felt that he was one of their last hopes. And I think that he had caught something of the resonance and flavor of the Negro poor.

HENRI GHENT: Speaking of the so-called Negro problem in America, have you ever encountered racial prejudice as a black artist?

ROMARE BEARDEN: Now you mean a particular prejudice or you mean prejudice in the world of art? How do you mean that?

HENRI GHENT: Prejudice in the world of art.

ROMARE BEARDEN: Well, my feeling is — I wouldn't say I think — my feeling is that it is there, but not, say, a direct prejudice or a sign saying don't come into this gallery, or don't do this, or we don't take Negroes in. Because Negro artists are in many of the galleries; but I think the prejudice may be an oblique one. Let me explain what I mean: The Negro artist is usually not what you might say "on the scene." He's not moving where a number of the better-known white artists are. I was in the Archives on Thursday and there I saw a photograph on the wall of Rauschenberg and a number of artists around him at what must have been an exhibition at a museum; and there were no Negroes in this group. You know, you ask a white artist or a critic, "Who are the Negro artists? Do you know any Negro artists?" He might know a friend, but the fact of a Negro "making the scene" or his compatriot, he doesn't think so. It just may not be in his consciousness. Just like I was talking to a critic, Irving Sandler, on a radio program once. He had been to the meetings of this club on Eighth Street. And he said, "Now that I think of it, too, I wonder why someone didn't invite some — you might have had a different point of view." You follow what I mean?

HENRI GHENT: Sure.

ROMARE BEARDEN: Also, the art critics . . . I read a number of art books on the history of American painting and it's very seldom that Negro artists are mentioned. For instance, in my opinion, Henry O. Tanner is one of the four or five great American painters. And you never see his name mentioned. In Barbara Rose's latest book on painting from 1900 to the present, nowhere is Tanner mentioned. And he's a better painter than Glackens or Prendergast; especially his late paintings, the ones he did in the late '10s and '30s, the small things. Mert Simpson has a number of them. Only Rouault is comparable. Well, this question that you raised about prejudice, maybe we can simplify that rather than leave it. I mentioned Barbara Rose's book. I don't think she did it out of any feeling that, well, I'm prejudiced and I'm not going to mention any. It's just not in the consciousness of a lot of people who are writing these things.

HENRI GHENT: Why do you think this is so?

ROMARE BEARDEN: I couldn't give a definite answer. But I think that Negroes themselves have to encourage . . . should have the same interest in artists that they might have in Negro basketball and baseball players, or now in politics and other things. This has to be pushed the same way. Just as I made the statement about Tanner. Maybe that would call someone's attention to him and they would really look into what this man accomplished. El Greco remained forgotten for three or four hundred years until around the turn of this century when he was rediscovered as one of the great masters of Baroque painting. So it's the same. Nor is the Negro ever equated in many of the paintings that I've mentioned in abstract expressionism. In this magazine which I received in the Archives it said, "Finally America arrives in the abstract expressionist painting." But no one, when you stop to think, has ever equated abstract expressionism as a movement with jazz music. It's based on improvisation. The rhythms, the personal involvement, all of this is part of the jazz experience. And many of the abstract expressionists would often play jazz music while they were painting, or at least were very interested in that art form. But here is an avenue I imagine that Negro critics themselves as they get into it are going to have to explore and open up these new dimensions to people.

HENRI GHENT: As is common with a great many artists, you have gone from one particular style to another, and more recently I believe you have concentrated on subject matter that is more or less directed to the Negro experience. How do you account for that?

ROMARE BEARDEN: Well, what I arrived at after a time was the space. And after I got a certain space that hasn't changed so much. But, a lot of the life that I knew in certain rural Negro surroundings is passing. And I set down some of my impressions of that life. It's in a certain sense historical and has certain affinities with many classical things that have happened before. For instance, I used to know a lady in Maryland where my grandfather had a church. And this lady made watermelon cake. And I don't know where she had gotten these baking pans from, her mother or what, or whether she made them. I was too young to think about that at the time. But anyway, she made this kind of red cake, the inside of the cake like a watermelon. And she'd cut out chocolate seeds and put them in this red batter. And over that would be a white batter, and over that striped green and white of the watermelon — this was iced. If you'd stand five or six feet away you'd swear that you were looking at a watermelon. And on weekends the wealthy people in Lutherville would order these watermelon cakes. And sometimes when I'd be visiting in Lutherville I would deliver the cakes for this lady. And her husband was a famous blind guitar player, a folk singer like blind Lemon Jeffries, and he used to play in Baltimore before they moved out to this place. Sometimes he'd go along with me just for a walk and hold on to me or to the wagon and he'd be walking down the country roads. He knew everybody's business, and when people saw him coming they would kind of run because he always had a dream. He'd say, "Oh, Mrs. Jones, I dreamt last night I saw you just laying in that coffin just as plain." Nobody wanted to hear him. So there he was and he'd be strumming on his guitar. It was kind of out of a Greek play. Leading the blind soothsayer, you know, the little boy leads him in and he makes a dire prediction for the city. And this had some of this element in it. If you equate a lot of the things that happened in Negro life you see there's a continuity with many of the great classical things that have happened before. And this is what I tried to find in my work, this connotation of many of the things that have happened to me with the great classical things of the past.

HENRI GHENT: You once said — if I quote you correctly — that you had not to go out and seek the Negro experience in order to paint the way you do because all you had to do was look out of your studio window on 125th Street in Harlem and there it was.

ROMARE BEARDEN: Yes, I was talking specifically about the people talking about Happenings and Surrealism. I said I didn't need to worry about Happenings or trying to make these things up. I'd just look out the window and every five minutes there'd be some Happening going on.

HENRI GHENT: Do you think that the Negro should now direct his efforts to the black community? That is, by exhibiting exclusively in black communities, colleges, universities, et cetera?

ROMARE BEARDEN: Well, I don't think that this should be exclusively done but, since so little of it has been done before, I think that a great deal of effort should be made in this direction to make the communities, to use a cliché, more art conscious, or more aware of the Negro artist. And I think that in time this will make for a better artist because the artist can learn some of the feelings of the community about his work. To make an artist you need many hands and all working together can make for something very meaningful. The Negro artists of the nineteenth century were not, you might say, Negro artists at all. They were people who were Negroes and artists and most of them lived abroad and their work was directed not to Negroes primarily, or with the Negro in mind, but it was directed, like that of other American artists, to the patrons of art. This is what I mentioned earlier about Courbet. He thought about these things: to whom his work would be directed, and something about the social responsibilities of artists. This was a consideration of his and I think in a way that this is why I revere Courbet. And certainly I think this is part of the thing that the Negro artist has to do. And with that I don't think that the Negro community then should be exposed just to Negro artists, but that they begin to be involved in all of art, that they will see Egyptian art, that they will be acquainted then with African sculpture, and involved in a number of artistic experiences.

HENRI GHENT: Speaking of Negro or black artists living and working abroad, if you had the opportunity personally, would you prefer to live in Europe, Africa, or any country other than this one?

ROMARE BEARDEN: Well, as I said before, I would like to live in the Caribbean — whether it would be on a full-time basis or not, I don't know. Because, after all, I am American, I guess. I was born in this country, I take aspirin if I have a headache, I ride the subway, I wear these clothes; and all this conditioning means something. And I'm more familiar with this milieu. And living abroad — now to a nineteenth-century artist like Tanner it was a very different thing. Tanner went to art school in Philadelphia. He had a great deal of trouble at the Philadelphia Academy. And I know in the '20s when I first began to be interested in art a number of art schools would not take Negro students. Some of the art schools that did take Negro students would not allow them into the life drawing classes. So you can understand why a number of Negro artists would prefer going to Europe where they could escape these kinds of silly prejudices and also have the opportunity for furthering their art. Tanner, for instance, studied with Benjamin Constant who in his day was like the Picasso of today, you know, was well-known. Gérôme was very interested in his work. He was right in the midst of, you might say, "the scene" or what was happening at that time. Now Paris is not the art scene as it was in the 1890s when Tanner went there. It was a place where all American artists had to go. The scene has shifted to New York City at the present time. Now how long this will remain, or what the meaning of that is, it is a fact. So the art schools that once refused to take Negroes do now. At Spelman College they were telling me that they had to accelerate their art program because a number of the students were going to Georgia State College where they have a very large art complex. So they're in competition. Where once Negro students just went to Atlanta University, now they can go to the other colleges, so that the Negro college has to offer something equally as good to attract the students. You follow what I mean?

HENRI GHENT: Yes, surely.

ROMARE BEARDEN: So it's the same thing with the Negro artist. Many of them seem more comfortable overseas. They had a show there about two or three years ago, "Twelve American Negro Artists Living in Europe." I'm sure there are many more but these twelve put on a very fine show. A friend of mine, Merton Simpson, tells me that he works with a great deal more facility in Paris than he does in New York City. It may be just something personal rather than a prejudicial thing. So I think that, so far, what I have done here is in response to the environment that I know best and I think at least for a time that I have to stay here, and if I did leave I'd always be echoing back to what I knew here.

HENRI GHENT: Yes. Your roots are here.

ROMARE BEARDEN: That's right.

HENRI GHENT: Do you have any hobbies or do any work which some people might call a hobby?

ROMARE BEARDEN: Well, painting to men like President Eisenhower or Churchill was a hobby and a very relaxing one. But it is not so to a very serious artist. Because your painting is constantly saying no to you. And this, you might say, dialogue between you and your art has to each day be renewed which often makes it taxing for the artist. I know a lot of artists just hate in a certain way to go to paint. So in that sense you can't call painting for a serious artist a hobby. It's a calling. And beyond that if you are a serious painter you don't have time. You read and you go to the theater and do a few things that are relaxing, but to have anything as a hobby — well, like playing chess — Marcel Duchamp gave up painting to be a chess player — it would demand that type of attention.

If I went into woodworking or anything I would give it that same degree of attention and I wouldn't be painting. You know, this happened to me when I was writing songs. So I don't bother with any hobby.

HENRI GHENT: You don't have time for it.

ROMARE BEARDEN: No. Because I would give it the same time to do it well as I do painting.

HENRI GHENT: In addition to being an artist, you are also a writer; you're writing a book, maybe two, no?

ROMARE BEARDEN: That is true. And after I've finished those that will be the end, if you can call that a hobby. But I've written a book with Carl Holty called *The Painter's Mind*. Carl Holty I mentioned before as being in the Kootz Gallery with me, or when I was with that gallery. It is a kind of an exegesis of structure and space in painting.

HENRI GHENT: I see.

ROMARE BEARDEN: And then after that I think Carl and I will do a second book, a continuation of this exploring the artist's vision. And I'm working on the notes now for a book on the history of the black artists in the United States.

HENRI GHENT: What period will that encompass?

ROMARE BEARDEN: Well, from the first artists whose work we have a record of — Joshua Johnston on to the contemporary scene.

HENRI GHENT: I see. Will this be commercially available?

ROMARE BEARDEN: Well, I hope so when I finish it. In a certain sense I'm trying to write the history of the black artists in this country in a way that will be understandable to people without a long analysis as I do in *The Painter's Mind*. A more popular book so I can acquaint people with the history of the Negro artists in this country.

HENRI GHENT: I see. There's a good possibility that this book will be used in schools and colleges, et cetera?

ROMARE BEARDEN: That's what I hope.

HENRI GHENT: So it'll be educational?

ROMARE BEARDEN: That's right, educational, entertaining, and I hope with some artistic merit.

HENRI GHENT: How much time do you devote to your work?

ROMARE BEARDEN: Painting?

HENRI GHENT: Yes. Do you have a schedule?

ROMARE BEARDEN: Yes. I paint on a kind of regular schedule. I usually don't paint in my studio, not for the last few years; I go to the place of a friend of mine in Long Island City. I go Monday, Wednesday, and Friday. And usually in my own studio I work a bit on the weekends. And I've left Tuesday and Thursday for writing, research, and the like for the books.

HENRI GHENT: I see. I gather than you're happiest when you're painting? Not that you're unhappy when you're writing, but you prefer to paint?

ROMARE BEARDEN: Yes, I prefer to paint because I don't know that much about writing. And a lot of the technical things that are no problem to me in painting are problems to me in writing. For instance, I know that yellow and blue make green. But the grammar, and those things — you say, well, you knew all the rules and you can forget them and have your own style. But I'm not that conversant as a writer. I just stumble on and hope the editor will assist me.

HENRI GHENT: Your colleague — Carl Holty — how extensive has his participation been in this literary venture?

ROMARE BEARDEN: *The Painter's Mind*? Well, Carl has a very brilliant mind and he's a little bit older than I am. And it was I who persuaded Carl to try to get down some of his ideas — that was how the book started. And so this collaboration developed and he was a great assistance to me.

HENRI GHENT: Let's talk about form or content of central interest to you in your work.

ROMARE BEARDEN: Well, in beginning a work now I first put down several rectangles of color some of which, as in a Rembrandt drawing, are in the same ratio as the canvas or the rectangle that I'm working on. You understand what I mean?

HENRI GHENT: Yes, of course.

ROMARE BEARDEN: Now, if I'm doing a collage, after I put down these rectangles I might paste a photograph, say, anything just to get me started, maybe a head, at certain — a few — places in the canvas that I've started. The type of photograph doesn't matter at all because this is going to be a hand or a little landscape that I put down just to get me started. As Delacroix said, a painting or drawing is developed by first putting down something and then the superimposition of ever more definite statements. That's how I start this thing: rectangles, pasting on this, and the superimposition of ever more definite statements. Now when I put this paper or the photograph on I try to move up and across the canvas, always moving up and across. If I tear anything I tear it up and across. What I'm trying to do then is establish a vertical and a horizontal control of the canvas. I don't like to get into too many slanting movements. When I do I regard this as a tilted rectangle and I try to find something that compensates right away for a slant or a tilt or a diagonal movement on the canvas. I like the language of what I'm trying to do to be as classical as possible but I don't want complete reductionism like a Malevich or white on white where you end up with an empty canvas. I am interested in flat painting and the things I told you that I studied—the Dutch, the early Sienese, or Byzantine painters; the great exponents of flat painting. Moreover, I try to incorporate some of the techniques of documentary film or the camera eye into the art of painting.

A lot of people have said to me that my use of overlapping planes and this flat space is similar to Cubism. Which is true. But however in the actual process of my composition I find myself as much involved with the methods of Dutchmen like de Hooch and Vermeer that I've mentioned as I do with any of the Cubists. What I like most about Cubism is this emphasis on the essentials of painting. And what I don't like about Cubism is I feel that a lot of it overcrowds the space. That is what sent me back to the Dutchmen, to the emphasis on this rectangle where I can stress these great vacant areas of the plane against the things that are busy—as in some of Picasso's collage drawings; or, of course, the work I told you I like so much, the Cubism and the neo-plastic work of Mondrian. Of course, in a lot of the things that I have done in my crowded urban street scenes with a lot of people in them and a multiplicity of images, I have tried to find other ways to get this plasticity that I want with my liking for the flat painting and the classical manner. Now also involved is the interplay between the photograph and the actual painting and I constantly find myself adjusting my color to the gray of the photograph so that there won't be too much disparity in color between them. However, I found that even in spite of the fact that I have to restrict my color, that just using a few colors can give me quite a range. For instance, in the Pompeian paintings they just used a red, a gray, and a black, and a few other colors; yet you feel the full range of color in those great paintings. In other words, what I try to do is relate all my colors to gray and then put in in a few places a few dissonant accents. I also have found that too bright a color—like in Art Nouveau and the rest—after a while these color harmonies that seemed so interesting at first begin to wear, and what stands up the longest almost are paintings where you feel the absence of color. Like the Chinese paintings, done with just washes of gray or a very little touch of color. Or the paintings of Zurbarán in gray, you know, where you don't tire of a color harmony. And I also find that I'm constantly adjusting my color to things that I paint; bright sections of color and also the photographs that I will use, all this must be related so you feel that a harmony has been arrived at. Now

I think that some of the things that underlie my process is the fact that a photographic image when it's taken out of its original content and put in a different space than you saw it in the magazine can have another meaning entirely. Just then a work of art is not life itself. There's a certain artificiality about it and by cultivating the artificiality, or, in other words, by cultivating what is art, you make what you're doing seem more real. And so while my initial thing has been one of shock — as we've mentioned — to a lot of people, I think that other people upon reflection have found a great deal of artistic merit in the work, and often a great deal of social meaning other than what I actually attempted to put into the work itself.

HENRI GHENT: In addition to your own activities as a professional artist, I know that you have been also active as director and co-director of several important shows here in New York and in other cities around the country. At the outset I would like to cite the recent show of, I believe it was called "The Evolution of Afro-American Art."

ROMARE BEARDEN: The "Evolution of Afro-American Artists 1800–1950."

HENRI GHENT: That was sponsored by City College?

ROMARE BEARDEN: It was sponsored . . . you could call it a tripartite sponsorship — by the City University of New York, the Urban League of Greater New York, and the Harlem Cultural Council.

HENRI GHENT: I see. And you are the Art Director for the Harlem Cultural Council, are you not?

ROMARE BEARDEN: Yes, I may be now. I was; I may be. I think if things that come that have to be done of a nature like this involving the Harlem Cultural Council, they usually call upon me. The first such show that Jim Love, a young interested person from Brooklyn, and I organized for the Harlem Cultural Council was a show called "Contemporary Art of the American Negro" in the summer of 1966.

HENRI GHENT: That was in Harlem, wasn't it?

ROMARE BEARDEN: Yes. On 125th Street in the basement of a furniture store which we made over into a very acceptable gallery — Riker's Furniture Store.

HENRI GHENT: That went over pretty well, I understand?

ROMARE BEARDEN: Oh, yes. It was the first big show of Negro artists in Harlem since the 1930s. And then the show that you mentioned was done the following year in October 1967 in the Great Hall of City College. This was a far more elaborate undertaking because it involved finding the work of a number of nineteenth-century artists' art starting with Joshua Johnston, Robert Duncanson, the sculpture of Edmonia Lewis, Edward Bannister, Henry Tanner, on to Richard Mayhew and Merton Simpson. We had, maybe, over two hundred works of art in the show. The Great Hall . . . when I first saw it, I was just thunderstruck with what could be done. But we had the services of a young Negro designer, James Mayo, from Washington, D.C.

HENRI GHENT: Didn't he design the show of Persian Art or something to that effect?

ROMARE BEARDEN: The Turkish show that was touring. And he designed some Persian work it is true, but it was for a permanent exhibit in Dumbarton Oaks.

HENRI GHENT: It was a beautiful design for the CCNY show.

ROMARE BEARDEN: Oh, he's marvelous. And he designed . . . because we had to set up these stanchions — the stanchions were in various pastel colors to break the monotony because the Great Hall is as big as a good football field.

HENRI GHENT: Yes, I know.

ROMARE BEARDEN: And this had to be lighted. He knew all the dimensions of the work that was going to the show and he made a scale model of the exhibit area and scaled the pictures to the size and put them around the way they should be. So when the work arrived you could hang it just like clockwork.

HENRI GHENT: It was a very beautiful show.

ROMARE BEARDEN: Oh, it was a tremendous show. And during the run approximately a quarter of a million people came to the show. And most of the schoolchildren of the City of New York were bussed in. Everyone asked when will this show travel? It was too bad that arrangements for traveling the show could not be made. We had a beautiful catalogue which is a collector's item now, listing at least one photographic reproduction of every artist in the exhibit, biographical information on every artist in the exhibit. And we had to make several printings and there are just a few of these catalogues left, I think, now at City University for institutions. The rest are all gone.

HENRI GHENT: I remember being especially impressed with some of the sculpture of Edmonia Lewis. And she I believe was a nineteenth-century artist, right?

ROMARE BEARDEN: Yes. Edmonia Lewis was of mixed Indian and Negro ancestry. She was educated at Oberlin and as a young girl went to Rome where she lived the rest of her life. She was friendly with people who you might call the jet set of her day. Robert Browning and Elizabeth Barrett Browning were her friends. One of her patrons was Prime Minister Disraeli of England. She did several commissions for Harvard University of Longfellow. She did a number of the leading personages of the time, like Seward, who was in Lincoln's cabinet; Ralph Waldo Emerson. She worked in this neoclassic style and was a very skillful and brilliant exponent of that style even though I think it is said you can't bathe in the same water twice and it was difficult to breathe life again into something of the Greeks of two or three thousand years ago, and the Early Renaissance. But she did it. She was very skillful as far as craftsmanship was concerned. And her life was very interesting.

HENRI GHENT: She was born in New York State, wasn't she?

ROMARE BEARDEN: Upper New York State. Living that kind of life and suddenly finding herself in the most sophisticated circles in Rome makes it very interesting. And working in the skillful manner that she did, you know, in the Western manner instead of . . . there's no Indian influence in her work, like totems or the type of things that they did.

HENRI GHENT: Was Duncanson in that show?

ROMARE BEARDEN: Duncanson was a Cincinnati artist and we had several of his canvases. We wanted to get a very famous one of his — *Flood Waters*, or *Blue Ho Little Miami River* I think is the full title, which, I think, is one of the great American landscapes. But the Cincinnati Museum said that this picture had been out on loan so much and so often requested that they felt that the people coming to the museum should have the privilege of seeing it so they didn't want to loan that painting.

HENRI GHENT: Tanner, of course, was represented?

ROMARE BEARDEN: Oh, we had ten or twelve paintings of Tanner. Very fortunate because it was just before the large Tanner show here, and so, through the Grand Central Gallery, we were able to get quite a few of the Tanners. Then after the nineteenth century we moved on to some of the painters in that period when there were so few Negro painters — from 1900 almost to the '20s: Albert Smith, probably the first American Negro Expressionist painter; a man named Braxton — William Braxton. And then on into the 1920s: Aaron Douglas, Palmer Hayden, Hale Woodruff, Ellis Wilson. I think we had a very large mural of Aaron Douglas's brought in for the show along with easel paintings of his. We had three or four of his paintings. He was beautifully represented. After that into the painters of the Depression years, like Charlie White, Jacob Lawrence, Charles Alston, Norman Lewis. Then to the painters that emerged up into the '50s: Richard Mayhew, Merton Simpson. I'm not mentioning all the names. I think in all it was a very worthwhile show. It opened a lot of people's eyes because they didn't realize the contribution that the Negro had made and how long he had been involved in art in this country. I've mentioned that I am writing a book. It is on this aspect that I'm basing the book, telling more in detail about the lives of these nineteenth-century artists, why it was necessary for them to go to Europe, who their patrons were, the difficulties that they had and some of the things that were less difficult for them, peculiarly enough, than many of the artists have at the present time. Like a man like E. M. Bannister who came from Nova Scotia, lived in Boston for a while, then moved to Providence. He was really involved in the life of Providence art circles and was one of the founders of the Providence Art Club, which still exists to this day. Now you don't hear much of Providence in art but at one time in the last century, in the 1880s and 1890s, it was a great force in American art. I mean the artists from Providence and the things that were going on there were important. And Bannister was a part of all this. I want to bring out all these facts. Each epoch had its various problems. Artists like Bannister, Duncanson, and Tanner, as I said before, happened to be Negroes but they were involved in the art of their time. Then when you get to Douglas and Woodruff you see them trying to depict Negro life, Douglas using Harriet Tubman for instance as a theme for a mural, Woodruff using as a theme the famous Amistad mutiny. This the artists of the nineteenth century didn't do. So they were coming to a consciousness of another identity or of identifying with their own history. And in the 1930s the Negro artist and his problems at that time with, let's say, the social revolution. Or the artists of the '50s into the more abstract thing, into the involvement of America with the full art of the West. And I want to point out some of these problems in the book which I hope I can do in an interesting way.

HENRI GHENT: What about your future plans?

ROMARE BEARDEN: I'm continuing painting. I have no one-man shows but several group shows planned for the fall. I also intend to go to a few of the colleges to talk in a symposium on some of the same problems that we have discussed in this tape — at the School of Visual Arts in New York — in the fall. And, as I said before, I hope by that time to be well along in the book about Negro artists. And I may in my next show, which will not be next season but probably the season after, have some oils again, without collages. And I would want to work these out rather carefully. So I think in the next couple of years I should be pretty busy. That's it.

PART II / WRITINGS

# THE NEGRO ARTIST
# AND MODERN ART

*Romare Bearden*

For a moment, let us look back into the beginnings of modern art. It is really nothing new, merely an expression projected through new forms, more akin to the spirit of the times. Fundamentally the artist is influenced by the age in which he lives. Then for the artist to express an age that is characterized by machinery, skyscrapers, radios, and the generally quickened cadences of modern life, it follows naturally that he will break from many of the outmoded academic practices of the past. In fact every great movement that has changed the ideals and customs of life has occasioned a change in the accepted expression of that age.

Modern art has passed through many different stages. There have been the periods of the Impressionists, the Post-Impressionists, the Cubists, the Futurists, and hosts of other movements of lesser importance. Even though the use of these forms is on the decline, the impression they made in art circles is still evident. They are commendable in the fact that they substituted for mere photographic realism a search for inner truths.

Modern art has borrowed heavily from Negro sculpture. This form of African art had been done hundreds of years ago by primitive people. It was unearthed by archeologists and brought to the continent. During the past twenty-five years it has enjoyed a deserved recognition among art lovers. Artists have been amazed at the fine surface qualities of the sculpture, the vitality of the work, and the unsurpassed ability of the artists to create such significant forms. Of great importance has been the fact that the African would distort his figures, if by so doing he could achieve a more expressive form. This is one of the cardinal principles of the modern artist.

It is interesting to contrast the bold way in which the African sculptor approached his work, with the timidity of the Negro artist of today. His work is at best hackneyed and uninspired, and only mere rehashings from the work of any artist that might have influenced him. They have looked at nothing with their own eyes — seemingly content to use borrowed forms. They have evolved nothing original or native like the spiritual, or jazz music.

Many of the Negro artists argue that it is almost impossible for them to evolve such a sculpture. They say that since the Negro is becoming so amalgamated with the white race, and has accepted the white man's civilization he must progress along those lines. Even if this is true, they are certainly not taking advantage of the Negro scene. The Negro in his various environments in America, holds a great variety of rich experiences for the genuine artists. One can imagine what men like Daumier, Grosz, and Cruickshanks might have done with a locale like Harlem, with all its vitality and tempo. Instead the Negro artist will proudly exhibit his "Scandinavian Landscape," a locale that is entirely alien to him. This will of course impress the uninitiated, who through some feeling of inferiority toward their own subject matter, only require that a work of art have some sort of foreign stamp to make it acceptable.

I admit that at the present time it is almost impossible for the Negro artist not to be influenced by the work of other men. Practically all the great artists have accepted the influence of others. But the difference lies in the fact that the artist with vision, sees his material, chooses, changes, and by integrating what he has learned with his own experiences, finally molds something distinctly personal. Two of the foremost artists of today are the Mexicans, Rivera and Orozco. If we study the work of these two men, it is evident that they were influenced by the continental masters. Nevertheless their art is highly original, and steeped in the tradition and environment of Mexico. It might be noted here that the best work of these men was done in Mexico, of Mexican subject matter. It is not necessary for the artist to go to foreign surroundings in order to secure material for his artistic expression. Rembrandt painted the ordinary Dutch people about him, but he presented human emotions in such a way that their appeal was universal.

Several other factors hinder the development of the Negro artist. First, we have no valid standard of criticism; secondly, foundations and societies which supposedly encourage Negro artists really hinder them; thirdly, the Negro artist has no definite ideology or social philosophy.

Art should be understood and loved by the people. It should arouse and stimulate their creative impulses. Such is the role of art, and this in itself constitutes one of the Negro artist's chief problems. The best art has been produced in those countries where the public most loved and cherished it. In the days of the Renaissance the towns-folk would often hold huge parades to celebrate an artist's successful completion of a painting. We need some standard of criticism then, not only to stimulate the artist, but also to raise the cultural level of the people. It is well known that the critical writings of men like Herder, Schlegel, Taine, and the system of Marxian dialectics, were as important to the development of literature as any writer.

I am not sure just what form this system of criticism will take, but I am sure that the Negro artist will have to revise his conception of art. No one can doubt that the Negro is possessed of remarkable gifts of imagination and intuition. When he has learned to harness his great gifts of rhythm and pours it into his art — his chance of creating something individual will be heightened. At present it seems that by a slow study of rules and formulas the Negro artist is attempting to do something with his intellect, which he has not felt emotionally. In consequence he has given us poor echoes of the work of white artists — and nothing of himself.

It is gratifying to note that many of the white critics have realized the deficiencies of the Negro artists. I quote from a review of the last Harmon exhibition, by Malcolm Vaughan, in the New York *American*: "But in the field of painting and sculpture, they appear peculiarly backward, indeed so inept as to suggest that painting and sculpture are to them alien channels of expression." I quote from another review of the same exhibition, that appeared in the *New York Times*: "Such racial aspects as may once have figured have virtually disappeared, so far as some of the work is concerned. Some of the artists, accomplished technicians, are seen to have slipped into grooves of one sort or another. There is the painter of the Cezannesque still life, there is the painter of the Gauguinesque nudes, and there are those who have learned various 'dated' modernist tricks."

There are quite a few foundations that sponsor exhibitions of the work of Negro artists. However praise-worthy may have been the spirit of the founders the effect upon the Negro artist has been disastrous. Take for instance the Harmon Foundation. Its attitude from the beginning has been of a coddling and patronizing nature. It has encouraged the artist to exhibit long before he has mastered the technical equipment of his medium. By its choice of the type of work it favors, it has allowed the Negro artist to accept standards that are both artificial and corrupt.

It is time for the Negro artist to stop making excuses for his work. If he must exhibit let it be in exhibitions of the caliber of "The Carnegie Exposition." Here among the best artists of the world his work will stand or fall according to its merits. A concrete example of the accepted attitude towards the Negro artist recently occurred in California where an exhibition coupled the work of Negro artists with that of the blind. It is obvious that in this case there is definitely created a dual standard of appraisal.

The other day I ran into a fellow with whom I had studied under George Grosz, at the Art Students League. I asked him how his work was coming. He told me that he had done no real work for about six months.

"You know, Howard," he said, "I sort of ran into a blind alley with my work; I felt that it definitely lacked something. This is because I didn't have anything worthwhile to say. So I stopped drawing. Now I go down to the meetings of The Marine and Industrial Workers' Union. I have entered wholeheartedly in their movement."

We talked about Orozco, who had lost his arm in the revolutionary struggle in Mexico. No wonder he depicted the persecution of the underclass Mexicans so vividly — it had all been a harrowing reality for him.

So it must be with the Negro artist — he must not be content with merely recording a scene as a machine. He must enter wholeheartedly into the situation which he wishes to convey. The artist must be the medium through which humanity expresses itself. In this sense the greatest artists have faced the realities of life, and have been profoundly social.

I don't mean by this that the Negro artist should confine himself only to such scenes as lynchings, or policemen clubbing workers. From an ordinary still life painting by such a master as Chardin we can get as penetrating an insight into eighteenth-century life, as from a drawing by Hogarth of a street-walker. If it is the race question, the social struggle, or whatever else that needs expression, it is to that the artist must surrender himself. An intense, eager devotion to present-day life, to study it, to help relieve it, this is the calling of the Negro artist.

## NOTE

From *Opportunity: Journal of Negro Life* XII.12 (December 1934) © Romare Bearden Foundation/Licensed by VAGA, New York, NY.

# THE NEGRO ARTIST'S DILEMMA

*Romare Bearden*

Several months ago, a young artist came to my studio to request a painting for an exhibition of Negro Art that was being sponsored by some suburban Community Council. While we were discussing the exhibition, he showed me a portfolio of his lithographs. Most of them depicted incidents he had experienced while in the Army. His more recent work, drawn somewhat in the manner of political cartoons, was an attack against racial injustice. He said that the medium of lithography offered him an excellent means of expressing his ideas, and especially those related to the ill-treatment accorded the Negro.

Finally I asked him: "Since you wish to combat intolerance with your drawings, why are you on the other hand collecting pictures for a segregated art exhibit?"

Following a discussion, he acknowledged he had been inconsistent, but he felt that this exhibit, and others of a like nature, were necessary to acquaint people with the accomplishments of the Negro in the fine arts.

This artist's attitude is not untypical of the disharmony between practice and ideals among the Negro artists. In fact, it is at the root of a serious problem affecting the Negro's mature status as an artist. Certainly what is needed is a reorientation of values and ideals. This is important at present, now that more and more Negro artists are appearing publicly, with correspondingly greater attention accorded them. To explain fully the reasons for this confusion would require an unraveling, not only of complex economic and social forces, but also of the distortions that years of oppression have ingrafted in the minority consciousness. Such is the tyranny of the mind that we carry, like Sinbad's "Old Man of the Sea," ideas and attitudes long beyond their period of relevancy. Since a condition of progress is the understanding of sources, it is expedient to explore the subtle causes and effects of the existing confusions in their historical context. I do not propose a detailed analysis. A few considerations should suffice for the purposes of this article.

The Negro, aside from his folk expressions, is a latecomer into the visual arts in America. As slave and serf, the Negro has had to struggle for his very existence. The visual arts are, in a sense, a sophisticated expression. During slavery, when there were actual laws prohibiting the education of slaves, there was no chance of their receiving either the necessary instruction or encouragement, if we except a few isolated individuals. Even now, it is difficult enough for most artists to buy the paints and canvas they need, and for the destitute Negro slave hand it was out of the question. That the innate capacities existed is evidenced in the elegant iron-grill work created by Negro slave artisans. About the only expression allowed the Negro was religion, so it is understandable that his first artistic achievement would be a vocal one — the spirituals.

During the Reconstruction days, the Negro fared little better than he had during slavery. He was forgotten by the majority of Northerners, whose previous concern over his slave status had been merely a disguise for their political and social machinations. The full energies of the North were directed toward growing industrialization and westward expansion. But the Negro stayed on the land with his mule, mortgaged to the vicious system of tenant farming.

It is a privilege of the oppressor to depict the oppressed. Consequently, the picture of the Negro that appealed to the South was that of a shiftless, dim-witted buffoon. This concept, pleasing to the Southern ego, was both a rationalization and one of the means of keeping the Negro in his dark corner. Pseudo-scientific books were written; ministers gave long-winded sermons to prove that the Negro was a creature driven by animal spirits, possessing only limited capacities, and best suited to a servile existence.

This concept was disseminated among the mass of people during those times mainly by the minstrel shows. It is ironical that white men, like those in the Christy and Virginia minstrels, made up in black-face, with woolly wigs and thickly painted lips, did so much in establishing the Negro stereotype in America. And a stereotype, once ingrained in the folk ways of a people, is difficult to change, as instanced in the present-day eye-rolling, grinning interpretation of the Negro on the screen by actors like Stepin Fetchit and Bill Robinson.

The portrayal of the Negro in visual art was but another manifestation of the main cultural pattern. The artists of this period either over-sentimentalized the Negro — as in the genre paintings of Eastman Johnson — or showed him ludicrously — as in the "head-in-the-watermelon" school of painters.

It is pitiful, when one considers the rich genre painting of Bruegel, Jan Steen, Adriaen Brouwer, and the other great Dutch and Flemish masters, that such feeble paintings resulted from the abundant materials offered in Negro life. I remember that when I was a young boy an old chromo called, I believe, "The Darktown Poker Club," used to hang in a number of Negro homes. Here was a group, such as Mr. Hoyle never imagined, gathered about a battered table on which rested a huge jug of corn whiskey, armed with razors and with stray aces hidden in shoes and hat brims. It is not surprising that so many Negroes hung this picture in their homes and got enjoyment from it as an amusing depiction of their lives. It can be explained in the fact that they were constantly exposed to false standards, and tended to adopt these as their own.

Too few of the Negro leaders of the Reconstruction era possessed the vigor and intellectual honesty of Frederick Douglass. They were not indigenous with the people, and their position of leadership usually derived from their acceptability to the powers in control. In fact, they added to the confusion and vulgarization of their people's minds. They advocated segregation and looked to Jehovah and the benevolence of their white friends as the instruments of advancement. One of them said: "I believe that the interests of my people lie with the wealth of the nation and with the class of white people who control it."

Many such men were the controlling forces in Negro education, which was adjusted at that period to the accepted fact that the Negro would be a ploughman or a mechanic. The opportunity to understand or appreciate, let us say, a sonnet by Drayton, or a painting by Titian, was not given to the Negro student. Now there are a few Negro colleges with adequate curricula and good teachers. Howard University, in Washington, D.C., has a large art department. Hale Woodruff, a competent artist, has done a sound job at Atlanta University. Nevertheless, dead ideas inconsistent with new circumstances still persist in most Negro colleges.

The enlightenment that was to aid the Negro in his struggle for full emancipation slowly filtered into the American consciousness, bobbing up and down like the seismographic needle, agitating men's minds and their society. French humanitarianism, the rights of the individual as espoused by Godwin, Thoreau, and Proudhon, the economic theories of Marx, and the scientific study of races found expression in the growing American labor and libertarian movements.

After 1900, there were constant, tangential shifts in the Negro population, away from the Southern centers of gravity, to answer the North's increasing demands for laborers. In the North, where he enjoyed greater educational opportunities and the right to vote, the Negro took his place in the heterogeneous working population and gradually began to make some impression on the tough matrix of American society.

The attitude of a man about himself and his fellow men will affect whatever expression he attempts. Accordingly, white artists who were the intellectual offspring of the libertarian movements were first to explore this subject matter of Negro life in a forthright manner. Then, too, the concept of naturalism — the most significant force in American arts during the first decades of the twentieth century — demanded that the artist envision his characters rationally and interpret his environment with some measure of social responsibility.

Among the foremost of the non-Negro artists who made earnest attempts to portray the Negro were: Robert Henri, George Luks, John Sloan, and George Bellows. Since he was of the same period, I will mention Henry O. Tanner, who — until the time of his death in 1937 — had been the best-known Negro painter. His was a special case. A student of Thomas Eakins at the Philadelphia Academy, he was able at an early age to go to Paris, where he painted capably, but not with great distinction, in the academic traditions of his time.

It was not until the twenties that the Negro entered the various fields of art in any substantial numbers. This period has been called both the "Negro Renaissance" and the "New Negro Movement." Among the poets and writers, Countee Cullen, Claude McKay, Langston Hughes, and Eric Walrond produced the most significant work. Beginning in 1928, the Harmon Foundation initiated a series of yearly exhibits of Negro painting and sculpture.

The Harmon Foundation exerted a considerable, if dilatory, influence on Negro art. Nearly all of the practicing Negro artists of the period exhibited their work in the seasonal shows. Insofar as the Harmon Foundation brought to public attention the work of such artists as Richmond Barthé, Aaron Douglas, Malvin Johnson, Sargent Johnson, William Johnson, James Porter, James L. Wells, and Hale Woodruff, it performed a worthwhile service.

But the attitude of the foundation toward the Negro artists was patronizing: it firmly established the pattern of segregated exhibits; it fostered artificial and arbitrary artistic standards, stemming from a sociological rather than aesthetic interest in the exhibitors' works. This concept of the Negro artist as an odd personality, rather than as a mature individual, has been both insulting and harmful.

I recall that during an exposition in California about ten years ago, the paintings of Negro artists who had been invited to show were placed in the same section with the handicrafts of the blind to show the accomplishments of "handicapped" people. On another occasion, films were made of some of the Negro painters at work. One of the artists filmed had once been a superintendent of a building in Harlem, so he was asked to stand painting before his easel in a pair of janitor's overalls.

Significantly, it was during the dog days of the Depression and the WPA Art Project that most of the younger painters of today emerged. As a whole, this group was more aware of their social and cultural responsibilities than any Negro artists had been heretofore. The number of artists is significant and includes such diverse talents as: Charles Alston, Henry Bannarn, Robert Blackburn, Elizabeth Catlett, Ernest Crichlow, Eldzier Cortor, Jacob Lawrence, Norman Lewis, Frank Neal, Charles Sebree, Charles White, and Ellis Wilson.

Of this group, Jacob Lawrence has had great success in the art world. Not yet thirty, he has held Rosenwald and Guggenheim Fellowships; his paintings have been exhibited in most of the leading museums; and, in 1943, he was honored with a one-man exhibit at the Museum of Modern Art in New York City. During the summer of 1946, he was invited to teach at Black Mountain College.

In considering critical opinion in relation to the Negro artists, I have observed three major concepts that constantly reappear:

The Negro should continue, or at least simulate, the traditions of African art.

The Negro artist should attempt a unique, nationalistic, social expression, closely akin in feeling to jazz music and the spirituals. (One critic stated in reviewing a group show of Negro artists: "We can say this of it: the farther removed the Negro is from copying the white man's style or subject matter, the better he is.")

The Negro's art should be a visual and trenchant reflection of his political and social aspirations, especially as it would focus attention on the exigency of his existence.

It would be highly artificial for the Negro artist to attempt a resurrection of African culture in America. The period between the generations is too great, and whatever creations the Negro has fashioned in this country have been in relation to his American environment. Culture is not a biologically inherited phenomenon. Just as no sane person would expect a Greek-American to carve in the manner of Phidias or Praxiteles, so should the Negro be encouraged in a contemporaneous expression compatible with himself.

However disinherited, the Negro is part of the amalgam of American life, and his aims and aspirations are in common with the rest of the American people. The survival of man is a history of his adaptability to new situations. Modern anthropological findings indicate that when people migrate to a new environment, they tend to adopt cultural patterns consistent with their new spatiotemporal circumstances.

African art was an anthropomorphic expression identified with tribal magic and ritual, with which the American Negro no longer has any affinity. Few Negroes believe that a statue can banish demons, else Negro artists would be overworked carving fetishes to keep landlords away from their peoples' doors.

Modigliani, Picasso, Epstein, and other modern artists studied African sculpture to reinforce their own design concepts. This would be perfectly appropriate for any Negro artist who cared to do the same. The critic asks that the Negro stay away from the white man's art, but the true artist feels that there is only one art — and it belongs to all mankind. Such an eminent historian as Toynbee stated:

> The idea is coming to be entertained that the fundamental social characters, when exhaustively analysed and defined, may prove to be nothing but an illuminating set of classificatory abstractions, which have never had any objective or independent existence at all in real life.

Examine the art forms of any culture and one becomes aware of the patterns that link it to other cultures and peoples. The Negro spirituals have a similar structural pattern to that of the English four-part hymn. The Negro had to master the playing of the white man's instruments before he could develop jazz music. Benny Goodman, Max Kaminsky, and Joe Sullivan, and other leading white practitioners of jazz music have not disdained to play in this idiom simply because it is essentially a Negro creation.

The work of the Negro artists reflects all the artistic trends of the times, ranging from the academic to the modern. There is no single characteristic that would stamp their individual works as having been done by a Negro. I mention a few artists, chosen because their work indicates the Negro artists' adherence to all the general art trends of today; however, it is not the purpose of this article to attempt a general criticism of their work.

Richmond Barthé continues the academic traditions of sculptors like Daniel French and St. Gaudens. Horace Pippin, who died recently, was one of the most unusual of American painters. A disabled veteran of World War I, he began to paint late in life as a hobby. While the classification of his work as primitive is not entirely accurate — just as it is not of Rousseau — there is a naïve quality in his oils, combined with a great clarity of color in his silhouetted forms that links him to that great French painter. Beauford Delaney [paints] in a swirling expressionistic manner. Charles White is concerned with the depiction of social problems, and his paintings are stylized, strongly modeled and dramatic. Norman Lewis creates out of broad semi-abstract planes, and there is a vein of good humor in his paintings.

Accordingly, there seems little reason for a continuation of all-Negro group shows. Aside from the fact that there are no ethnical characteristics that warrant such exhibitions, they tend to hamper the Negro painters by fostering dual standards. The liberal critic's perspective is often blurred in his efforts to be sympathetic. He is inclined to gloss over the work as a whole and look for redeeming features in the creations of individual artists. Then, too, an artist profits by association and competition with other artists, which the racial shows drastically limit.

The last and most perplexing problem is the evident pressure exerted on the Negro artist to use his art as an instrument to mirror the social injustices inflicted upon his people. However, the danger in this type of expression is that the artist tends to either limit his point of view or become subservient to a political ideology, rather than to the dictates of his own concepts of right and wrong. It is not necessary that the Negro artist mirror the misery of his people. Since freedom of expression is a prerequisite for any artist, there is no reason why the Negro artist should not paint whatever moves him. His greatest service consists in making his individual creations as strong as he possibly can.

Before the war, the National Association for the Advancement of Colored People sponsored an exhibition of paintings that would show the brutality of lynching and mob violence. I recall that few of the works of either the white or Negro exhibitors — depicting lynchings, floggings, and like incidents — possessed any artistic merit, which was irrelevant considering the function of the exhibition. Most of the works were lachrymal and filled with self-pity and sentimentality. On the other hand, Goya — working with like material — endowed the particular incidents of the French invasion that he depicted with a universal and tragic meaning, independent of race, time, or locale.

Recently, a number of artists were invited to show their paintings and graphic works in Detroit in an exhibition aimed at combating the rising tide of racial intolerance in that industrial city. In view of the previous statements regarding segregated exhibitions, it is amusing to note that this exhibition was divided into two sections of paintings and graphic arts, and the works of the white artists restricted to the latter category.

The social purpose of both the Detroit and NAACP shows was a good one, but it is a question whether the fine arts could best fulfill that purpose. Again, should a painting be judged as meritorious because it enlists more people's support to the anti-lynch bill?

For purposes such as these exhibitions, either literary means or a ratiocinative art like the political cartoon would be more suitable. True, the artist works in relation to certain ideals, but he searches for values that are permanent and relevant to all men and not those related to the fluctuating needs of any group, or the transitory social situation. A good painting has its own world. What ideas it arouses are integral and in relation to itself.

The traditions of Western humanitarianism are dying, and the scorching days of the Atomic Age are at hand. We cannot calculate what new forms will emerge, but the artist, of whatever race, must explore with integrity and sensitiveness the processes of life that he sees and feels. The Negro artist must come to think of himself not primarily as a Negro artist, but as an artist. Only in this way will he acquire the stature which is the component of every good artist.

## NOTE

From *Critique: A Review of Contemporary Art* (November 1946) © Romare Bearden Foundation/Licensed by VAGA, New York, NY.

# THE JOURNAL OF ROMARE BEARDEN 1947 TO 1949

*Romare Bearden*

AUGUST 14TH, 1947

Two problems in my painting give me a great concern at the moment, especially the fashioning of the middle and bottom sections of the pictures. Last night I noticed that in a group of sketches I had made, all the legs and drapes of the figures were ending on the bottom edge of the paper. I looked at some reproductions of Duccio's *Life of Jesus*[1] and I got some fruitful ideas. His under edges are constantly varied. If on one side, legs are bunched, and in movement, the other side is open, etc. One enters his pictures through a series of staggered rectangular planes from the sides, with dynamic movements right and left, and closed horizontal and vertical rests to hold all the movements at rest.

During the afternoon I visited Holty at his studio.[2] Both of us went in to chat with Miró, who was working on his mural for Cincinnati.[3] . . . Miró had begun the mural by toning the entire canvas a cobalt blue. This was done in the manner of a house painter applying calcimine to a rough exterior wall. The strokes moved in all directions, and this was important in Miró's manner of working, since the accidental tracks of the brush gave him ideas for the final design.

On the blue tone Miró made a careful charcoal drawing, filling in his black areas neatly with charcoal. He painted in these areas directly over the charcoal, since I imagine this must give him a textural quality that he likes. Seemingly he works in one color at a time; rather than spotting all the colors throughout the canvas at once, in the manner of Cézanne. His procedure, while tentative and arbitrary, seems well suited to his particular talents.

Carl said his (Miró's) compositional trick was to get one or two movements in perfect balance, and then swing the other motifs around these. So his paintings have an effect such as fish swimming about a flat aquarium.

AUGUST 16TH

A style is achieved by an artist through his introduction of personal forms into the grand style of his period.

AUGUST 18TH

Went to see Sam (who had just returned from France).[4] He told me that he asked Picasso if he thought that Braque, Léger, Matisse, and he himself did not overshadow the younger painters today. Picasso said, "The younger painters have it easy today, for when I was young Renoir, Lautrec, Monet, and Cézanne were the competition the young artist had to go against."

AUGUST 20TH

Looked through the latest edition of the *Cahiers d'Art* that Sam had brought back from Paris. There was a complete treatment in the issue of Paul Klee.[5] Klee was a fine imaginative artist, but with such a personal style you feel that you should have known Klee to really understand the work. Since in his case, the work is not the whole man, but rather a series of different facets of his personality.

There were also a number of reproductions of Picasso's drawings for his piece of sculpture *The Shepard* [sic].[6] Picasso is undoubtedly the best sculptor of this era. . . . However, his feeling for the round [three-dimensionality], in some instances makes for jarring disturbances in his pictures. That is, some sections will rise off the picture plane. Carl seems to believe that Picasso does this purposefully to create dramatic effects. It was for this reason that Mondrian always said that Picasso was too pictorial.

AUGUST 21ST

. . . The other night an artist showed me a copy of an issue of the *Cahiers d'Art* which was devoted to Picasso. There were reproductions of the *Guernica* mural as it progressed.[7] It was amazing to see the changes that Picasso made, strengthening his rhythms and shapes, always allowing the development of the painting to progress out of the body of the work. Matisse works in the same manner, with the initial lay-in often having no relation to the final statement. And this is the true manner of working — since the artist takes what he finds.

Started on the "lay-ins" for this year's paintings. On some canvases I put a thin Venetian red wash of turpentine, and these I heightened with half tempera, half oil. Then I will varnish these and begin to glaze on colors. On others, I just layed [sic] on three or four colors, and I'll build these entirely in oil, using these under colors as a ground. My canvas is so absorbent that it's necessary that I build up a solid body of paint.

In working my paintings this year I intend to build them up through a series of approximations . . . I'll just set up the colors in a rough idea of my watercolor sketch and then see how I can expand the oil. I see now that the initial sketch is but a graphic representation of the artist's first thoughts and should by no means limit him in the continued development of the picture. (See Plate 2.)

Perhaps my paintings will look worse than they previously did, but this is to be expected when one attempts to work on a higher level.

When I gather my means these technical aspects of the problem should be easier. But I want a method that will allow for a great deal of expansion. As fine a painter as Miró is, I feel that he has imposed too many limitations on himself, as regards his approach. Naturally an artist cannot be all inclusive, but if possible he should try for some sort of universal touch. . . .

Went to see Carl. Had a soda at Carl's studio with him, Alonso,[8] and Miró. Miró had just finished putting in the reds on his mural, and seemed very animated.

Carl had me look at his paintings. They are very colorful in the lay-in, and will no doubt come along fine. However, it was too early for me to give Carl an opinion. . . .

... Worked fairly well on an oil: *Two Prophets Before the Burning City.*[9] I had heightened a red ground with half oil and tempera and lightly glazed the oil color over. This seems like a very effective method of painting.

... There has hardly been any great portrait painted in the 20th century of a *particular individual.* And this is almost impossible. The faces and souls of people are not invested with those qualities that make great portraits possible.

Rembrandt took beggars, draped them in exotic garments and painted them as kings. They were kings, but his greatness consists in the fact that you can see that they were also beggars. The qualities you can see in the faces of Rembrandt's sitters, that inner feeling of security, is not part of the consciousness of modern man.

Went to The Cloisters to see the Unicorn tapestries.[10] ... It would be impossible for an artist to have conceived such an intricate design today because the peace of mind that would allow for such an effort simply does not exist.

That does not mean that great works of art are impossible of creation today, but rather that the modern artist has recourse to other elements. Matisse, in many of his grandest efforts, has used the most simple means — large flat areas of color that are powerful in themselves and must be looked upon from an entirely different point of view than one would consider the Unicorn tapestries or Persian miniatures. ...

Talked with Carl about the disciples of pure painting. Where these painters make their mistake is in considering that they can at once start out to achieve a pure style. Pure painting is always an end product. Mondrian's work was in a large sense a result of the man's whole way of life. ...

... I had a good talk with Stuart.[11] He feels that for the time being Europe is through as an art force. [That] is, Europe is squeezed in between America and Russia, the two main forces in the world today. Stuart felt that the European artists like Picasso, Matisse, and Miró were leftovers and that it would be difficult for the new generation of artists since they were losing the strong basis of their culture.

SEPTEMBER 3RD

... There are always attempts to incorporate primitive designs in dresses, pottery, and even in the fine arts, but it always appears as if a steamroller had been run over the work. Naturally the same objections cannot apply to those artists like Picasso and Miró who have used certain structural elements in primitive art forms to complement their own work. These artists did not attempt literal copies of primitive forms.

In a like manner it will be necessary for the American artist to attempt a synthesis of our native forms. The old circus posters were wonderful for the daring use of what amounted to an abstract use of color. Pink, red, yellow, and blue were the predominant colors, with the idea of attracting immediate attention. It is quite possible that American artists will make use of these garish and strident colors, so that the paintings will be shocking to Europeans. . . .

SEPTEMBER 5TH

I am trying to develop my new paintings very slowly. First, I want to lay-in approximately what I've got on the sketch and then destroy this effort to search for better forms. Painting is like a man being in love — an adventure one plunges into without knowing how you will fare.

SEPTEMBER 6TH

Went to see Wm [William] Carlos Williams in Rutherford, New Jersey. Sam is doing a book on the "Women,"[12] with reproductions of the gallery group's paintings. He is planning forewords by noted writers and he suggested Dr. Williams for me.

Dr. Williams made me feel at ease immediately. The first thing he did was to show me his collection of art. He had Sheelers, Demuths, and Hartleys[13] along the walls of his living room. These painters had all been friends of Dr. Williams and he was quite proud of their work.

Later, I discussed ideas with him. He grasped at once that I was trying to humanize the structure of abstract painting. But when he told me that he disliked Picasso's distorted faces my heart fell and I was apprehensive about showing him my own efforts. However, he seemed very enthusiastic. In fact he said that the sheer brilliance of the color blew away the paintings on his wall. I gave him the sketch I had done for my painting in the "Women" show and both he and his wife, who had come in the room during the conversation, were delighted.

. . . In relation to my sketches, Dr. Williams said that he thought they came to grips with reality. . . .

SEPTEMBER 7TH

There is unfortunately no bridge between the fine arts and the arts of commerce. The artist must decide which of the two endeavors is most compatible to his talents and personality. . . .

SEPTEMBER 8TH

Talked with Vytlacil[14] at Carl's studio. He said that a number of his students ask if they can bring their paintings for him to criticize. All of them want to know if they have enough talent to become successful artists.

This is always a difficult thing to advise a student about. There are so many other factors that determine the complete artist other than the possession of artistic talent. Who can tell whether or not the young artist can bear all the vicissitudes of the artist's life, not only standing up under the blows, but turning them to his own artistic advantage?

Many of the artists are talking about the problem of when a painting is finished — someone has said that a painting is finished when the intention of the artist is realized. I would go beyond this, for quite often the initial intention of the artist is rather puerile and will change as the painting progresses. I saw a reproduction of a Crucifixion by Dünwegge[15] . . . that was tremendously involved. Yet out of all the involvements one gets a monumental feeling of unity. What is it that allows some artists to go on and on, continually strengthening their design, so that at the end, instead of the picture looking crabbed and overworked it appears as fresh as a mountain stream. It's quite true that a painting is never finished, only, at some point along the way the artist relinquishes it.

Imagine a factory whistle blowing through your spine, and consider how long you could stand this shrill discordance. Then, this is in effect tantamount to the effort of intense creation. The greater artists have been able to stand this whistle and steam blowing their insides apart a little while longer than the others. A mechanic can step up the revolutions of a motor and listen, with his head almost in the bearings, for the engine defects. Likewise the great artist can destroy form after form, constantly seeking the unique twist that will appear in the end as if he *owned* the entire array of shapes and colors.

SEPTEMBER 9TH

. . . I have looked for hours at Rembrandt's great self-portrait at the Frick Museum.[16] How noble is this man framed there in his declining years. The ambivalence prevails. He is at once a god, but then look at the mouth and he is Lucifer. The agony is there, contained as it was with Christ at Gethsemane, yet he understands the soldier who ran his spear through Christ's side. He is filled with the Immaculate Conception, but could plant the seed in the Virgin's womb. He is the wet and the dry. He is solid as a pillar, yet as your understanding increases the more he is revealed to you. The eternal black horse of despair romps through his mind, however, he is chained and bridled to the radiant and calm white charger. Here are the four corners of the winds of life roaring and cataclysmic and by the interaction of their own forces producing the vortex — the calefacient calm of the middle.

SEPTEMBER 10TH

Sometimes when the artist has trouble with his painting it is helpful to draw for a period, then in returning to his painting the problems may have means of simple solution.

A painting is seldom sustained from the point of its inception to its completion in a steady progression of work; rather, the painting jumps ahead in the artist's inspired moments, or falters for lack of such inspiration. An artist can hope to get about two hours in which he is "on the surface," and it is in this period that the feeble beginnings and unrelated shapes are brought together.

I read some of Mondrian's essays on paintings.[17] Here is a great artist who succeeds in spite of certain fallacies in his thinking. Mondrian [equated] his strict use of horizontal and vertical lines with the forces of good and bad which he felt would have to be brought to an [equilibrium]. Thus, Mondrian used symbols even as the Surrealists, although he constantly decried literature in painting.

Then to propose absolute values of good and bad is [Platonic], and impossible in these times. Such a concept is puritanical and medieval in the sense that one would imagine such absolute ideas as arising from a static society. However, I understand that Mondrian's work was the embodiment of the whole man. His was a life of poverty and self-denial. . . .

Psychologically and externally, all the factors of Mondrian's life made for the sparse, cathartic character of his art.

It was Miró who freed painting from the tight Cubist form. He said "I forsook the structure and listened to the voice of poetry."[18]

I have found recently that my ideas have become much clearer and more coherent. In talking to people I haven't had to stumble searching for the right word, or the orderly arrangement of my thoughts. My drawings, while they are less crowded, seem to convey my intention, and Carl says my space sense is becoming oriented with my ideas.

The artist's sense of space is something at which he gradually arrives, and then usually keeps intact the rest of his life. Picasso achieved his space with Cubism, and despite the many phases of his creation, he has held to his space ideal.

The sense of space has not so much to do with distances in art, as it has with the feeling of fullness of design, drawing, color, and concept.

I feel that my drawings are perhaps clearer, because what knowledge I may have is beginning to soak through to my hands. Then, too, if an artist is going to make rich drawings he must *devoutly want to do so.*

I see difficult times ahead for myself in relation to my finding those who will either understand, or make the effort to understand, my painting. The sincere artist would hope to address his work to those capable of intellectual comprehension — but where are the intellectuals of today? This is a land, a wilderness, peopled by the middle class. Where is the Baudelaire, incorruptible and right, who can speed to the defense of the true artist? . . .

Chirico[19] has painted some fine pictures, especially those during the period 1913–1918, but in spite of this he actually misunderstood the modern movement. He juxtaposed strange elements, like trees growing in living rooms. He painted people without faces as a comment on this age. His long perspectives set the pattern for Dalí and the other Surrealist painters. (It seems odd that the Surrealist painters have to such a great extent used the same deep space, since the paintings are supposed to be compounded from dream symbols and the material offered by the unconscious. Have all the Surrealists dreamed the same dreams?)

Actually then, in spite of the bizarre combinations, Chirico's space and form sense is that of the Renaissance. Unlike the great Renaissance masters, he most often fails to compensate for the havoc that deep thrusts through the center planes [of] the picture can cause.

The artist must be careful to try and bring both his drawing and painting to an even keel. Drawing is a tool. Sometimes to draw better than one can make use of this knowledge in painting is a deterrent.[20] (See fig. 4.)

Miró came by my studio[21] with Carl. I showed him a great deal of my paintings and he was very interested. My latest paintings were so undeveloped that I imagine it was impossible for him to get any idea of what they would be like. Through Carl, I explained to him that I was now working very tentatively in oil in an attempt to build the form and color gradually. He said the method was probably all right — it was just a matter of an artist's temperament that would determine his working habits. Later, Carl told me that he had said I was a gifted artist. . . .

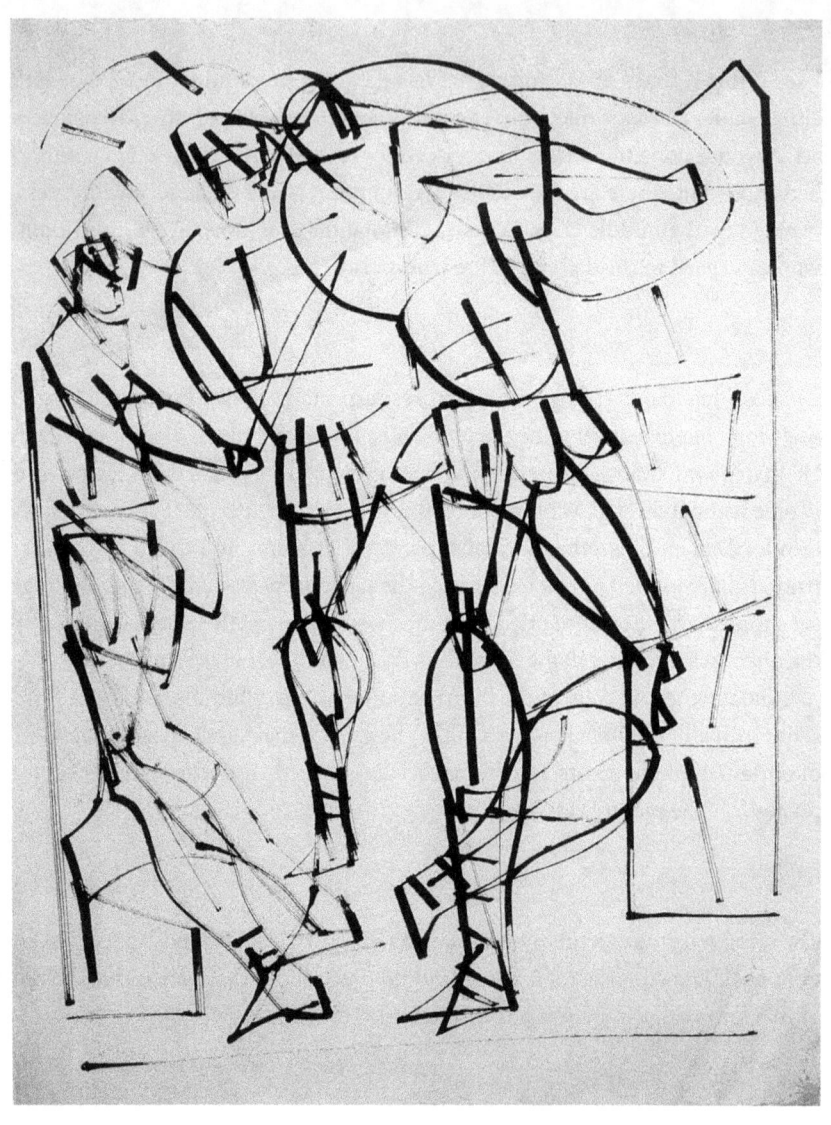

FIGURE 4 Romare Bearden, *Trojan War*, pen and ink on paper, 1948.
Art © Romare Bearden Foundation/Licensed by VAGA, New York

Went to see Carl at his studio, and later had dinner with [him], Jean,[22] Ethel,[23] and Baziotes.[24] Carl was ill and could not get by the studio to see my work. How much I owe him for any progress I have made with painting. He has really taught me what I know of the formal elements and has done this with such a patient and generous spirit. Carl is a fine man full of the joy of giving. This is an evangelical spirit that delights in the confraternity of his fellow men. He has inspired me to a real appetite and love for the art of painting. One of my reasons for keeping a journal has been to note certain ideas and thoughts for whose inspiration I am so much indebted to him. The pity is that few people will understand him, for few people cherish the generous nature.

You will find a certain selfishness in all true artists in the sense that they hoard their gifts so that in the end they may give all. That is one reason it is difficult to study with the greatest masters.

How I admire Baziotes his feeling for the beautiful. The nightingale of Keats flies to his shoulders. But I have to hunt this little ephemeral bird in such devious ways through the light, the dark, on plains and crags, and with every contrivance. I've never even glimpsed her as yet, only heard on occasion the melody of her song. I know I must pursue her through the dark roads of Goya, Greco, and Dante. If I find her I shall crush her to death for causing me such torment and because she has my heart.

. . . Shakespeare and Dante were both great humanists, but Dante pierced deeper into the shades of the mind. . . . He has explored ultimate facets of the human character. . . .

The work of the lyric poets like Keats, Heine,[25] [Marc] Chagall, and Miró is always more easy for immediate comprehension. These men tell beautiful stories, or make beautiful images. The great artists like Dante and Cézanne speak of themselves, and their relation to life, so that we are often repelled by the horrors, as well as enriched by the grandeur of their concepts.

Had a pleasant evening Friday with Stuart. Ralston Crawford[26] came by and he and Stuart had a lively session as the flow of rye loosened the tongues. Stuart, who so often talks in analogies and around a subject, rode Ralston about the straight lines in his paintings. Naturally, Stuart meant that Ralston should loosen up so that his work would not appear so ice-bound. There is quite a difference in Ralston's approach and that of Mondrian who was able to summon his entire attitude toward life in a straight line.

Stuart made an interesting observation. He said that we all have a roll of camera film within us, and that it is the province of the real artist to do more than just expose it. He will take care to achieve the proper lighting and do a little retouching. . . .

Today I painted out all the starts I had made on my oils. Nothing can satisfy me any longer. At best I can achieve certain passages that are pleasing, but I'm unable to sustain the total effect.

Perhaps if I ever find what I'm searching for they'll take me to the hospital with fits of hysterical laughter, since the solution will have been so easy.

Carl told me that Mondrian said the reason van Gogh cut off his ear was [that] . . . he and Gauguin were arguing as to what was worse, physical or spiritual pain. Van Gogh argued that spiritual pain was the worse to endure and to prove his point cut off his ear. Mondrian said he would have done the same thing as a young man, for to defend his painting he would have gone to the death.

Discussing the magic of line with Carl, he made a pertinent comment, saying that lines took on a magic quality when they were so placed as to be *most* helpful in advancing the *whole* composition. That is, lines should never be thought of as merely boundaries of local objects, but as forces acting across the entire picture plane.

Studied some reproductions of Bonnard's[27] paintings in relation to my own work. In his last years Bonnard became a very fine painter. Artists do not consider him very much since he always made the understatement in modern art. His later paintings can be most instructive to anyone interested in the real art of painting. He used tracks of colors across his surfaces to the best advantage. It is important that the painter spread his colors up and down and across the canvas, never making the definitive, or intense, statement in color until the end. In his greatest canvases Bonnard was hardly equaled among contemporary painters in this respect.

The great German mystic Meister Eckhart[28] felt that it was always more profound to consider the aspects of any thing or situation in its essence, or whole, instead of in terms of particular attributes or qualities. Therefore to him the feeling for color [as an entity] was to be preferred to red, yellow, or blue. In Bonnard's paintings one does get a sensation for color, and it would be difficult to think of his paintings (the later ones) as being a red-gray, a blue-green, or a pink-blue conception. Rather the feeling is that the canvas is saturated with color.

I have been looking for hours at my drawings hung about the wall. Good painting will come from good drawing. Drawing is indeed the mother of the visual arts. The artist must determine how he can make the transition from drawing to painting. . . .

. . . I listened last evening to a Spanish Moorish record. It started as a bugle call, a theme common to French and Spanish legion posts. Then began an ominous death wail. The trumpets were out of Old Carthage. The entire piece had a most startling effect on me, because out of death these people had made a real work of art. Art in its ultimate always celebrates the victory. Such is the difference between the paintings of executions by Goya and those of Gropper[29] and Evergood.[30]

Whatever subject the artist chooses he must celebrate in it the triumph. He has so many forms of oppression, why should we make of art another.

An artist who attempts to make a *particular* statement will always have difficulty, because it must be very strong and perfect or else the errors in the conception will show glaringly. In these days, with no current tradition to work out of, the problem is enormous. This is why the paintings of the tonalists look often much better and more complete than the work of those artists who attempt something definitive in form and color. . . .

An artist must at a certain point of his development bring his work to a synthesis. Now with all his talent and great knowledge one cannot but feel that Picasso has skirted this problem. Too often he relies on a shock appeal to achieve which he has had to relinquish the great unity of the picture surface. . . .

More and more painters will begin to find it fruitful to compose out of the big ornaments of the object, rather than to seek from impressions. The days of the strict Cubist disciplines are over, yet many painters who would not even acknowledge Cubism as a source, use arbitrary shapes and forms in the manner that the Cubists used certain shapes as symbols for bottles, guitars, tables, etc. What is more integral is to find, as did Cézanne, the peculiar and unique ornaments on the picture plane that by closely contrived movements and countermovements will eventually spell out tables, guitars, and bottles.

With the overemphasis these days of various surface techniques I think of Poussin's words, "A painting should be a delight for the eye, but the artist should never begin with the intention of making it so."[31] Before van Gogh, painters did not work in very heavy impasto. What might give the appearance of heavy paintings was usually a tempera under priming over which were laid their glazes, with certain parts of the pictures accented.

Now the treatment of the surface has gone to ridiculous extremes, not only esthetically, but the methods are technically ruinous. Some painters have taken to pouring gasoline over their paintings and then lighting the gasoline to achieve a murky surface effect. A murkiness that is most often a reflection of their own minds and attitudes towards the artistic creation.

DECEMBER 11TH

Can great paintings be done here in America? Everything apparently is against such an accomplishment.

I have noticed in Japanese prints that the artists often contrive to so place the neck and head as to not have the head set on the middle of the shoulders. Picasso, in breaking up his faces to show many different aspects of the face on one plane, is concerned with the same problem.

If the movements and countermovements are correct, and if the artist makes allowance for scale, and abstract equivalents for the form, anything is possible. If the painting is plastically sound the distortions will appear correct. . . .

DECEMBER 19TH

There is really no such thing as a "negative space." In a well-organized picture all the spaces must be considered as being positive functions towards the ordering of the whole. . . .

DECEMBER 22ND

. . . Mondrian [equates] his use of horizontal and vertical lines with good and evil. These forces he feels must be brought to an [equilibrium] . . .

Perhaps it is to Mondrian's credit that he was able to offer a modern equivalent for such a basic idea. For after all, art has concerned itself with these simple basic emotions during the entire development of world culture, the differences of style developing from the varying perspectives in which artists in different eras surveyed these forces.

DECEMBER 26TH

It is the function of art to show, not to describe. . . .

Looked over Sam's book *The Woman*.[32] I see now how bad my painting really is, my rhythms could have been extended so much further, so that the tracks across my figures would have given the masses greater volume.

I can't think that Baziotes's painting is successful in terms of a woman.[33] The shape supposed to be a woman simply is not convincing. One cannot be impressed by an odd shape as having a particular identity. The greater fantasy is that which takes off from an object and shows it to the beholder in a new way and yet does this out of the component elements of the object. . . .

UNDATED ENTRIES, 1949

. . . A sketch is hard to transpose into an oil, because the artist must always consider the scale of the sketch and [that of] the oil, which are not the same.

I have studied Giotto and the Ravenna mosaics[34] and find that the shapes of the figures are quite simple. In fact, Giotto's figures are in some respect like big sacks of potatoes. Giotto, and the mosaic makers, made their figures bold by the great passages through the separate figures, that gave them great involvement. How cursed the modern artist is to have had an early training in the error of mechanical perspective. In composing the picture it is best not to think in terms of separate figures (if the artist is using the human figure) but to consider the big movements, and counter-rhythms that in the end can be easily established as one or more figures.

In the Duccio (see fig. 5)[35] the black of Christ's garment extends as a plane to the cloak of Pilate on the right. Each figure involves another in a flowing linear movement. At the end, as with the red lines, the figures can be delineated. Where several reds are used in a painting, apparently only one of the tones will function as red, with the other reds becoming tans and browns.

Let's never make the mistake of believing that a real artist ever paints a picture. The true artist paints something. . . .

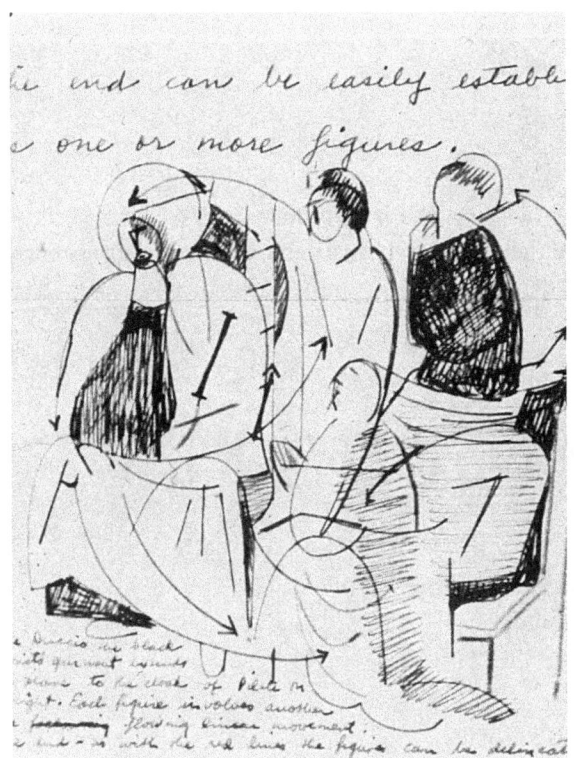

FIGURE 5  Sketch of painting by Duccio from the journal of Romare Bearden. Art © Romare Bearden Foundation/Licensed by VAGA, New York

Painting is a great storm cellar, not only as a place of refuge, but a place where one can do things free from the censoring minds of little people. The world is never a big enough or free enough place to contain the artist's laughter — or understand his sorrows.

Silly for the "pure form" boys to say "this or that line in a painting shouldn't be moved." The test of a good painting is that it can be shifted.

To come in to the studio and start to paint just cubes and circles is in a sense to deny everything one has seen all day.

So much of the modern artist's affection for the primitives is because the primitive work gives support to their ideas. But Titian, and Tintoretto, had as much abstract formulation as did the primitives — plus more vitality. . . .

Structure is a necessity to the artist, for the artist's feelings must have a measure.

The artist looks for a vision, not an idea.

The artist's vision is transcendental.

So many of our institutions and ideas have become forms of oppression. The artist must be careful not to let his art become another.

Every exaggeration should take the direction of nature, and of the idea. . . .

## NOTES

From Cynthia Jo Fogliatti, ed., *Romare Bearden: Origins and Progressions: The Detroit Institute of Arts, September 16–November 16, 1986*, exh. cat. (Detroit, MI: The Institute, 1986). The following notes are by Fogliatti and include information obtained during interviews with Bearden from March to May 1986.

1. Duccio di Buoninsegna, Italian (active 1278–1318), *Maestà* altarpiece, 1308–11, Museo dell'Opera del Duomo, Siena.

2. Carl Holty (1900–1973), an American abstract painter, was Bearden's mentor and close friend. Born in Germany in 1900, Holty studied painting at the Art Institute of Chicago, at the National Academy of Design, and with Hans Hofmann in Munich. He was a member of the Abstraction-Création group in Paris in 1931–32, was a founder of the American Abstract Artists group, and was included in the first group of artists to show at Samuel Kootz's gallery (see note 4). He and Bearden co-authored the book *The Painter's Mind: A Study of the Relations of Structure and Space in Painting* (1969), as well as several other articles. Holty's studio in 1947 was located at 149 East 119th Street in New York.

3. The Spanish artist Joan Miró's (1893–1983) mature works combine elements of Surrealism, Primitivism, abstraction, and fantasy. During Miró's first trip to the United States in 1947 he worked at Holty's studio in New York on a commission for Cincinnati's Hotel Terrace Plaza. The commissioned painting, *Mural*, is now in the collection of the Cincinnati Art Museum.

4. Samuel Kootz (1899–1982) was one of New York's most prominent modern art dealers and an early advocate of Abstract Expressionism. He opened his first gallery in 1945 at 15 East 57th Street, giving Bearden his first one-person show in that same year. Bearden showed regularly at the gallery in both one-person and group shows until 1948, when the gallery closed. When it reopened a year later, Bearden was not included in the group of artists to exhibit.

5. See *Cahiers d'Art* 20è–21è années (1945–46): 9–74. This issue includes articles on Paul Klee by Christian Zervos, Georges Duthuit, Pierre Mabille, Tristan Tzara, Joe Bousquet, Georges Bataille, Roger Vitrac, Will Grohmann, and Valentine Hugo, and poems by René Char and Jacques Prévert.

6. The drawings and plaster cast for Picasso's *L'homme au mouton* (*Man with Sheep*) (1944) were published in Christian Zervos, "L'homme à l'agneau de Picasso Juillet 1942–Octobre 1943," *Cahiers d'Art* 20è–21è années (1945–46): 85–113. The work was not cast in bronze until after World War II.

7. Picasso's *Guernica*, a work commissioned by the Spanish Republican Government for the Spanish Pavilion at the 1937 Paris World's Fair, was published in Christian Zervos, "Histoire d'un tableau de Picasso," *Cahiers d'Art* 12è année, nos. 4–5 (1937): 105–56.

8. Unidentified.

9. The current location of this work is unknown.

10. One of the most prized holdings of The Cloisters, a branch of the Metropolitan Museum of Art specializing in medieval art, is *The Hunt of the Unicorn* (also known as *The Unicorn Tapestry*), a series of six Franco-Flemish tapestries and fragments of a seventh woven about 1500. The influence of these tapestries on Bearden was enormous:

in *The Painter's Mind* Bearden and Holty analyze their compositional structure in depth as a paradigm to be followed by artists.

11. Stuart Davis (1894–1964) was an American Modernist painter whose works often incorporated jazz themes and elements of abstraction and Cubism. Bearden met Davis through Ad Bates, a black modern dancer who had come into contact with numerous artists when he was a model at the Art Students League during the 1930s. Although Bearden met Davis before World War II, their close friendship developed after the war.

12. See *Women: A Collaboration of Artists and Writers* (New York: Samuel M. Kootz Editions, 1948). This publication documents an exhibition, on view at the Kootz Gallery in September of 1947, of paintings of women executed by the artists in Kootz's stable. After the exhibition had opened, Kootz brought together artists Picasso, Georges Braque, Fernand Léger, William Baziotes, Romare Bearden, Byron Browne, Adolph Gottlieb, David Hare, Hans Hofmann, Carl Holty, and Robert Motherwell with authors Lewis Galantière, Paul Goodman, Clement Greenberg, Weldon Kees, Benjamin Péret, Harold Rosenberg, Jean-Paul Sartre, Barry Ulanov, Tennessee Williams, William Carlos Williams, and Victor Wolfson to collaborate on this unique publication. The book was designed by Paul Rand. Williams wrote "Woman as Operator" to accompany Bearden's painting *Women with an Oracle* (1948; current location unknown).

13. Charles Sheeler (1883–1965) and Charles Demuth (1883–1935) were both painters who practiced a form of Cubism, native to the United States, called Precisionism. Marsden Hartley (1877–1943), also an American painter, was influenced by Divisionism, Expressionism, Cubism, and Constructivism at various times in his career. He was a member of the group of artists to show regularly at Alfred Stieglitz's "291" gallery in New York.

14. Vaclav Vytlacil (1892–1984) was an American Modernist painter and one of the founders of the American Abstract Artists group in 1936. Holty, who was a close friend of Vytlacil, introduced him to Bearden.

15. *The Crucifixion of Christ,* Collection Bayerische Staatsgemäldesammlungen (Alte Pinakothek), Munich, was initially believed to be by Viktur and Heinrich Dünwegge, School of Cologne (active late 15th/early 16th centuries), but has been reattributed to the German artist Derick Baegert (ca. 1440–ca. 1515).

16. Rembrandt Harmensz. van Rijn, Dutch (1606–1669), *Self-Portrait*, 1658, The Frick Collection, New York.

17. In 1945 the first complete compilation of all the essays written in English by Dutch artist Piet Mondrian (1872–1944) was published. Bearden acquired a copy of the book for his library upon the recommendation of Carl Holty, who had become friendly with Mondrian in Paris in the early 1930s. See Piet Mondrian, *Plastic Art and Pure Plastic Art, 1937, and Other Essays, 1941–43*, in the series *The Documents of Modern Art*, general ed. Robert Motherwell (New York: Wittenborn and Company, 1945).

18. This is Bearden's interpretation of a statement in an article by Miró titled "Je rêve d'un grand atelier," which was published in *XXè Siécle* 1, no. 2 (May 1938): 25–28.

19. Giorgio de Chirico (1888–1978) was an Italian painter who founded the Scuola Metafisica, or metaphysical school of painting. He strove to present familiar objects in a manner that removed from them their traditional associations, such as in his *Piazze d'Italia* series. Bearden knew de Chirico's work from the permanent collections of the Museum of Modern Art, New York. He was also familiar with James Thrall Soby's book on the artist, *The Early Chirico* (New York: Dodd, Mead & Company, 1941).

20. Bearden meant that an artist's manner of drawing should reflect his style of painting rather than imitating that of an accepted master, especially if the latter's style is not compatible with one's own.

21. Bearden's studio at the time was located at 243 West 125th Street, New York.

22. Unidentified friend of Carl Holty.

23. Wife of William Baziotes.

24. William Baziotes (1911–1963) was an American Abstract Expressionist painter whom Bearden met through Samuel Kootz. Baziotes, who regarded his paintings as reflections of his state of mind at the time of their creation, was one of the first Abstract Expressionist artists to show at Kootz's gallery.

25. Heinrich Heine (1797–1856) was a German Romantic poet and critic whose works include *Buch der Lieder* (1827), *Romanzero* (1851), and *Neue Gedichte* (1853–54).

26. Ralston Crawford (1906–1978) was an American Precisionist painter whose work, like Sheeler's, centered upon industrial subjects that had been reduced to their most elemental shapes. He met Bearden through the American Social Surrealist painter Walter Quirt. In turn, Bearden introduced both Baziotes and Crawford to Stuart Davis.

27. Pierre Bonnard (1867–1947) was a French painter of *intimisme*, or scenes, usually of interiors, that draw the viewer into an intimate setting. Bearden had several discussions with Stuart Davis about Bonnard's work, especially following the exhibition of that artist's work organized by the Museum of Modern Art in 1948 in collaboration with the Cleveland Museum of Art.

Christian Zervos's article, "Pierre Bonnard: est-il un grand peintre?" appeared in the same issue of *Cahiers d'Art* (22è année [1947]) as a review of the 1947 Galerie Maeght exhibition "Introduction à la Peinture Moderne Américaine sous le Patronage des United States Information Services: Baziotes, Bearden, Browne, Gottlieb, Holty, Motherwell," and may have inspired Bearden's interest and comparison.

28. Meister Eckhart (Johannes Eckhart) (ca. 1260–ca. 1328) was a German mystic, Christian theologian, and author of *Talks of Instruction* (1300?) and *The Book of Divine Consolation* (1308?).

29. William Gropper (1897–1977) was an American Social Realist painter and political cartoonist. Bearden knew Gropper's work because by 1947 several of his pieces were included in such major New York museum collections as the Metropolitan Museum of Art, the Whitney Museum of American Art, and the Museum of Modern Art.

30. Bearden became familiar with work by the American Social Realist painter Philip Evergood (1901–1973) through the annual exhibitions of contemporary art organized by the Whitney Museum, in which Evergood's paintings had been included since 1934.

31. Bearden had knowledge of Poussin's ideas and work through André Gide's monograph on the artist published in 1945 by Au Divan, Paris. Only the first phrase of this quotation can be directly attributed to Poussin; Bearden found it in Gide's catalogue entry (no. 42) on the painting *L'Hiver* (1660–64, Musée du Louvre). The remainder of the quotation is Bearden's personal response to Gide's text. See Jacques Thuillier to Davira S. Taragin, April 16, 1986 [source unknown].

32. See note 12.

33. See William Baziotes's *Night Form* (1947, Collection Washington University, St. Louis). Kootz had chosen Harold Rosenberg to collaborate with Baziotes on the *Women* project; Rosenberg's poem *Smoke of Circe* accompanied Baziotes's painting in the publication.

34. Bearden was most impressed with the mosaics of Sant'Apollinare Nuovo in Ravenna, Italy. By studying them he learned the importance of counterbalancing forms to give symmetry to a composition.

35. The sketch is based upon a detail from the *Crowning with Thorns*, a scene in Duccio's *Maestà* altarpiece (see note 1).

# RECTANGULAR STRUCTURE IN MY MONTAGE PAINTINGS

*Romare Bearden*

I

When I first started to make pictures I was particularly interested in using art as an instrument of social change. As far as I was concerned at the time, which was in the mid-1930s, art techniques were simply the means that enabled an artist to communicate a message — which, as I saw it then, was essentially a social, if not a political one. My original objective as an artist was to become a political cartoonist. I was an undergraduate majoring in mathematics at New York University when I started producing a steady stream of caricatures and satirical sketches for *The Magpie*, the campus magazine of humor; by the time I received my degree I had already become something of a semiprofessional cartoonist with a weekly feature in the Baltimore *Afro-American*, a Negro newspaper of nationwide reputation and circulation.

It was my search for better ways of getting a social message into my cartoons which led me to the works of Daumier, Forain, and Käthe Kollwitz, to the Art Students League and to George Grosz. The artists in the 1930s were deeply conscious of social problems, and Diego Rivera, José Orozco, and David Siqueiros in Mexico, and Thomas Hart Benton, John Steuart Curry, and Grant Wood in the United States were then at the height of their popularity. But what impressed, engaged, and challenged me most were the corrosive line drawings and the watercolors of Grosz.

It was during my period with Grosz, under whom I began studying several months after graduating from New York University, that I began to regard myself as a painter rather than a cartoonist. The drawings of Grosz on the theme of the human situation in post–World War I Germany made me realize the artistic possibilities of American Negro subject matter. It was also Grosz who led me to study composition, through the analysis of Bruegel and the great Dutch masters, and who in the process of refining my draftsmanship initiated me into the magic world of Ingres, Dürer, Holbein, and Poussin.

I had decided that I wanted to make painting, not mathematics, my life's work, but it was not until several years after leaving the League that I managed to do a group of paintings with any stylistic continuity. The subject matter of almost all of these paintings was drawn from Negro life. This is also true of my painting now, but at that time my emphasis was more on the rural South of the United States, than the urban North. Everything that I have done since then has been, in effect, an extension of my experiments with flat painting, shallow space, Byzantine stylization, and African design.

All of my first paintings were done in tempera. I completed about twenty before going into military service in 1942. When I returned to civilian life in 1945, I began a series of watercolors based on such themes as the Passion of Christ, the Bullring, and the *Iliad*. My temperas had been composed in closed forms and the coloring was subdued, mostly earthy browns, blues, and green. When I started working with watercolor, however, I found myself using bright color patterns and bold, black lines to delineate semi-abstract shapes. I never worked long on a painting with this method or made many corrections. I had not yet learned that modern painting progresses through cumulative destructions and new beginnings.

When I started to paint in oil, I simply wanted to extend what I had done in watercolor. To do so, I had the initial sketch enlarged as a photostat, traced it onto a gessoed panel, and with thinned color completed the oil as if it were indeed a watercolor.

Later on I read Delacroix's *Journal* and felt that I, too, could profit by systematically copying the masters of the past and of the present. Not wanting to work in museums, I again used photostats, enlarging photography of works by Giotto, Duccio, Veronese, Grünewald, Rembrandt, de Hooch, Manet, and Matisse. I made reasonably free copies of each work by substituting my own choice of colors for those of these artists, except for those of Manet and Matisse when I was guided by color reproductions. The Rembrandt I chose, *Pilate Washing His Hands*, gave me the most difficulty.[1] While studying this masterpiece, I found so many subtle rhythms and carefully planned relationships that I finally surrendered the work, having learned that there are hidden, mysterious relationships which defy analysis.

## II

In 1950, I went to Paris on the GI Bill for eighteen months. During that time, however, I was much too busy visiting museums, galleries, and studios to get any actual painting done. But I was undergoing a change in my thinking nevertheless, and when I returned to New York I began experimenting in a radically different way. I started to play with pigments, as such, in marks and patches, distorting natural colors and representational objects. I spent several years doing this, until I gradually realized the tracks of color tended to fragment my compositions. That was when I went back to the Dutch masters, to Vermeer and De Hooch in particular, and it was then I came to some understanding of the way these painters controlled their big shapes, even when elements of different size and scale were included within those large shapes. I was also studying, at the same time, the techniques which enable Chinese classical painters to organize their large areas, for example: the device of the open corner to allow the observer a starting point in encompassing the entire painting; the subtle ways of shifting balance and emphasis; and the use of voids, or negative areas, as sections of pacivity [*sic*] and as a means of projecting the big shapes.

As a result, I began to paint more thinly, often on natural linen, where I left sections of the canvas unpainted so that the linen itself had the function of a color. Then in a transition toward what turned out to be my present style, I painted broad areas of color on various thicknesses of rice paper and glued these papers on canvas, usually in several layers. I tore sections of the paper away, always attempting to tear upward and across on the picture plane until some motif engaged me. When this happened, I added more papers and painted additional colored areas to complete the painting.[2]

When I begin a work now, I first put down several rectangles of color, some of which, as in a Rembrandt drawing, are of the same proportion as the canvas. I next might paste a photograph, perhaps of a head, in the general area where I expect a head to be. The type of photograph does not matter, as it will be greatly altered. At this stage I try only to establish the general layout of the composition. When that is accomplished, I attempt ever more definite statements, superimposing other materials over those I started with. I try to move up and across the surface in much the same manner as I had done with the torn papers, avoiding deep diagonal thrusts and the kind of arabesque shapes favored by the great baroque painters. Slanting directions I regard as tilted rectangles, and I try to find some compensating balance for these relative to the horizontal and vertical axes of the canvas.

I do not burden myself with the need for complete abstraction or absolute formal purity but I do want my language to be strict and classical in the manner of the great Benin heads, for example. In that sense, I feel my work is in the tradition of most of all the great exponents of flat painting. I have drawn on these styles, which I feel are timeless and historically durable, to control my images in pictorial space. I have incorporated techniques of the camera eye and the documentary film to, in some measure, personally involve the onlooker. Without going too far beyond selected aspects of reality, I try to transform them, often as they are perceived conventionally, into an intense aesthetic statement.

Some observers have noted that the apparent visual basis of my current work, through the use of overlapping planes and of flat space, is similar to Cubism. In the actual process of composition, however, I find myself as deeply involved with methods derived from De Hooch and Vermeer, as well as other masters of flat painting, including the classic Japanese portrait artists and the pre-Renaissance Siennese masters, such as Duccio and Lorenzetti. What I like most about the Cubism of Picasso, Braque, and Léger is its primary emphasis on the essentials of structure. Nevertheless I also find that for me the Cubism of these masters leads to an overcrowding of the pictorial space. This accounts for the high surface of the frontal planes, so prevalent in some of the most successful early works of the Cubists. In fact, such exceptions as the collage drawings of Picasso in which emptier areas are emphasized, only point up what is otherwise typical. Much of the agitation in Juan Gris' *Guitar and Flowers*, for instance, is the result of the violent diagonal twist of his planes away from the stabilizing rectangle of the surface. Even the early Cubism of Mondrian, who was in many ways a descendant of De Hooch and Vermeer, contains a number of small bricklike, rectangular shapes which strike me as being more a concession to the manner of the time, than essential to his austere conception of space and structure.[3]

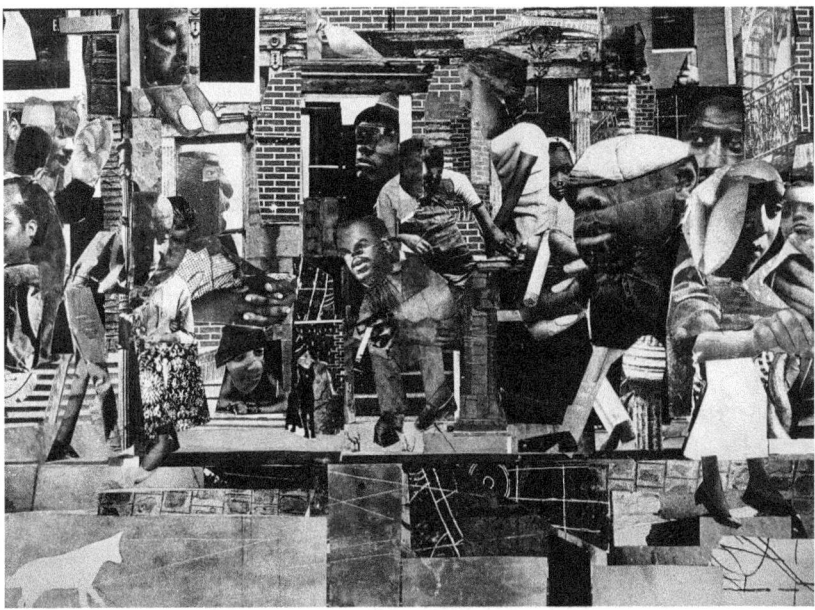

FIGURE 6 Romare Bearden, *The Dove (Projection)*, 1964. Montage painting (photostat on board), 35 × 48 in. (88.9 × 121.9 cm). Art © Romare Bearden Foundation/Licensed by VAGA, New York

Although I find I am increasingly fascinated by the possibilities of empty space on a canvas, in *The Dove (Projection)* (fig. 6) and *The Street (Projection)* (fig. 7) I was working for maximum multiplicity, without the surface fragmentation which I object to in the early Cubist paintings. Both of these works, which I call Projections, were first done in a size not much larger than a sheet of typing paper, then the original was enlarged photographically and dry mounted on Masonite board. The subjects are drawn from crowded urban street-scenes but in *The Dove* the variety of the scale in the human figures is such that some of the faces really function as areas of pacivity [*sic*]. The robes in *The Baptism (Projection)* (fig. 8) fulfill a similar function in the counterpoint of occupied and empty areas. Zurburán, in some of his great figural compositions, employed flatly modeled drapery for the same purpose. *The Baptism* is a recollection of the fact that during the warm weather the shallow streams in the Southern states were frequently used for baptismal purposes. In this picture, the train represents the encroachment of another culture.

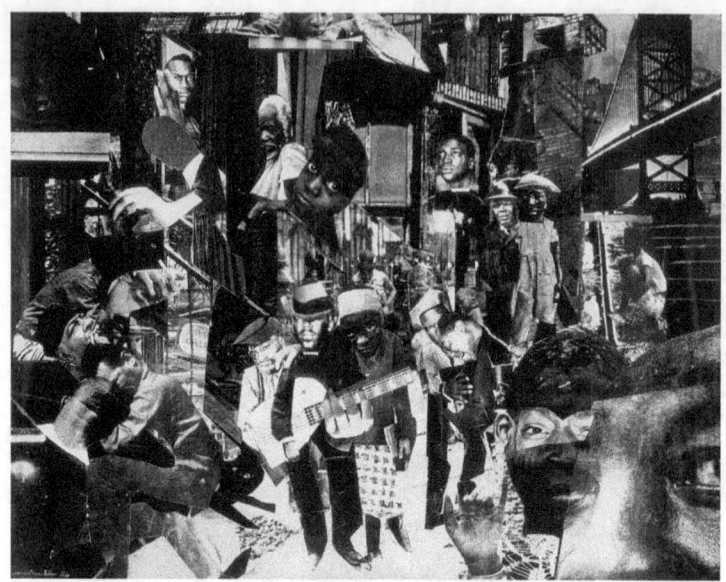

FIGURE 7 Romare Bearden, *The Street (Projection)*, 1964. Montage painting (photostat on board), 38.5 × 54.5 in. (97.8 × 138.4 cm). Art © Romare Bearden Foundation/Licensed by VAGA, New York

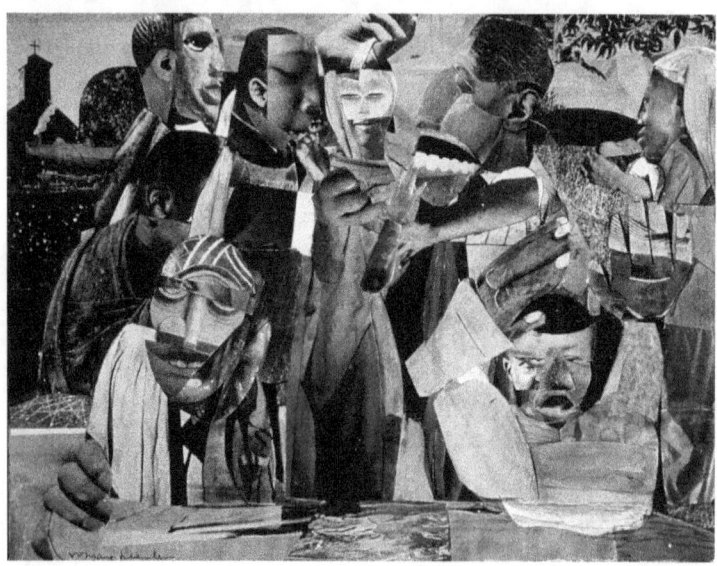

FIGURE 8 Romare Bearden, *The Baptism (Projection)*, 1964. Montage painting (photostat on board), 34 × 48 in. (86.4 × 121.9 cm). Art © Romare Bearden Foundation/ Licensed by VAGA, New York

# III

One of the technical problems with which I am now involved is the interplay between a photograph and an actual painting so that I find myself adjusting color to the grays of the black-and-white photograph. This adjustment to an overall gray is, of course, not new to the art of painting. Even in what remains of some Pompeian frescos it appears apparent that in spite of the orange-red backgrounds, the figures and drapery were painted in tones of black, white, and gray, with the flesh tints glazed over this gray range of colors. The deep browns and reds, which we associate with the great frescos of the Casa Misteria [Villa dei Misteri] in Pompeii, actually emanate from a merging of the background with the grayed figures and objects. Before full color methods of printing were established in the early decades of this century, the old two-color process had a more extensive range of color than one would have thought possible because of a similar interaction of colors.

In many of my paintings I use either a blue-gray or a green color to harmonize with the gray, since I feel both of these colors are intimately related to gray. Sometimes, in order to heighten the character of a painting, I introduce what appears to be a dissonant color, as in *The Approaching Storm* (fig. 9), where the reds, browns, and yellows disrupt the placidity of the blues and greens. I found, when I was working on this painting, in which various colored papers were mounted directly onto Masonite, that these dissonant colors gave an entirely new significance and character to the other colors and forms. Therefore, in order to unify the composition, I was obliged to both emphasize certain colors and shapes and to mollify others.

Similarly, the heavy red in the ground and upper right-hand areas in *The Folk Musicians* (fig. 10) was called for by the brightly colored orange guitars of the musicians. The figures in this painting are, for the most part, painted in oil. The relations of the other colors and shapes to the bright orange, which is certainly the most dominant color, produced some unusual effects. The figure on the far right is quite ghostlike, probably because of the contrast with the red brick wall and, also, because of the opposition of the more solid appearing central figure, which is both light and dark in value.

On the other hand, the simple whites of the blouses on the two figures in the gray, white, and blue painting, *The Old Couple* (Plate 3), hold their place in a decidedly more reticent manner. I think it is worth observing that most of the background in *The Old Couple* is painted in oil and that throughout the

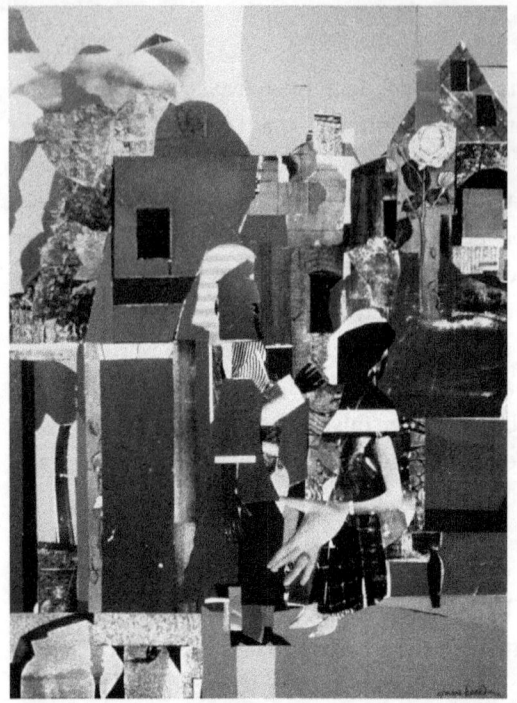

FIGURE 9 Romare
Bearden, *The Approaching Storm*,
1967. Montage
painting, 48 × 30 in.
(121.9 × 76.2 cm). Art © Romare
Bearden Foundation/
Licensed by VAGA, New York

FIGURE 10 Romare
Bearden, *The Folk Musi-
cians*, 1967. Montage painting,
44 × 56 in. (111.8 × 142.2 cm). Art
© Romare Bearden
Foundation/Licensed by VAGA,
New York

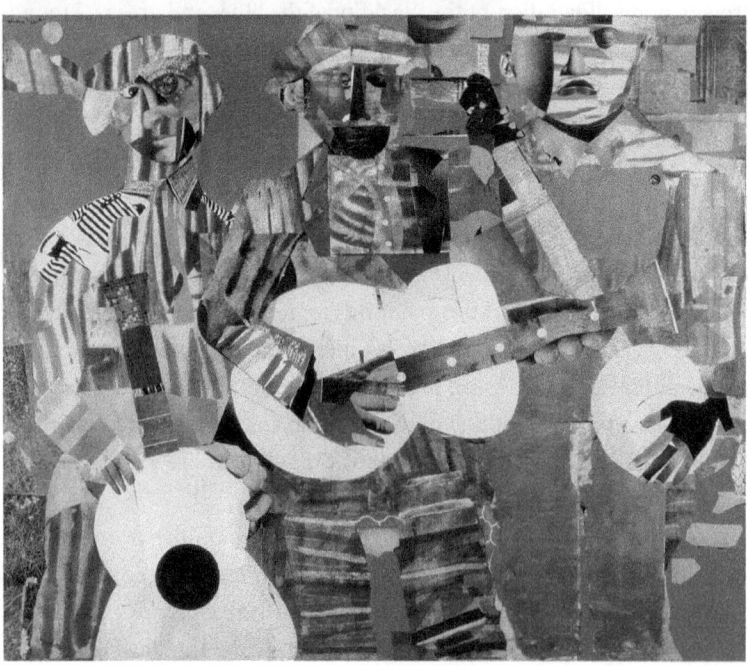

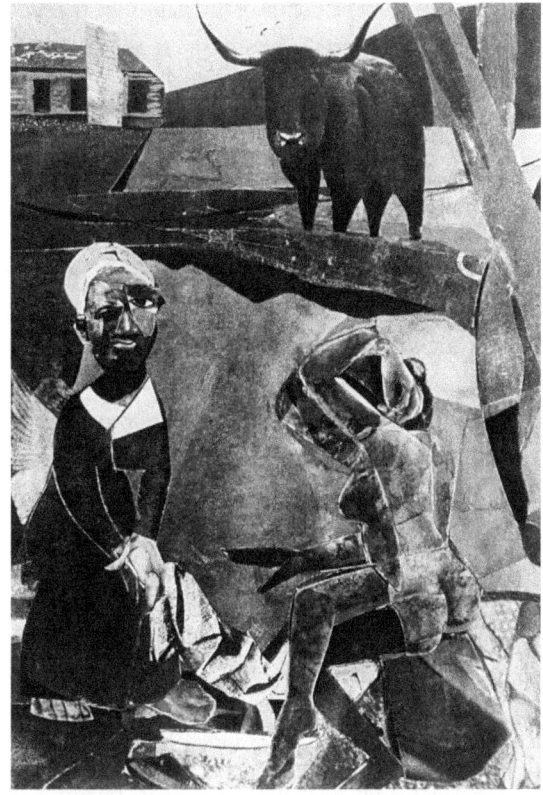

FIGURE 11 Romare Bearden, *Conjur Woman as an Angel*, 1964. Montage painting, 40 × 30 in. (101.6 × 76.2 cm). Art © Romare Bearden Foundation/Licensed by VAGA, New York

painting there is an interchange between the photographic material and what is painted.

This is also true in *Conjur Woman as an Angel* (fig. 11), where the nude figure of the young woman was freely painted and the photographic components were imposed afterwards. A conjur woman was an important figure in a number of southern Negro rural communities. She was called on to prepare love potions; to provide herbs to cure various illnesses; and to be consulted regarding vexing personal and family problems. Much of her knowledge had been passed on through the generations from an African past, although a great deal was learned from the American Indians. A conjur woman was greatly feared and it was believed that she could change her appearance.

Much of the material used in the abstract elements of my paintings (particularly in the construction of faces) are often parts of photographs as in *Illusionists at 4 PM* (Plate 4), where the faces of the women are related to African masks.

## IV

Two fundamental assumptions underlie my attitude to my work. First, I feel that when some photographic detail, such as a hand or an eye, is taken out of its original context and is fractured and integrated into a different space and form configuration, it acquires a plastic quality it did not have in the original photograph. In most instances in creating a picture, I use many disparate elements to form a figure, or part of a background. I rarely use an actual photograph of a face but build them for example, from parts of African masks, animal eyes, marbles, corn, and mossy vegetation. In such a process, often something specific and particular can have its meaning extended toward what is more general and universal but never at the expense of the total structure. In this connection, the thumb of the woman on the far left has as much to do with integrating the painting as a whole, as with representing the "handness" of hands. And in *Two Women in a Courtyard* (fig. 12), I try to show that the courtyard was as important to American southern life, as indeed it was in the Holland of de Hooch, ter Borch, and Vermeer.

Also involved in the process of fracturing, as I conceive it, is its purpose in extending the larger rhythms of the painting. For instance, also in Plate 4, the way the lower section of the standing woman's face is cut, corresponds to the horizontal rhythms that stretch across the top of the painting.

Secondly, I think a quality of artificiality must be retained in a work of art, since, after all, the reality of art is not to be confused with that of the outer world. Art, it must be remembered, is artifice, or a creative undertaking, the primary function of which is to add to our existing conception of reality. Moreover, such devices of artificiality as distortion of scale and proportion, and abstract coloration, are the very means through which I try to achieve a more personal expression than I sense in the realistic or conventionally focused photograph. The initial public reaction to my work has generally been one of shock, which appears to rise out of a confrontation with subject matter unfamiliar to most persons. In spite of this, it is not my aim to paint about the Negro in America in terms of propaganda. It is precisely my awareness of the distortions required of the polemicist that has caused me to paint the life of my people as I know

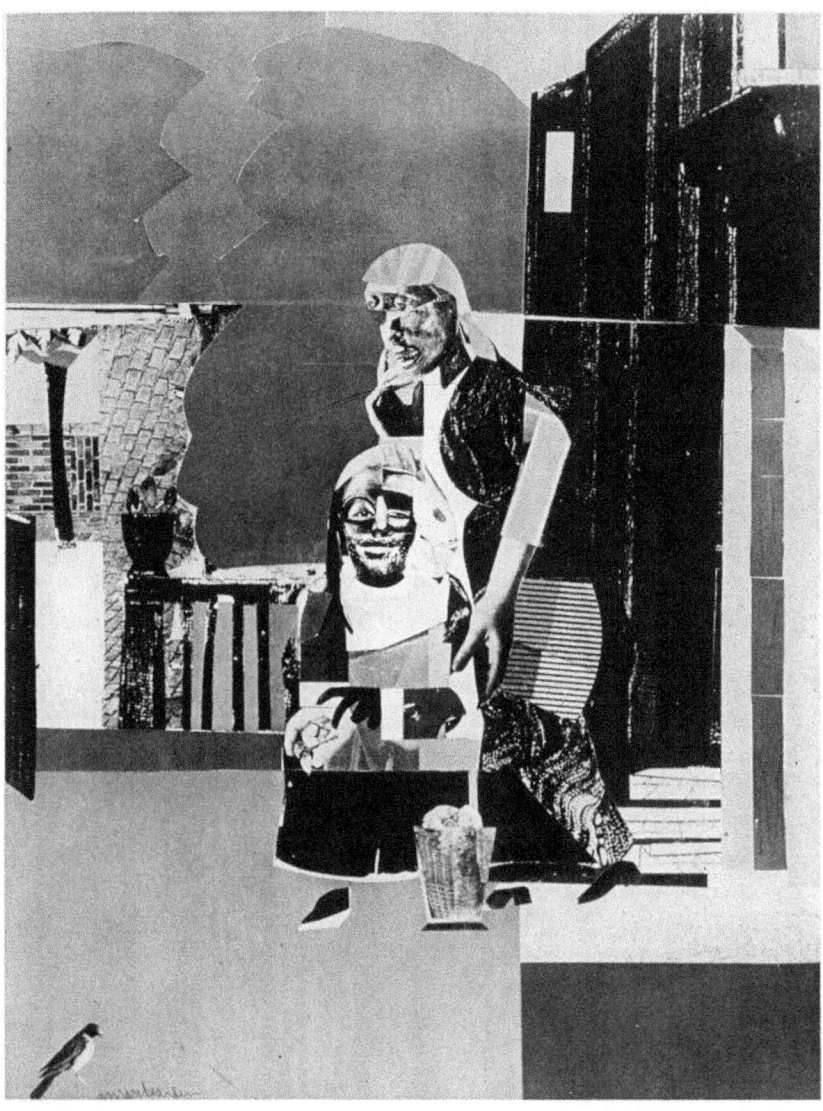

FIGURE 12 Romare Bearden, *Two Women in a Courtyard*, 1967. Montage painting, 40 × 30 in. (101.6 × 76.2 cm). Art © Romare Bearden Foundation/Licensed by VAGA, New York

it — as passionately and dispassionately as Bruegel painted the life of the Flemish people of his day. One can draw many social analogies from the great works of Bruegel — as I have no doubt one can draw from mine — my intention, however, is to reveal through pictorial complexities the richness of a life I know.

I am afraid, despite my intentions, that in some instances commentators have tended to overemphasize what they believe to be the social elements in my work. But while my response to certain human elements is as obvious as it is inevitable, I am also pleased to note that upon reflection many persons have found that they were as much concerned with the aesthetic implications of my paintings as with, what may possibly be, my human compassion.

## NOTES

From *Leonardo* 2.1 (January 1969).

1. This painting is in the Metropolitan Museum of Art, New York.

2. References: R. Michau, "Les collages de peinture ou pictocollages," *Leonardo* 1 (1968): 35; A. Verlon, "Montage-painting," *Leonardo* 1 (1968): 383.

3. References: H. Rosenberg, *Introduction à la peinture modern américaine* (Paris: Galerie Maeght, 1947); C. Childs, "Bearden: Identification and Reality," *ARTnews* (October 1964); D. Ashton, "Romare Bearden: Projection," *Quadrum*, no. 17 (1965); F. Geitlein, "Confrontation at the Corcoran," *Washington Star* (October 14, 1965); J. Canaday, "Romare Bearden Focuses on the Negro," *New York Times* (October 14, 1967); R. Pomeroy, "Black Persephone," *ARTnews* (October 1967); C. Childs, "The Artist Caught Between Two Worlds," *Tuesday Magazine* (April 1967); L. Roberts, "A Gallery of Eight" (special issue, "The Negro in the American Arts") *Topic*, no. 5 (1966); "Patchwork Nostalgia," *Time* (October 27, 1967).

# THE TWENTIES AND THE BLACK RENAISSANCE

*Romare Bearden and Harry Henderson*

World War I made it clear that the United States had emerged as a world power. Yet, except for overly idealized "patriotic" versions, American history was neither widely known nor understood. In fact, many European-oriented academicians still argued that America had no history — paralleling what they said about Africans. The idea that there was an American literature, music, theater, or art was not widely recognized either in this country or abroad.

This historical situation opened the way for development of an American cultural identity that was not dominated by European concepts. As a writer in *The Freeman*, one of the leading intellectual magazines of the day, put it: "The great hope of culture in America lies in the fact that we in this country have not yet agreed upon a definition of 'American culture.' The greatness of our opportunity consists in the very fact that thus far we have set up no definite boundaries of nationality where culture is concerned."[1]

From the perspective of today, it would seem that African Americans recognized this situation as their opportunity to participate in the evolving American culture and way of life. In contrast to the many young writers and artists who felt disillusioned and alienated by World War I and who went to Paris in search of an acceptable identity as Americans, most black people had a proud sense of being Americans. And they strongly felt it was time to shuck off the stereotyped limitations imposed on them historically, including the old denial of their artistic ability. The emergence of a number of young black artists reflected this profound change among African Americans. They knew that spirituals had won worldwide respect, and they saw that jazz had America up and dancing. They believed, as one analyst of the period, Nathan Irvin Huggins, has put it, that they "were on the threshold of a new day."[2]

Three major factors had given rise to this new attitude among African Americans. First, some 200,000 black men had served in the savagery of World War I, and the black 369th Infantry from New York, alone among United States troops, had been decorated en masse by the French government with the Croix de Guerre for its heroism. The old ways were gone forever for these men, their families, their friends, black leaders, and intellectuals.

Second, millions of poor black people had silently, both individually and in family groups, left the South in a determined effort to improve their lot in northern cities. In 1910 eight of ten black Americans had resided in the eleven former Confederate states, with 90 percent living in rural areas with almost no schools. Jobs in northern factories, mills, and mines during World War I started this great migration, but it continued between 1920 and 1925, when some two million African Americans left the South. The black population of Chicago rose from 44,102 persons in 1910 to 233,903 by 1930. New York, with 91,709 black persons in 1910, had 327,706 by 1930. Harlemites proudly called it "the black capital of the world."[3]

This major change in their economic and cultural circumstances, from rural to urban, contributed to African Americans' general feeling that, despite difficulties, they were not helpless, that they were moving ahead. The mass migration helped provide a psychological basis for the optimistic feeling of "renaissance," the rebirth of black people as effective participants in American life. Leaving the South prompted individual and collective examinations by African Americans of who they were, of their own thoughts and feelings, as well as their rights as Americans and the complexity of their abilities and aspirations.

Without this migration, the development of a significant group of African-American artists in the 1920s could not have occurred. In earlier periods, there had been only a few, isolated black artists. As long as the overwhelming majority of African Americans lived in the impoverished rural South, there could not be a substantial number of black artists. Most of the African-American artists who developed in the 1920s — Palmer Hayden, Malvin Gray Johnson, Richmond Barthé, James Lesesne Wells, Ellis Wilson, and Augusta Savage, to mention a few — were born in small southern towns.

Pride in African-American soldiers, whose frontline courage had been expected to end the denial of full citizenship rights for all black people, and the mass migration, in which nearly every African-American family participated in some way, contributed to the third factor — the great outpouring of creative energy by many talented African Americans in all the arts, most noticeably in music and the theater. While it may be seen as an aspect of the fundamental change in African Americans' attitudes toward themselves and their participation in American life, this creative activity had a synergistic effect, particularly on the demand for better conditions, education, and the encouragement of talented individuals. Even a poor, uneducated migrant could see that some African Americans were now musical and theatrical "stars." To African Americans as a group, this development meant great heights could be scaled. Intellectuals optimistically believed that discrimination and prejudice could be ended by demonstrating that African Americans were capable doctors, judges, lawyers, writers, and artists. Their work, creating a bridge across ignorance and prejudice, was expected to win respect and full rights for black people.

Although this creative period has been generally called the "Harlem Renaissance," the term is a misnomer. Harlem's creativity was simply the most publicized and most diverse. The same kind of activity went on in Philadelphia, Chicago, Boston, Baltimore, and San Francisco, where the sculpture of Sargent Johnson was winning prizes. These efforts made many influential Americans aware of African-American poets, writers, musicians, artists, and theatrical stars. It was something new and disturbing to old ideas about the role of African Americans in American life.

Although northern cities gave these aspiring artists some opportunities to see works of art, to visit museums and libraries, prejudice still kept them from receiving technical training at many art schools. The Art Students League, the National Academy of Design, and Cooper Union in New York and the Art Institute of Chicago were among the few schools that accepted black students. African Americans were made to feel unwelcome at many art galleries and some libraries.

However, the artists' first concern was survival, not art. Hard work, long hours, and poor pay left little time for museums. W. H. Johnson labored as a longshoreman on the docks; Augusta Savage was a laundress. Cloyd L. Boykin worked as a janitor, and Palmer C. Hayden did odd jobs and cleaned apartments. All were constantly advised by people of both races to give up their hopes of becoming artists. Many were forced to do so. Carleton Thorpe, for example, exhibited paintings in a 1921 Harlem library show but was told he had no chance of becoming an artist because he was black. He took a darkroom job with Peter A. Juley, a specialist in photographing art, and gave up painting.[4]

A handful of older black artists encouraged and sometimes taught younger ones. Among them were William E. Braxton, a skilled and much-published Chicago illustrator; William McKnight Farrow, originally from Ohio, who acquired his own training while a curator's assistant at the Art Institute of Chicago, became an expert etcher, and taught etching there;[5] William Edouard Scott, who had studied with Henry Ossawa Tanner in France and become an illustrator and muralist; and Laura Wheeler Waring, originally from Hartford, Connecticut, who trained at the Pennsylvania Academy of Fine Arts, studied in Rome and in Paris with Auguste Rodin, and taught at the Cheyney Training School for Teachers near Philadelphia. Having achieved some recognition, these older artists were admired by younger ones and served as their guides.

African-American identity was enhanced by the recognition that jazz was changing the nation's music — was indeed becoming its music. This was something very different from the sympathetic appreciation of religious spirituals. The rhythms of jazz set people to dancing; "we're living," people said, "in the Jazz Age." A new, fascinated awareness of black people, their spirit, and their capacity to live spread across America.

This helped to stimulate interest in the visual arts created by black artists. Between August 1 and September 30, 1921, the first large exhibition of work by African-American artists was displayed in the Harlem branch of the New York Public Library.[6] Nearly 200 paintings and sculptures, including some from Boston and Washington, D.C., had been assembled by an enthusiastic Harvard graduate, Augustus Granville Dill, whose Harlem bookstore became a mecca for young black writers. Tanner sent a painting to encourage younger artists. Five engravings by Patrick Reason, a lithographer during the 1830s, gave many New Yorkers their first inkling that there had been black artists in America long before the Civil War.

Other exhibits followed, such as the 1921 Tanner Art League show at the Dunbar High School in Washington, D.C., and the 1922 Wabash YMCA show in

Chicago, which included the work of Farrow, Charles C. Dawson, Arthur Wilson, and Ellis Wilson, who later made Haitian landscapes and people his central themes. In 1927 a major show was held at the Art Institute of Chicago under the sponsorship of the Chicago Women's Club. Called "The Negro in Art Week," it included African art as well as that of contemporary Chicago artists, work by Tanner, Edward M. Bannister, and Edmonia Lewis.[7] At this show Richmond Barthé was so successful with his clay portraits that he turned from painting to sculpture. Other exhibitors included Farrow, Scott, William A. Harper, Arthur Diggs, Aaron Douglas, John Hardrick, Hale A. Woodruff, Edwin A. Harleston, Leslie Rogers (the *Chicago Defender* cartoonist), and photographer King Ganaway. An unusual aspect of this show was its wide community sponsorship. In addition to the Chicago Women's Club, it was supported by other women's groups of both races, religious groups, the National Association for the Advancement of Colored People, and the Urban League. Among its patrons were nationally known Chicagoans, including attorney Clarence Darrow, sculptor Lorado Taft, attorney Harold Ickes, poet Carl Sandburg, and social worker Jane Addams. This sponsorship guaranteed wide publicity.

Long before this, W. E. B. Du Bois, who had known Tanner in Philadelphia, had begun publishing African-American artists' work on the cover of the NAACP magazine, *The Crisis*. The weekly *New York Age* and the Urban League's publication, *Opportunity*, also reproduced their work. Citing the example of Tanner, Du Bois particularly championed the development of artists.

Until these publications and exhibits appeared, few Americans had any idea that black artists existed. For the African-American artists, the exhibitions provided direct encouragement, and they demonstrated another aspect of the renaissance to African Americans in general.

In New York the exciting spirit of self-discovery in this period was heightened by the concentration of the African-American community. It then occupied a narrow section of Manhattan, less than a fourth of Harlem today. This narrow strip above 125th Street — then a Jim Crow street, where many restaurants barred black people — provided a physical intimacy and identification with people and events. A newcomer from Georgia or the Carolinas might find himself walking side by side with the dignified Du Bois, the vivacious Florence Mills, or Noble Sissle and Eubie Blake, whose all-black musical *Shuffle*

*Along* was making Broadway history. At the 135th Street branch of the public library one might find a display of paintings by black artists or see Arthur A. Schomburg arranging a display of African masks. Or one might glimpse James Weldon Johnson, the NAACP leader who had dramatized the need for a federal antilynching law, talking with Godfrey Nurse, one of the city's leading African-American physicians.

On most evenings the newcomer could hear street speakers, including Marcus Garvey calling for self-help and militant self-assertion in establishing an African nation. At the Gray Shop, Wallace Thurman, a novelist and managing editor of the labor-oriented *Messenger,* ran an almost continuous forum of writers and artists. Outside the Lafayette Theater, one might see famous performers like Bill "Bojangles" Robinson.

On 138th and 139th streets, between Seventh and Eighth avenues, many black professionals lived in handsome homes, some of which were designed by Stanford White. Off Lenox, in a block-size lot, Colonel Hubert Fauntleroy Julian was preparing a plane for a transatlantic flight; when he tested the engine, all Harlem heard it. On 137th Street one could dance at the Renaissance Casino and sometimes see the "Renaissance Five," whose ball handling dazzled the leading basketball teams of the era.

To many Harlemites, the renaissance meant the rebirth of a great black culture that had once created golden kingdoms in Africa. And just about everybody was participating in it. There were frequent parades by fraternal groups, such as Masons, Elks, Odd Fellows, and Moose, as well as religious and political organizations, with their members resplendent in uniforms, swinging down Seventh Avenue behind marching bands. In the evening thousands enlivened their social life by strolling along Harlem's main streets. "This is not simply going out for a walk," wrote James Weldon Johnson, "it is more like going out for an adventure."[8]

Artists like W. H. Johnson and Augusta Savage (fig. 13), who came from small southern towns, were greatly nourished and stimulated by what they found in Harlem — by a new sense of black identity and importance, of community, of power and talent. When she had tried to get portrait commissions among middle-class black people in Florida, Savage had been turned down. But in New York she did busts of both Du Bois and Garvey, the outstanding black leaders of the day, with critically divergent views, enormously different backgrounds, and sharply contrasting personalities. Each offered ideas and programs that appealed to tens of thousands, providing a cultural richness in their bitter rivalry

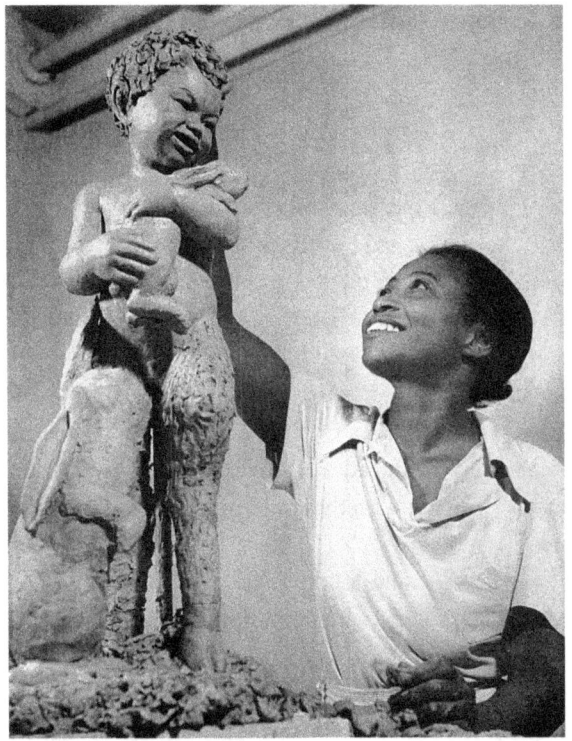

FIGURE 13
Augusta Savage with
her sculpture of a faun,
*Life* (Oct. 3, 1938).

unknown to African-American artists only a few years earlier. That both men considered artists important and arranged time to sit for an unknown black woman artist gave all of Harlem's black artists a sense of pride and of their importance in the development of their own people's influence on American history.

The city's greater social and personal freedom and the resultant spiritual and artistic freedom and sense of initiative also contributed to individual development, according to Hale Woodruff, a newcomer to New York whose drawing of young black artists at their easels appeared on the August 1928 cover of *The Crisis*. "I can't tell you how free I felt just being in the city," he said.[9]

Yet Woodruff also pointed out that, unlike the jazz musicians they were constantly advised to emulate, young black artists did not have opportunities to get together for regular exchanges, to give each other the support, response, and stimulation that foster a sense of artistic group identity. According to Woodruff, the young artists' work schedules as they struggled to earn a living, usually at menial jobs, and their differing levels of aesthetic experience worked against such exchanges.

In 1924 the editors of *Survey Graphic* magazine asked Alain L. Locke, the first African-American Rhodes scholar and head of the philosophy department at Howard University, to prepare a "Harlem" issue of their magazine. Drawing upon the work of many African-American writers, artists, and critics, Locke assembled a wide range of material that included poetry, drama, music, fiction, black history, folklore, literary criticism, discussion of the problems of black women, Du Bois's vision of the relationship of the colored peoples of the world, and other historical, sociological, and educational studies. In this way African Americans themselves imaginatively and aesthetically presented what is now called "the black experience."[10]

The impact of this issue was far-reaching. Within a year, *The Crisis* published a symposium on "the criteria of Negro art," with many African-American writers and leaders presenting their views.[11] *The Nation* extended this discussion. Wilham E. Harmon, a wealthy real estate developer, set up the Harmon Foundation to provide "Negro Achievement Awards," including one for art, and a group of New York black writers and artists attempted to organize their own avant-garde magazine, *Fire!!* But nothing more objectively conveys the impact of the "Harlem" issue of *Survey Graphic*, published in March 1925, than the reprinting of its nucleus as a book in November because the demand for it was so great. Titled *The New Negro,* the book was enhanced by six distinctive African-based design panels by Aaron Douglas, representing his first efforts to create lyric, silhouette-style black figures in action (see fig. 14). Their vitality immediately demonstrated how different the "new Negro" was. "The day of the 'aunties,' 'uncles,' and 'mammies' was done. Uncle Tom and Sambo have passed on," Locke wrote in his introduction.[12] For many influential Americans, *The New Negro* was the first demonstration of the rich cultural capabilities of African Americans in fields other than music and the theater.

Two articles in *The New Negro* dealt specifically with black artists. One was written by Albert C. Barnes, one of the book's few white contributors, who had assembled a great collection of modern and African art on his estate outside Philadelphia. As proof of the creativeness of the African-American, Barnes cited songs and poetry as "the true infallible record of what the struggle [against oppression]

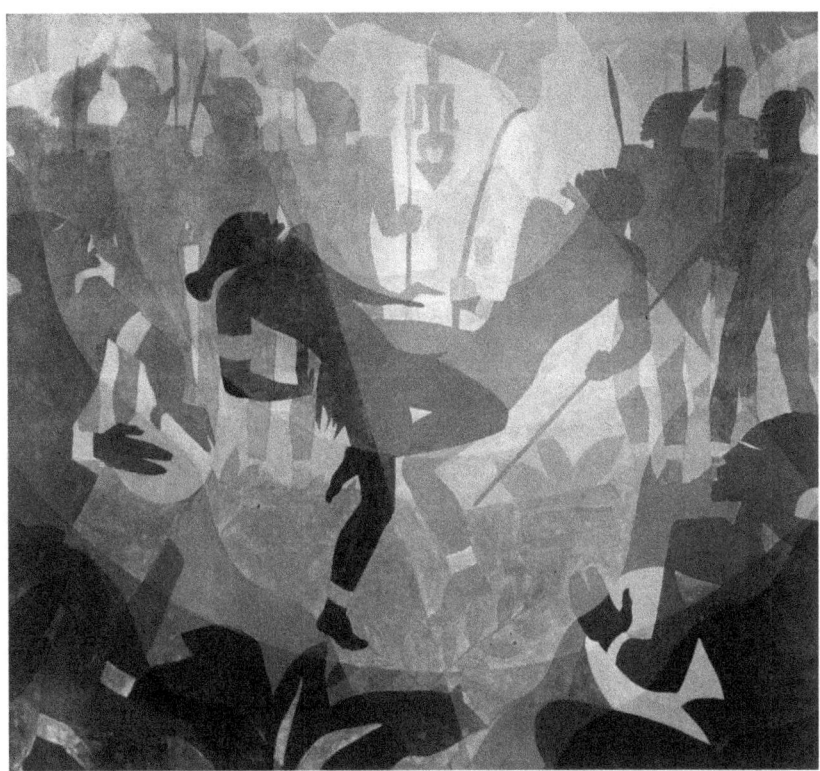

FIGURE 14 Aaron Douglas, *Aspects of Negro Life: The Negro in an African Setting*, 1934. Oil on canvas. The New York Public Library, Schomburg Center for Research in Black Culture, Art and Artifacts Division.

has meant to his inner life. . . . This mystic, whom we have treated as a vagrant, has proved his possession of a power to create, out of his own soul and our own America, moving beauty of an individual character whose existence we never knew."[13]

The second article was Locke's essay on "the legacy of the ancestral arts," which strove to influence the direction of African-American artists. Locke was one of the relatively few Americans at the time who were aware that Pablo Picasso and Georges Braque had utilized African sculpture in developing Cubism in 1909. By illustrating his essay with photographs of African art, he hoped to stimulate a link between this ancient art and the development of African-American artists. While debatable in many respects, Locke's essay touched on vital, complex issues confronting the black American artist, and it remains a primary document in their history.

"The characteristic African art expressions are rigid, controlled, disciplined, abstract, conventionalized," Locke wrote. In contrast, he saw the work of black American artists as "free, exuberant, emotional, sentimental, human." He stressed that the "spirit of African expression, by and large, is disciplined, sophisticated, laconic, and fatalistic. The emotional temper of the American Negro is exactly the opposite. What we have thought primitive in the American Negro — his naiveté, his sentimentalism, his exuberance, and his improvising spontaneity — are then neither characteristically African nor to be explained as an ancestral heritage. They are the result of his peculiar experience in America and the emotional upheaval of its trials and ordeals," essentially derived from environmental influences rather than "original artistic temperament."[14]

Locke knew that the African-American artist at that time felt no connection with African art. But because African art had influenced modern European art, he suggested,

> There is the possibility that the sensitive artistic mind of the American Negro, stimulated by a cultural pride and interest, will receive from African art a profound and galvanizing influence . . . the valuable and stimulating realization that the Negro is not a cultural foundling without his own inheritance. Our timid and apologetic imitativeness and overburdening sense of cultural indebtedness have, let us hope, their natural end in such knowledge and realization. . . . If the forefathers could so adroitly master these mediums . . . why not we?[15]

In addition to decreasing feelings of inferiority, what could be gained from African art was, Locke said, "the lesson of a classic background, the lesson of discipline and style of technical control pushed to the limits of technical mastery. A more highly stylized art does not exist than the African. If after absorbing the new content of American life and experience, and after assimilating new patterns of art, the original artistic endowment can be sufficiently augmented to express itself with equal power in more complex patterns and substance, the Negro may well become what some have predicted, the artist of American life."[16]

Through his optimistic essay and his personal access to patrons, important foundation heads, and educators, Locke shaped attitudes that influenced the development of African-American artists. At many levels, from art teachers to artists and philanthropists, he made many distinguished Americans aware of the emergence of African-American artists as a group. He also deepened the artists' own awareness of their cultural heritage. Visiting New York, Philadelphia, Chicago, and other cities, Locke often met with African-American artists.

He provided them with an orientation and sense of direction in their relationships with one another and their own people, increasing their confidence in their potential to sound a new note in American art.

Although some of the concepts presented by Barnes and Locke lay beyond their technical skills, for most African-American artists *The New Negro* was a landmark. That black people had a history as artists and that their ancestors' art influenced modern art were facts of enormous psychological importance in erasing negative images of themselves and in shaping their own positive identity. Years later Hale Woodruff recalled his excitement as an isolated young art student when, in 1924, a sympathetic Indianapolis book dealer gave him a German book on African art. Until then Woodruff had not known, beyond his own inner feelings, that any black person could create anything of artistic value.

One idea that flowered during the Black Renaissance was that racial prejudice could be greatly reduced and alleviated by art, that the artist could refute the myth of racial inferiority. This idea, derived from the widespread acceptance of spirituals, was particularly advocated by James Weldon Johnson. He asserted that "through his artistic efforts the Negro is smashing [an] immemorial stereotype faster than he has ever done . . . impressing upon the national mind the conviction that he is a creator as well as a creature . . . helping to form American civilization."[17]

On an individual level, talent did seem to mitigate the painful sore of prejudice. The idea of the artist as a lever for achieving interracial socializing became very popular in some New York circles in the mid-1920s. Interracial socializing soon became the most publicized aspect of the Renaissance. At A'Leila Walker's salon, "The Dark Tower," white intellectuals, publishers, producers, and rich socialites could meet talented black writers.

However, few young African-American visual artists took on this role. Except for Aaron Douglas and Bruce Nugent, who was both a writer and an artist, they were infrequent visitors at "The Dark Tower." Some, like W. H. Johnson and Augusta Savage, never came, for they were too busy working to survive and trying to learn how to solve technical problems. Their working hours already limited their visits to museums, galleries, and libraries.

While James Weldon Johnson's concept had some validity, it applied to relatively few individuals. Most young black artists and writers were concerned with the fundamental problem of being black in white America and the need for broader economic and social changes that Johnson's concept promised. Meeting in Douglas's apartment one night in 1926, a group of seven, including Nugent, Langston Hughes, Wallace Thurman, Zora Neale Hurston, Gwendolyn Bennett, and John P. Davis, decided to publish a quarterly magazine "devoted to the younger Negro Artists" and entitled *Fire!!*

Hughes outlined their goal: "We young Negro artists who create now intend to express our individual dark-skinned selves without fear or shame. If white people are pleased, we are glad. If they are not, it doesn't matter. If colored people are pleased, we are glad. If they are not, their displeasure doesn't matter."[18]

Few people, however, saw the one issue of *Fire!!* that was published. In it, contradicting Johnson's concept, the young artists and writers expressed their belief that the barrier of racial prejudice had to be overcome by economic, social, and political pressure — it could not be overcome by art alone. As Hughes's statement makes clear, the creators of *Fire!!* were struggling with their dependency on both black and white audiences. This complex, biracial dependency was at the core of the struggle to establish an African-American identity.

While Johnson's goal was the admission of African Americans to American life, Du Bois offered a more complex view. He suggested that the unique understanding and insight gained by black experience could change the qualities of American life. Addressing the NAACP convention, Du Bois asserted that it was not only civil rights that "we are after. . . . We want to be Americans, full-fledged Americans, with all the rights of other American citizens. But is that all? Do we simply want to be Americans? Once in a while through all of us flashes some clairvoyance, some clear idea of what America really is. We who are dark can see America in a way that white Americans cannot. And seeing our country thus, are we satisfied with its present goals and ideals?"[19]

For young black artists, Johnson's and Du Bois's ideas raised disturbing questions about their feelings and identity as African Americans, their African heritage, and their role in American life. In addition to coming up with the rent and acquiring technical knowhow, they had to confront the controversial question of how their people should be portrayed.

Debate about how African Americans should be depicted arose in many quarters and took many forms after publication of *The New Negro*. Centuries of abuse had made many African Americans extremely self-conscious and suspicious about portrayals of their lives. A novel, play, or painting that depicted black people gambling, dancing, drinking, loitering, sloppily dressed — anything that seemed to support the stereotypes applied to black people — was certain to be attacked regardless of aesthetic truth. In their search for an acceptable identity as Americans, some black people wanted to see their lives glorified. A similar phenomenon can be found in some Irish people's reaction to their portrayal by Sean O'Casey and James Joyce, who illuminated their weaknesses as fallible human beings as well as their strengths.

Du Bois particularly concerned himself with this question, writing in 1920:

> It is not that we are ashamed of our color and blood. We are instinctively and almost unconsciously ashamed of the caricatures done of our darker shades. Black is caricature is our half-conscious thought and we shun in print and paint that which we love in life. . . . We remain afraid of black pictures because they are cruel reminders of the crimes of the Sunday "comics" and "Nigger" minstrels. Off with these thought chains and inchoate soul-shrinkings, and let us train ourselves to see beauty in "black."[20]

Du Bois was not alone in raising the question of how African Americans should be portrayed. During the twenties, many intellectuals, writers, and artists of both races debated this issue and whether African-American artists were under any obligation to portray black people in a positive way — a question that came sharply into focus with Archibald J. Motley, Jr.'s portrayal of night life in what he called "Bronzeville."

Du Bois formalized this debate by publishing a long series of responses to this question in *The Crisis*, beginning in March 1926.[21] The poet Countee Cullen believed that black artists did have such an obligation, but that each artist had to "find his treasure where his heart lies."[22] Vachel Lindsay, who had attempted to capture the speech rhythms of black people in his poetry, felt what mattered most was the artist's "own experience and his inmost perceptions of truth and beauty, in its severest interpretation, should be his only criteria."[23]

H. L. Mencken, the twenties' most influential critic, who had published many articles and stories favorable to black people in *Smart Set* and the *American Mercury*, felt this was not the time to worry about how black people were presented. He urged a satiric attack on the racial foolishness and inconsistences of the majority. He asserted that "the remedy of the Negro is not to bellow for justice — that is, not to try and apply scientific criteria to works of art. His remedy is to make works of art that pay the white man off in his own coin. The white man, it seems to me, is extremely ridiculous. He looks ridiculous to me, a white man myself. To the Negro, he must be a hilarious spectacle indeed. Why isn't the spectacle better described? Let the Negro sculptors spit on their hands. What a chance!"[24]

Related to the question of how African Americans should be portrayed was the question of a distinct racial style urged by Locke. In *The New Negro* he had argued that the contemporary black artist lacked a mature tradition to follow and appealed for a consideration of African art as the real heritage of African-American artists. He wrote:

> There is a real and vital connection between this new artistic respect for African idiom [in "modern art"] and the natural ambition of Negro artists for a racial idiom in their art expression. . . . Only the most reactionary conventions of art, then, stand between the Negro artist and the frank experimental development of those fresh idioms. This movement would, we think, be well under way . . . but for the conventionalism which racial disparagement has forced upon the Negro mind in America. . . . The Negro physiognomy must be freshly and objectively conceived on its own patterns if it is ever to be seriously and importantly interpreted. . . . We ought and must have a school of Negro art, a local and racially representative tradition.[25]

Although he never precisely defined a "school of Negro art," Locke wrote many essays reiterating his plea, and he exhibited art from the Congo to stimulate awareness of the "legacy of the ancestral arts." He was supported by others, such as Arthur A. Schomburg, curator of the 135th Street branch of the New York Public Library and founder of the great collection of African-American history that bears his name. Schomburg argued: "History must restore what slavery took away."[26]

A different perspective on the nature of African-American art was expressed in *The Nation* by the conservative black journalist George S. Schuyler:

> The Aframerican is merely a lampblacked Anglo-Saxon. If the European immigrant after two or three generations of exposure to our schools, politics, advertising, moral crusades, and restaurants becomes indistinguishable from the mass of Americans of older stock (despite the influence of the foreign language press), how much truer must it be of the sons of Ham who have been

subjected to what the uplifters call Americanism for the last 300 years. . . . As for the literature, painting, and sculpture of Aframericans, such as there is, it is identical in kind with the literature, painting, and sculpture of white Americans; that is, it shows more or less evidence of European influence.[27]

Schuyler, who modeled his literary style on that of H. L. Mencken, was attacking Locke's concept of a "racial school of art" and the idea that African-American artists could produce an art that differed from that of other American artists. There was some truth in what he said. What was considered art in America had been determined by the white majority. Young black artists, struggling to learn their craft, unable to obtain formal training, scrambling to exist, were simply trying to gain some acceptance as artists by doing traditional work. In a day when white-sheeted Klansmen were marching in many parts of the country, they were challenging the prevailing stereotype which denied that African Americans could be artists. Most of them exhibited in churches and at state fairs, where their work was often displayed with the needlework of the "handicapped." This in some ways was a recognition of the deprivations suffered by African Americans, and an other ways an insulting continuation of the racial stereotype.

Schuyler did not deal with the fact that the more talented the artists were, the more they were subjected to pressure to paint in ways that the majority perceived as "primitive." That perception required — indeed, demanded — a degree of awkwardness or crudity, violent color, and sensuality. Catering to that idea became the easiest way for an African-American artist or writer to gain attention from dealers, influential collectors, and publishers — the gatekeepers of recognition and acceptance.

Pressure on African-American artists to work in a "primitive" style was intensified by social and cultural factors, specifically by the presentation of warped, sensationalized black characters in novels and plays such as Julia Peterkin's novel *Scarlet Sister Mary,* Dorothy and DuBose Heyward's *Porgy,* and Eugene O'Neill's *Emperor Jones.* Their emotionally distorted black characters derived from — and fostered — the stereotype that African Americans were unschooled, ignorant, superstitiously religious, immoral, incapable of forethought or intelligence, and controlled by sensuality and fear. These characters were, in varying degrees, racist caricatures, not based on objective observation or insight into the African-American character.

Because these novels and plays were successful, African-American writers and artists were expected to follow such models — and to be even more "primitive."

Fortunately, there were other models. The translations in the mid-1920s of René Maran's *Batouala*, an absorbing story of African village life, deeply impressed many black artists and intellectuals. Maran was a Frenchman of African descent. Winning the Goncourt prize in 1921, his book was, in some respects, a forerunner of Zora Neale Hurston's authentic and penetrating presentation of African-American folkways.

In addition, the naturalism that characterized the writings of Theodore Dreiser, Frank Norris, and Upton Sinclair, as well as the art of John Sloan, George Luks, and others, was a rapidly growing force. A tenet of naturalism was that artists should represent people and events with objectivity, without preconceptions, and this viewpoint increasingly began to inform African-American critical writing.

Rebelling against prevailing preconceptions, Langston Hughes refused the demand of a patron who had rejected his poem satirizing the idle rich, saying, "it's not you," and had asked him to write something different. As Hughes explained: "She wanted me to be primitive and know and feel the intuitions of the primitive. But, unfortunately, I did not feel the primitive surging within me, and so I could not live and write as though I did. I was only an American Negro — who had loved the surface of Africa and the rhythms of Africa — but I was not Africa. I was Chicago and Kansas City and Broadway and Harlem."[28]

Similarly, Aaron Douglas and other artists who had patrons were sometimes told their work was "not you." Some patrons looked upon the education and professional training of black artists as destructive to their "natural" abilities.

The demand for the African-American artist to be "primitive" has persisted to this day, and it has been the source of much misunderstanding and confusion. In the 1920s, the word *primitive* tended to isolate black artists from other American artists, and yet it became, in the 1920s, what was expected of them.

Because the term *primitive* continues to be used inappropriately, clarification of its meaning in relation to African-American artists is essential. The word, which is derived from the Latin *primus*, meaning "first," came to be used in reference to archeology and anthropology. In brief, these disciplines applied the term to early, original, and basic forms of societal and cultural organizations as well as to housing and craft products. Then ethnologists, describing the cultural artifacts of past societies, applied the term to objects fashioned with crude tools and, ultimately, to peasant handicraft work. Initially such objects, including religious and symbolic statues and pictorial representations, were preserved for their ethnological interest. However, after the discovery of the ancient African, Aztec, and Inca cultures, which were demonstrably advanced and had developed sophisticated ceramic, mineral, and metallurgical technology, it was gradually recognized that these objects were not "primitive" but based on disciplined artistic and cultural concepts and traditions, and required aesthetic consideration.

By the 1920s, the word *primitive* in relation to the arts meant to be unschooled and indifferent to moral and legal codes, without thought or intellectual substance. Freudian concepts of the repression of an individual's natural sexual instincts by "civilization" were popular in American intellectual circles at the time, and an oversimplification of these concepts contributed to the demand for "primitive" expression by African-American artists, with particular emphasis on violent color and sensuous expression. To many white intellectuals and artists, the black American was the opposite of dehumanizing industrialization — a natural man, unfettered by the customs, morals, and character of the organization of modern society. In works like *Emperor Jones,* when a black man goes against his "primitive" nature, he meets with disaster.

Generally, to whites, the term came to mean a style that was crude and unschooled in the "stilted affectations of the more cultured styles and conceptions," as V. F. Calverton phrased it in the thirties.[29] This misuse of the term arose from a distorted perception of black people, dating back to the days of slavery.

Today, similar misuses continue and the term *primitive* has lost any clear meaning.[30] What does it mean, for example, to refer to African sculpture, a highly sophisticated art form, as "primitive art," and then use the same term for the work of Grandma Moses and other folk artists? In this and other contexts the term carries a note of disparagement — implying that this is not "real" art.

African-American artists were continually confronted with the question: Who would buy their work? Directing their work to either a black or a white audience carried severe limitations. In seeking appreciation from a white audience, they faced possible suppression of their inner feelings and convictions. On the other hand, the black audience had its own particular taboos about subject matter. It also offered considerably fewer opportunities for support.

Artists' responses to this situation varied. Some, notably Sargent Johnson, Aaron Douglas, Richmond Barthé, and James Lesesne Wells, experimented with African styles. James A. Porter and others felt that the "self-conscious pursuit of the primitive" would further separate Negro art and artists from American art and artists. They "insisted that the Negro [artist] should encompass all experience, not attempting to suppress non-Negro influence, for such suppression meant intellectual and aesthetic negativism."[31]

Hughes rejected any denial of racial experience, recalling a young man who said to him, "'I want to be a poet—not a Negro poet.'... And I was sorry the young man said that, for no great poet has been afraid of being himself. And I doubted that, with his desire to run away spiritually from his race, this would ever be a great poet. But this is the mountain standing in the way of any true Negro art in America—this urge within the race toward whiteness, the desire to pour racial identity into the mold of American standardization, and to be as little Negro and as much American as possible."[32]

None of the spokesmen for these varying views abandoned his point. Locke continued to be a persistent, important influence, and his endorsement often meant a foundation grant. He jabbed, goaded, and held up the popularity of jazz as an inspiration. Jazz musicians were basking "in the sunlight and warmth of a proud and positive race-consciousness" while "our artists were still for the most part in an eclipse of chilly doubt and disparagement."[33] However, Locke's plea for a return to "the legacy of the ancestral arts" was challenged in 1927 by the African-American sociologist E. Franklin Frazier. He pointed out that developing group experiences and traditions and utilizing such experiences in artistic creativity "is entirely different from seeking in the biological inheritance of the race for new values, attitudes and a different order of mentality." Biological inheritance could not provide a "unique culture."[34]

African-American artists' difficult struggle to achieve identity was evident in exhibitions by the Harmon Foundation between 1928 and 1935.[35] Although it presented achievement awards to African Americans in nine areas of endeavor, including religion and business, the Harmon foundation is remembered today only for its recognition of African-American artists. An expression of the idea that art could help break down racial prejudice, the foundation's touring shows frankly accepted segregation in the South in trying to win recognition for black talent. The exhibitions helped African-American artists become aware of one another, and to gain some public attention. By 1935 some 400 black artists from all over the nation were "in regular touch with the foundation."[36]

The Harmon exhibitions accepted all kinds of work—traditional, naive, academic, abstract, and experimental. Porter, who exhibited, later remarked that the jury's selections for prizes showed "too liberal taste in subject matter and too little concern for execution."[37] Although disclaiming any point of view, the foundations' catalogs urged black artists "to create a genuine interpretation of racial background" and published Locke's exhortations on the "ancestral arts." Each successive show exhibited not only more work than earlier exhibitions, but also more black subject matter—a significant, if oversimplified, indication of growing self-acceptance.

The Harmon exhibitions were the largest and most publicized effort at the time to encourage African-American artists and show what they were doing. What was confusing, both aesthetically and in terms of black identity, was the assembling of very different types of work at all levels of achievement—bringing together a Cubist, a Romantic, an illustrator, and a naive—and calling them all representative of "Negro art" simply because the artists were black.

The situation drew criticism from African-American artists with the first public exhibition in 1928 (earlier competitions were not public). The artist-poet Gwendolyn Bennett, later a leader of the Harlem Artists Guild, complained that the works shown "lack the essence of artistic permanency. . . . There can be no cultural contribution unless something distinctive is given, something heightened and developed within the whole form that did not exist before the artist's hand took part in its molding. But where in this exhibition is there any such deftness of hand?"[38]

A few years later, in 1934, Mary Beattie Brady, the director of the Harmon Foundation and selector of its juries, was stung when Romare Bearden, a young Harlem artist, severely criticized its exhibitions as misguided, however well intentioned, because they lacked artistic standards and no unified aesthetic or social philosophy existed among African-American artists. Under the title "The Negro Artist and Modern Art," he argued for abandoning the "outmoded academic practices of the past," which most black artists were following in seeking acceptance as artists, and for the creation of an art that genuinely reflected the black artist's life and character. He condemned the Harmon Foundation:

Its attitude from the beginning has been of a coddling and patronizing nature. It has encouraged the artist to exhibit long before he has mastered the technical equipment of his medium. By its choice of the type of work it favors, it has allowed the Negro artist to accept standards that are both artificial and corrupt.

It is time for the Negro artist to stop making excuses for his work. If he must exhibit, let it be in exhibitions of the caliber of "The Carnegie Exposition." Here among the best artists of the world his work will stand or fall according to its merits. A concrete example of the accepted attitude towards the Negro artist recently occurred in California where an exhibition coupled the work of Negro artists with that of the blind. It is obvious that in this case there is definitely a dual standard of appraisal.[39]

Yet whatever its faults aesthetically and from an African-American viewpoint, the Harmon Foundation brought encouraging public attention to the development of African-American artists in a critical period.[40] Without its activities, exhibitions, and publicity, many artists would not have survived as artists, and its awards often identified important leaders among them. It particularly stimulated the formation of art departments in African-American colleges through its traveling shows, which generally had a higher artistic level than the exhibitions themselves.

The Harmon shows demonstrated that there were many African-American artists and that black subject matter — the lives, activities, and portraits of African Americans — was a legitimate, valuable, and unique part of American life, worthy of artistic expression and the unique province of black artists. How some of the significant black artists of the twenties developed — their problems, what they created, what influenced them, how individual they each were, and how they survived — provides insight into many aspects of American cultural life in that period.

## NOTES

From Romare Bearden and Harry Henderson, *A History of African-American Artists: From 1792 to the Present* (New York: Pantheon Books, 1993). © Romare Bearden Foundation/Licensed by VAGA, New York, NY, and Harry Henderson. The text was completed after Bearden's death by Henderson.

1. G. T. Robinson, *The Freeman Book* (New York: B. W. Huebsch, 1924), 97.

2. Nathan Irvin Huggins, *Harlem Renaissance* (New York: Oxford University Press, 1971), 5.

3. For migration's impact on Chicago, see St. Clair Drake and Horace R. Cayton, *Black Metropolis* (New York: Harper & Row, 1962), 52. For its impact on New York, see Gilbert Osofsky, *Harlem: The Making of a Ghetto* (New York: Harper & Row, 1968), 128.

4. Thorpe, who was listed in the catalog of the 1921 exhibition at the 125th Street branch of the New York Public Library, told this to the authors in 1967, when they were searching Juley's files for photographs of Tanner's work.

5. For background on Farrow, see *The Negro in Chicago, 1779–1927,* vol. 1 (Chicago: Washington Intercollegiate Club, 1927), 96. Also, Theresa Dickson Cederholm, ed., *Afro-American Artists* (Boston: Trustees of the Boston Library, 1973).

6. There were much earlier shows. In October 1905 the Colored Men's Branch of the Brooklyn YMCA on Carleton Avenue exhibited forty-five paintings by William E Braxton, Samuel O. Collins, W. O. Thompson, and Clinton DeVillis. Another exhibition was held there in 1913 and the NAACP held an exhibition in its New York offices that year in conjunction with its annual meeting. In 1917 the Arts and Letters Society of Chicago exhibited paintings and drawings by Charles Dawson, William M. Farrow, William Harper, and Archibald J. Motley, Jr. In August 1918 the Negro Library Association exhibited work by Braxton, Collins, DeVillis, Thompson, Robert H. Lewis, Robert H. Hampton, Albert A. Smith, Ella Spencer, Laura Wheeler Waring, Richard Lonsdale Brown, and William Edouard Scott. This exhibition also included books, manuscripts, and twenty-one African sculptures from the Modern Art Gallery of Marius de Zaya. In 1919 the Tanner Art Students Society at Dunbar High School in Washington, D.C., exhibited some thirty paintings and six sculptures by Scott, Waring, Julie Abele, Meta Vaux Warrick Fuller, May Howard Jackson, and John E. Washington. See Beryl J. Wright, "The Harmon Foundation in Context," in *Against the Odds: African-American Artists and the Harmon Foundation* (Newark, NJ: Newark Museum, exhibition catalog, 1989), 13–25.

7. "The Negro in Art Week" was suggested by Alain L. Locke to Zonia Baber of the University of Chicago and Chicago Women's Club. It was scheduled from November 16 to 27, 1927. When attendance averaged eight hundred a day, the institute extended the show to December 4 (*The Negro in Chicago*, vol. 1–2, 27).

8. James Weldon Johnson, *Black Manhattan* (New York: Atheneum, 1968), 163.

9. Hale A. Woodruff, undated letters to authors, c. 1971.

10. W. E. B. Du Bois, "The Criteria of Negro Art," *The Crisis* 32 (Oct. 1926): 290. This was his speech at the NAACP convention. It followed a questionnaire (*The Crisis* [Feb. 1926], p. 165) on "how to treat the Negro in art," which was sent to leading publishers, writers, and artists of both races who responded in subsequent issues. Among them were Sherwood Anderson, Benjamin Brawley, Charles W. Chesnutt, Countee Cullen, J. Herbert Engbeck, Jessie Fauset, DuBose Heyward, Langston Hughes, Georgia Douglas Johnson, Robert T. Kerlin, A. A. Knopf, Sinclair Lewis, Vachel Lindsay, Otto F.

Mack, Haldane McFall, H. L. Mencken, Mary W. Ovington, Julia Peterkin, William Lyon Phelps, Joel E. Spingarn, Walter White, and Carl Van Vechten.

11. Alain L. Locke, ed., *The New Negro* (New York: Albert Charles Boni, 1925; reprint, New York: Atheneum, 1968).

12. Locke, *The New Negro*, 5.

13. Locke, *The New Negro*, 21, 24.

14. Locke, *The New Negro*, 254.

15. Locke, *The New Negro*, 256.

16. Locke, *The New Negro*, 258.

17. Johnson, *Black Manhattan*, 283–84.

18. Langston Hughes, in *Fire!!*, vol. 1, no. 1; quoted in his reminiscing account, "The Twenties: Harlem and Its Negritude," *African Forum* 1 (Spring 1966): 11–20.

19. Du Bois, "Criteria," 290.

20. W. E. B. Du Bois, "Opinions of W. E. B. Du Bois: In Black," *The Crisis* 20 (Oct. 1920): 263–64.

21. W. E. B. Du Bois, "The Negro in Art," *The Crisis* 32 (March 1926): 219.

22. Countee Cullen, in *The Crisis* 32 (Aug. 1926): 193.

23. Vachel Lindsay, in *The Crisis* 32 (May 1926): 35–36.

24. H. L. Mencken, in *The Crisis* 32 (March 1926): 220. Although Mencken used racist terms at times, he was sympathetic to African Americans in the 1920s and corresponded with Du Bois, George S. Schuyler, and James Weldon Johnson. In 1922 he suggested to Johnson, "a history of ragtime, establish names and dates accurately . . . It ought to be done. Then you might do similar essays on negro poets, and negro painters and sculptors, and so have a second book on the negro as an artist." (See Charles Scruggs, *The Sage in Harlem: H. L. Mencken and the Black Writers of the 1920s* [Baltimore: Johns Hopkins University Press, 1984], 191, n. 16.)

25. Locke, *The New Negro*, 262–66.

26. Locke, *The New Negro*, 231.

27. George Schuyler, "The Negro Art-Hokum," *The Nation* 122 (June 16, 1926): 663–64.

28. Langston Hughes, *The Big Sea* (New York: A. A. Knopf, 1945; reprint, New York: Hill & Wang, 1968), 312–30.

29. V. F. Calverton, in *America Now: Civilization in the United States*, ed. H. E. Stearns (New York: Scribner's, 1938), 496.

30. For example, Peter and Linda Murray, eds., *Penguin Dictionary of Art and Artists* (Harmondsworth, England: Penguin Books, 1978), describe *primitive* as "a word that is now almost meaningless," noting that it originally applied to Netherlandish and Italian artists before 1500, and all Italian painters between Giotto and Raphael, although these artists have "no obvious connection with the naïve, unsophisticated, unspoilt vision consistent with amateur, or 'Sunday' painter status." They cite Edward Hicks, Jean-Jacques Rousseau, and Grandma Moses as examples of how the definition has blurred.

31. James A. Porter, *Modern Negro Art* (New York: Dryden Press, 1943), 100.

32. Langston Hughes, "The Negro Artist and the Racial Mountain," *The Nation* 122 (June 23, 1926): 662–64.

33. Alain Locke, *Negro Art: Past and Present* (Washington, DC: Associates in Negro Education, 1936; reprint, New York: Arno Press and *The New York Times*, 1969), 119.

34. E. Franklin Frazier, "Racial Self-Expression," in *Ebony and Topaz*, ed. C. S. Johnson (New York: Opportunity, 1927; reprint, Freeport, NY: Books for Libraries Press, Black Heritage Library Collection, 1971), 119.

35. The Harmon exhibitions were not yearly and initially not public, although there were juries and awards in 1926 and 1927. The first public exhibition was in 1928, followed by exhibitions in 1929, 1930, 1931, and 1933. The 1935 exhibition was limited to the work of three artists — Richmond Barthé, Malvin Gray Johnson, and Sargent Johnson.

36. *Negro Artists: An Illustrated Review of Their Achievements* (New York: Harmon Foundation, exhibition catalog, 1935), 5.

37. Porter, *Modern Negro Art*, 107.

38. Gwendolyn Bennett, in *The Southern Workman* 57 (March 1928): 111–12.

39. Romare H. Bearden, "The Negro Artist and Modern Art," *Opportunity* 12 (Dec. 1934): 371–73. For the full text, see pp. 87–90, in this volume.

40. See David Driskell, "Mary Beattie Brady and the Administration of the Harmon Foundation," in *Against the Odds: African-American Artists and the Harmon Foundation* (Newark, NJ: Newark Museum, 1990), 59–69.

# THE 1930S
## AN ART REMINISCENCE

*Romare Bearden*

Last summer I was approached by a group of young Black students who were attending the summer session of the Yale Art School. They were full of questions concerned with finding their relevance to the Black community. Their questions led me to think that some of the experiences which such Black artists as Charles Alston, Henry Bannarn, Selma Burke, Ernest Crichlow, Elizabeth Catlett, Vertis Hayes, Jacob Lawrence, Norman Lewis, Elba Lightfoot, Charles White, and I, among others, underwent during the Depression of the 1930s may have some special significance for young Black artists of today.

First of all, there were the Federal Art Projects through which the federal government provided assistance to the arts as never before in the history of the Republic. While it seems very ironical that this should occur during the country's worst economic depression, the aid was a boon to all artists. But to Black artists, it was of marked importance.

Black artists were able to work at their craft, with materials and other facilities provided, and paid for doing so. They explored various technical methods of painting, sculpture, and printmaking. They learned all the various procedures and problems, as an instance, for preparing a large mural. Artists came together and exchanged ideas and experiences. Aside from the salary, very few Black artists could have afforded the practical schooling provided on the projects alone.

In former times Black artists had more or less worked in isolation from one another. Joshua Johnston, a portrait painter of the Colonial era, lived in Baltimore and considering the restrictive laws that ordained the behavior of Black people in that city and state, it is amazing how he was able to learn his craft and pursue his career. Three mid-nineteenth-century artists — Robert Duncanson of Cincinnati, an excellent landscape painter; Edward Bannister of Providence, who won a medal at the great Philadelphia Centennial Exposition of 1876; and Edmonia Lewis, who attended Oberlin and did most of her sculptures in Rome — apparently did not even know of each other.

One of the reasons that Henry O. Tanner, the first Afro-American artist to gain international recognition, remained in Paris is because he enjoyed a communion with artists there he could not find in his own country. During the 1920s, the so-called period of the Harlem Renaissance, New York was a magnet for such well-known artists of the time as Richmond Barthé, Palmer Hayden, Malvin Gray Johnson, William H. Johnson, and Augusta Savage. However, there was little contact between them. Certainly nothing to compare with the kind of relationship between Picasso, Braque, Gris, Modigliani, and other artists of the Paris school in a similar time.

Because meaningful contacts between artists are so important, especially during their formative years, I consider the formation of the Harlem Artists Guild another extremely important event which occurred during the 1930s. Never before, and never since, has there been such a large representative organization of Black artists. The first meeting of the Guild was held during the mid-1930s. Aaron Douglas, whom we younger artists looked up to as the Dean of Afro-American painters, was elected chairman. I was astonished to find nearly fifty artists present, since I had no idea there were that many Black artists in the entire country. My surprise was shared by most of the other artists, because until then we had been isolated.

Once we came to know each other, we clustered at "306" — actually 306 West 141st Street. Here Alston and Bannarn had studios. Depending on how close it was to when the Federal eagle flew, after work a group of artists could also be found at Joe's on 136th and 7th Avenue, at Patsy's on 140th Street and 8th Avenue, and at Dick Huey's next to the YMCA on 135th Street (where Dick, who was also a rather well-known actor, made really great barbecue), and very late at Mom Young's on West 133rd Street, where you could get a bowl of chili and a coffee can filled with homemade beer for a quarter.

This movement from place to place wasn't only a pleasure trip, it was a learning process also, similar, as I have explained, to the importance the Impressionists and Moderns attached to their meetings in various Parisian cafes. In our peripatetic exchange we were liable to run into Langston Hughes, Claude McKay, Ted Ward, and other writers. The actors Canada Lee, Jack Carter, and Servus Bell, who helped make the production of a Black "Macbeth" at the Lafayette Theater so exciting, knew most of us very well. The composers Frank Fields and Joshua Lee were always with artists. Charlie Buchanan, who managed the Savoy Ballroom, let a number of us in free of charge, so besides enjoying the music of Chick Webb, Count Basie, Jimmy Lunceford, Fess Williams, Duke, and all the great bands of the era, we saw some of the greatest dancing imaginable. We exhibited our works at the local Y's, the 135th Street Library, and at the federally financed art school on Lenox Avenue and 125th Street, where Augusta Savage, and later Gwendolyn Bennett, were the directors. We actually became so well established within our community that whenever any Black persons in the arts came to New York, they were likely to show up at 306.

In addition, we had a sense of community awareness, which antedates that quality of community concern sought by a number of young artists today. We realized quite well whom we were painting for then. Of course, in a community economically depressed, we could not expect much financial reward for our works, but we did find sympathy, interest, and sometimes understanding.

I remember how Claude McKay, who had broad interests and knowledge in all the arts, so admired the work of Jacob Lawrence. He acquired one of Jacob's early temperas, a scene of tenements, which he prized and would look at for long periods. Every so often a group of ladies descended upon Bannarn's studio and made it tidy for a rent party to help him out. Ad Bates, one of the first Black dancers in the modern idiom, gave me my first one-man exhibit at his studio.

I must confess that sometimes this interest came from unexpected sources. Once I somehow got a commission to do a portrait of a racket man's children. I got a down payment and a promise of real money if my client was satisfied — and he fully intended to be satisfied. I worked hard on the painting from several photographs of the children. The father came by my studio on 125th Street every now and then to check on the progress of the work. I could tell he wasn't satisfied at all. One day a friend of mine, Warren Smith, visited me and when he saw the effort I was making he told me that what I was doing was all wrong. He advised me to go to a place where I could get the photograph of the children enlarged and superimposed right onto a canvas. I did this and Warren had a girl he knew, who worked as a photo-retoucher, color the painting. The result looked ghastly, as if the children were made up for internment at Forest Lawn Cemetery. Warren advised me, however, not to ruin it by putting in any artistic touches. I awaited my client's visit in some despair.

When he came he looked at the painting, if it could be called that, with the strangest expression. Then he broke out in tears.

"My children," he sobbed, "they're here in this room."

He pulled out a wad of bills and paid me and gave me something extra, but he came back with the painting a few minutes after he left. I wondered if he had shown it to someone who knew something of art?

"My God," he said, "you're like all artists, you paint a masterpiece and you forget to sign it."

I did sign it for him — Eramor Nedraeb.

Perhaps an inevitable result of our coming together as artists was to consider a useable Black heritage. In this, a key figure for a number of artists who served their apprenticeship during the 1930s was Mr. Charles Seifert, who if I remember correctly was a contractor by trade. The rooms of Mr. Seifert's home on West 138th Street, however, were filled with books on Negro and African history. From these volumes, many of which were as rare as those in the Schomberg Collection, a number of us caught our first glimpses of African history and culture. Perhaps the quality of this collection is indicated by the fact that, following Mr. Seifert's death, it was presented by Earle Sweeting to one of the principal educational institutions in Ghana, where it was enthusiastically received as an indispensable addition to their national collection.

Mr. Seifert's devotion to his interest was boundless and he was overflowing with knowledge about Africa. He made a special point of passing this on to painters and sculptors, as no formal institution did in those days. Often some of the artists, and other interested persons, would gather in Mr. Seifert's living room for informal discussions. As a result of Mr. Seifert's influence, Sweeting and Robert Pious did many paintings of episodes related to African and Afro-American history.

I recall going with Mr. Seifert one Sunday to the Museum of Modern Art to see the first large, comprehensive show of African sculpture in this country. Mr. Seifert had a dignified posture and he dressed for this occasion in formal morning wear. There were few books and little information concerning African art at that time and a large crowd of interested viewers soon gathered around us and followed Mr. Seifert as he explained the various pieces to me. I particularly remember him pointing out that the Dahomey war god, as represented in a rare piece, was actually an antecedent of the axe-holding Norse god Thor.

Artists don't necessarily paint or sculpt what they actually see — an apple, a tree, a person's face. They try to come to terms with their feelings about such things. Consequently, Mr. Seifert was influential in directing some artists to think, and to feel in the fullness of their hearts, about themselves and their history. I was too young at the time to evaluate Mr. Seifert's scholarship. But, whatever, to some of us he came as a much-needed, exceptional man. To the world, I'm afraid, he came somewhat in advance of his time.

Our interest in our past was neither academic nor an escape into romantic fantasy, for we were nothing if not socially conscious and politically committed. We soon learned to work together for economic advantage. The involvement of most project artists was actually as much political as it was aesthetic. There were constant demonstrations to secure better working conditions and, above all, to try to protect the jobs. So artists learned not only the proper way to stretch a canvas, but also how to make effective posters for the endless picket lines. For most Black artists this was the first time they struggled in common cause with their white compatriots. An old 1938 leaflet printed for project artists and their sympathizers read in part: "Our Christmas present is here again and plenty early too. Our Santa Claus is the Administration and he has placed Layoffs on the Christmas Tree."

An overall result of this struggling, studying, and self-searching was not to make us effete exponents of "art for art's sake" on the one hand, nor unartistic political hacks on the other. Anyone, for example, who knows the work of Jacob Lawrence can see deep commitment to human values, yet he never sacrifices artistic integrity. Any true artists will be concerned with the enduring qualities of their art; it is precisely that which endures, and will in the long run provide man with his most useful information.

By no means am I implying that all the artists who emerged during this period had the same kind of social commitment in their art as did Lawrence. Norman Lewis, who was no less actively engaged, is an artist whose approach is primarily lyrical and abstract. Both Lawrence and Lewis would agree though that every sincere artist, regardless of his subject matter, must acquaint himself with the broader nature of the art experience.

The connections between a great deal of what is happening now and the 1930s are explicit. Current efforts to bring art directly to the people, whereby museums and other institutions have established community galleries; the nationwide proliferation of store-front galleries; the Walls of Pride painted on buildings in depressed areas; are, for the most part, carryovers from that generation.

The point of all this is that there is an existing tradition of a community-oriented art among Black people here in the United States. We need not go back very far to find it. The 1930s are only four decades away. As a matter of fact, many of the key figures are still very active and available.

What I hope is that young artists will spend at least as much time acquainting themselves with their immediate past, as many now spend searching for historical connections with an ancient African past. By not doing so, some artists are already repeating some of the avoidable mistakes we made during the 1930s. But, by doing so, they can greatly enrich their own relation to art and society and so proceed on a firmer basis.

After all, an older generation expects to find themselves extended and refined in the works of the younger artists.

## NOTE

From *New York Amsterdam News* (September 18, 1971).

# HUMILITY

*Romare Bearden*

PITTSBURGH — Alfred North Whitehead was convinced of the indispensable relationship of science, technology, art, and religion. I can believe that the administration and faculty of Carnegie-Mellon University have based your training on assumptions entirely compatible with Whitehead's imperatives. They have invited me, an artist, to speak to you [graduating students], who are for the most part in various scientific and technological disciplines.

After all, when we talk about the human ends of science and technology we are concerned with aesthetics — indeed the world of art. Science is greatly absorbed with mankind's perceptions of the objective world. Art, whether it be literature, dance, music, or painting, sculpture, and the graphic arts, is concerned with the conceptions men and women have of themselves, and of their relation to the world around them. However, neither the scientist, nor the technologist, nor the artist works in a vacuum; all are involved with human ends. That is to say, human impulses, drives, urges, desires, motives, and ideals.

Thomas Mann has described man as the means through which nature becomes aware of itself. Mankind, then, is nature with consciousness, and men and women are aware of themselves, and those things around them, to a greater extent than any other form of life on this planet. In acquiring consciousness we also acquired a conscience, which is a concern about the consequence of action, and, naturally, a desire for that which is most serviceable to mankind.

I like to believe for all the specialized demands of your chosen fields, you do not lose sight of human ends, which are of primary importance to the artist. Before our age of specialization, the artist, scientist, technician, and religious servant often existed in one person as a matter of course. In the Western world, this was the time of the Renaissance, and with Leonardo da Vinci, we certainly have the embodiment of all these faculties.

Among his many other accomplishments, Leonardo devised something similar to our modern submarine. When Leonardo was once asked to build this device and use it to set fire to an enemy fleet blockading an Italian city, Leonardo refused because he felt that water was a divine element and should not be violated by subterfuge. Since Leonardo, in all he did, never lost sight of human ends, in this instance, I'm sure, his conscience told him not to use his submarine in the way suggested.

While it may be easy for the scientist and technologist, busy in their own efforts, to ignore the artist, the artist cannot ignore them, because they are constantly altering the world the artist must relate to.

As students you are part of a generation that has been much involved with social and political change. The desire to participate in improving our world is most commendable; but, from the recent mishaps around the world, it should be apparent, change is most effective when we have an understanding of what we intend to change. No one is going to alter our world for the better anymore with technology alone, or with military might, which is a force of technology, often placed in the wrong hands. The demands of the world require much more than good intentions — they require insight and wisdom. For wisdom in the face of complexity is likely to produce the necessary humility that keeps mankind human.

And all this is to say that great productive changes never occur through the influence of one dominant force, whether it be art, science, or religion, but through a confluence of many forces, which in unison have the power to transcend the contributions of all individual elements. For the highest order of the human experience is in building a fit world where we can all live in peace.

## NOTE

From *The New York Times* (June 21, 1975) © Romare Bearden Foundation/Licensed by VAGA, New York, NY. This op-ed was illustrated with a black-and-white version of Bearden's *The Train* (see fig. 39, this volume).

# ENCOUNTERS WITH AFRICAN ART

*Romare Bearden*

My interest in African art goes back to a show at the Museum of Modern Art in the 1930s, when I was a young boy. There was a gentleman in Harlem on 138th Street named Mr. Seifert. We used to call him Dr. Seifert. Dr. Seifert — he was a contractor, I think — had a great collection of books on Africa and Afro-American art and history, almost rivaling that of the Schomburg Collection. He was very interested in meeting young artists. And on this particular day he put on a morning suit, and he took some of us down to the museum for the show.

One of the pieces I recall very well was a kind of a war god holding an ax. Dr. Seifert, in his own way, ethnologically traced the name of this particular god, to the ax god Thor of Northern mythology. We gathered around and went after him from piece to piece. African art, you know, didn't have wide popularity then, and there weren't many books, like we have now.

When I began to study certain things, I began to look — in my own work — at African sculpture. But that was much later. A lot of magazines — even black magazines — wouldn't print this art. It seems people had the idea that this was something that was primitive or belonged to magic and things that people might want to forget. If it wasn't Titian or Ingres or classical Renaissance, people had no interest. And then came African sculpture, and it was looked upon as curios, ethnological things to study, not art.

I had to search out African art on my own to understand it. I didn't know how to go about looking at that time, or just how to incorporate it. And also — let us say if you look at a Titian or an El Greco, just two names that come first — the mythology of what they are talking about, or their intent, the religion, was right there: a virgin holding a baby — motherhood; or Rembrandt, the woman by the well or religious things that he did. But this African art was something else that I wanted to look at and see what the philosophy was, discover what were some of the ideas that emanated from this work. I wanted to try and understand the African vision of the world — because there were so many varying African forms: some might be rather realistic like Benin bronze, and some very abstract. But this is the thing: to get a sense, a feeling — not just looking at them and admiring them as décor to put some place. But to discover what is it that motivated the art.

African art appeals to me because it has offered another dimension, a way of looking at the world. I have been permeated by African art by looking at and trying to understand the design: how is it possible to simplify in a drawing — to see a head just as an oval shape; how to understand its symbolic quality — in my own terms. So I had to put the books down and just look at how I felt about it. The books get in the way sometimes.

We are faced with chaos in life. Or could be, anyway. To the artist, when he looks at something — Monet at a haystack, or an African at a tree trunk — he is trying to look at the particular chaos and be redemptive about it; to find something in there and bring some passion, where it can move people. The demagogue on the other hand, says, "now you're dealing with chaos, just vote for me — you may lose some of your liberties" — but he sees chaos as his opportunity for power; the artist, on the other hand, sees it as a chance for redemption. The thing about art that all of these people have in common is that they look at chaos. The thing about art that is different from science or most anything else is that it could have been stopped at any time, and you would have had a complete art, even with the caveman. But all of our epochs have the power of completing their intent. And then we move on to some other resolution of how people dealt with the world before one had ambition.

When I was a boy in the South, in North Carolina, around spring, every Sunday morning they would have baptisms in the streams. So I tried to depict or imagine one of these events in collage. I used various parts of African masks for parts of the features of the people. I am very interested in myth and ritual. I used various kinds of African sculptures, because the people — when they were brought here from Africa — came from various tribes. So I tried a little bit of this, a certain fragmented depiction of an event that was happening in, let's say, Mecklenburg County, North Carolina, and also extended — artistically and mythologically — to a certain past. That is the way I have often used the African sculpture — the baptism for example, to bring it back by working in some event, some remembrance I have of Charlotte and Mecklenburg County. In this particular instance it didn't matter to me how the pieces were originally used; probably it should, but it didn't. I might have, say, a Dan head for the nose or mouth, or use something else realistically. It was all mixed up to show Afro-American.

I continue, quite often, to use African images in my work. There was a man who was a great guitar player in Charlotte, named Jefferson Cooley. And I was looking at something in St. Martin (W.I.), a reproduction in a magazine, and I said, gee, this reminds me of him. So I just cut it out and put it down, and then I doctored it — changed this and that; but that brought me right back to Jefferson.

I judge African art by looking at the pulses. I look at it as a melody. And pulses — see, if I did this and played this where my fingers are [he says, holding up his left hand, fingers spread evenly apart, so as to represent a musical instrument], and I did this [he continues, using his right hand as the hand that plays the instrument his left hand has become] da da da da [he sings in a monotone] and if I keep on doing that, well, that would just drive you nuts. But if I do this [he adds, spreading one finger apart from the others] I'm changing the pulses or the intervals in between. So I look at African sculpture for the pulses and the intervals — and after that, the melody which calls for repetition.

I learned, I hope, a lot about painting from listening to Earl Hines. I listened and listened and listened to Earl Hines until I couldn't hear the music, only the silences — in order to pick up the intervals of his playing. All of this in jazz music, all of this — when you ask about it — comes from the drum. I see all this art in drum beats: let's say you are listening to Louis Armstrong — da de dah dah de dah — you're hearing the rhythms of the drum. These pieces of African art are the plastic expressions of the drum.

## MBAGANI MASK

Here you have a mask that can protect you from the chaos I mentioned earlier. I can see it as that. Beyond the design and the other qualities, I see the question: how do I deal with chaos, the nature of evil, and other things in the world? When I saw this, I thought: that would protect you against *anything*: you put that on, and you're well-protected!

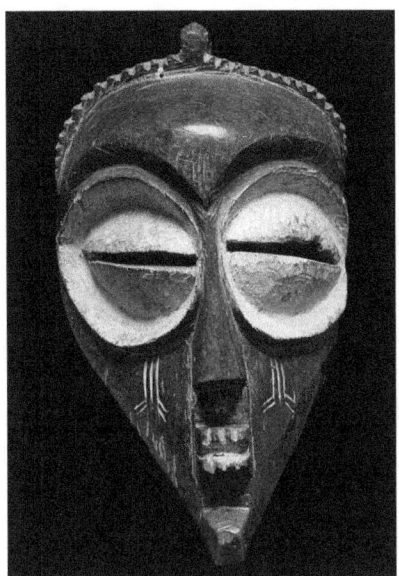

FIGURE 15 Mbagani Mask

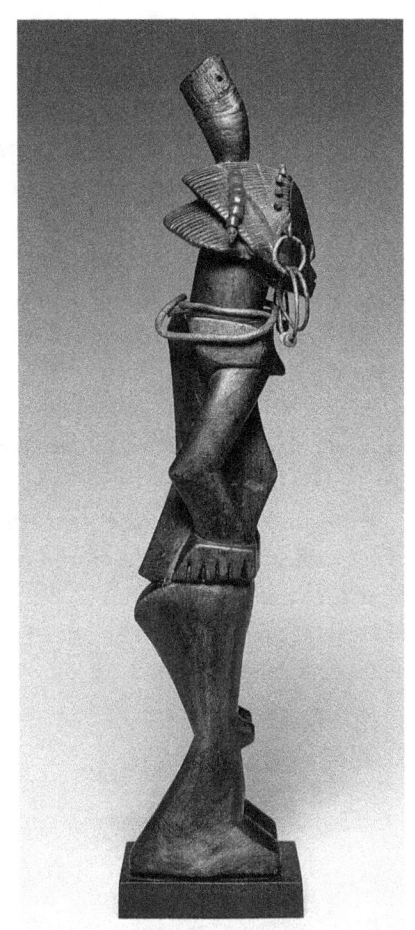

FIGURE 16 Luba-Shankadi Figure

In all of these pieces, the first thing I look at is design. The very presence of this has to do with somebody looking at you like this. It must have been used for some kind of initiation purpose. I admire the curvilinear movement, the very shaping of this like a tear drop — the form seems to catch a certain spirit with this great drop.

## LUBA-SHANKADI FIGURE

The thing about this that struck me is that you have this Early American design — the Shaker, with the chairs. They seem so functional: you sat down in a chair with no fancy decoration, it was just a certain plainness that you felt — where everything had to be just right. I felt the same about this. The shapes and the very simplicity of it have some kind of relation to the Shakers — although I don't think the Shakers would see this.

I guess there is something in great carvers and great men that see this. I also like the headdress's relation to the earrings and the relationship to shapes — when you look at the profile, the beautiful stance like this. It's hard to describe something like this because every element in it seems to flow so well into the next. I like all the elements because of how they are related to everything else.

This would be a more square melody. I don't mean in the sense of the slang expression — but I mean more compact, more contained. This is more within itself, so it wouldn't run all over the place. Firm beating, and constant coming back and playing the repetitions at a higher pitch. The legs, the hips are so firm; it's right on the ground, it's so compact. Bap bap bap bap — a firm, solid beat.

I would like to know what the artist had intended. Like Monet's haystacks or his cathedral: it meant a great deal to *him*. But a lot of people just see the light, the color, and other things. But why he chose them, or why the man who made this sculpture chose this, or another artist chose a tree — it is sometimes a meaning that they would not know themselves.

## SENUFO FEMALE FIGURE

I think that this is one of the most intricate pieces of carving in my selections. Again, every element and every aspect of this seems to float so well into the other. It also reminds me of some American Indian figures. For a female, it is so strong. I wonder, at the top of her head, what the little animal means. It's a work of great force. The whole aspect, the whole thrust of the figure; the way she's standing — but there's also this feeling that she could be seated, the way the back of her buttocks is here. Say if she was on a chair, she could be resting on that. This is what's so interesting, the curvature. It has this forceful power. It seems to be *bursting* with power, as if she's a woman going out hunting or something. She's holding a gourd in her right hand, something she could shake; and this in her left is some kind of a stave. Whether this is a part of a dance, I wouldn't know. When they say it's a female figure, and then to see on the chin what looks like a goatee, and the scarifications on her face and body — it gives this lady a tremendous force and power. Look at her shoulders and her neck: she is very animated. It's almost like someone on guard. I mean, if something needed to be actually or symbolically protected, you put this figure up, and oh, you wouldn't go near it.

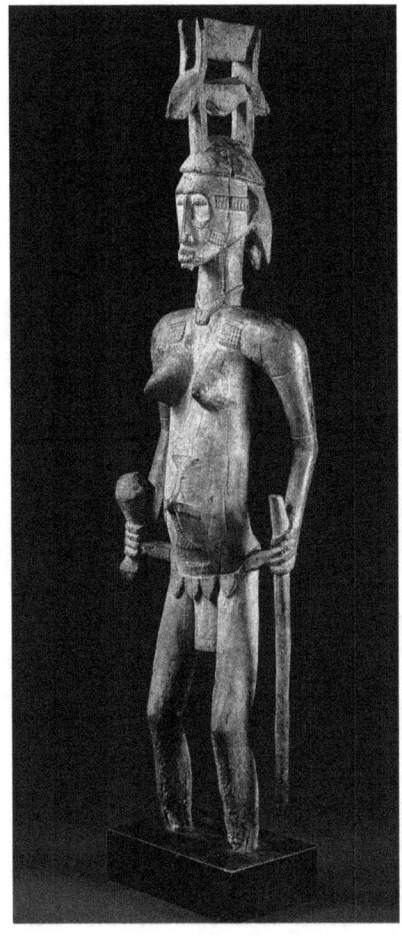

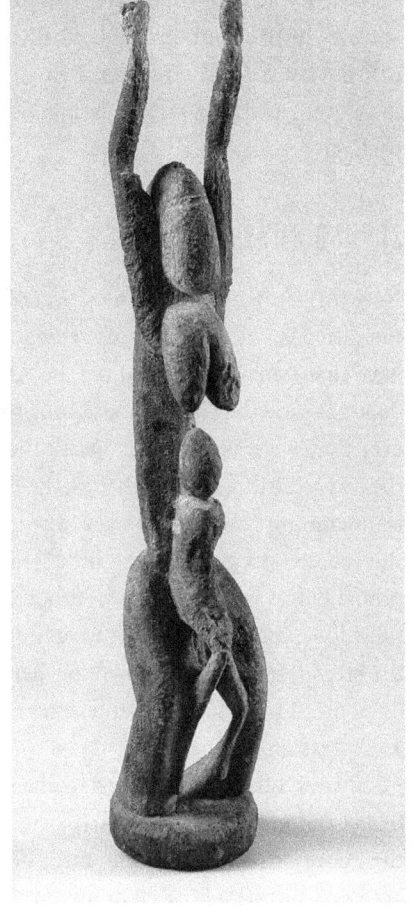

FIGURE 17  Senufo Female Figure          FIGURE 18  Dogon Mother and Child

## DOGON MOTHER AND CHILD

What interested me about the Dogon Mother and Child was the simple beauty of the silhouette. You see, again, it's fashioned out of these repetitions — the bottom is a smaller version of the top. Not as a fact of design, but the child that is so low here, has a symbolic quality to it. Because most of the people would have held the child up here, to the breast. So you have the feeling that the child is also coming out of the womb and climbing up someplace. That concept interests me. And the very straight back of the mother — it gives such beautiful support to the child, like a tree which he can climb. I also like what I see as the security of the mother. Symbolically, instead of holding him up, it's showing that the child is a child who is being held, but who has also just emerged from the womb. And almost, in a certain way, the mother is laid down with her arms back, giving birth.

## SENUFO RHYTHM POUNDER

Now this is a whole different aspect of the female figure, as differentiated from the other Senufo figure. This seems more composed. Both are abstract, they have that same design quality. The African sculpture has this great expressive quality — and they had — something to tell you about the female or about whatever they were carving. Again, it's the rhythms of this which are so beautiful: the head, the three gourd shapes, the head and the two breasts, the length of the arms coming down to her waist. The head seems to be just a little tilted off from the center — to give it just a little irrationality. This is a peaceful woman, and probably this was carved to beat out a rhythm. While both women are beautifully done, you can see this one continues to turn on itself the way the head turns, the breasts, from the top down to where it culminates in the fingers of the hands. They didn't let naturalistic appearances conflict with what they had to do as far as expression is concerned.

Always, I think, in great art, some part of it must be left for the imagination of the onlooker to complete. It's the simple and expressive things that make the figure. Also, the gaze is inward. If you look at the French monuments, they are very much looking right at you: "why weren't you in church?" they seem to demand. But this gaze is inward. Inward are the spiritual aspects that I see.

## IGBO IKENGA FIGURE

Here you have this headdress of this figure. The way the shape moves around in that curve — I see it again, that same movement, connected in the legs. This is developed — the whole piece of sculpture — on the straights and on the curves. [With his hand on the photo, beginning at the top and continuing down to the base, he melodically sings.] See: curve, curve, curve — the same way — curve, curve, curve; the going *against* the curve [his hand is upon the figure's legs] curve here, the curve, the straight, the straight, *this* is like *this*, and you see that

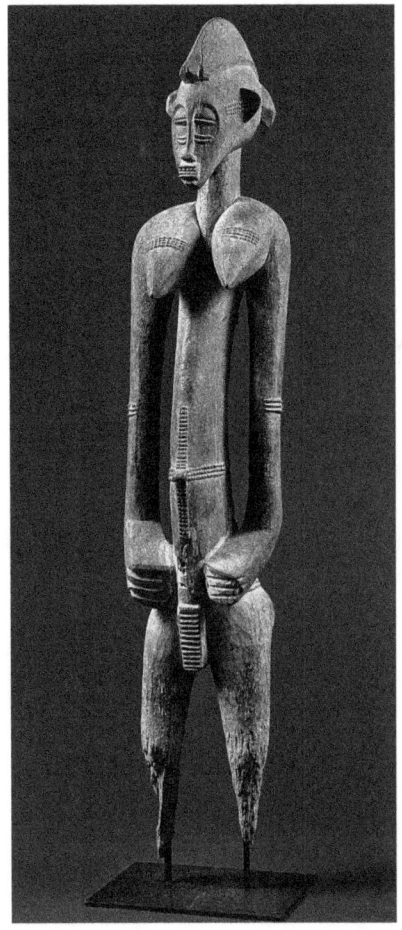

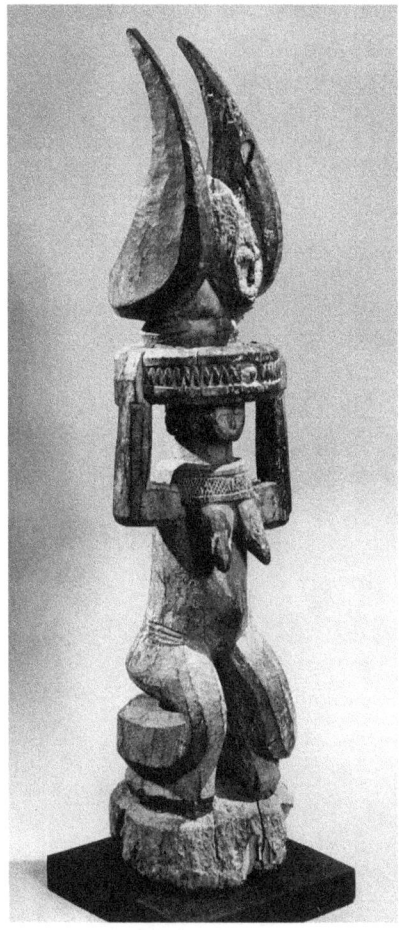

FIGURE 19  Senufo Rhythm Pounder          FIGURE 20  Igbo Ikenga Figure

these things are all based upon this curving movement and it's held by these two horizontals — that's the first thing; I would look at this melody — and then I'd see if I could play it.

It would not be a very good melody for so-called jazz, I don't think, because it's too circular. It's more like French music, where people are constantly turning in French country dancing. But in jazz — or so-called Afro-American classical music, it's a linear music that's going someplace straight, no matter what the digression. In a certain way, I can hear the drumming in this. Dum dum

dum — Bum Bum bohm — and going back and taking it in another way — this is a D curve, D-ump. That's why I mean a melody. And when I hear it, I can play it like that. It has a sense of balance, but the sense of pulse and rhythm is what's important. It's the intervals between sizes; repetitions, the change of pulses.

## NOTE

From *Perspectives: Angles on African Art* (New York: The Center for African Art, 1987); excerpt of interview with Romare Bearden by Michael John Weber.

# PART III / REFLECTIONS ON A LAYERED LEGACY

# BEARDEN
## BLACK LIFE ON ITS
## OWN TERMS

*August Wilson*

In 1965, as a twenty-year-old poet living in a rooming house in Pittsburgh, I discovered Bessie Smith and the blues. It was a watershed event in my life. It gave me a history. It provided me with a cultural response to the world as well as the knowledge that the text and content of my life were worthy of the highest celebration and occasion of art. It also gave me a framework and an aesthetic for exploring the tradition from which it grew. I set out on a continual search for ways to give expression to the spiritual impulse of the African American culture which had nurtured and sanctioned my life and ultimately provided it with its meaning. I was, as are all artists, searching for a way to define myself in relation to the world I lived in. The blues gave me a firm and secure ground. It became, and remains, the wellspring of my art.

In 1977, I made another discovery which changed my life. I discovered the art of Romare Bearden. I was then a thirty-two-year-old poet who had taken his aesthetic from the blues but was unsure how to turn it into a narrative that would encompass all the elements of culture and tradition — what Baldwin had so eloquently called "the field of manners and ritual of intercourse" that sustains black American life. My friend Claude Purdy had purchased a copy of *The Prevalence of Ritual*, and one night, in the fall of 1977, after dinner and much talk, he laid it open on the table before me. "Look at this," he said. "Look at this." The book lay open on the table. I looked. What for me had been so difficult,

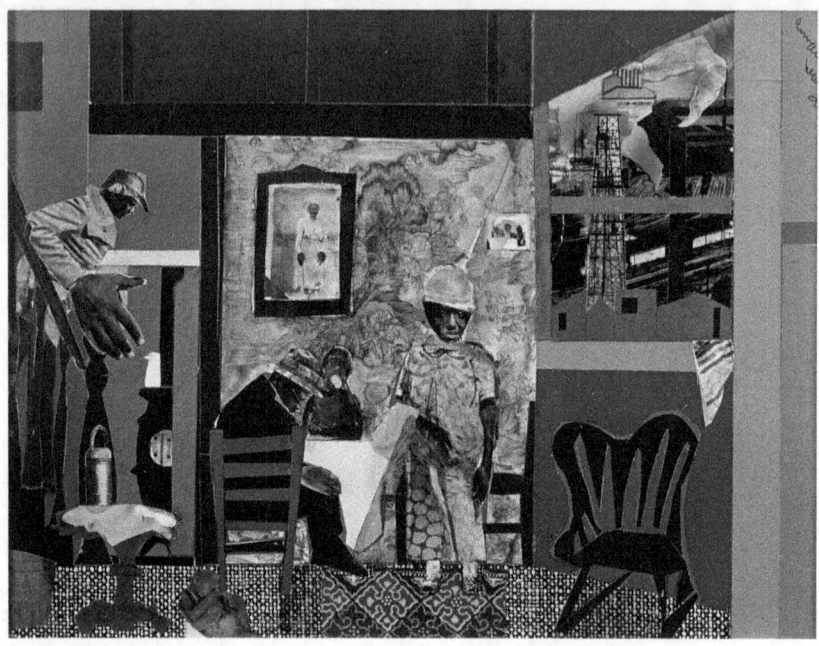

FIGURE 21 Romare Bearden, *Profile/Part I, The Twenties (Pittsburgh Memories): The Mill Hand's Lunch Bucket*, 1978. Watercolor and collage on board, 14×18 in. (35.6×45.7 cm). Art © Romare Bearden Foundation/Licensed by VAGA, New York. When first shown, this collage, like the others in Bearden's Profiles series, bore a caption co-composed by his friend Albert Murray, handwritten on the gallery wall: "The mills went 24 hours a day with three 8-hour shifts." It inspired August Wilson's play *Joe Turner's Come and Gone* (first staged in 1984), which in draft was titled "Mill Hand's Lunch Bucket."

Bearden made seem so simple, so easy. What I saw was black life presented on its own terms, on a grand and epic scale, with all its richness and fullness, in a language that was vibrant and which, made attendant to everyday life, ennobled, affirmed its value and exalted its presence. It was the art of a large and generous spirit that defined not only the character of black American life, but also its conscience. I don't recall what I said as I looked at it. My response was visceral. I was looking at myself in ways I hadn't thought of before and have never ceased to think of since.

In Bearden I found my artistic mentor and sought, and still aspire, to make my plays the equal of his canvases. In two instances his paintings have been direct inspirations. My play *Joe Turner's Come and Gone* was inspired by Bearden's *Mill Hand's Lunch Bucket*, a boardinghouse setting in Pittsburgh. I tried to incorporate all of the elements of the painting in the play, most notably the haunting and brooding figure at its center, whom I named Herald Loomis. The names of the characters, Seth and Bertha, were taken from another Bearden painting, *Mr. Seth and Miss Bertha*. The title of my play *The Piano Lesson* was taken from a painting of the same title. (See fig. 21.)

I never had the privilege of meeting Romare Bearden. Once I stood outside 357 Canal Street in silent homage, daring myself to knock on his door. I am sorry I didn't, for I have never looked back from that moment when I first encountered his art. He showed me a doorway. A road marked with signposts, with sharp and sure direction, charting a path through what D. H. Lawrence called the "dark forest of the soul." I called to my courage and entered the world of Romare Bearden and found a world made in my image. A world of flesh and muscle and blood and bone and fire. A world made of scraps of paper, of line and mass and form and shape and color, and all the melding of grace and birds and trains and guitars and women bathing and men with huge hands and hearts, pressing on life until it gave back something in kinship. Until it gave back in fragments, in gesture and speech, the colossal remnants of a spirit tested through time and the storm and the lash. A spirit conjured into being, unbroken, unbowed, and past any reason for song — singing an aria of faultless beauty and unbridled hope.

I have often thought of what I would have said to him that day if I had knocked on his door and he had answered. I probably would just have looked at him. I would have looked, and if I were wearing a hat, I would have taken it off in tribute.

August Wilson
Saint Paul, Minnesota

## NOTE

From Myron Schwartzman, *Romare Bearden: His Life and Art* (New York: Harry N. Abrams, 1990), foreword.

# ABRUPT STOPS AND UNEXPECTED LIQUIDITY
## THE AESTHETICS OF ROMARE BEARDEN

*Toni Morrison*

In order to get to the crux of my views on the art of Romare Bearden—on the discourse of African American art in general—I have to go back a bit, for my own sake if not for yours, to put my remarks in context.

Extraordinary things were happening in and among African Americans in the Sixties. The realm of political change during that period has received, as it should, minute, even exhaustive, attention. Yet in spite of some singular critiques of African American art at the moment of origin, and many more expansive ones later on, it seems to me that the exploration of visual art as it relates to other genres in African American culture is still tentative.

Where analysis of cross-genre aspects of black expression does exist, it relies on terms like "inspiration," "similarity," "spirit," "vibrancy," "intensity," "drama," "liveliness," and "shared cultural values." There are a number of reasons for that rather vague emotional vocabulary. Artists are notoriously evasive about their creative process. They speak about the consequences of the art, but not about the creation. Also, it takes a certain amount of nerve, if not faith, for a scholar like myself to assert connections, echoes across disciplines, if she does not feel expert in all these ways of making art. After all, aesthetic ramifications are very difficult to iterate.

More importantly, the early attention of scholars of African American literary and other art was engaged in canon formation—taking its cue from the mainstream's established format for the ranking of art production. The alternative canon that the new black critics urged had several goals: nationalism, revolutionary success, cultural hegemony. Among those goals was an aesthetic put to the service of a strong political agenda and/or a cohesive cultural flowering. Aesthetics were understood to be a "corrective" to a "polluted American mainstream," or a "sister" to the Black Power movement. Artists were encouraged and judged by the nation-building uses to which their work could be put. The groundswell of those who understood this to be the work of their work is legend, as any review of Sixties and later poetry will reveal. And there is no question that matters of "authenticity," of representing the lived life and concerns of black people, are still the sine qua non of virtually all African American art—from rap music to film to novels to visual arts. How successfully, how distorted, how even triumphantly this authenticity expresses itself is still much of the drive of criticism.

Although the explosion of creative energy was overwhelming in the Sixties, its criticism did not, perhaps could not, refuse to wrestle with the eternal (and eternally irrelevant) argument about how and whether the art of a black artist could be, should be, considered "universal"—meaning "mainstream," "race-transcendent," agenda-free, and so on. The heart of that argument implied that if what was produced was merely political, it was not art; if it was merely beautiful, it was not relevant. Thus the critiques focused on the accuracy of the sociology and/or the inspirational "self-help" value of the work. Some work was championed as representative, authentic; other work was deemed unacceptable if it was less than uplifting; other work was dismissed as crude protest or propaganda. Virtually every African American writer in the near and distant past—James Baldwin, Zora Neale Hurston, Ralph Ellison, Richard Wright, Gwendolyn Brooks, Phyllis Wheatley—has been called upon, or felt called upon, to explain what it meant to be a Negro artist or a black artist. The sheer idiocy of that call has been enough to force artists angrily, or with annoyance, I suspect, to respond to it.

Romare Bearden was working long before the Sixties and had traveled widely, studied carefully the ancient and the new. His homes included the South, the North, Europe, the Caribbean, country landscapes, porches, urban streets, clubs, churches. So it was with some delight that I read a comment by him on the subject of race or social factors embedded in his work. "I am afraid," he said, "despite my intentions, that in some instances commentators have tended to overemphasize what they believe to be the social elements in my work. But while my response to certain human elements is as obvious as it is inevitable, I am also pleased to note that upon reflection many persons have found that they were as much concerned with the aesthetic implications of my paintings as with what may possibly be my human compassion." The operative words for me are, "my response to certain human elements is as obvious as it is inevitable." How, he is asking, can a human artist *not* be responsive to human things, which are, by their nature, social things? He takes for granted the humanity of his subject matter, and as has been said, this in itself is a radical act in a country with a history of purposefully and consistently dehumanizing the black population.

Bearden was also pleased to refer to his work's "*aesthetic* implications." That is to say, there is information, truth, power, and beauty in his choice of color, form, in the structural and structured placement of images, in fragments built up from flat surfaces, in the rhythm implicit in repetition, and in the medium itself—each move determining subsequent ones, enabling the look and the fact of spontaneity, improvisation. This is the appropriate language employed to delineate his work, and to suggest its relationship to another genre, music. Which is very interesting since, whatever the view of aesthetics and criticism, it has traditionally confined itself to explorations *within* an art form, not *among* them. It is odd, considering how affected artists are by other disciplines, that this approach, which so closely resembles traditional critique, maintains in spite of the insistence of the art itself on its wider sources and its far more interdisciplinary dialogue. The cross-fertilization among artists within a genre is a subject well examined; less so are instances where the lines between genres are implicit. The influence and representation of African American music is a mainstay in commentary on Romare Bearden's work, as is the relationship between the plays and sensibility of August Wilson. The influence of and alignment with music has been a common observation in criticism of my own work as well, and of course I have acknowledged this relationship with music, myself.

What I want to describe this evening are other ways in which artists of disparate disciplines fold into, energize, and transfer the aesthetics of one another. Let me linger for a moment on some aspects of my own process, which are indeed responsive to the work of Romare Bearden. I must say I've been very generous to myself in getting ideas from painters other than Bearden—although they are usually just scenes or figurative arrangements on canvas. With Bearden I am struck by the tactile sensuality of his work, the purity of the gesture, and especially the subtext of the aggressive, large-as-life humanity of his subject matter. This latter is no small thing, when the urgency of de-stereotyping is so strong it can push easily into sentimentality. The edge of the razor that I see embedded in Bearden's work prevents—or ought to prevent—easy, self-satisfying evaluations of his subject matter. Among the aspects of his work that appeal to me, that is one that is primary: lack of condescension. Another aspect of my own process involves the composition of the text: the layered exercise that I consistently undergo which has more elements in common with painting than with literature.

I need three kinds of information to complete, sometimes even start, a narrative. Once I've settled on an idea and the story through which to examine it, I need the *structure*, the *sound*, the *palette*—not necessarily in that order. The sound of a text clearly involves the musical quality of the dialogue and the language chosen to contextualize it. Elsewhere I have written about my choices for the opening of *Beloved*; I will repeat my comments here. With the opening—"124 was spiteful. Full of a baby's venom."—I was careful to illustrate the rhythm I thought necessary, and the quality of a spoken text: "There is something about numerals that makes them spoken, heard, in this context, because one expects words to read in a book, not numbers to say, or hear. And the sound of the novel, sometimes cacophonous, sometimes harmonious, must be an inner-ear sound or a sound just beyond hearing, infusing the text with a musical emphasis that words can do sometimes even better than music can." I go on to explain why the second sentence—"Full of a baby's venom."—is really a dependent clause that I have given the status of a sentence simply to mandate a stress on the word "full." In an effort to understate the strangeness of an infant ghost so the reader will understand its presence as normal, as the household does. The remarkable thing being its power (*full*) rather than its presence. In describing at such length the crucial nature of sound to my work, I hoped to focus attention not on a kind of forced poetry or lyricism, but rather on what meaning can be gleaned and communicated from sound, from the aural quality of the text.

I only want to suggest that this is more than being influenced by blues or jazz. It is plumbing the music for the meaning that it contains. In other words, the "aesthetic implications" of which Bearden spoke ought to include what is usually absent from aesthetic analysis. Most often the analysis is about how successful a technique is in summoning pleasure—a shocking, or moving, or satisfying emotional response. Seldom does it center on the information, the meaning, the artist is communicating by his style, via his aesthetics.

It can be said, has been said, that the collage technique employed by several modernist artists was taken to new levels by Bearden, and reflects the "fractured" life he depicts: an intervention into the flat surface that repudiates as it builds on the Cubism of earlier periods. And that collage was representative of the modernist thrust of African American life as well as its insurgency. Both structure and improvisation inform this choice—the essence of African American music. The attraction to me in this technique is how abrupt stops and unexpected liquidity enhance the narrative in ways that a linear "beginning, middle, and end" cannot. Thus I recognize that my own abandonment of traditional time sequence—and then and then and then—is an effort to capitalize on modernist trends. And to say something about the layered life—not the fractured or fragmented life of black society—but the *layered* life of the mind, the imagination, and the way reality is actually perceived and experienced.

The third, palette, or color, is one of the last and most the crucial of my decisions in developing a text. I don't use color to "prettify" or please, or provide atmospherics. but to imply and delineate the themes within the narrative. Color *says* something, directly or metaphorically. The red-white-and-blue strokes at the beginning of *Song of Solomon* should lie quietly in the mind of the reader as the American-flag background the action is commenting on. The withholding of color in *Beloved*, its repudiating of any color at all until it has profound meaning to the character: Baby Suggs's hankering for some; Sethe's startle when she's able to let it come into view; the drama of one patch of orange in a quilt of bleak grays. These studied distributions of color or its absence, the careful placement of white for its various connotations—the bridal dress of the figure praying next to Sethe; the dresses of the church ladies at the pie table in *Tar Baby*; the repetition of a collection of colors chosen to direct the reader to specific and related scenes in *Paradise*—do not mimic the choices of a Romare Bearden, but are clearly aligned with the *process*.

I am convinced that among the reasons Bearden must be widely viewed in galleries, should occupy the burgeoning attention of scholars to African American art is only partly canon formation, is only minimally the quenching of nationalistic desire, is supplementally a tribute to his genius. The more significant reason, in the exploration of the resonances, alignments, the connections, and intergenre sources of African American art, is the resounding aesthetic dialogue among artists. Separating art forms, compartmentalizing them, is convenient for study, instruction, and institutions. But it is hardly representative of how artists actually work. The dialogue between Bearden and jazz music and musicians is an obvious beginning. The influence writers acknowledge is a further step. The borders established for the convenience of study are, I believe, *not just porous, they are liquid.* Locating instances of this liquidity is vital if African

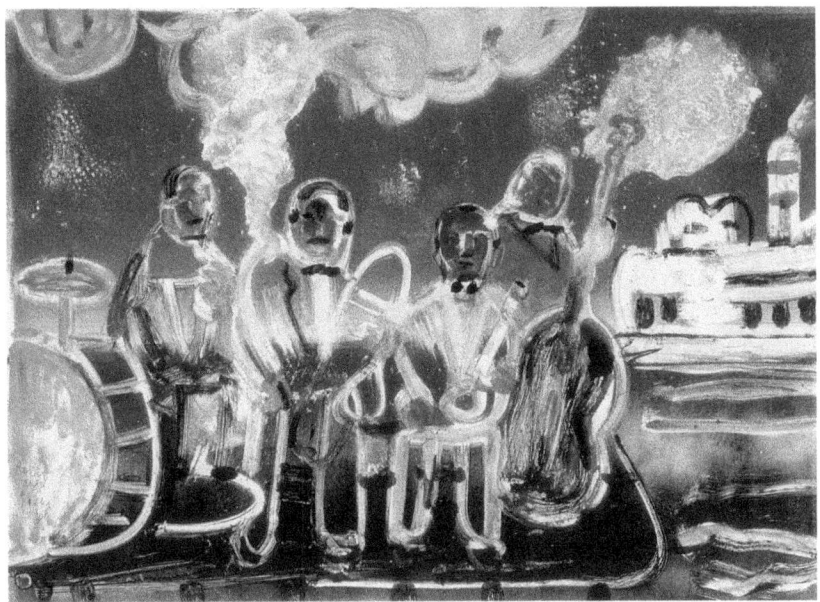

FIGURE 22 Romare Bearden, *Riverboat Musicians*, watercolor, n.d. The author acquired her similar work ca. 2000. Art © Romare Bearden Foundation/Licensed by VAGA, New York

American art is to be understood for the complex work that it is and for the deep meaning it contains.

Romare Bearden sat in an airplane seat once, and told me that he was going to send me something. He did. An extraordinary, completely stunning portrait of a character in one of my books. Not his Pilate of 1975, but the Pilate in *Song of Solomon* (Plate 5)—part of a series, I gather. Imagine my surprise at what *he* saw—things I hadn't seen or known when I invented her. What he made of her earring, her hat, and her bag of bones—far beyond my word-bound description, heavy with the life that both energized and muted her; solitary, daring anyone to deprive her of her symbols, her history, her purpose. I had seen her determination, her wisdom, and her seductive eccentricity, but not the ferocity he saw and rendered.

Later on, I acquired a watercolor of his: a row of Preservation Hall–type musicians standing before a riverboat, all in white, with their traditional sashes of color (see fig. 22). For the first time in a representation of black jazz musicians I saw stillness—not the active, frenetic, unencumbered physical movement normally seen in renderings of musicians, but the quiet at the center. It was, in a word, sacred, contemplative. A glance into an otherwise obscured aspect of their art. That kind of insight is rare. Displaying it, underscoring it, analyzing it is far more compelling than merely enjoying it. The legacy we are here to celebrate enjoins us all to think deeply about what Romare Bearden has given us and what African American art is imploring us to discover.

## NOTES

Transcribed talk, presented at Columbia University conference on Romare Bearden, October 16, 2004.

1. Romare Bearden, "Rectangular Structure in My Montage Paintings," *Leonardo* 2.1 (January 1969): 18; see full text in this volume, pp. 121–32.

2. Toni Morrison, *Unspeakable Things Unspoken: The Afro-American Presence in American Literature* (Ann Arbor: University of Michigan, 1989), 160.

# THE GENIUS OF ROMARE BEARDEN

*Elizabeth Alexander*

It is difficult to imagine twentieth-century American art without Romare Bearden, and it is equally challenging to settle on a single topic when presented with the opportunity to write about his work. Do we choose a little-researched period in the artist's work, or in his life as a painter who was also a social worker, songwriter, traveler, intellectual? Or do we abandon scholarly methods and instead rhapsodize, exalt in the magnificent and meticulous scope of any given Bearden work? Do we think about the art in the context of New York City, Pittsburgh, Paris, St. Martin/St. Maarten, or Mecklenburg County, North Carolina? Do we focus on the medium of prints or consider also his early abstract oils? Dare we neglect the magnificent Bearden collage?

Grant Hill has wisely collected a dazzling group of Beardens that span the artist's career, from the early gouache paintings *Serenade* (1941) and *They That Are Delivered from the Noise of the Archers* (1942) to the great collages of the 1980s. Those early paintings give fascinating indications of what he achieves later on. We see his proclivities as the master colorist he fully becomes in the collage form; his interest in the (black) figure seen in geometric components; and important Bearden icons such as the guitar. The 1979 collage in the collection, *Time for the Bass*, gives us Bearden in his exhaustive jazz mode. These works translate the energy, rhythm, and movement of jazz music into the flat form. This collection also shows us Bearden's urban and rural modes of

Mecklenburg County and Harlem. Bearden's work displays great intimate understanding of those landscapes that outline the movement of so many black people from South to North in the Great Migration.

The Grant Hill Collection gives an opportunity to see not only the span of Bearden's career but also a generous selection of his collage work. For Bearden's work comes into its most mature form in collage, and it is not hyperbole to state that as a collagist he is without parallel. I want to focus on collage here first by discussing the work itself but then by thinking about how the Bearden collage gives us a way to think about the complexities of African-American identity. In that regard, we can look at Bearden as an important twentieth-century African-American theorist as well as one of its most magnificent visual artists.

Bearden refigured collage via European cubism, African-American quilting, and idioms of jazz and the blues. His subject matter has ranged from a retelling of *The Odyssey,* in vibrant blacks and blues, to scenes from the North Carolina of his early childhood. His iconography is magically commonplace: trains seen through doorways, roosters, doves, saxophones, trumpets, washtubs, clouds. Bearden moved through phases of abstract oils and cubist watercolors but found his fullest voice in the 1960s, when he began to work extensively in collage. His work combines any number of media, from newspaper and magazine pictures, to brightly colored paper, to fabric, watercolor, and thick black "Speedball" pens.

Everything you read and the stories people tell about Bearden say that he was a very clever man, analytical and dazzlingly well-read, humble without being self-effacing, respectful, and aware of himself in relationship to myriad traditions. While writing a paper about him in college, I decided I wanted to speak to him, found him in the New York City phone book, called him, and found him, answering the phone and willing to entertain my questions. By the end of the conversation he had sent me to Sun Tzu's *The Art of War,* any stained glass windows I could find, and Earl "Fatha" Hines's music, so that I might better understand his own work. Bearden had digested a wide range of influences to arrive at the specificity of his vision.

Here is a quotation from Bearden, on his own identity: "I think of myself first as an American, and being an American means four things. One, being a student in the tradition of Emerson, Emily Dickinson, Melville, Walt Whitman. Second, you have to have the spirit of the whole Negroid tradition. The third tradition is the frontiersman, like Mark Twain and Bret Harte, and the fourth tradition is the Indian."[1] W. E. B. Du Bois wrote these lines in 1903, in *The Souls of Black Folk*: "One ever feels his twoness — an American, a Negro; two souls, two thoughts, two unreconciled strivings; two warring ideals in one dark body, whose dogged strength alone keeps it from being torn asunder."[2] "One ever feels his two-ness" would become a veritable mantra to legions of students of blackness and Du Bois's image of an ineffably split African-American consciousness, and of bifurcation as the major twentieth-century trope for African-American consciousness, remains resonant today.

But over one hundred years later, the "two-ness" trope must be revised. If the African-American intellectual consciousness is split, it is split multiply rather than doubly, and that so-called fragmentation, arisen from the fundamental fragmentation of the Middle Passage, has become a source of our creative power. The complex coexistence of a spectrum of black identities in a single space — think of Bearden's own self-description above, for example — represents a particular strength and coherence of African-American cultural production. Formal conflict is the locus of true innovation such as that which is evident in the twentieth-century African-American tradition from *Souls* back to Anna Julia Cooper's *A Voice from the South* to *Cane* (Jean Toomer), to *Invisible Man* (Ralph Ellison), to *Mumbo Jumbo* (Ishmael Reed), to *The Bluest Eye* (Toni Morrison), among others. In order for Du Bois to make a space for his "type" on the literary continuum, that type being the twentieth-century heretofore unimagined African-American intellectual who would write a book with the formal multiplicity and referentiality of *Souls*, he had to "make" a multiple self in the text at hand. In other words, the structural hybridity of the book *Souls* necessarily makes the written space in which he can fully explore aspects of what I would call his "collaged" identity. And collage, as developed and employed by Bearden, is my model to describe the presentation of self-identities in African-American literature and culture. Critics have used collage to talk about the literary works of modernist writers such as Joyce, Pound, and Eliot, as well as in Dadaist novels and various postmodern forms, but the Bearden collage offers a more necessarily historical — and culturally particular — context for twentieth-century African-American literature and culture.

Collage lets us think about identity as a spoked wheel or gyroscope on which its aspects spin and recombine. Collage also allows us to see African-American creative production as cohesive rather than schizophrenic. In other words, the disparate aspects of personalities and of influence that might seem contradictory can actually coexist in a single personality, or a single identity. When the process of cutting and pasting is visually evident, as it is in the cut and torn edges within Bearden's collages, yet obscured — by the fact of the unified whole the picture represents — creative/constructive process itself is valorized as a crucial and *aesthetic* component of the path to artistic coherence, and, indeed, an avenue to understanding how "coherence" itself is evaluated.

Collage, in both the flat medium as well as more abstractly in book form and as a metaphor for the creative process, is a continual cutting, pasting, and quoting of received information, much like jazz music, like the contemporary tradition of rapping, and indeed like the process of reclaiming African-American history (or of any historiography). African-American culture from the Middle Passage forward is of course broadly characterized by fragmentation and reassemblage, sustaining what can be saved of history while making something new. Collage constructs wholes from fragments in a continual, referential dialogue between the seemingly disparate shards of various pasts and the current moment of the work itself, as well as the future the work might point toward. Ralph Ellison said about Bearden:

> Bearden has sought here to reveal a world long hidden by the clichés of sociology and rendered cloudy by the distortions of newsprint and the false continuity imposed on our conception of Negro life by television and much documentary photography. Therefore, as he delighted us with the magic of design and teaches us the ambiguity of vision, Bearden insists that we see and that we see in depth and by the fresh light of his creative vision. Bearden knows that the true complexity of the slum dweller and the tenant farmer requires a release from the prison of our media-dulled perception and a reassembling in forms which would convey something of the depth and wonder of the Negro American's stubborn humanity.[3]

And here, a quotation from Picasso on collage: "If a piece of a newspaper can become a bottle, that gives us something to think about in connection with both newspapers and bottles, too. The displaced object has entered a universe for which it was not made and where it retains, in a measure, its strangeness. And this strangeness was what we wanted to make people think about because we were quite aware that our world was becoming very strange and not exactly reassuring."[4] Picasso's displaced "object" could be thought of as the African body, then the African-American body in migration, and collage as the process through which that "body" makes sense of itself in a hostile and unfamiliar environment.

Any discussion of the African-American collage must include a discussion of the quilt. Quilts embody the simultaneous continuity and chaos that characterize African-American history in all spheres. If African-American creativity is always in some way grappling with African-American history by trying to knit together the fragmentation that forms its core and the paradox of fragmentation as a center, quilting is a motif for a creative response to that history. Romare Bearden himself understands how quilting fits into African-American social, creative, and visual history. He has represented the act of quilting in his work, and his collages allude to strip weaving, quilts, and textiles. He also utilizes actual scraps of fabric. He has called his collage-making "precisely what the ladies (at the quilting bee) were doing."[5] The bits and pieces that make quilts as well as collages all refer to their uses and places in other lives; the life of the quilt is the aggregate of those pieces, and the work then becomes a referential discussion of both past and present at once.

West African, Mande-influenced strip weaving, in which narrow strips of cloth, sometimes as many as one hundred, were sewn together to make larger pieces of cloth or garments, was a crucial precursor to the African-American quilt. The patterns that made their way into the African-American tradition were the so-called crazy quilt patterns, seemingly irregular contrasts of color and line. These West African fabrics were collaged in the sense of being disparate pieces put together, though they do not have the same system of diverse referents as New World collages; once these textile traditions reached the Americas, they arose of different material and historical circumstances, and the textile work, as with other arts and crafts, reflected those new circumstances. Still, the concept of the process of putting pieces together and the improvisational possibilities inherent in the different color and pattern contrasts relate to the concept of collage. Strip weaving and quilting are not the same as cutting a pattern for a dress, where each piece is predetermined and the end outcome of the whole can be anticipated. Rather, when strips of cloth are sewn together, like strips in a quilt, the creative process continues throughout that act, through the matching and setting of color to color and pattern to pattern.

Fon-influenced appliquéd textiles also found their way to the African-American quilting tradition. Those African textiles set up intricate symbolist landscapes and told stories, strongly derivative of Egyptian hieroglyphics. African-American story quilts, in particular Harriet Powers's story quilts between 1886 and 1898, blend the New World necessity of sewing bed covering with Old World information about textile work, a New World manifestation of ancestral motifs and narrative impulses.[6]

An African-American quilt might be made from pieces of blanket wool, worn cotton from an apron, a soft piece of calico from a fourth-hand dress, made of the materials of the new place, but could nonetheless reflect the patterns of an ancestral heritage, just as slaves made instruments from whatever was at hand — washtubs, broom handles, even their own bodies in hambone and spoons. A washboard could make sound and music but was also, or had been, an instrument of work, a historical referent of the condition of the creator. The object had its contemporary life and meaning as well as its ulterior "lives," all in the same site. If nothing else was available, when even the body was not legally one's own, the body nonetheless could become a site for creative assemblage.

Composite visual works are ancient and cross-cultural. In the twelfth century Japanese calligraphed poetry was made of cut and pasted pieces of delicate paper. Thirteenth-century Persian artists cut leather into flowers for bookbinding. In the early seventeenth century and quite probably earlier Mexican feather mosaic pictures were made, and in the same century in Europe mosaic pictures were made of such earthly objects as beetles and corn kernels. Eighteenth-century European collages were made from butterfly wings, and in midcentury the still-familiar British tradition of Valentines commenced. According to art historian Herta Wescher, there is "nothing very new about the essential idea of collage, of bringing into association unrelated images and objects to form a different expressive identity."[7] Eddie Wolfram observes, "Besides their functional reality, some mundane objects have always held the potential of an 'inner,' more magical reality that is connected with man's wonder about the nature of existence and his own destiny."[8]

Collage, per se, entered the art historical lexicon in the early part of this century, as an outgrowth of cubism, and cubism, of course, developed as its practitioners were becoming familiar with and consequently inspired by different kinds of African art. Gregory Ulmer calls collage "the single most revolutionary formal innovation in artistic representation to occur in our century,"[9] and states that the innovation broke with traditional realism in its interplay between what Bearden called "mosaic-like joinings" and the unified image viewed from a greater distance. Wescher insists that twentieth-century collage was scarcely influenced by these earlier developments by "craftsmen, folk artists, and amateurs," folk and religious artists, which seems dubious, but certainly this was the first time that collage was employed by creative artists as the outgrowth of a specific artistic movement.

The word *collage* comes from the French *coller*, meaning to paste, stick, or glue. Claude Lévi-Strauss would play with that root when in *The Savage Mind* he used the term *bricoleur*, for he or she who made do with whatever was at hand, "with a set of tools and materials which is always finite and is also heterogeneous."[10] The first collages recognized as such were Pablo Picasso's *Still Life with Chair Caning* and George Braque's *Fruit Dish*, both made in 1912. There is some dispute over who made the first of what we now call collages, Picasso or Braque;

both claimed credit, and Picasso may have "pre"-dated *Still Life* to place himself first. But at this point of the cubist movement both artists had similar aims.

In cubism, painters attempted to show their subjects from as many sides or perspectives as possible at the same time. This concept revolutionized the world of possibilities in modern art by introducing the concept of simultaneity and a departure from the flat, literal surface. Collage juxtaposed seemingly disparate elements into a new context and a new whole. Braque said that in collage he could separate color from form, thus allowing both to "emerge in their own right" or exist simultaneously together and apart.[11]

The displaced "object" Picasso mentions in the above quotation is, in African-American terms, first and foremost the displaced African body. There is also a "displaced," or, to riff on Carter G. Woodson, "mis-placed," galaxy of cultural and historical references that the African-American cultural worker draws upon. Historical distortions are deliberate and not at all haphazard; we are displaced in that we were taken from Africa, and we are misplaced in that we have been put in a place, both literally and figuratively, that does not acknowledge the full complex dimensions of our existence. Culture workers must then continually strive to create, validate, and keep in circulation written evidence, traces, of actual cultural existence. The quilt or collage creates something new that is simultaneously what it was and what it might be, due to its referentiality. The finished product is always a reflected breakdown of selections, the mechanics of choosing. The act of making is inherent in the finished thing itself.

When Bearden cuts colored paper rather than representational newspaper and magazine images, the shapes he makes from the paper become repeated motifs, his ritual shapes and images that continually call attention to a depth and a life behind the canvas itself. Bearden has said:

> In most instances in creating a picture, I use many disparate elements to form either a figure, or part of a background. I build my faces, for example, from parts of African masks, animal eyes, marbles, mossy vegetation, [and corn] . . . I then have my small original works enlarged so the mosaic-like joinings will not be so apparent, after which I finish the larger painting. I have found when some detail, such as a hand or eye, is taken out of its original context and is fractured and integrated into a different space and form configuration it acquires a plastic quality it did not have in the photograph. (Romare Bearden, 1911–1988, 26)

Evidently Bearden first ventured into collage in the mid-fifties with *Harlequin* (ca. 1956) and *A Land Beyond the River* (1957), both composed of colored papers with ink, paint, and graphite on paper.[12] He experimented with Egyptian hiero-glyphics in a "Hierographs" show in the forties as well as pointed shapes and a con-cern with black, line, and color that would recur in later collages.[13] It was not until the 1960s that he was fully involved in collage as his primary art form.[14] His water-colors in the forties and early fifties are frequently separated by heavy black lines; he was playing with the idea of blocks or patches of color that would resurface in the collages. But the crucial difference in collage is the concept of overlapping. Separated spaces and blocks of color do not represent an integration of disparate segments in the same way that overlap and consequent recombination underpins the very concept of collage, especially as I am using collage to talk about identity formation. I am arguing for an African-American identity that is not segmented but rather a curious whole. Collage becomes a way to remember — and the pro-cess of remembering and refiguring, whether literal or metaphorical, is inherent in the African-American literary critical enterprise — and find a vehicle in the act. A look at the process of piecing together in Bearden's work will provide a bridge to understanding the same process at work later in African-American written works.

*Untitled: Duke and Billy*, which appears to be the earliest of Bearden's pub-lished collages, is a whimsical postcard (the catalog lists "size unknown").[15] A dutiful Billy Strayhorn and a jaunty Duke Ellington stroll by a Paris book stand in a snapshot on the left side of the plane. On the right, Bearden has made ink line drawings of cliché Paris postcard scenes: the Eiffel Tower reaching to the clouds, a bridge over the Seine, a *jeune homme* in ankle-pants and striped sailor shirt. The background is green, and red, white, and blue stripes to suggest the French flag govern the frame in titled rectangles. "Duke and Billy" is handwritten in red and blue underneath the photograph. What makes this collage most inter-esting is that Bearden has pasted cut sections of photo contact sheets of Elling-ton and Strayhorn in what looks like a Parisian train station. The contact sheet represents time in the collage — the sense of a whirlwind trip as exemplified in the rapid shifts between the frames — as well as an intimacy: Was Bearden there? Did he take the pictures?[16] They are not posed portraits but rather snapshots; how did he come upon them? Bearden leaves off the last names of his subjects to suggest that either he is intimate with them or that we should be intimate with the subjects, "Duke" and "Billy" to all. The public France of the postcard moves quickly to the intimate France, and the larger cultural juxtaposition is one of these two black American musical greats bringing their black jazz to Europe. This minor collage illustrates how referentiality embedded in the objects juxta-posed on the page opens up the fields of meaning in the work itself.

In Bearden's collages, you see the simultaneous referentiality — the "past life" of the cut or torn fragment — as well as the contemporary moment or whole that these reintegrated fragments create. Bearden's 1971 collage *The Block I* is a long horizontal rectangle, setting up a sense of the forward movement of narrative from the start. Though Palmer Hayden and Archibald Motley are the artistic parents of the African-American street scene, Bearden was the first to go behind the façade of the block inside his subject's homes and lives. For the buildings he has used plain brown papers, bricks he has painted himself, and what looks to be brick-patterned Contac paper, reminiscent of the wood grain paper used by Picasso in those first collages. He has "cut" into the buildings not solely in the regular spaces where windows would be but rather at random spots, as though cutting through the brick. In this way the viewer feels less like a Peeping Tom than like a privileged observer placed squarely in the middle of life lived. The irregularity of the cuts adds to the element of spontaneity and therefore "authenticity." Yet he also makes a viewer aware of this status of invasion, of looking in without having asked permission. Additionally, because we do not see into every room, the viewer is aware that choices have been made of what to reveal and what to keep private. The grave boy looking out might be asking, Who are you? as the viewer asks the same questions. The angels burst from the brick at the top of the work, making us aware of the constructed frame that defines and sometimes constricts a community as well as the spiritual necessity of imagining movement beyond those boundaries.

In the Grant Hill Collection, we see a similar scene in *The Street* (watercolor and collage on board, 1985). The sense of a public black life and the private life beyond is made clear. The haunting black faces cut out from other places find themselves at home on this street. Yet their eyes speak of elsewhere, referring again, perhaps, to the Great Migration that was part of Bearden's own experience and that he understood as emblematic to black people in this country as they have moved and reassembled from one country to another, one region to another, even one block to another, adapting and evolving with each geographic shift.

Bearden's interiors also give us a sense of the intimacy with which he knew and saw black life, and his use of collage adds dimension to that sense of intimacy. In *Morning Gingham* (1985) two women prepare for the day, one bathing and the other preparing water or food. They occupy the same space, faced in opposite directions, each performing her own ablutions, distinct yet together. The gingham in the collage is actual fabric that serves both to represent a woman's skirt and a window curtain, but also to allude to a culture where nothing is wasted, where materials are recycled, and where stories are embedded in objects or materials.

The recent Whitney Museum exhibit "The Quilts of Gee's Bend" magnificently showcases women who work together intimately — so in a sense this is collective or communal work — but their individual voices and aesthetics are also blazingly clear. The so-called Negro spirituals came from a collective context and collective authorship, yet they made space for the solo voice to be heard, individuality out of community.

You don't have to believe in magic to believe that objects carry something from one person to another. Think of the old wedding tradition that a bride should wear something old, something new, something borrowed, and something blue. The "something borrowed" is meant to bring good luck and blessings to the bride from the person who first wore the brooch or carried the handkerchief. Few would dare break with such tradition. So it isn't a leap to understand that the bits of cloth that came from garments someone actually wore bring a bit of that person with them. To translate this to Bearden's artistic practice, as one imagines that many of these previous owners were unknown to him, he is bringing something of the actual spirits of black people into his work in a way that paint alone never could. In the Grant Hill Collection we see this especially in *Morning Charlotte* (1985) and *The Evening Guitar* (1987). For what is Du Bois's double consciousness but the sense that we are scrutinized even as we make private space, what we are imagined even as we imagine ourselves? Bearden understood that paradox profoundly, and he managed the feat of making it visibly manifest in his collaged work. He also gave us a world of its own integrity, that could be spectated, if you will, at the same time that it enjoyed the free play of imagination and self-invention. Most importantly, it managed to convey profound intimacy. Bearden's genius is placed in context of a long and fruitful career in this collection.

## NOTES

From *Something All Our Own: The Grant Hill Collection of African-American Art*, exh. cat. (Durham, NC: Duke University Press, 2003).

1. *Romare Bearden, 1911–1988: A Memorial Exhibition*, exh. cat. (New York: ACA Galleries, 1989), 3.

2. W. E. B. Du Bois, "The Souls of Black Folk," in *W. E. B. Du Bois*, ed. Nathan Huggins (New York: Library of America, 1986), 364–65.

3. Ralph Ellison, "The Art of Romare Bearden," in *Going to the Territory* (New York: Random House, 1986), 234; see full text in this volume, pp. 196–203.

4. Pablo Picasso in conversation with Francoise Gilot, quoted in Marjorie Perloff, "The Invention of Collage," in *Collage* (New York: New York Literary Forum, 1983), 5–47.

5. *Romare Bearden: Origins and Progressions* (Detroit, MI: Detroit Institute of Arts, 1986), 41.

6. John Michael Vlach, *The Afro-American Tradition in Decorative Arts* (Athens: University of Georgia Press, 1990), 45–48. See also Gladys-Marie Fry, *Stitched from the Soul: Slave Quilts in the Ante-Bellum South* (New York: Dutton Studio Books, 1990); Robert Farris Thompson, "Round Houses and Rhythmic Textiles: Mande-Related Art and Architecture in the Americas," in *His Flash of the Spirit: African and Afro-American Art and Philosophy* (New York: Random House, 1983), 193–224; Maude Southwell Wahlman and John Scully, "Aesthetic Principles in Afro-American Quilts, in *Afro-American Folk Arts and Crafts*, ed. William Ferris (Jackson: University Press of Mississippi, 1983), 79–97; and Alvia Wardlaw's introduction to John Beardsley et al., *The Quilts of Gee's Bend* (Atlanta: Tinwood, 2002).

7. Herta Wescher, *Collage* (New York: Harry N. Abrams, 1972), 8.

8. Eddie Wolfram, *History of Collage: An Anthology of Collage, Assemblage and Event Structure* (New York: Macmillan, 1975), 7.

9. Gregory Ulmer, "The Object of Post-Criticism," in *The Anti-Aesthetic: Essays on Post-Modern Culture*, ed. Hal Foster (Seattle: Bay Press, 1983), 84.

10. Claude Lévi-Strauss, *The Savage Mind* (Chicago: University of Chicago Press, 1966), 17.

11. Perloff, "The Invention of Collage," 24.

12. This sentence is modified to correct an error in Alexander's original essay drawn from *Romare Bearden, 1911–1988*, where the collage *Untitled: Duke and Billy* is dated 1951. It is, in fact, part of an early 1980s "Paris Blues" project that involved the writer Albert Murray and the photographer Sam Shaw, whose photographs from 1960 appear in the collage (see Sam Shaw Archives, New York). Information on Bearden's earliest collages comes from Ruth Fine et al., *The Art of Romare Bearden* (Washington, DC, and New York: The National Gallery of Art and Abrams, 2003), 27, 92, 256.

13. *Ten Hieroglyphic Paintings by Sgt. Romare Bearden* (Washington, DC: G Place Gallery, 1944).

14. Mary Schmidt Campbell writes: "In 1964, [Bearden] abruptly abandoned his non-objective oil paintings . . . when he began making his collages . . . Having lived with a number of different ideas of art, he had come back to the subject matter he started out with — Black American life as he remembered it in the South of his childhood in North Carolina, and in the North of his coming of age in Pittsburgh and Harlem, and, later in life, the Caribbean island of St. Martin." *Memory and Metaphor: The Art of Romare Bearden, 1940–1987* (New York: Studio Museum in Harlem, 1991), 8.

15. *Romare Bearden, 1911–1988*, 21. This publication mistakenly dates *Untitled: Duke and Billy* to 1951. See note 12.

16. The photographs are by Sam Shaw. See note 12.

# THE ART OF ROMARE BEARDEN

*Ralph Ellison*

*I regard the weakening of the importance given to objects as the
capital transformation of Western art. In painting, it is clear that a
painting of Picasso's is less and less a "canvas," and more and more
the mark of some discovery, a stake left to indicate the place through
which a restless genius has passed . . .*
— André Malraux

This series of collages and projections by Romare Bearden represents a triumph
of a special order. Springing from a dedicated painter's unending efforts to master the techniques of illusion and revelation which are so important to the craft
of painting, they are also the result of Bearden's search for fresh methods to
explore the plastic possibilities of Negro American experience. What is special
about Bearden's achievements is, it seems to me, the manner in which he has
made his dual explorations serve one another, the way in which his technique
has been used to discover and transfigure its object. In keeping with the special
nature of his search, and by the self-imposed "rules of the game," it was necessary that the methods arrived at be such as would allow him to express the tragic
predicament of his people without violating his passionate dedication to art as a
fundamental and transcendent agency for confronting and revealing the world.

To have done this successfully is not only to have added a dimension to the
technical resourcefulness of art, but to have modified our way of experiencing
reality. It is also to have had a most successful encounter with a troublesome
social anachronism which, while finding its existence in areas lying beyond the
special province of the artist, has nevertheless caused great confusion among
many painters of Bearden's social background. I say *social*, for although Bearden
is by self-affirmation no less than by public identification a Negro American,
the quality of his *artistic* culture can by no means be conveyed by that term. Nor

does it help to apply the designation "black" (even more amorphous for conveying a sense of cultural complexity), and since such terms tell us little about the unique individuality of the artist or anyone else, it is well to have them out in the open where they can cause the least confusion.

What, then, do I mean by anachronism? I refer to that imbalance in American society which leads to a distorted perception of social reality, to a stubborn blindness to the creative possibilities of cultural diversity, to the prevalence of negative myths, racial stereotypes and dangerous illusions about art, humanity and society. Arising from an initial failure of social justice, this anachronism divides social groups along lines that are no longer tenable, while fostering hostility, anxiety and fear, and in the area to which we now address ourselves it has had the damaging effect of alienating many Negro artists from the traditions, techniques and theories indigenous to the arts through which they aspire to achieve themselves.

Thus in the field of culture, where their freedom of self-definition is at a maximum, and where the techniques of artistic self-expression are most abundantly available, such artists are so fascinated by the power of their anachronistic social imbalance as to limit their efforts to describing its manifold dimensions and its apparent invincibility against change. Indeed, they take it as a major theme and focus for their attention, and they allow it to dominate their thinking about themselves, their people, their country and their art. But while many are convinced that simply to recognize social imbalance is enough to put it to riot, few achieve anything like artistic mastery, and most fail miserably through a single-minded effort to "tell it like it is."

Sadly, however, the problem for the plastic artist is not one of "telling" at all, but of *revealing* that which has been concealed by time, custom, and our trained incapacity to perceive the truth. Thus it is a matter of destroying moribund images of reality and creating the new. Further, for the true artist, working from the top of his times and out of a conscious concern with the most challenging possibilities of his form, the unassimilated and anachronistic — whether in the shape of motif, technique, or image — is abhorrent evidence of conceptual and/ or technical failure, of challenges unmet. Although he may ignore the anachronistic through a preoccupation with other pressing details, he can never be satisfied simply by placing it within a frame. For once there, it becomes the symbol of all that is not art and a mockery of his powers of creation. So at his best he struggles to banish the anachronistic element from his canvas by converting it into an element of style, a device of his personal vision.

As Bearden demonstrated here so powerfully, it is of the true artist's nature and mode of action to dominate all the world and time through technique and vision. His mission is to bring a new visual order into the world, and through his art he seeks to reset society's clock by imposing upon it his own method of defining the times. The urge to do this determines the form and character of his social responsibility, spurs his restless exploration for plastic possibilities, and accounts to a large extent for his creative aggressiveness.

But it is here precisely that the aspiring Negro painter so often falters. Trained by the circumstances of his social predicament to a habit (no matter how reluctant) of accommodation, such an attitude toward the world seems quixotic. He is, he feels, only one man, and the conditions which thwart his freedom are of such enormous dimensions as to appear unconquerable by purely plastic means, even at the hands of the most highly trained, gifted and arrogant artist. "Turn Picasso into a Negro and *then* let me see how far he can go," he will tell you, because he feels an irremediable conflict between his identity as a member of an embattled social minority and his freedom as an artist. He cannot avoid, nor should he wish to avoid, his group identity, but he flounders before the question of how his group's experience might be given statement through the categories of a nonverbal form of art which has been consciously exploring its own unique possibilities for many decades before he appeared on the scene. It is a self-assertive and irrelevant art which abandoned long ago the task of mere representation to photography and the role of storytelling to the masters of the comic strip and the cinema. Nor can he draw upon his folk tradition for a simple answer. Beginning with the Bible and proceeding all the way through the spirituals, blues, novels, poems, and the dance, Negro Americans have depended upon the element of narrative for both entertainment and group identification. Further, it has been those who have offered an answer to the question, always crucial in the lives of a repressed minority, of who and what they are in the most simplified and graphic terms, who have won their highest praise and admiration. Unfortunately there seems to be (the African past notwithstanding) no specifically Negro American tradition of plastic design to offer him support.

How then, he asks himself, does even an artist steeped in the most advanced lore of his craft and most passionately concerned with solving the more advanced problems of painting as *painting* address himself to the perplexing question of bringing his art to bear upon the task (never so urgent as now) of defining Negro American identity, of pressing its claims for recognition and for justice? He feels, in brief, a near-unresolvable conflict between his urge to leave his mark upon the world through art and his ties to his group and its claims upon him.

Fortunately for them and for us, Romare Bearden has faced these questions for himself, and since he is an artist whose social consciousness is no less intense than his dedication to art, his example is of utmost importance for all who are concerned with grasping something of the complex interrelations between race, culture, and the individual artist as they exist in the United States. Bearden is aware that for Negro Americans these are times of eloquent protest and intense struggle, times of rejection and redefinition, but he also knows that all this does little to make the question of the relation of the Negro artist to painting any less difficult. If the cries in the street are to find effective statement on canvas, they must undergo a metamorphosis. In painting, Bearden has recently observed, there is little room for the lachrymose, for self-pity or raw complaint, and if they are to find a place in painting, this can only be accomplished by infusing them with the freshest sensibility of the times as it finds existence in the elements of painting.

During the late thirties when I first became aware of Bearden's work, he was painting scenes of the Depression in a style strongly influenced by the Mexican muralists. This work was powerful, the scenes grim and brooding, and through his depiction of unemployed workingmen in Harlem he was able, while evoking the Southern past, to move beyond the usual protest painting of this period to reveal something of the universal elements of an abiding human condition. By striving to depict the times, by reducing scene, character and atmosphere to a style, he caught something of both the universality of Harlem life and the "harlemness" of the national human predicament.

I recall that later, under the dual influences of Hemingway and the poetic tragedy of Federico García Lorca, Bearden created a voluminous series of drawings and paintings inspired by Lorca's *Lament for Ingacio Sánchez Mejías*. He had become interested in myth and ritual as potent forms for ordering human experience, and it would seem that by stepping back from the immediacy of the Harlem experience, which he knew both from boyhood and as a social worker, he was freed to give expression to the essentially poetic side of his vision. The products of this period were marked by a palette which, in contrast with the somber colors of the earlier work and despite the tragic theme with its underlying allusions to Christian rite and mystery, was brightly sensual. But despite their having been consciously influenced by the compositional patterns of the Italian primitives and Dutch masters, these works were also resolutely abstract.

It was as though Bearden had decided that in order to possess his world artistically, he had to confront it not through propaganda or sentimentality, but through the finest techniques and traditions of painting. He sought to re-create his Harlem in the light of his painter's vision, and thus avoided the defeats suffered by many of the aspiring painters of this period who seemed to have felt that they had only to reproduce, out of a mood of protest and despair, the sense and surfaces of Harlem in order to win artistic mastery and accomplish social transfiguration.

It would seem that for many Negro painters even the *possibility* of translating Negro American experience into the modes and conventions of modern painting went unrecognized. This was, in part, the result of an agonizing fixation upon the racial mysteries and social realities dramatized by color, facial structure, and the texture of Negro skin and hair. Again, many aspiring artists clung with protective compulsiveness to the myth of the Negro American's total alienation from the larger American culture — a culture which he helped to create in the areas of music and literature, and where in the area of painting he has appeared from the earliest days of the nation as a symbolic figure — and allowed the realities of their social and political situation to determine their conception of their role and freedom as artists.

To accept this form of the myth was to accept its twin variants, one of which holds that there is a pure mainstream of American culture which is "unpolluted" by any trace of Negro American style or idiom, and the other (propagated currently by the exponents of *Negritude*) which holds that Western art is basically racist, and thus anything more than a cursory knowledge of its techniques and history is irrelevant to the Negro artist. In other words, the Negro American who aspired to the title "artist" was too often restricted by sociological notions of racial separatism, and these appear not only to have restricted his use of artistic freedom, but to have limited his curiosity about the abundant resources made available to him by those restless and assertive agencies of the artistic imagination which we call technique and conscious culture.

Indeed, it has been said that these disturbing works of Bearden's (which literally erupted during a tranquil period of abstract painting) began quite innocently as a demonstration to a group of Negro painters. He was suggesting some of the possibilities through which commonplace materials could be forced to undergo a creative metamorphosis when manipulated by some of the nonrepresentational techniques available to the resourceful craftsman. The step from collage to projection followed naturally, since Bearden had used it during the early forties as a means of studying the works of such early masters as Giotto and de Hooch. That he went on to become fascinated with the possibilities lying in such "found" materials is both an important illustrative instance for younger painters and a source for our delight and wonder.

Bearden knows that regardless of the individual painter's personal history, taste or point of view, he must nevertheless pay his materials the respect of approaching them through a highly conscious awareness of the resources and limitations of the form to which he has dedicated his creative energies. One suspects also that as an artist possessing a marked gift for pedagogy, Bearden has sought here to reveal a world long hidden by the clichés of sociology and rendered cloudy by the distortions of newsprint and the false continuity imposed upon our conception of Negro life by television and much documentary photography. Therefore, as he delights us with the magic of design and teaches us the ambiguity of vision, Bearden insists that we see in depth and by the fresh light of his creative vision. He knows that the true complexity of the slum dweller and the tenant farmer requires a release from the prison of our media-dulled perception and a reassembling in forms which would convey something of the depth and wonder of the Negro American's stubborn humanity.

Being aware that the true artist destroys the accepted world by way of revealing the unseen, and creating that which is new and uniquely his own, Bearden has used Cubist techniques to his own ingenious effect. His mask-faced Harlemites and tenant farmers set in their mysteriously familiar but empathetically abstract scenes are nevertheless resonant of artistic and social history. Without compromising their integrity as elements in plastic compositions, his figures are expressive of a complex reality lying beyond their frames. While functioning as integral elements of design, they serve simultaneously as signs and symbols of a humanity that has struggled to survive the decimating and fragmentizing effects of American social processes. Here faces which draw upon the abstract character of African sculpture for their composition are made to focus our attention upon the far from abstract reality of a people. Here abstract interiors are presented in which concrete life is acted out under repressive conditions. Here too the poetry of the blues is projected through synthetic forms which visually are in themselves tragicomic and eloquently poetic. A harsh poetry this, but poetry nevertheless, with the nostalgic imagery of the blues conceived as visual form, image, pattern and symbol — including the familiar trains (evoking partings and reconciliations) and the conjure women (who appear in these works with the ubiquity of the witches who haunt the drawing of Goya) who evoke the abiding mystery of the enigmatic women who people the blues. Here too are renderings of those rituals of rebirth and dying, of baptism and sorcery which give ceremonial continuity to the Negro American community.

By imposing his vision upon scenes familiar to us all, Bearden reveals much of the universally human which they conceal. Through his creative assemblage he makes complex comments upon history, society and the nature of art. Indeed, his Harlem becomes a place inhabited by people who have in fact been *resurrected*, re-created by art, a place composed of visual puns and artistic allusions where the sacred and profane, reality and dream are ambiguously mingled. Resurrected with them in the guise of fragmented ancestral figures and forgotten gods (really masks of the instincts, hopes, emotions, aspirations, and dreams) are those powers that now surge in our land with a potentially destructive force which springs from the very fact of their having for so long gone unrecognized and unseen.

Bearden doesn't impose these powers upon us by explicit comment, but his ability to make the unseen manifest allows us some insight into the forces which now clash and rage as Negro Americans seek self-definition in the slums of our cities. There is beauty here, a harsh beauty that asserts itself out of the horrible fragmentation which Bearden's subjects and their environment have undergone. But, as I have said, there is no preaching; these forces have been brought to eye by formal art. These works take us from Harlem through the South of tenant farms and northward-bound trains to tribal Africa; our mode of conveyance consists of every device which has claimed Bearden's artistic attention, from the oversimplified and scanty images of Negroes that appear in our ads and photojournalism, to the discoveries of the School of Paris and the Bauhaus. He has used the discoveries of Giotto and Pieter de Hooch no less than those of Juan Gris, Picasso, Schwitters, and Mondrian (who was no less fascinated by the visual possibilities of jazz than by the compositional rhythms of the early Dutch masters), and he has discovered his own uses for the metaphysical richness of African sculptural forms. In brief, Bearden has used — and most playfully — all of his artistic knowledge and skill to create a curve of plastic vision which reveals to us something of the mysterious complexity of those who dwell in our urban slums. But his is the eye of a painter, not a sociologist, and here the elegant architectural details which exist in a setting of gracious but neglected streets, and the buildings in which the hopeful and the hopeless live cheek by jowl, where the failed human wrecks and the confidently expectant explorers of the frontiers of human possibility are crowded together as incongruously as the explosive details in a Bearden canvas—all this comes across plastically and with a freshness of impact that employs neither sociological cliché nor a raw protest.

Where any number of painters have tried to project the "prose" of Harlem, a task performed more successfully by photographers, Bearden has concentrated upon releasing its poetry, abiding rituals and ceremonies of affirmation, creating a surreal poetry compounded of vitality and powerlessness, destructive impulse and the all-pervading and enduring faith in their own style of American humanity. Through his faith in the powers of art to reveal the unseen through the seen, his collages have transcended their immaculateness as plastic constructions. Or to put it another way, Bearden's meaning is identical with his method. His combination of technique is in itself eloquent of the sharp breaks, leaps in consciousness, distortions, paradoxes, reversals, telescoping of time and surreal blending of styles, values, hopes and dreams which characterize much of Negro American history. Through an act of creative will, he has blended strange visual harmonies out of the shrill, indigenous dichotomies of American life, and in doing so has reflected the irrepressible thrust of a people to endure and keep its intimate sense of its own identity.

Bearden seems to have told himself that in order to possess the meaning of his Southern childhood and Northern upbringing, and to keep his memories, dreams, and values whole, he would have to re-create and humanize them by reducing them to artistic style. Thus in the poetic sense these works give plastic expression to a vision in which the socially grotesque conceals a tragic beauty, and they embody Bearden's interrogation of the empirical values of a society that mocks its own ideals through a blindness induced by its myth of race. All this, ironically, by a man who visually, at least (he is light-skinned and perhaps more Russian than "black" in appearance), need never have been restricted to the social limitations imposed upon easily identified Negroes. Bearden's art is therefore not only an affirmation of his own freedom and responsibility as an individual and artist, but is an affirmation of the irrelevance of the notion of race as a limiting force in the arts. These are works of a man possessing a rare lucidity of vision.

## NOTE

"Introduction" to *Romare Bearden: Paintings and Projections*, exh. cat. (Albany: Art Gallery of the State University of New York at Albany, 1968); reprinted as "The Art of Romare Bearden" in Ralph Ellison, *Going to the Territory* (New York: Random House, 1986).

# BEARDEN

*Ralph Ellison*

Let me begin by saying that Romie frequently got me into trouble. Nothing physical, mind you, but difficulties arising out of our attempts to make some practical sense of the relationship between art and living, between ideas and the complex details of consciousness and experience. Of course there can be no final answers to such questions, and so today I find Romie challenging me from beyond the limits of death and dying.

It was my good fortune to know Romie from my early days in New York. I met him when I was a fledgling writer working (some would say "boondog-gling") on the Federal Writers Project, and when he was an unknown painter who worked for the New York Department of Welfare. At the time I knew very little about painting as such, but thanks to having taken a class in sculpture at Tuskegee and to my exposure to avant-garde magazines, I had developed a more than casual interest in the visual arts. I became even more interested once I realized that I had found in Romie an artist who could talk knowledgeably about my own passion, which was literature.

At the time I was very much involved with the poetry and plays of Federico García Lorca. I discovered that Romie knew a great deal about García Lorca. I was interested in the poetry of Eliot and the fiction of Hemingway, and I was delighted that they too had aroused his interest. Indeed, I soon discovered that

Romie knew about many matters that I in my naiveté hadn't expected a painter to know, and when I accepted this fact my life was unexpectedly enrichened.

Earlier today I tried to think back to the circumstance through which I was prepared for my relationship with Romie, and by what stroke of fate I had been made ready for this impact upon my sensibilities. (Incidentally, I have no concrete idea about how *Romie* was prepared for his contact with such an oddball as myself, but I suspect that reading played a part.) Nevertheless, as I thought back I realized that there had indeed been a forerunner of Romie in my life, and that my interest in drawing and painting went directly back to an older boy who lived next door.

This was in Oklahoma City, and that boy, that hero of my childhood, filled his notebooks with cartoon characters who acted out visual narratives that I found far more interesting than those provided by the newspaper comic sections. More interesting because they were about *us*, about Negro boys like ourselves. He filled his notebooks with drawings which told stories of Negro cowboys and rodeo stars like Bill Pickett, of detectives and gangsters, athletes, clowns and heroes. Indeed, he created such a variety of characters and adventures that our entire neighborhood took on a dimension of wonder. But for me the most amazing part was the fact that all this was done by someone I knew, by the fellow living just next door who allowed me to look on as he gave form to figures, scenes and adventures on page after page of notebook paper. But then as my friend and I grew older, Fate, the old "good-bad," struck our lives in its ever ambiguous way.

There came a day when his father sat us down beneath their towering apricot tree and proceeded to teach him the trumpet and me the alto horn. For me this was a stroke of good fortune, but there's a question about whether that was true for my friend. While our community was highly enthusiastic in fostering music, it lacked adults who might have encouraged my friend's artistic talents. Thus it was that he went on to become a musician and barber like his father. So it was in Romie that I found the fulfillment of my earlier friend's promise and the continuation of that stimulating friendship. However, it was no mere duplication of past experience, for while Romie was more mature and intellectually curious, he was no less generous in sharing his talent and in discussing his struggle for mastery with me.

I can remember visits to Romie's 125th Street studio during which he stood at his easel sketching and explaining the perspectives of the Dutch and Italian masters. At other times he played with the rhythms of Mondrian and related them to the structure of jazz, and on still other occasions he explained some of the magic by which color became space, space became perspective, and color became form. He also had much to say about the nature of African sculpture.

It was his generosity in sharing such knowledge that made Romie Bearden such an affirmative figure in my own struggle to acquire writing skills. True, among my friends there was a world-famous writer, and another, with whom I held endless discussions of our mutual craft, who would soon be widely acclaimed, but Romie's approach to art and his line of development seemed closer to my own. Thus when it seemed impossible that I would ever get anywhere with my writing, I could talk with him, take heart from his progress and feel encouraged. Better, I could observe and discuss his search for more effective techniques with which to give artistic form to his conception of our general experience. Each of us was concerned with the relationship between artistic technique and individual vision, and we were especially concerned with the relationship between our racial identity, our identity as Americans, and our mission as writer and artist.

Romie's father was a teller of tales, and Romie, whose art even at its most abstract retains an element of narrative, enjoyed regaling his friends with folk tales. These arose out of a need to impose form upon experience, and Romie's delight in them led me to realize that here again we shared a stream of Afro-American culture which I had received from my Oklahoma background and Romie from living in North Carolina, Pennsylvania, and New York. This shared ancestral lore made for a level of unspoken communication which connected the past to the present, and of course we shared many of the wide variety of experiences that were available during the thirties. New York was a center of opportunity in which the aspiring could form contacts with recognized artists and writers. Libraries, art galleries and museums were there to be used by those with the curiosity and interest to use them, and we did.

Those were also days of great excitement in Harlem, for in many ways it was still a place of glamour. Those were the days of the swinging big bands, days when the streets of Harlem were filled with celebration every time Joe Louis knocked somebody out in the ring, days when we danced the lindy at the Savoy Ballroom, and nights when new stars were initiated on the stage of the Apollo Theater.

Yes, but those were also the days of the Depression, days of *dispossession* and of protest marches. Harlem was growing edgy, and Romie observed its effects most intimately through his work with the Welfare Department. There was a great turbulence growing in American society, much of it racial, and it became a subject both of our discussions and our artistic efforts. The question was, how did one express it in art? How sharpen its impact and render it artistically effective? How transform dismal sociological facts into art? Many attempts were being made, and certain ideological formulas were recommended as solutions, but I myself felt that they were reductive, that they overemphasized the negative aspects of our condition while leaving unnoticed the tragic-comic transcendence through which we had survived and remained hopeful, both as individuals and as a people. Most of all, such ideological formulas sought to reduce our complex American identity to the single aspect of race. I suspected, and Romie's work affirmed, that perhaps there were other ways of going about giving expression to the times. Perhaps the solution lay in other, more eclectic approaches. Art itself was a form of freedom, and there was a world of art complete with all the styles and complex techniques through which artists had confronted experience and given it artistic form. That world was ours to draw upon. Yes, and there were the rituals — religious, fraternal, social — through which our people had imposed order upon the chaos of their lives. There were the interrelations between such rituals that were shared by Americans of various backgrounds to be drawn upon. Therefore the image of American society presented by the newspapers, magazines, and radio often missed much of the sheer human complexity of the life we knew. That life was marked by a ceaseless resistance against all attempts to reduce its complex humanity, whether by force or ideology, and by example it pointed a direction for the writer and artist. Thus each of us decided in his own way to find the artistic means with which to express our complex sense of American and Afro-American variety and diversity, discord, and unity, and we decided that to do this one had to draw upon one's own unique experience. One had to discover one's means and direction by going into the self, and by identifying one's self with all that claimed one's respect and aroused one's sense of wonder. In brief, we came to believe that it was the role of the artist to confront and impose his own artistic sense of order upon the world.

Since there are hundreds of you gathered here who knew those times and who shared their hopes and disappointments, there is no need for me to continue with this bit of background. You know very well how it worked out for Romie. Some of the results, the paintings, are here in this cathedral. Some are in magazines, in books, and in many museums. They are in many places, and in all their settings they speak eloquently of a promise which goes far beyond the designs and figures displayed within their frames.

Over the years we have come to speak of Romie as "Bearden" and we recognize him as a great master of collage. Now perhaps we should remind ourselves that we are a *collage of a nation*, and a nation that is ever shifting about and grousing as we seek to achieve the promised design of democracy. Therefore one of the reasons that *we* revere Romie is for his discovery that one of the ways of getting at many of the complex matters which we experience, but seldom find recorded in official history, is through art. Art is the mystery which gets left out of history.

We are thankful to have known him, and to have shared some of his discoveries. Of this we are certain: we shall be discovering more and more about Bearden and his work as we discover more about — and accept the responsibility of confronting — the wonderful complexity of American life.

## NOTE

Eulogy delivered on April 6, 1988, at the Cathedral of St. John the Divine in New York City; published in *Callaloo* 36 (Summer 1988).

# BETWEEN THE SHADOW AND THE ACT

*John Edgar Wideman*

*In Bearden I found my artistic mentor and sought, and still aspire, to make my plays
the equal of his canvases. . . . I never had the privilege of meeting Romare Bearden.
Once I stood outside 357 Canal Street in silent homage, daring myself to knock on his
door. I am sorry I didn't. . . . I probably would just have looked at him. I would have
looked, and if I were wearing a hat, I would have taken it off in tribute.*
— August Wilson, "Bearden: Black Life on Its Own Terms"

Romare Bearden, the world-famous painter who attended Peabody, the same
high school in Pittsburgh my sister, my incarcerated brother, and I attended,
said that at the beginning of the Italian Renaissance some artists resisted the
demands of their patrons for paintings that conformed to fashionable rules of
perspective. Artists feared the new science and math of rendering space. Feared
deep thrusts cutting into their canvases. Tintoretto, for example, screwed up on
purpose. He believed the illusory holes in a painting could become real holes
in which the gaze, maybe the gazer's body and soul, might plunge and be lost
forever. Who knew? The point is resist. Painters might tumble in too.

Romare Bearden's collages remind me of how my mother talked, still talks
to me today, years after she's been gone. Her stories flatten and fatten perspective. She crams everything, everyone, everywhere into the present, into words
intimate and immediate as the images of a Bearden painting. When she's going
good my mom manages to crowd lots and lots of stuff into a space that doesn't
feel claustrophobic. She fills space to the brim without exhausting it. Without
surrendering the authority of her long life, she always talks about a precise moment she's inhabiting. Makes her moment present and large enough, thank
goodness, to include everybody listening. Bearden's collages and my mother's
narratives truly democratic — each detail counts equally. Every part matters as
much as any grand design. Size and placement don't highlight forever some

items at the expense of others. Meaning equals point of view. Stop. I sound like a museum audiocassette guide when all I really need to say is "dance" — my mom talking or Bearden at the turntable mixing cutouts with paint with fabric with photos with empty space are works-in-progress inviting me to dance.

No one's fault, Romare Bearden supposes, if a gift doesn't fit in the box it was meant to fill with love. He tilts the collage board. Lets fragments arranged for gluing to the board slide back onto the worktable. Discovers they no longer quite fit on the table. Board empty. Table overflowing. He must start again. Decide again what to include or discard. He believes his life depends on each choice. Working on collage is too hard, impossible really, unless he hears something resembling music whose rhythms guide his eyes, hands. His feet shuffle beneath the work table's edge like Monk's feet under a piano.

Not surprising that, given the scope of his ambitions, Bearden misremembers occasionally the dimensions of a board he's preparing for collage or forgets how large a medley of ingredients he has assembled to glue, nail, sew to a board. Anyone observing him labor could have told him he's undertaking an impossible task. Too many things gathered on the table, limited room after all within a frame. Bearden's extremely smart so he must know better, too, but he is seduced by the privilege of paying absolute attention, piece by piece, to every item he selects. If pushed, he'd probably insist that losing track of the bigger picture also a mercy, even a momentary state of grace, especially when you're an older man, he might go on to say. Why not linger over a swatch of antique, patchwork Alabama quilt alive under his gaze as he rotates and rubs it, discovering new, mellow harmonies among its once brightly colored threads. Sweet funk of it as he brings it closer to his eyes. Dream of its perfection and dream of mounting it perfectly gone, but such dreams are worth the risk of disappointment. He will start over, though it means putting aside a particular gleaning until he finds a better fit for it. He will listen again, awhile longer for a silent tune that animates and clarifies what must be done next.

Every simple collected thing, unique. Each has endured rupture, transition, the terror of disappearance within an unfamiliar context where individual identity may materialize or not.

Collage should prepare brand new space, Bearden believes, not abandon items within a space defined by its previous occupants. Thinks collage envisions new pasts as well as new futures, and wonders if *thinking* is the proper word to express how he decides, separates, tests the possibility of packing an imaginary vehicle with material things he salvages.

To find what comes next Bearden must raise his gaze from the board upon which a collage is forming. Ask his eyes to perform the impossible magic of being in two places at once. He recalls Alberto Giacometti lamenting a fatal division of focus as he sculpted the face of his brother, Diego Giacometti. His brother's features disappear and rearrange themselves into a different face every time Alberto shifts his gaze from Diego to the image of him he's attempting to render in clay. No matter how swiftly his eyes travel from flesh and blood brother to clay and back, Alberto wrote, he confronts the enigma of a Diego whose face changes. Never the face seen an instant before. Often the face of a stranger. Mysteriously troubling as my brother's face can appear to me after six months, nine, a year between visits to the prison.

Space framed within collage is at least as elusive as any human face, Bearden has learned. Each time Bearden's eyes study an element he considers adding to a collage — a color, a photo, a triangle of denim — the composition vanishes. To see the whole again, his eyes must relinquish their grip on the element. The same way I lose my brother when I exit prison walls. The way I must exit the world outside prison bars to visit my brother.

Well, how does an artist resolve this dilemma, Maestro? This perpetual losing battle, this shifting back and forth, this absence, this oblivion between a reality the senses seize and a reality the imagination seizes.

*You guess. You believe,* Bearden would probably respond to anyone curious and serious enough to ask. A kind of wishful thinking, he might admit to himself. Each step of building collage unleashes unforeseeable energies. All choices precarious. Revelation. Loss. With something concrete in your hand, you leave this *inextricable place* as Samuel Beckett called it, and revisit a remembered space. You understand the fragment of material you grasp is as fragile, fallible as a memory. Understand no former place remains fixed, unchanged. But you guess, hope a space will be there. Not waiting patient as a prison cell, but a familiar, generous place offering room for what you bring.

Bearden worries about things that may have slipped from worktable to floor. He's unable to explain why removal of things from an array sometimes makes the array more plentiful not smaller. Nor explain how a board upon which he's arranging things becomes more spacious as he packs it. He learns to live with the necessity of letting go. Enjoys the idea of himself being as surprised as a stranger opening one of these gift boxes he prepares.

Or Bearden might explain that since any surface is fickle, never a done deal, always more or less than it seems, collage doesn't start there. Collage starts with nakedness inside a bare board. With swirling atoms, molecules, elementary particles, primal colors and combinations. Builds layer upon layer of skin to reach the skin people think they see because they notice it first. And that surface skin usually enough to keep most people busy. All that most of us will ever see unless someone — a fabricator of collage, for instance — does his or her work well. Undresses appearance. Denies its claims. Reminds people that what they see as real, as solid and confirmed, is only a layer, only partially, momentarily visible as layer succeeds layer, shifting, ascending and descending. Dying, being born. Playing across a screen fluid as a river into which no person's eyes gaze twice at the same place.

Human beings readily observe waves rippling the sea. But exactly where is a wave? Quantum mechanics offers an explanation. Unlike a particle, a wave is not localized at a single place, but is a disturbance that carries energy through a medium. Like people taking part in a stadium-wave. Single water molecules bobbing up and down are what we see as waves rippling. Bearden's collages agitate elements that compose them. Make waves.

Or Bearden might say: Let me give you a less abstract example of how collage constructed. Start with the bare-bones plot of a story. It begins with me and two other colored boys beating up on Eugene, a crippled white boy — my grandmother intervenes — rescues the crippled boy and he becomes my best friend — Grandma discovers he lives in a brothel with a prostitute mother and rescues him again — he comes with his birds to live with us a short year then dies. My collage is layer upon layer of questions about this simple story.

One luxury of growing old, Bearden continues, is more time to ask questions about simple stories we make up. Stories that make us up. Will I be born again? Live again once this particular allotment of time runs out? Is a city called Pittsburgh still reachable by catching a train north from Carolina or a train south from Harlem that climbs over and tunnels through many mountains, rounds a gigantic horseshoe curve? If Pittsburgh continues to exist within a golden triangle cordoned by bridges and three rivers, clinging to steep hills like Rome, and if I reach Pittsburgh and walk its streets, am I a boy there or old like I am here and now, still asking a boy's questions? What names did Eugene give his birds? How much did Eugene's mom charge for a piece of pussy? Did she earn more or less in a year than the price one of my collages commands today?

Is teasing my bald head with idle questions a less forgivable luxury now than when I was a boy? If I return to the Pittsburgh I'm remembering, would

I carry knowledge allowing me to pose questions a boy couldn't ask because he had no idea of what he yearned to know? Just yearned. A boy with meager experience, few words to name his yearnings, few ideas beyond "yearning" to enable him to decide exactly what he desires to ask. No one to whom he could address his most nagging questions, even if he'd been able to articulate them. Man and boy hemmed in by circumstance, time, whether innocent of time or intimidated by evidence of time's imminent expiration. Doomed either way, now or then. Stuck with a habit of spending, perhaps wasting, his precious time daydreaming. As if living and questioning never ends. As if simple questions might stump time, buy time, stop time long enough for a boy, a man, to slip past the conductor and ride back and forth to Pittsburgh on a beam of light without paying the price of a ticket.

Anyway, Bearden confides, my first drawings not very nice. I learned from my friend Eugene how to draw the nasty stuff we spied on through rotting floorboards of the attic room he shared with his mother over a whorehouse that sat down Spring Street and around the corner from my grandmother's boarding house. One Saturday Grandma saw us extremely busy, busy drawing on large, blood-spotted sheets of brown paper chicken came wrapped in from the butcher and she marched over, *What you boys up to? Why you all so quiet over here?* When she saw what we were up to, her eyes got wide. She hollered. Snatched our drawings. Ripped them up and rained the tiny pieces into a kitchen garbage pail.

I expected a good whack or two. My grandmother one of those large bosomed, colored women who love children dearly, especially me. But if you made her mad, watch out. *Pow.* Trouble was Grandma so nice and easy most the time you don't notice her getting mad. First sign of mad — *Pow.* Then it's too late to move out her way cause with Grandma getting mad also a matter of getting even. Fact is, I didn't exactly understand why she might be hitting mad when I saw her coming over to where we were busy at the kitchen table. Even though I sort of knew the pictures Eugene and I were drawing had something very secret, very private about them I surely didn't want Grandma of all people to see.

What I had peeked at between the raggedy floor boards scared me. People hurting one another my first thought. Noisy, ugly thrashing about. Mean grabbing, mean pushing and squeezing, spilled whiskey, dirty sheets, cigarettes. Bare skin of grown-up body parts I'd never seen before. More scary because it was colored bodies and white bodies down there mixed up closer than I ever saw colored and white mixing on Spring Street and the little checkerboard, briar-patches of neighborhood around Spring and the Rolling Mill where a few lucky colored folks had regular jobs. All kinds of people living in the neighborhoods around the Mill. Poor the one requirement. Mixing on one hand, but on the other hand definitely not mixing. No trespassing the Golden Rule. Only colored men rented my grandmother's rooms, and different houses, different blocks, different barbers, different churches for white and colored because people believed in sticking to their own kind. Even kids believed it, so the first time I met up with Eugene, it was me, Mumps and Bo, the three of us teasing him, beating on him unmercifully because what the hell a white boy think he's doing standing there staring, ugly as a fresh knot on somebody's head got conked by a rock. Probably him being crippled as much as being the wrong color (though it was my skin's color, too, by the way) made us jump him, smack him so he'd go away and never bring his pitiful self back to the alley behind Spring where we played.

My grandmother had busted in that time in the alley, too. Setting down her shopping bags on the cobblestones, yelling *Stoppit, Stop that, you bad boys,* and whacking whoever she could lay her hands on, running us away from that skinny white kid. Whacking Mumps and Bo like she whapped me because that was how it worked back then around Spring Street. You were everybody your color's child and if you got caught doing wrong by any adult your color they had the right to whip your behind and send you home for another good beating because you should know better and not shame yourself, shame your people by doing wrong in public as if you hadn't been raised to know better.

Anyway, going back to that other time, later, after she tore up those butcher paper drawings and shredded them or maybe burned them to ashes in the kitchen sink, Grandma calmed down and asked me and Eugene what in Jesus name did we think we were doing and where'd we get the idea of those terrible drawings. We told her about the room under the attic room Eugene shared with his mama and a hole in one corner of the floor covered over with just a ratty piece of linoleum we lifted to spy on the goings on below. Told Grandma in which particular house Eugene resided around the corner from Grandma's, the house I went to almost every day after school and most evenings, too, if Grandma said ok.

*Oh, my. My-oh-my. Good Lord, have mercy,* Grandma groaned and snatched Eugene by the hand after she let go the ear she was pinching, and he gimped off beside her. I know Eugene didn't hardly want to go home, but he knew he better go and did, dragging his bad leg to slow things down as much as he dared

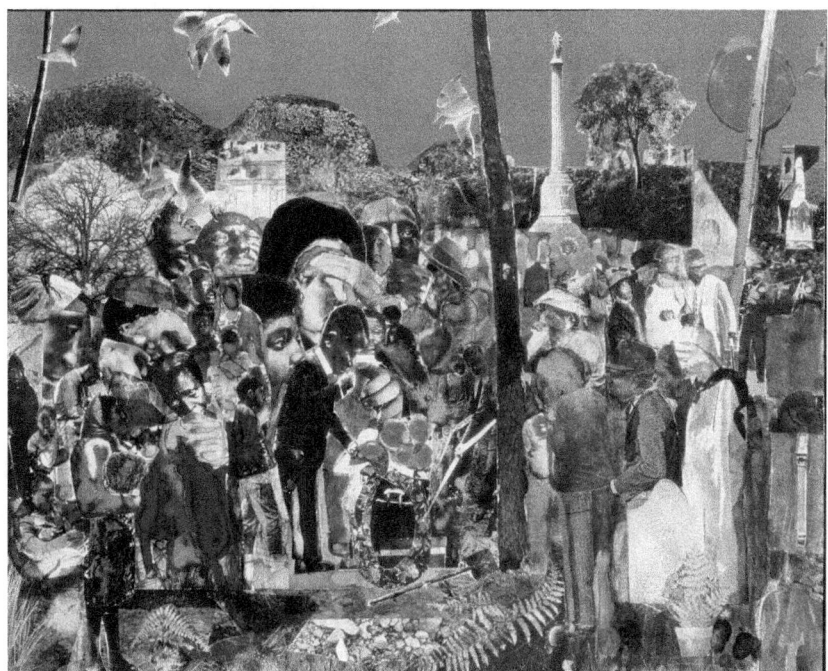

FIGURE 23 Romare Bearden, *Profile/Part I, The Twenties (Pittsburgh Memories): Farewell Eugene*, 1978. Collage of various papers with paint, ink, graphite, and bleached areas on fiberboard, 16 1/4 × 20 1/2 in. (41.3 × 52.1 cm). Laura Grosch and Herb Jackson. Art © Romare Bearden Foundation/Licensed by VAGA, New York

without letting on he was scared or stubborn or just plain didn't want to go. But off he went with Grandma and when she came back to our house, I sure was surprised to see she still got Eugene by the hand and he got a little plaid, cardboard suitcase and Grandma carrying his birdcage and Eugene stayed with us till he got sick and passed.

1927 when Eugene buried, Bearden says, and in 1978 I tried to pack all that Eugene story and Homewood, East Liberty, Pittsburgh story, the whole damned known world and probably the unknown too, Bearden smiles, in a 16¼" by 20½" collage pasted on board I titled *Farewell Eugene* (fig. 23). All those worlds as they appeared to me fifty years afterwards in my memories of how crowded a moment, a city, a boy's universe can be every single second if you teach yourself to look closely and practice patiently for a lifetime the skills of cutting and painting, gluing down textures, fabrics, colors, layer after layer to picture what the past might have been and how it rises again, solid and present as the bright orange disc of sun I put at the top right corner of *Farewell Eugene*.

Same sun shining almost red over Eugene's funeral one day fifty years ago with everybody on Earth in attendance or at least nobody missing who should be there. Eugene's friends, his people, mine, his pigeons, Grandma, me. We're all there in the collage, in the crowd back then and this time, too, if I got it close to right. All of us remembered, revived beneath an orange sun coloring the city, coloring bright flowers Eugene's pale mother holds. Same old sun, same old Pittsburgh, same old simple questions asking to be asked. The crowd of us then and now, living and dead saying our goodbyes, our hellos to Eugene. As many of us you could say as in the number religious thinkers in the Middle Ages used to bicker over if someone asked them how many angels fit on the point of a pin.

# ROMARE BEARDEN
## AFRICAN AMERICAN MODERNISM
## AT MID-CENTURY

*Kobena Mercer*

Romare Bearden's participation in the Spiral group was the catalyst for the *Photomontage Projections* he began in 1964. While individual works such as *Pittsburgh Memories* are widely appreciated as part of a distinctive contribution to postwar American art (fig. 24), it may be said that the significance of Bearden's collage practice has eluded deep interpretive understanding. Bringing a cultural studies approach to art historical and aesthetic concerns, this study sets out to examine the underlying montage principle of Bearden's work as a key turning point in African American modernism.

First identified by Ralph Ellison in his 1968 catalogue essay, "The Art of Romare Bearden," the montage principle of dialectical cut-and-mix has a broader significance in African American art history as it resonates with the assemblage art practiced by Betye Saar, David Hammons, and Noah Purifoy in the late 1960s. Drawing on Mikhail Bakhtin's concept of the dialogic imagination to examine the importance of collage in diaspora aesthetics, my aim is to elaborate upon Ellison's insight that "what is special about Bearden's achievement is . . . the way in which his technique has been used to discover and transfigure its object."[1] Bearden and Ellison enjoyed a close rapport throughout their lifelong conversation on the interplay of literary and visual strands in African American modernism. As well as stylistic affinities, they shared a similar generational background — Bearden was born in 1911 in Mecklenburg County, North

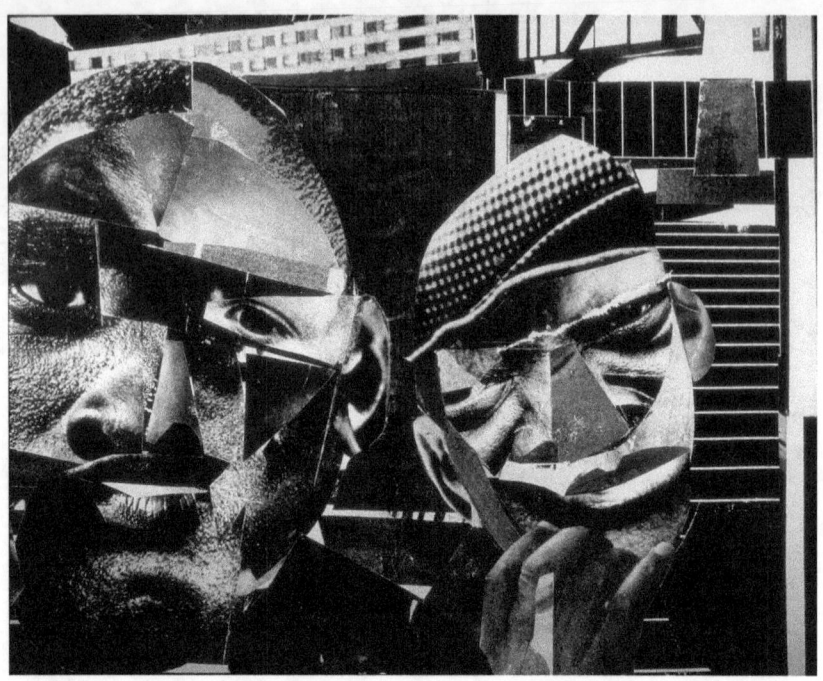

FIGURE 24  Romare Bearden, *Pittsburgh Memories*, 1964. Photomontage, 27 1/2 × 35 7/8 in.
(68.6 × 88.9 cm). Art © Romare Bearden Foundation/Licensed by VAGA, New York

Carolina, and Ellison was born in 1914 in Oklahoma City. After graduating
in the mid-1930s, each moved to New York City, and both participated in the
passionate debates on art and politics in the 1940s that formed the historical
backdrop to Ellison's classic novel, *Invisible Man* (1952).

Where Ellison got close to the "inner dialectical quality"[2] that animates
Bearden's collage, his insights shed light on the artist's struggle with the double-
binds of "race" and representation that underpinned what Bearden had called
the "Negro artist's dilemma." Working through aspects of this dilemma in the
vernacular realism of his early gouaches and then with his deepening interest
in post-Cubist pictorial space, Bearden found a synthesis in collage and photomontage that reconciled his commitments to the high modern ethos of individuality and complexity, on the one hand, and to the call-and-response ethos
in black American "folk" culture, on the other.

Sharing a mutual interest in what happens in the hyphen that articulates
African and American to form a distinctively composite identity, Bearden's

and Ellison's rapport was based on an implicit critique of realism in favor of a dialogical approach that sought to enter the inner world of black subjectivity so as to reveal its emotional, as well as social, realities. Hence, when Ellison states that "the true artist destroys the accepted world by way of revealing the unseen,"[3] I suggest that Bearden's dynamic fragmentation of pictorial space inscribes the creative presence of the "cut," which James Snead identified as a distinctive feature of diaspora aesthetics.[4] In contrast to the "folksy" humanism that characterizes prevalent interpretations of Bearden's work,[5] this reading seeks to restore the controlled negativity of the dialectical "cut" to the *Photomontage Projections*. Observing the Rabelaisean presence of the carnivalesque and the grotesque in Bearden's figurative vocabulary, in which the iconography of the "African" mask plays a presiding role, I suggest that a closer reading of his individual trajectory, from the 1940s to the 1960s, reopens a range of unresolved issues in the historiography of African American art.

Where successive generations encounter the "Negro artist's dilemma" in the form of an institutional double-bind that arose when ideologies of "race" were in conflict with the freedom of expression that was taken as axiomatic for modernism as a whole, criticism and scholarship repeatedly comes up against what Michele Wallace calls "the problem of the visual in Afro-American culture."[6] The problem was not simply that cultural difference was regarded, throughout most of the twentieth century, as something that had to be subordinated to modernism's core values of originality, individuality, and complexity, as immediate particularity is said to be subordinated to abstract universality, but that the visual index of "race" was itself based, as Frantz Fanon revealed,[7] on a symbolic code that made the optical realm of the gaze central to the politics of social recognition.

Looking at the Spiral moment in the context of the broad ruptures of the 1960s as a whole, this study identifies two issues that cast the "problem of the visual" into an altered light. One concerns the out-of-joint quality that arises in the uneven relationship between minority art histories and the big story of twentieth-century modernism, which I touch on by showing how Bearden's individual story personifies a wider, generational story about the mid-century shifts that resulted in the passage from late modern to postmodern. The other concerns an equally discrepant quality in the surrounding discourse whereby a rift often arises between what black artists are doing in the work and what intellectuals, advocates, and patrons seem to want them to be doing in society at large. These issues demand a critical revision of the modern art story that is able to enter into the dialogic spaces of the diaspora imagination. Understood as a place of "discrepant engagement,"[8] whose iconology remains unwritten, Bearden's art and Ellison's ekphrasis illuminate these hitherto unseen dimensions of hybrid modernity.

## UPTOWN LOOKING DOWNTOWN

Bearden's journey began at the tail end of the Harlem Renaissance in the late 1930s. Having graduated from New York University in 1936, while also enrolled at the Art Students League, he contributed editorial cartoons to such newspapers as the *Baltimore Afro-American*, and worked as a city welfare department caseworker from 1938 onward. His first studio was on West 125th Street, where Claude McKay was a neighbor, and his second was in the basement of the Apollo Building, shared with the photographers Morgan and Marvin Smith. Drawn toward the circle of artists who met at the 306 West 141st Street studio run by sculptor Henry Bannarn and painter Charles Alston, where his first exhibition was held in May 1940, Bearden had found a supportive environment. It was among the 306 group that he first met fellow painters Norman Lewis and Jacob Lawrence, and where he also crossed paths with Ralph Ellison, who had initially contemplated becoming a sculptor, having briefly studied with Richmond Barthé after leaving Tuskegee Institute.[9]

As the Pan-African imagery of the Harlem Renaissance gave way to scenes of rural Americana in the Depression era, Bearden was outspoken on issues of "race" among American art-world institutions. His viewpoint was informed by a strong interest in the wide-ranging debates on the "social responsibility of the artist" that arose against the background of the Popular Front platform announced at the 1935 Communist International, on the one hand, and the Federal Art Project of the Works Progress Administration, from 1939 to 1941, on the other. In dialogue with the views of Stuart Davis, who led the American Artists Congress (1935–36), as well as those of Augusta Savage, who formed the Harlem Arts Guild (1935–41) along similar lines, Bearden's approach was shaped by a dual commitment to the political imperatives of black representation and the expressive possibilities of modernist painting. Early paintings, such as *Cotton Workers* (1942), sought to reconcile artistic freedom and social responsibility by turning to the working-class "folk" cultures of the South, and such choices aligned Bearden with the vernacular realism embraced by Elizabeth Catlett (b. 1915), Charles White (b. 1918) and John Biggers (b. 1924). Where

White depicted a sharecropper's eviction in *Hear This* (1942), Bearden's *Rite of Spring* (1941–42) adopted a similar theme in its portrayal of a factory boss handing a termination notice to a despondent mother. The stylized distortion that characterizes the factory owner's exaggerated hands and massive face highlights an anti-naturalistic emphasis that was influenced by George Grosz, who was Bearden's tutor at the Art Students League. The influence of Diego Rivera and José Orozco further accentuated an internationalist outlook, which Bearden shared with Catlett, who had relocated to Mexico City in 1940, designing litho prints and posters at the Taller de Gráfica Popular.

In two important articles of this period — "The Negro Artist and Modern Art" (1934), published in *Opportunity*, the journal of the Urban League, and "The Negro Artist's Dilemma" (1946), published in *Critique*, the short-lived avant-garde journal — Bearden took a sharply critical view on the politics of "race" and representation.[10] Acknowledging the achievement of the 1920s, which lay in the recognition of black American expressive culture as an artistic subject and as a source of stylistic inspiration, he nonetheless rejected Alain Locke's ancestralist paradigm on the grounds that "to try and carry on in America where African sculpture left off would be to start on a false basis — the gap of the years, the environment, and ideology is too great."[11]

Where the 1934 article was critical of the "timidity of the Negro artist" and the distorted self-perception whereby minorities felt they had to emulate outmoded models of academic competence, it expressed Bearden's view that modernism and the African American vernacular were not mutually incompatible. From his opening premise that "the post-Impressionists, the Cubists, the Futurists, and hosts of other movements . . . are commendable in the fact that they substituted for mere photographic realism, a search for inner truths"[12] to his conclusion that the "Negro artist . . . must not be content with merely recording a scene as a machine. He must enter wholeheartedly into the situation he wishes to convey,"[13] the argument highlighted Bearden's immersive commitment to a vernacular realism in which expressive standpoint took precedence over the duty of depiction that was implicitly assigned to black artists on account of "race."

Indeed, the 1946 essay pinpointed insidious pressures created by three prevalent assumptions, namely: "1. The Negro should continue, or at least simulate, the traditions of African art. 2. The Negro artist should attempt a unique, nationalistic, social expression closely akin in feeling to jazz music and the spirituals . . . 3. The Negro's art should be a trenchant reflection of his social and political aspirations."[14] The burden of critique was directed toward what Bearden saw as an implicit double standard in the reception of black artists. Between 1926 and 1933 the Harmon Foundation's annual awards, Distinguished Achievement among Negroes, had played a major role in providing exhibition opportunities for the 1920s generation, but its philanthropic agenda compounded the perception of "Negro art" as "peculiarly backward"[15] in its relationship to modern art as a whole. Highly critical of such double standards, Bearden's view was that "the attitude of the Foundation towards Negro artists was patronizing; it firmly established the pattern of segregated exhibits [and] it fostered artificial and arbitrary artistic standards, stemming from a sociological rather than aesthetic interest in the exhibitors' works."[16] To the extent that Bearden's position was framed by a broad historical understanding of the political character of the relations of "race" and representation, his awareness of a struggle for access into art-world institutions aligned him with the hard-won insights of earlier generations. After reviewing nineteenth-century stereotypes in American art, his assertion that "it is the privilege of the oppressor to depict the oppressed"[17] echoed with the analysis put forward by W. E. B. Du Bois in "Criteria of Negro Art."[18] From his starting point that "the Negro, aside from his folk expressions, is a latecomer into the visual arts,"[19] his account overlapped with the historical survey that Alain Locke had curated in *The Negro in Art: A Pictorial Record of the Negro Artist and of the Negro Theme in Art.*[20] Although Bearden had questioned Locke's initial embrace of modernist primitivism, both shared the view that "culture is not a biologically inherited phenomenon."[21] Hence, Bearden's view that "the Negro is part of the *amalgam* of American life,"[22] actually confirmed Locke's later position, which re-accentuated the nineteenth-century term "amalgamation" so as to stress the hyphenated character of American Negro identity. Concluding his 1942 review entitled "Who or What Is 'Negro'?", Locke declared: "There is, in brief, no 'The Negro,'" for where "we stress the dominant flavor of the blend [it] is only in this same limited sense that anything is legitimately styled 'Negro'; actually it is Afro- or Negro-American, a hybrid product of Negro reaction to American cultural forms and patterns."[23] Hence, as he put it in his motto for black Atlantic modernity: "To be Negro . . . is to be distinctively composite."[24]

It was precisely this multi-accentual approach to the composite realities of African American life that Ellison picked up on and pinpointed as the locus of Bearden's distinctive stylistic signature when he wrote:

> During the late thirties when I first became aware of Bearden's work, he was
> painting scenes of the Depression in a style strongly influenced by the Mexican

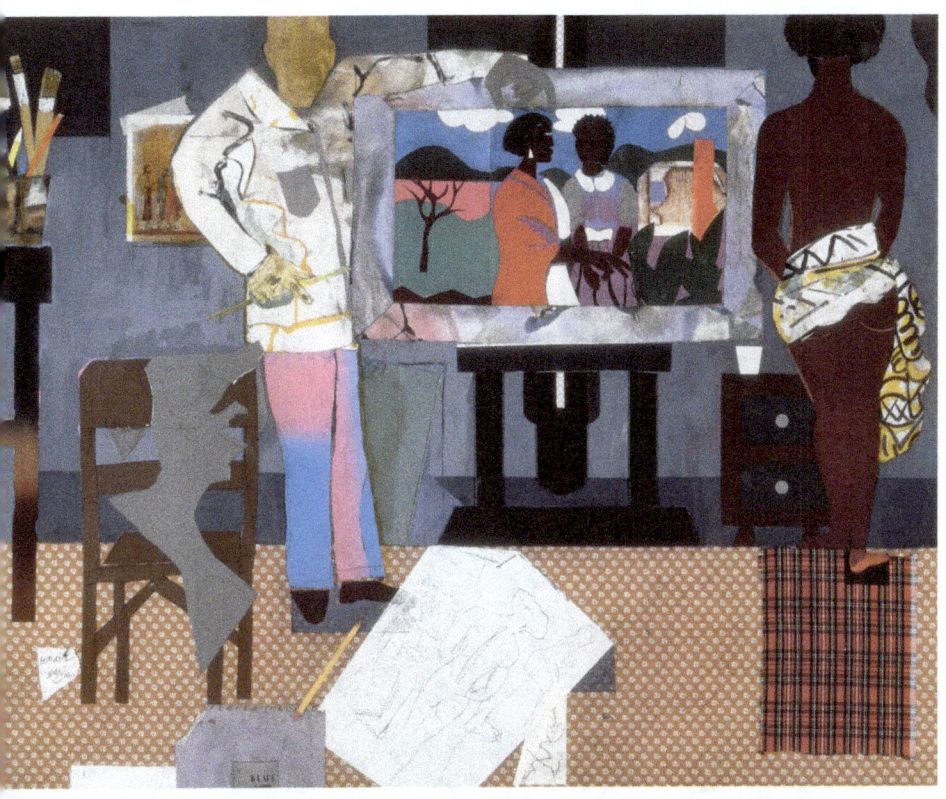

PLATE 1 Romare Bearden, *Profile/Part II, The Thirties: Artist with Painting and Model*, 1981. Collage on board, 44 × 56 in. (112 × 142.2 cm). High Museum of Art, Atlanta (2014.66). Art © Romare Bearden Foundation/Licensed by VAGA, New York

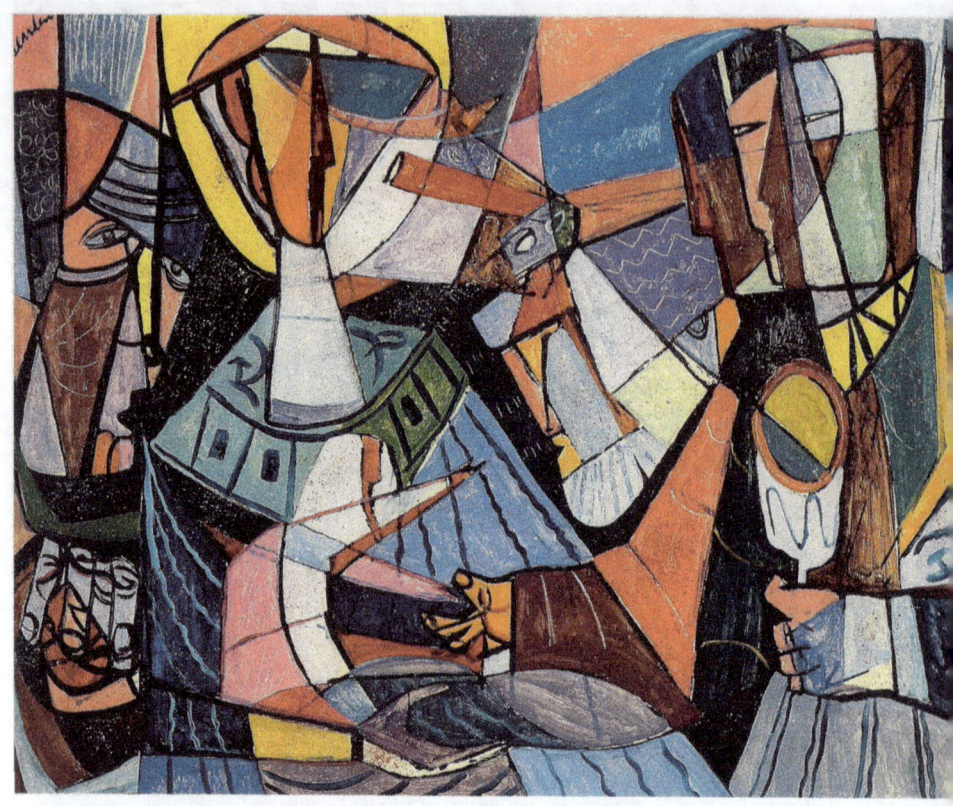

PLATE 2  Romare Bearden, *Adoration of the Wise Men*, 1945. Oil on Masonite, 24.5 × 30.5 in. (62.2 × 77.5 cm). Newark Museum, Gift of Mr. and Mrs. Benjamin E. Tepper, 1946 (46.164). Art © Romare Bearden Foundation/Licensed by VAGA, New York

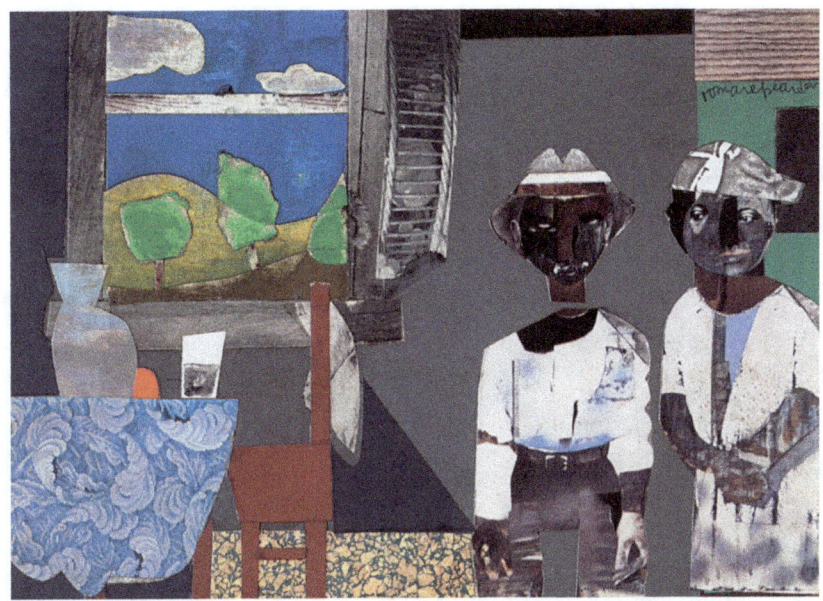

PLATE 3  Romare Bearden, *The Old Couple*, 1967. Montage painting, 30 × 40 in. (76.2 × 101.6 cm). Art © Romare Bearden Foundation/Licensed by VAGA, New York

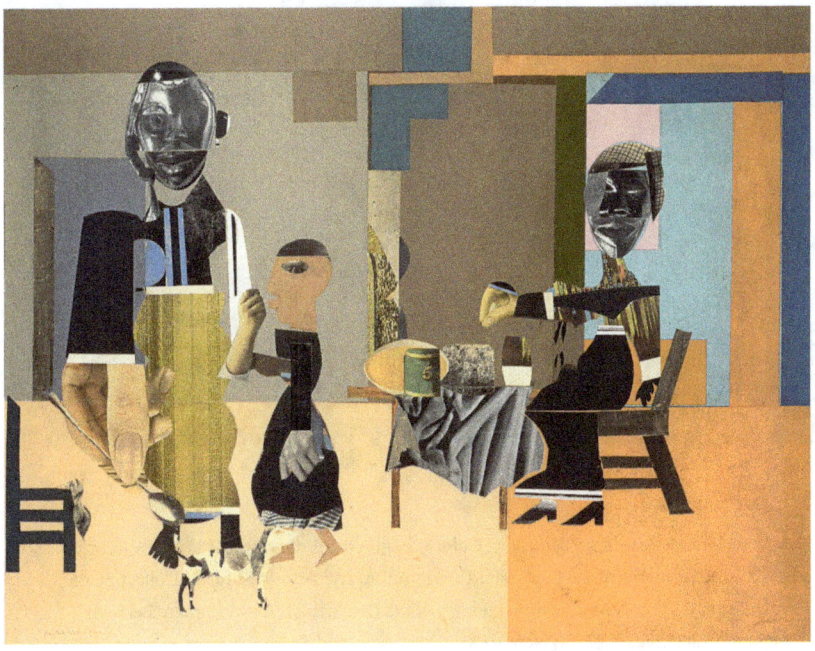

PLATE 4  Romare Bearden, *Illusionists at 4 PM*, 1967. Collage on board, 30 × 40 in. (76.2 × 101.6 cm). Collection of halley k Harrisburg and Michael Rosenfeld. Art © Romare Bearden Foundation/Licensed by VAGA, New York

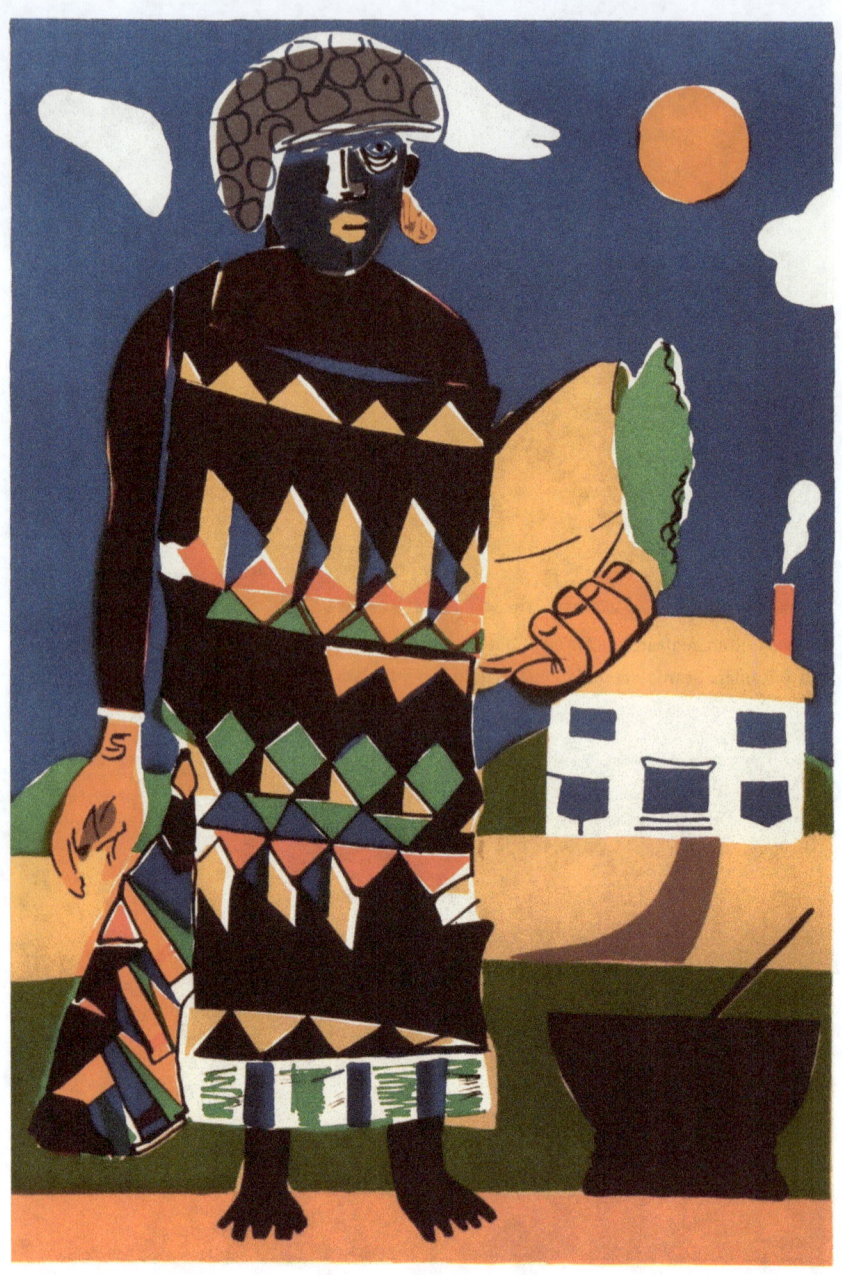

PLATE 5  Romare Bearden, *Pilate*, 1979. Color lithograph, ed. 7/25, 26 × 15 in. (66 × 38.1 cm). Pennsylvania Academy of the Fine Arts, The Harold A. and Ann R. Sorgenti Collection of Contemporary African-American Art, Philadelphia (2004.20.3). Art © Romare Bearden Foundation/Licensed by VAGA, New York

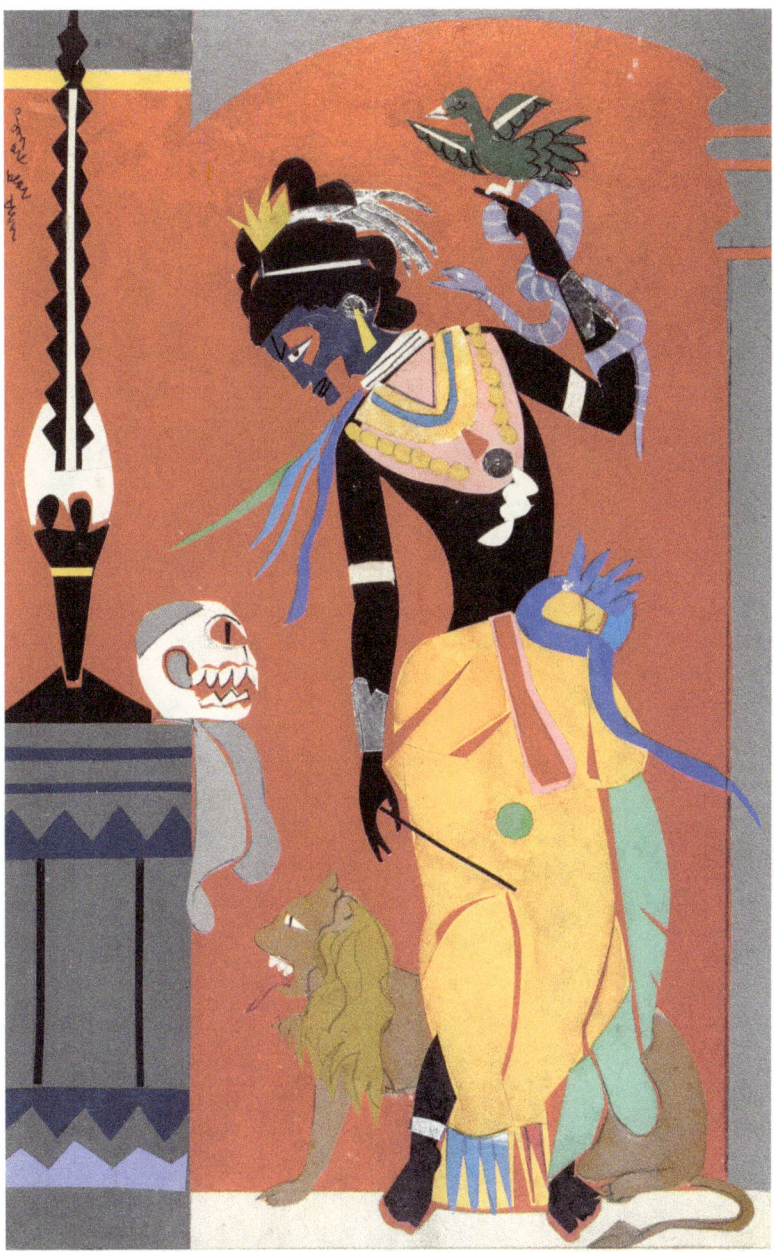

PLATE 6  Romare Bearden. *Untitled* ("*Black Circe*"), 1977. Collage on board, 15 × 9 3/8 in. (38.1 × 23.8 cm). Art © Romare Bearden Foundation/Licensed by VAGA, New York

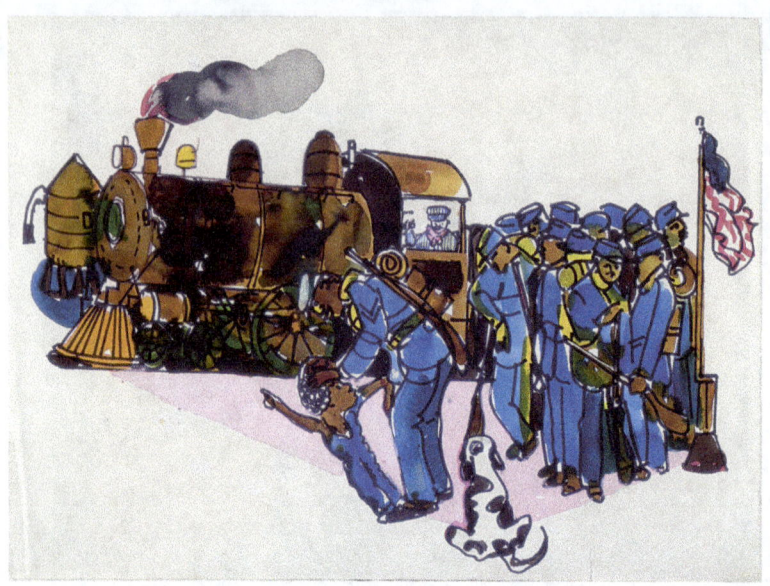

PLATE 7 Scipio tells L'il Dan, "Be brave, you're the mascot now for Company E," 1983. Watercolor illustration for *L'il Dan the Drummer Boy: A Civil War Story* (New York: Simon & Schuster, 2003). Art © Romare Bearden Foundation/Licensed by VAGA, New York

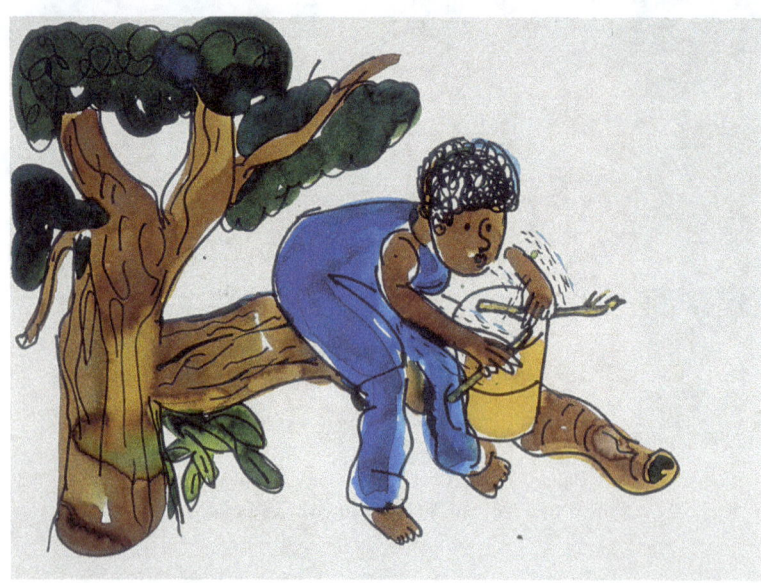

PLATE 8 L'il Dan improvises with sticks to mimic the sound of cannon fire, 1983. Watercolor illustration for *L'il Dan the Drummer Boy: A Civil War Story* (New York: Simon & Schuster, 2003). Art © Romare Bearden Foundation/Licensed by VAGA, New York

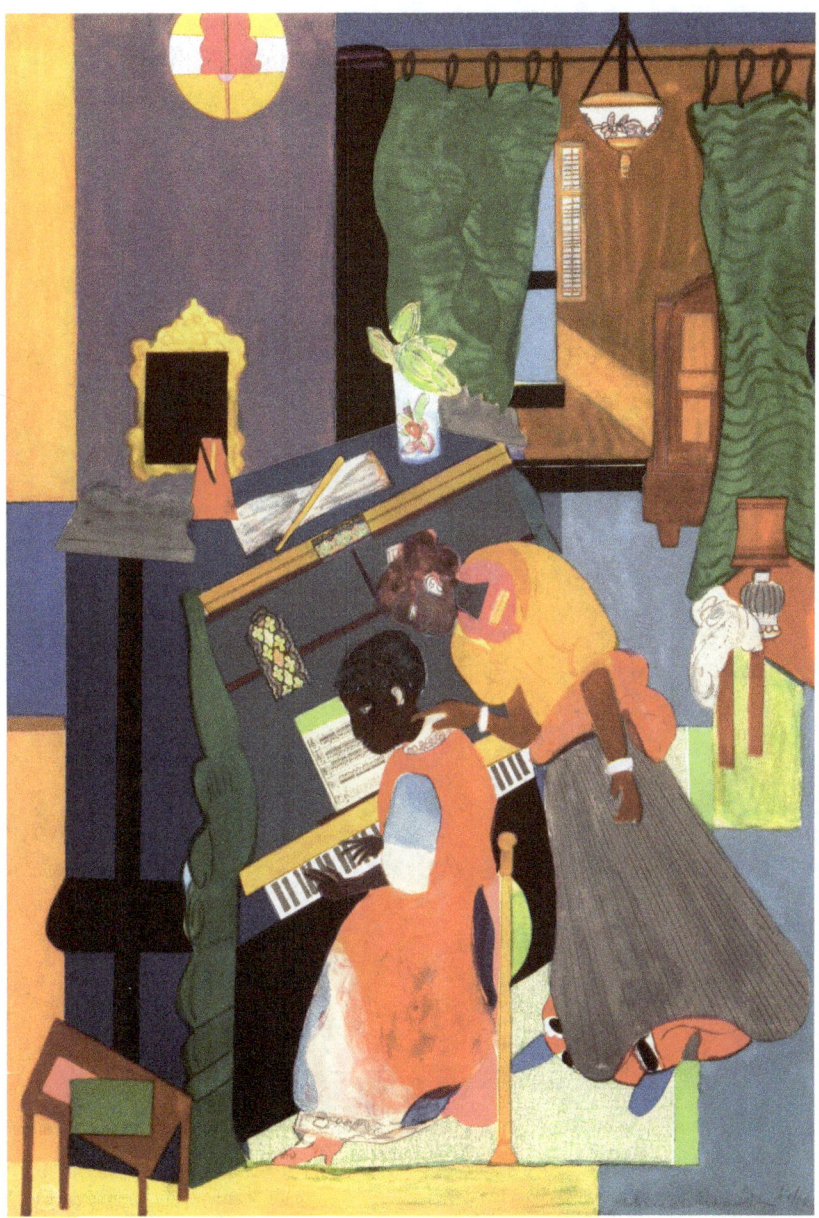

PLATE 9  Romare Bearden, *Homage to Mary Lou*, 1984. Color lithograph, 29 1/2 × 20 1/2 in. (74.93 × 52.07 cm). Pennsylvania Academy of the Fine Arts, The Harold A. and Ann R. Sorgeni Collection of Contemporary African-American Art, Philadelphia (1999.17.1). Art © Romare Bearden Foundation/Licensed by VAGA, New York

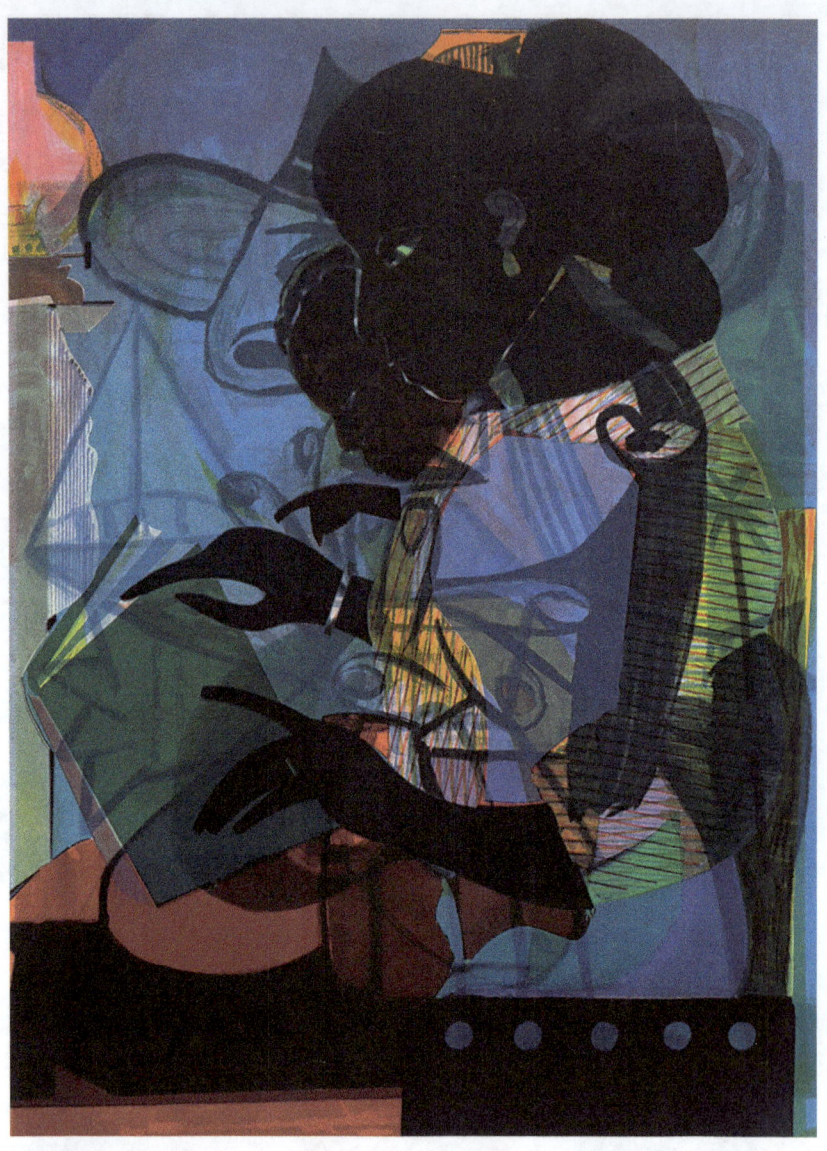

PLATE 10  Romare Bearden, *Woman and Child Reading*, ca. 1984, unique lithograph on paper. Collection of Professor and Mrs. David C. Driskell. Art © Romare Bearden Foundation/Licensed by VAGA, New York

muralists. This work was powerful, the scenes grim and brooding, and through his depiction of unemployed workingmen in Harlem he was able, while evoking the Southern past, to move beyond the usual protest painting of the period to reveal something of the universal elements of an abiding human condition. By striving to depict the times, but reducing scene, character, and atmosphere to a style, he caught something of both the universality of Harlem life and the "harlemness" of the national human predicament.[25]

Before we open up Ellison's trope of chiasmus, or doubling, which has important implications for grasping the "double knot" of Bearden's style, as it were, it is crucial to take account of Bearden's passage through the mid- to late 1940s and to understand the double-binds he was obliged to negotiate with the advent of Abstract Expressionism.

During the period between 1944 and 1947, when he was represented by Samuel Kootz Gallery on East 57th Street, following solo exhibitions such as *The Passion of Christ* (1945) at Caresse Crosby's G Place Gallery in Washington, D.C., Bearden sought to resolve the dilemmas he had previously identified by turning to literary sources. Taking inspiration from García Lorca's *Lament for a Bullfighter* for a 1946 solo exhibition of watercolors and oils, he followed it with another series, including *Poor Thirsty Souls* and *Some Drink! Some Drink!* (1946), inspired by Rabelais's *Gargantua and Pantagruel* which was in turn followed by a series based on *The Iliad*. Some individual pieces from each of these series featured in the Whitney Annual exhibitions of 1945 to 1947 and *He Is Arisen* (1945) was purchased by the Museum of Modern Art.

Bearden's narrative choices may be read as an effort to reconcile the perceived particularity of the black vernacular with the universalist values arrogated by modernism. Rabelais and Lorca, who evoked the Old World "folk" cultures of the European peasantry and popular classes, were aligned with Bearden's passion for Goya's *Disasters of War* which he viewed in the 1946 essay, against the propagandistic or sentimental pitfalls of mere protest, as an exemplary articulation of art and politics. His interest in tragedy would also account for the selection of those moments of biblical narrative, namely the Crucifixion and Resurrection, central to the black Protestant church. Finally, such works as *Blues Has Got Me* (1946), contributed to a group show at Kootz entitled *Homage to Jazz*, indicated both the dialogue that Bearden was striving for as well as the fresh dilemmas that arose with the shift from figurative to abstract expressionism.

Placed at the Kootz gallery alongside Adolph Gottlieb, Robert Motherwell, William Baziotes, Carl Holty, and Byron Browne, Bearden's uptown-to-downtown journey had much in common with other African American artists of his generation. Between 1941 and 1953 Jacob Lawrence had six solo exhibitions at Edith Halpert's Downtown Gallery, which also held exhibitions by Horace Pippin; William Henry Johnson had shows at the Wakefield Galleries in 1943 and 1944 during Betty Parsons's tenure; and Norman Lewis was represented by Marian Willard from 1946 to 1964.[26] What happened next, however, serves to reveal the inadequacy of the exclusion/inclusion couplet in accounting for the historical interaction between African American artists and the institutions of metropolitan modernism. In 1946 Samuel Kootz organized a touring exhibition with sponsorship from the United States Information Service entitled "Advancing American Art." Although intended to demonstrate modern art's migration to postwar New York, when the show arrived in Paris and was derided as retardataire rather than avant-garde, the response precipitated the closure of Kootz's gallery in July 1948. When Kootz reopened in September 1949, with a new roster of artists that included Willem de Kooning, Mark Rothko, and Jackson Pollock, Bearden found that, like Byron Browne and Carl Holty, he had been dropped. Responding to the displacement by withdrawing from painting, Bearden took a nine-month study leave in Paris, but even after his return to New York in 1952 he experienced a crisis of confidence that persisted until the early 1960s.

Looking back on that period, Bearden recalled: "I had two worlds, two different polarities: the blues up here, the downtown scene there with Kootz. At some point this had to coalesce."[27] But it didn't. Or rather, it was not until the popular ruptures of the 1960s that the cultural and political conditions were created for such a coalescence. Hence, although Ellison was keenly aware of the double-binds that black artists were placed in as a result of opting for representational realism, he overlooked the twist to the "Negro artist's dilemma" that arose during the heyday of American abstraction. Observing that the black artist "feels an irremediable conflict between his identity as a member of an embattled social minority and his freedom as an artist,"[28] Ellison was excoriating in his view of the 1940s generation, for he argued that: "while many are convinced that simply to recognize social imbalance is enough to put it to riot, few achieve anything like artistic mastery, and most fail miserably through a single-minded effort to 'tell it like it is.'"[29] Adding that the "highest praise and admiration" was won by "those who have offered an answer to the question — ever crucial in the lives of a repressed minority — of who and what they are in the most simplified and graphic terms,"[30] which may be understood as an allusion to Jacob Lawrence, Ellison's voluntarist emphasis nonetheless underplays the structural conditions of monocultural consensus that conditioned individual choices during the still-segregated era of the 1950s.

Ann Gibson points out that the inclusion at the center of such artists as Charles Alston, Hale Woodruff, and Norman Lewis — who participated in the Artist's Sessions at Studio 35 — did not preempt the perception of their work as marginal.[31] Where action painting exalted bebop improvisation as a generative analogue for the spontaneous gestural stroke, musical antiphony was understood as a call-and-response patter in which "no single instrumentalist established absolute dominance"[32] over the composition: yet in the drive toward painterly purity that led, say, from Piet Mondrian's *Broadway Boogie Woogie* (1942) to Franz Kline's *Dahlia* (1959), for example, such works as Norman Lewis's *Jazz Musicians* (1948) or Charles Alston's *Blues Singer I* (1952) were seen as manifestations of stylistic centrism. Forms of directed abstraction that retained referential signification were seen to stop short of high modernist values which held that "expressionistic brushwork was an authentic index of an artist's emotional honesty."[33] Hence African American artists who also practiced stylistic variation within their work were seen to betray "a lack of sincerity or conviction."[34] On the other hand, as Bearden himself put it in a 1980 interview: "For me, the trouble is the word 'abstract.' . . . A lot of these painters painted with jazz sounds filling their studios . . . *Now I was lost in this* . . . At my studio in the Apollo I found the music more interesting, and although I couldn't see any painterly equivalent at the time, I did try some experiments with Holty in the use of color — that it sometimes broke open the picture for me — that it seemed to run away and not stay on the canvas. So I just began to work in bigger chords of color. . . . Then just as the color was getting away from me, so did painting as a whole. Like the surveyor of Kafka's Castle, it always seemed to elude me."[35] To the extent that visual studies might seek to explain the conflicted inclusion of black artists in the 1950s by examining the discursive valence of "folk art" in the nascent hegemony of American art-world institutions as formations of both a national and international culture of modern art, it would do well to take account of Gibson's insights into the prevailing sublation of cultural difference during this period. Gibson relays a telling anecdote in which "Sculptor Philip Pavia recalls Hale Woodruff as being a friend of Ad Reinhardt's, a paying member of the Club, and a good painter. . . . 'One night we had a minstrel show,' said Pavia, '[Woodruff] didn't like it, and he complained to me about it. He didn't like the idea of jazz as folk art, either,' adding, 'We didn't have any color prejudice . . . I don't think he liked us very much, but we liked him.'"[36] During his final days at Kootz, Bearden contributed to a limited edition publication entitled *Women: A Collaboration of Artists and Writers* (1948), and in it, as Gibson reveals, the author of the text, William Carlos Williams, wrote: "because Bearden was a Negro, he could understand Woman, because he alone among men resembles her."[37] Such underlying equivalences confound the view that antimimetic or nonrepresentational practices somehow transcend the social inscription of difference in the optical realm.

Turning now to Spiral's 1960s moment, I shall echo Ralph Ellison's question — "How then does an artist passionately concerned with solving the more advanced problems of painting *as painting* address himself to the task (never so urgent as now) of defining Negro American identity, of its pressing claims for recognition and for justice?"[38] — to suggest that the answer Bearden discovered in the montage principle was a dialogic mode of double voicing which would loosen and undo the double-binds of "race" and representation that had created the impasse of the "Negro artist's dilemma."

## SPIRAL AND THE CUT

Following the 1963 March on Washington, union leader A. Philip Randolph called for a meeting with Bearden and Woodruff, asking how artists might respond to the Civil Rights movement.[39] The Spiral group held its first meeting on 5 July 1963 at Bearden's Canal Street loft. "As a symbol for the group, we chose spiral," said Woodruff, "a particular kind of spiral, the Archimedean one: because, from a starting point, it moves outwards embracing all directions, yet constantly upward."[40]

With Alston and Lewis from the Studio 306 era alongside younger artists such as Reginald Gammon (b. 1921), William Majors (b. 1930), Richard Mayhew (b. 1934), and Emma Amos (b. 1938), Spiral's cross-generational composition underlined its ambition to combine artistic freedom and political commitment. Having leased a gallery at 147 Christopher Street with a view to a group homage to slain Civil Rights activists in the South, which was to have been entitled *Mississippi 1964*, members were wary of the potential misperception of the initiative as mere documentary or protest. In the ensuing debate, an alternative idea was adopted in which it was proposed that works would be produced within the stricture of a monochrome palette. Hence, during its brief existence from 1963 to 1965, Spiral staged its first and only exhibition, *Black and White*.

Emma Amos recalled that Bearden arrived one evening with "an enormous picture file, all cut out in shapes and stuffed in a bag. He brought it to the Spiral meeting place on Christopher Street and spread it out on the floor, suggesting that we make a collaborative piece."[41] Although Amos and Mayhew joined in, with a view to making a mural along the lines of Picasso's *Guernica*, Bearden's idea for a collective collage proved unworkable and was subsequently dropped.

*Black and White* featured paintings directly inspired by the March on Washington, such as Reginald Gammon's *Freedom Now* (1965), based on a press photo by Moneta Sleet, Jr.; and Norman Lewis's *Processional* (1965), an abstract work whose diagonal thrust vividly evoked the era's optimism in a coalitional politics of progressive movement, a theme previously portrayed in Charles Alston's *Walking* (1958). As the setting in which the *Photomontage Projections* were first exhibited, *Black and White* not only provided the catalytic context for Bearden's individual breakthrough, but marked the turn to collage aesthetics as a decisive shift among African American artists of the 1960s as a whole. Forming the basis of Bearden's first museum retrospective at the Corcoran Gallery of Art in 1965, the twenty-one Projections also featured in the 1968 *Paintings and Projections* exhibition, which was the occasion for Ellison's insightful ekphrasis. Illuminating the dialectics of negation and affirmation at play in the work, he reveals how montage creates a hyphenated interval between painting and photography. Ellison recognized that what Bearden broke through was the impasse whereby the black artist's burden of representing the race was at odds with the modernist ideal of expressive freedom, which had liberated modern art from the duty of depiction. His trope of chiasmus thus offers a guiding thread into the work's labyrinthine mise-en-scène, for to catch "something of the universality of Harlem life and the 'harlemness' of the national human predicament," is to subvert the absolute "either/or" dichotomy that Fanon identified in the "Manichean delirium" installed into the visual by the optical polarities of the gaze.[42] Such doubling breaks open the closed or saturated codes of "race" as a representational problem that once equated the universal and the particular with the arbitrary signs of skin, blood, and bone and brings a "both/and" logic of hybrid inventiveness into the mix.

Bearden spoke of "arriving at the space" when asked about the subject matter of the Projections: "A lot of the life that I knew in certain rural Negro communities is passing, and I set down some of my impressions of that life," he said.[43] Beyond the biographical enclosure that has often limited previous interpretation, once we observe how Bearden's iconography roams and shuttles across urban and rural spaces, often enjoined by the motif of the train, we get closer to the dynamic relationship between his "cubist techniques"[44] and the photographic material he took as found. Cutting and pasting images that were literally torn out of such magazines as *Life, Ebony,* and *Ladies' Home Journal* onto small 8-by-11-inch Masonite boards, Bearden employed dechirage and papier collé, which he had been quietly experimenting with since the late 1950s, to underline the cut or the paper tear as both a stylistic signature and a mark of critical discrepancy between different regimes of representation.

"Suggesting some of the possibilities through which commonplace materials could be forced to undergo a creative metamorphosis when manipulated by . . . non-representational techniques," writes Ellison, "he has sought to reveal a world long hidden by the clichés of sociology and rendered cloudy by the distortions of newsprint and the false continuity imposed on our conception of Negro life by television and much documentary photography."[45] *The Street* (see fig. 7) and *The Dove* (see fig. 6) imply a highly motivated choice of scene, for where Aaron Siskind's candid reportage of the 1930s, for example, had indeed become a cliché of postwar photojournalism, the problem-oriented depiction of the "ghetto" had saturated the genre with connotations of poverty, injustice, and despair. Whereas Archibald Motley's *Black Belt* (1934) had performed an unstable inversion of Edward Burra's *Harlem* (1934) by substituting values of community and conviviality into the contested space of the street, Bearden's disarticulation of photographic realism was all the more subversive in its implication that social reality is itself composite and contradictory. "A harsh beauty . . . asserts itself out of the horrible fragmentation which Bearden's subjects and their environment have undergone,"[46] says Ellison, who adds: "Where any number of painters have tried to project the 'prose' of Harlem — a task performed more successfully by photographers — Bearden has concentrated on releasing its poetry, its abiding rituals and ceremonies of affirmation, creating a surreal poetry compounded of vitality and powerlessness, destructive impulse and enduring faith."[47] The mural-like scale of the works further highlights Bearden's oblique, rather than oppositional, relationship to photography. Taking up Gammons's suggestion to enlarge the original paper collages to a scale of 3 by 4 or 6 by 8 feet by means of the photostat process, which rendered a continuous monochrome surface in keeping with Spiral's black-and-white proposal, such photo-

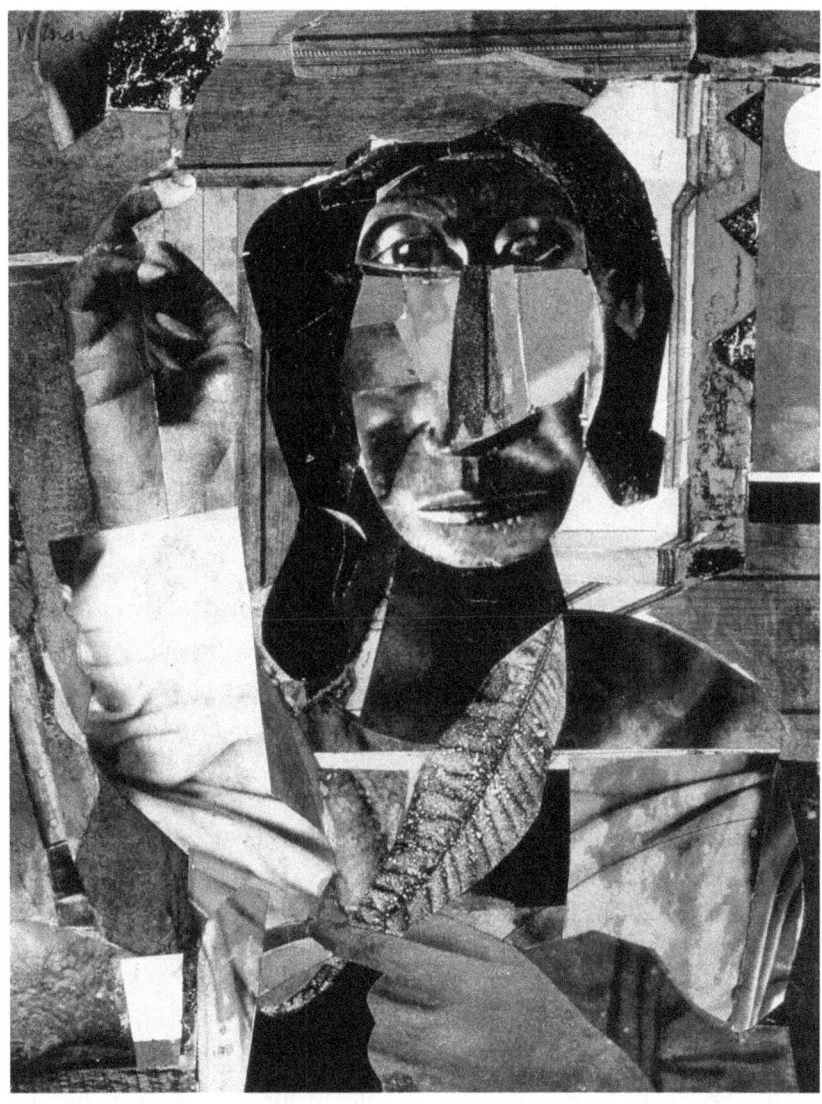

FIGURE 25  Romare Bearden, *Prevalence of Ritual: Conjur Woman*, 1964. Collage of various papers with foil, ink, and graphite on cardboard, 9 3/8 × 7 1/4 in. (23.8 × 18.4 cm). Art © Romare Bearden Foundation/Licensed by VAGA, New York

mechanical translation elevated the small, box-like "masters" into the realm of history painting, while also lending them to mass reproduction where they continue to circulate in the form of posters and prints.

Secondly, with regards to the figurative vocabulary of "mask-faced Harlemites and tenant farmers"[48] we find across *Mysteries* or *Conjur Woman* (fig. 25), for example, Ellison's emphasis is on the synthetic moment of re-assemblage, whereby the photographic fragments that Bearden pulled out of his sources are cancelled out and yet legibly preserved in their rearticulation "as signs and symbols of a humanity that has struggled to survive the fragmentizing effects of American social processes."[49] As he continues: "Through this creative assemblage . . . his Harlem becomes a place inhabited by people who have in fact been *resurrected*, re-created by art, a place . . . where the sacred and profane, reality and dream are ambiguously mingled. And resurrected with them in the guise of fragmented ancestral figures and forgotten gods (really masks of the instincts, hopes, emotions, aspirations and dreams) are those powers that now surge in our land with a potentially destructive force which springs from the very fact of their having for so long gone unrecognized, unseen."[50] Where social relations of "race" and representation overdetermined portraiture as one of the most saturated genres in which depictions of the ex-African face and body were remorselessly subjected to the iron mask of the stereotype, Ellison's insights are to be offset against a reception context in which Dore Ashton found Bearden's figures to be "accusing," and in which Robert Hughes merely perceived "crowded figures, shouting . . . *Here I am! Notice me!*"[51] On the contrary, Ellison's repeated evocation of the Fanonian trope of the mask draws attention to the inner realities whereby "faces which draw on the abstract character of African sculpture for their composition are made to focus our attention on the far from abstract reality of a people. Here abstract interiors are presented in which concrete life is acted out under repressive conditions."[52] Although Ellison overlooks the stylistic exaggeration Bearden gives to human hands — itself a legacy from the 1930s, where it was appropriated from socialist realism's concern with the dignity of manual labor — he insightfully observes that "these works give plastic expression to a vision in which the socially grotesque conceals a tragic beauty."[53] Adumbrating his conclusion that the Projections "embody Bearden's interrogation of the empirical values of a society that mocks its own ideals through a blindness induced by the myth of race,"[54] I must end with some remarks about the dialogic role of the cut in Bearden's dialectical photomontage.

Far removed from Alain Locke's idiom of "amalgamation," and much closer to the dicey pluralism that characterized Albert Murray's sociological overview in *The Omni-Americans*,[55] Ellison nonetheless points to an interactive space of antiphony as the very setting in which Bearden's collage principle activated a restlessly interrogative dialogue with the cornerstones of the European canon. "He has used the discoveries of Giotto and de Hooch no less than those of Juan Gris, Picasso, Schwitters, and Mondrian ... and has discovered his own uses for the metaphysical richness of African sculptural forms," wrote Ellison in yet another chiastic fold of double-consciousness; "In brief, Bearden has used (and most playfully) all of his artistic knowledge and skill to create *a curve of plastic vision* which reveals to us something of the mysterious complexity of those who dwell in our urban slums."[56] It is exactly this "curve of plastic vision" that slices through Bearden's storytelling picture space, as curator Lowery Stokes Sims observes.[57] When Ellison ends by saying, "Bearden's meaning is identical with his method. His combination of technique is in itself eloquent of the sharp breaks, leaps in consciousness, distortions, paradoxes, reversals, telescoping of time, and surreal blending of styles, values, hopes and dreams which character-ize much of Negro American history,"[58] such insight calls out to the aleatory conception of "the cut" that James Snead briefly sketched in "Repetition as a Figure of Black Culture." Engaging with Hegel's view of history as develop-mental rather than cyclical, Snead argued that, where "European culture does not allow 'a succession of accidents and surprises' but instead maintains the illusions of progression and control at all costs ... Black culture, in the 'cut,' builds 'accidents' into its coverage, almost as if to control their unpredictabil-ity. ... [T]his magic of the 'cut' attempts to confront accident and rupture not by covering them over but by making room for them inside the system itself."[59] Moving through music, dance, and language to describe what the "cut" does in folk song, in sermon, and in jazz improvisation, Snead saw a strange affin-ity between Freud's notion of repetition compulsion and the way in which "in black culture, the thing (the ritual, the dance, the beat) is 'there for you to pick it up when you come back to get it.' If there is a goal in such a culture, it is always deferred."[60]

If it is by virtue of such cultural deferral or difference that blackness falls behind the beat, into the place of the "syncope" where punctual meter goes missing in the rhythm, then I suggest that what Bearden's *Photomontage Projec-tions* did, in their double-voiced dialogue between the compositional elements of line, plane and color in post-Cubist pictorial space and the heterogeneous cuts and folds of diaspora subjectivity, was to issue a "coupre" or break to the boundary that once separated African and American as if they were mutually exclusive identities. "It's the spacing of what you leave out that makes what is *in* there," said Bearden. "A good illustration is the Greek vase . . . The spaces between these Attic figures counted even more than the figures themselves. It was one of the few art forms in which not just the figures, but I want to say the components, seem to be torn apart. What holds it all together is that the spacing between the various elements seems to be more important than the figures or objects themselves."[61] Interspersed with his memories of conversations with Stuart Davis about the role of the interval in the music of Earl Hines, these remarks confirm the point that the thing is there for you to pick up when you come back to get it, for we should also know that the photostat apparatus was already there during the 1940s, when Bearden enlarged textbook reproductions to conduct his own compositional analyses of ancient ceramics, European paintings, Chinese landscapes, and much else besides.[62] Continuing the conversation on the analysis of picture-making space via correspondence with Carl Holty, what resulted was *The Painter's Mind*, a coauthored book published in 1969.[63]

By way of coda: Bearing in mind the highly volatile climate of the times, Spiral's outlook was rapidly overshadowed by the Black Arts movement, which saw the emergence of such artists' groups as Africobra, formed in 1968 in Chicago by Jeff Donaldson and others, and the Black Emergency Cultural Coalition, formed by Benny Andrews in New York in 1969. From his apparently conservative-liberal late-modern standpoint, Ellison was implicitly writing against the grain of such voices as those of Amiri Baraka, Ron Karenga, and Larry Neal, who espoused what Addison Gayle called "the black aesthetic."[64] The paradox was not merely that, in its populist demand for identifying black content, the Black Arts movement was merely repeating the Popular Front demand for social realism, but that, more broadly, in its highly didactic tone, the essentialist discourse of the black cultural nationalists was compulsively repeating the three prescriptive pressures Bearden had pinpointed in 1946, namely that black artists "should continue the traditions of African art . . . should attempt a unique, nationalistic, social expression . . . should [provide] a trenchant reflection of [his] political aspirations." As Bakhtin had put it, and as Bearden worked it through, substituting "image" for "word," as it were, when he realized that the inner dialectical quality of the sign comes out fully into the open in times of social upheaval, as it did in the 1960s: "The word is language as half someone else's. It becomes one's own . . . only when the speaker appropriates the word, adapting it to his own semantic and expressive intention. Prior to this moment of appropriation the word does not exist in a neutral or impersonal language . . . rather it exists in other people's mouths, serving other people's intentions: it is from there that one must take the word and make it one's own."[65]

## NOTES

From Michael Ann Holly and Keith P. R. Moxey, eds., *Art History, Aesthetics, Visual Studies* (Williamstown, MA: Sterling and Francine Clark Art Institute, 2002).

1. Ralph Ellison, "Introduction," in *Romare Bearden: Paintings and Projections*, exh. cat. (Albany: The Art Gallery, State University of New York, 1968), reprinted as "The Art of Romare Bearden," in *Going to the Territory* (New York: Random House, 1986), 221; see full text in this volume, pp. 196–203. On Bearden's and Ellison's dialogue, see Paul Rogers, "Ralph Ellison, the Collages of Romare Bearden and Race: Some Speculations," *International Review of African American Art* 10, no. 3 (1994): 7–10.

2. V. N. Volosinov, *Marxism and the Philosophy of Language* (1929; reprint, Cambridge, MA: Harvard University Press, 1973), 23.

3. Ellison, "The Art of Romare Bearden," 234.

4. James Snead, "Repetition as a Figure in Black Culture" in *Black Literature and Literary Theory*, ed. Henry Louis Gates, Jr. (New York: Methuen, 1984), 59–79.

5. Kinshasha Holman Conwill, Mary Schmidt Campbell, and Sharon F. Patton, eds., *Memory and Metaphor: The Art of Romare Bearden, 1940–1987* (New York: Oxford University Press and Studio Museum in Harlem, 1991).

6. Michele Wallace, "Modernism, Post-Modernism, and the Problem of the Visual in Afro-American Culture," in *Out There: Marginalization and Contemporary Cultures*, ed. Russell Ferguson, Martha Gever, Trinh T. Minh-ha, and Cornel West (New York: New Museum of Contemporary Art, 1990), 39–50.

7. Frantz Fanon, *Black Skin, White Masks* (1952; reprint, New York: Grove Press, 1967).

8. Nathaniel Mackey, *Discrepant Engagement: Dissonance, Cross-Culturality, and Experimental Writing* (Cambridge: Cambridge University Press, 1993).

9. Mark Busby, *Ralph Ellison* (Boston: Twayne Publishers, 1991), 11.

10. Romare Bearden, "The Negro Artist and Modern Art," *Opportunity* (December 1934), 271–72; see full text in this volume, pp. 87–90. Romare Bearden, "The Negro Artist's Dilemma," *Critique* (November 1946), 16–22; see full text in this volume, pp. 91–98.

11. Romare Bearden, letter to Walter Quirt (20 January 1942), quoted in Myron Schwartzman, *Romare Bearden: His Life and Art* (New York: Abrams, 1990), 121.

12. Bearden, "The Negro Artist and Modern Art," 371.

13. Bearden, "The Negro Artist and Modern Art," 371.

14. Bearden, "The Negro Artist's Dilemma," 20.

15. Malcolm Vaughn, *New York American* (1927), quoted in Bearden, "The Negro Artist and Modern Art," 372. See also Gary Reynolds and Beryl Wright, eds., *Against the Odds: African-American Artists and the Harmon Foundation* (Newark, NJ: Newark Museum, 1989).

16. Bearden, "The Negro Artist's Dilemma," 19.

17. Bearden, "The Negro Artist's Dilemma," 17.

18. W. E. B. Du Bois, "The Criteria of Negro Art," *The Crisis* (October 1926): 290–97.

19. Bearden, "The Negro Artist's Dilemma," 16.

20. Alain Locke, *The Negro in Art: A Pictorial Record of the Negro Artist and of the Negro Theme in Art* (Washington, DC: Associates in Negro Folk Education, 1940).

21. Bearden, "The Negro Artist's Dilemma," 19.

22. Bearden, "The Negro Artist's Dilemma," 19.

23. Alain Locke, "Who or What Is 'Negro'?" *Opportunity* (February and March, 1942), reprinted in Jeffrey C. Stewart, ed., *The Critical Temper of Alain Locke: A Selection of His Essays on Art and Culture* (New York: Garland Publishing, 1983), 311.

24. Locke, "Who or What Is 'Negro'?," 311.

25. Ellison, "The Art of Romare Bearden," 231–32.

26. Ann Gibson, *Abstract Expressionism: Other Politics* (New Haven, CT: Yale University Press, 1997), 120.

27. Romare Bearden, in Schwartzman, *Romare Bearden: His Life and Art*, 146.

28. Ellison, "The Art of Romare Bearden," 230.

29. Ellison, "The Art of Romare Bearden," 229.

30. Ellison, "The Art of Romare Bearden," 230.

31. See chapter 6, "Painting Through Primitivism" in Gibson, *Abstract Expressionism*, 114–32.

32. Matthew Rohn, *Visual Dynamics in Jackson Pollock's Abstractions* (Cambridge: MIT Press, 1987), quoted in Gibson, *Abstract Expressionism*, 32.

33. Gibson, *Abstract Expressionism*, 101.

34. Gibson, *Abstract Expressionism*, 101.

35. Romare Bearden, in Schwartzman, *Romare Bearden: His Life and Art*, 173.

36. Gibson, *Abstract Expressionism*, 122.

37. Gibson, *Abstract Expressionism*, 76.

38. Ellison, "The Art of Romare Bearden," 230–31.

39. Gail Gelburd, "Romare Bearden in Black and White: The Photomontage Projections of 1964," in Gail Gelburd and Thelma Golden, eds., *Romare Bearden in Black and White: Photomontage Projections 1964* (New York: Whitney Museum of American Art/ Abrams, 1997), 18.

40. Hale Woodruff, "Foreword," to *Spiral*, exh. cat. (Long Island University, 1965), quoted in Floyd Coleman, "The Changing Same: Spiral, the Sixties, and African-American Art," in William E. Taylor and Harriet G. Warkel, eds., *A Shared Heritage: Art by Four African Americans* (Indianapolis, IN: Indianapolis Museum of Art, 1996), 148–49.

41. Emma Amos, in Schwartzman, *Romare Bearden: His Life and Art*, 210.

42. Fanon, *Black Skin, White Masks*, 183.

43. Romare Bearden, in Schwartzman, *Romare Bearden: His Life and Art*, 179.

44. Ellison, "The Art of Romare Bearden," 234.

45. Ellison, "The Art of Romare Bearden," 234.

46. Ellison, "The Art of Romare Bearden," 236.

47. Ellison, "The Art of Romare Bearden," 236.

48. Ellison, "The Art of Romare Bearden," 234.

49. Ellison, "The Art of Romare Bearden," 234–35.

50. Ellison, "The Art of Romare Bearden," 235.

51. Dore Ashton, *Romare Bearden: Projections*, exh. cat. (Washington, DC: Corcoran Gallery of Art, 1965), and Robert Hughes, *Time* (June 1991), quoted in Gelburd and Golden, *Romare Bearden in Black and White*, 21.

52. Ellison, "The Art of Romare Bearden," 235.

53. Ellison, "The Art of Romare Bearden," 237.

54. Ellison, "The Art of Romare Bearden," 237.

55. Albert Murray, *The Omni-Americans: New Perspectives on Black Experience and American Culture* (New York: Dutton, 1970).

56. Ellison, "The Art of Romare Bearden," 236 (emphasis added).

57. Lowery Stokes Sims, *Romare Bearden* (New York: Rizzoli Art Series, 1988).

58. Ellison, "The Art of Romare Bearden," 237.

59. Snead, "Repetition as a Figure of Black Culture," 67.

60. Snead, "Repetition as a Figure of Black Culture," 67.

61. Romare Bearden, in Schwartzman, *Romare Bearden: His Life and Art*, 110.

62. "When I started to paint in oil, I simply wanted to extend what I had done in watercolor. To do so I had the initial sketch enlarged as a photostat . . . Later on I read Delacroix's *Journal* and felt that I too could profit by systematically copying the masters . . . I again used photostats." Romare Bearden, "Rectangular Structure in My Montage Paintings," *Leonardo* 2.1 (January 1969): 12; see full text in this volume, pp. 121–32.

63. Romare Bearden and Carl Holty, *The Painter's Mind: A Study of the Relations of Structure and Space in Painting* (New York: Crown Press, 1969).

64. Addison Gayle, Jr., *The Black Aesthetic* (New York: Doubleday, 1971).

65. Mikhail Bakhtin, *The Dialogic Imagination* (Austin: University of Texas Press, 1981), 293–94.

# BEARDEN
# PLAYS BEARDEN

*Albert Murray*

## I

As striking as the figurative and thematic dimensions of most of the paintings and collages of Romare Bearden[1] so often are, the specific forms as such — however suggestive of persons, places, and things and even of situations and events, actual or mythological — are by his own carefully considered account always far more a matter of on-the-spot improvisation or impromptu invention not unlike that of the jazz musician than of representation such is the stock in trade of the portrait painter, the illustrator, and the landscape artist of, say, the Hudson River School.

Not that there is ever anything casual, random, or merely incidental about his choice of subject matter. Except for his completely nonobjective works of the late 1950s and early '60s, the raw materials he processes into aesthetic statement either come directly from or in some way allude to or otherwise reflect historic, geographic, or idiomatic particulars of Afro-American experience. Nor is it at all unusual for works in any given one-man exhibition[2] to be so closely and deliberately interrelated in subject matter as well as style as to constitute a series, or even a sequence, that is undeniably not only narrative and anecdotal in nature but also intentionally so.

But even when a series or sequence comes as close to illustration as the twenty collages in the exhibition titled "Odysseus,"[3] the images as such, for all their evocation of characters and episodes of a long-established and well-known story line, were seldom preconceived. More often than not they began simply as neutral shapes with contours that were simply what they happened to be. What each original shape eventually became was always determined only as each collage evolved.

Sometimes, as in the case of the autobiographical suite of twenty-eight collages titled "Profile/Part I: The Twenties,"[4] the theme of childhood recollection was agreed upon in advance. But even so, the specific reminiscences that now seem so integral to each picture actually came only after each composition began to click into focus as an aesthetic statement. It was, he reports, more as a matter of saying this looks like a garden, so why not Miss Maudell Sleet's garden,[5] rather than saying now I'm going to recreate Miss Maudell's garden.

Of course, once such a painting is completed an artist can say any number of interesting and essentially literary things about it (as Bearden has done on request on not a few occasions). But although sometimes he may talk as if about an illustration, what he is referring to is a painting, a system of organized forms; and in the process of pulling it together he was far more concerned with such aesthetic elements as decorative and ornamental effect than with narrative or dramatic impact. Indeed, as charming as such remarks can be, the picture as a painting would not be changed one bit if he called Maudell Sleet Miss Emily Ellison and reminisced about how after her husband died she used to bury her savings in an Alaga syrup[6] bucket. In the case of *Farewell Eugene* (see fig. 23), Bearden tells a touching and informative anecdote about a boyhood friend in Pittsburgh and about how Eugene, who taught him how to draw, used to make pictures of houses in which the interior activities could be seen from the street. *But the painting does not tell that story at all!*

Each of his paintings is evolved out of what the juxtaposition of the raw materials at hand brings to mind as he plays around with them in much the same as, say, Duke Ellington in search of a tune or in the process of working up an arrangement or composing a fully orchestrated blues sonata begins by playing around with chords, phrases, trial runs, and potential riff patterns on the keyboard. The exact imitation of nature is irrelevant to the aesthetic statement Bearden wishes the picture to make. That statement, however, is altogether dependent upon the ornamental and decorative quality achieved.

"You have to begin somewhere,"[7] he has said. "So you put something down. Then you put something else with it, and then you see how that works, and maybe you try something else and so on, and the picture grows in that way. One thing leads to another, and you take the options as they come, or as you are able to perceive them as you proceed. The fact that each medium has its own special technical requirements doesn't really make any fundamental difference. My point is that my overall approach to composition is essentially the same whether I'm working with the special problems and possibilities of the collage, or with oils, watercolors, or tempera. As a matter of fact I often use more than one medium in the same picture."

"Once you get going," he has also said, "all sorts of things begin to open up. Sometimes something just seems to fall into place, like the piano keys that every now and then just seem to be right where your fingers happen to come down. But there are also all those times you have to keep trying something over and over and then when you finally get it right you wonder what took you so long. And of course there are also times when you have to give it up and try something else. But sometimes it turns out just great as the beginning of another, totally different picture. By the way, this sort of thing is much more likely to have to do with how something fits into the design or ornamental structure of the painting than with its suitability as subject matter."

Nor is Bearden unaware of the relationship of his procedures to those of jazz musicianship. He is conscious not only of beginning by vamping as if till ready for the downbeat and the first chorus of each composition, but also of hitting upon and playing around with details of both color and form as if with visual riff phrases. Nor is he any less aware of working in terms of relating solo-like structural elements to ensembles, sometimes as call-and-response patterns, sometimes as in jam session leapfrog sequences and sometimes as in full band interplay of section tonalities (trumpets with or against trombones, reeds, or piano, and so on).

That he learned to work in his own way with the separations between colors and with the different values of a given color by studying the expressive use of interval in the piano style of Earl Hines[8] is a matter of record. And he has also said that his application of what he learned from Hines led him to appreciate the visual possibilities of Ellington's absolutely fantastic use of blues timbres, down-home onomatopoeia, urban dissonance, and cacophony in numbers such as "Daybreak Express" and "Harlem Airshaft"; to Chick Webb's accentuations on "Stomping at the Savoy"; to rhythmic extensions of Count Basie's deceptively simple abbreviations of ragtime and Harlem stride; to the instantly captivating distortions and disjunctures of Thelonious Monk, and in due course also to the realization that his basic orientation to aesthetic statement had been conditioned by the blues idiom in general and jazz musicianship in particular all along.

Nor was anything more consistent with his background as an Afro-American who came of age between 1914 and 1935. His background in point of historical fact is hardly distinguishable from that of the great majority of the outstanding blues idiom musicians of his generation and of the preceding generation as well. He spent his early years in the bosom of the church, as the old folks in the pews used to say, down home in Mecklenburg County, on the outskirts of Charlotte, North Carolina; and in a transplanted down-home neighborhood in Pittsburgh, Pennsylvania, where he, exactly like those destined to grow up to become leaders and members of the great orchestras that conquered the world for American music, heard and absorbed the spirituals, the traditional hymns, gospel songs, and amen corner moans in context and conjunction with the prayers, sermons, shouts, testifying shuffles, and struts that make up the service or ritual that gave rise to them in the first place. As he also imitated and in some instances choreographed for playground purposes the work chants, railroad rhymes, and field hollers that, along with the music of the kitchen, the wash place, the fire circle, the street corner, the honky-tonks and the dance halls, were the secular complements to church music.

Not even the New Orleans of young Louis Armstrong himself during the first and second decades, or the Kansas City of young Charlie Parker during the 1930s, was dominated more definitively by music and musicians than was the Harlem that was Bearden's briar patch and stamping ground as a schoolboy and young adult. He spent his puberty and adolescence in the very Heart of Harlem, as the incurably square ofay radio announcers back during that time, which was the heyday of the uptown cabarets, used to say. The legendary rent party sessions, for instance, were regular, though informal, neighborhood events that were so much a part of his childhood awareness that he took them for granted much the same as if they were church suppers and socials, or even sandlot baseball games.

Such celebrated stride time piano players as James P. Johnson, Willie "The Lion" Smith, and Lucky Roberts, among others, were not only immediately recognizable as everyday figures on the sidewalks of the neighborhood, but were in most instances also instantly identifiable by the personal nuances that were their signatures as artists. Fats Waller, as a matter of fact, was a very close friend of Bearden's family. And so among many others was Flournoy Miller of the famous Miller and Lyles vaudeville team, whose reputation was comparable to that of Williams and Walker, and Sissle and Blake. The performers working in such smash hit Broadway revues of the period as *Shuffle Along, Chocolate Dandies, Hot Chocolates,* and *Lew Leslie's Blackbirds* were inseparable parts of the musical life of the neighborhood.

As were such headliners from the Columbia, Keith, and TOBA circuits[9] and/ or the world of phonograph records as Ethel Waters, Alberta Hunter, Mamie Smith, Lucille Hegamin, Perry Bradford, John Bubbles, and so many others. The stage entrance to the Lafayette Theatre was just across the street from the Bearden apartment on 131st Street. The main entrance was around the corner, on Seventh Avenue. The Lincoln Theatre[10] was only a few blocks away, on 135th Street off Lenox Avenue. Before Florence Mills,[11] the star of *Blackbirds,* became the sensation of Broadway and London, she had established her reputation at the Lincoln as well as the Lafayette; and when she died suddenly at the very peak of her triumph, all Harlem grieved as if for a most darling member of the household, and as the funeral procession slowly wound its way through the streets, young Bearden was among the hundred and fifty thousand mourners who are said to have lined the streets while thousands more waved farewell from windows and rooftops, and he also remembers that people came back from the burial talking about how one airplane flew over the ceremony and released a flock of blackbirds and another came scattering roses.

When the Savoy Ballroom opened at 140th Street on Lenox Avenue, about ten blocks away Bearden was not quite twelve years old. But even before that, the patterns of sound coming from such not-faraway spots as the Renaissance Casino, Smalls Paradise, and the Nest Club were no less a part of the local atmosphere than were the voices of the woofers and jive shooters and tall-tale tellers and signifiers in the various neighborhood lunch counters, poolrooms, and barbershops.

Then almost as if overnight the big orchestras of Fletcher Henderson, Duke Ellington, Chick Webb, Cab Calloway, Charlie Johnson, Claude Hopkins, Jimmie Lunceford, McKinney's Cotton Pickers, and the Savoy Sultans had either evolved on the scene, or had come to Harlem from elsewhere. Thus, during the time of the now-epical battles of the great bands and jam sessions, Bearden was a very curious, gregarious, and devilishly mannish adolescent of good standing in most social circles in Harlem, and not only was impeccable musical taste an absolute requirement for growing up hip, urbane, or streetwise, but so was the ability to stylize your actions — indeed, your whole being — in terms of the most sophisticated extensions and refinements of jazz music and dance.

"Regardless of how good you might be at whatever else you did," he has said more than once, "you also had to get with the music. The clothes you wore, the way you talked (and I don't mean just jive talk), the way you stood (we used to say *stashed*) when you were just hanging out, the way you drove an automobile or even just sat in it, everything you did was, you might say, geared to groove. The fabulous old Harlem Renaissance basketball team, like the Globetrotters that succeeded them, came right out of all that music at the Renaissance Casino." Nor were the Globetrotters unrelated to the fox trotters at the Savoy Ballroom. Incidentally, when Ellington's "It Don't Mean a Thing if It Ain't Got That Swing" came out, Bearden was eighteen and very much the fly cat about town and on campus as well.

## II

But obviously he did not learn to paint by listening to music. He learned to paint by looking at and responding to many paintings. Even when he listens to music on the radio while at work in his studio, his specific objectives and procedures are exclusively those of a painter, and accordingly his efforts are best understood and most fully appreciated in terms of and in the context of the works of the visual artists, not the musicians he admires and attempts to extend, elaborate, and otherwise refine, and those he rejects either in part or on the whole, and so ignores or feels compelled to counterstate.

Each painting, that is to say, is a visual statement that is a reference or allusion to another or other paintings, to which in effect it either says yes and also and also and perhaps also; or it says no or not necessarily or on the other hand or not as far as I for one am concerned. Not that musicians don't do exactly the same thing. Ellington's unique voicings, for example, began by saying yes in some instances and no in others to King Oliver, Jelly Roll Morton, Fletcher Henderson, and even the likes of Paul Whiteman and the saw-fiddle Tin Pan Alley extensions of George Gershwin. Such, after all, are the dynamics of the creative process. But the point is that as visual artists, painters must proceed in terms of existing *visual* statements. It is precisely thus that they participate in the ongoing dialogue that makes their métier what it continues to be.

Indeed, as should surprise no one, it was a painter who made Bearden realize, as only a painter could have, that elements of blues idiom musicianship could be applied to visual composition. During the days when he was still a young journeyman, so to speak, he used to visit the studio of Stuart Davis, an American master of post-Cubist persuasion, who had studied in Paris, and in the course of discussions about the approaches of Picasso, Matisse, Braque, and Juan Gris, among others, Davis, who had a large collection of jazz records, kept coming back to the music of Earl Hines and kept trying to make him see visual devices in terms of the way Hines did things on the piano. Davis, who was no less deeply involved with native U.S. techniques, raw materials, and attitudes than with avant-garde experimentation, also told him that the subject matter of painting includes the materials of expression.

But his friendship with Davis, who, by the way, was not native to the blues idiom, came not at the beginning of Bearden's career as an artist, but (as stated above) a few years later. It was not what motivated him to become a painter. It was rather advice from an older and more accomplished fellow professional, and it gave him new insight into, and eventually a greater facility with, the ideas and techniques he had already acquired in the normal course of his apprenticeship to visual expression. As his earliest works show, he was already trying to process raw material from the blues territory, as it were, into art long before he met Davis. What Davis said made him realize that the jazz aesthetic itself was applicable to visual statement.

At the outset of his career as a serious painter, there was George Grosz at the Art Students League. "It was during my period with Grosz,"[12] he has written, "under whom I began studying several months after graduating from New York University, that I began to regard myself as a painter rather than a cartoonist. The drawings of Grosz on the theme of the human situation in post–World War I Germany made me realize the artistic possibilities of American Negro subject matter. It was also Grosz who led me to study composition through the analysis of Bruegel and the great Dutch masters, who in the process of refining my draftsmanship initiated me into the magic world of Ingres, Dürer, Holbein, and Poussin."

His apprenticeship at the League also put him in an environment where his fellow students and his instructors lived in terms of visual art much the same as so many of the people among whom he had grown up in Harlem lived with, by, and for music. It was through them and their dialogues, debates, enthusiasms, and put-downs that he was to come to know and frequent the great midtown galleries and museums and also the small galleries and certain ateliers in Greenwich Village as young jazz musicians used to know and frequent the Harlem nightclubs, dance halls, practice rooms, and showcase theaters. Young painters at the League and at parties shared their excitements over the ongoing explorations and achievements of Picasso, Matisse, Braque, Klee, and so on to Hans Hofmann with the same sense of direct involvement, even if not quite with the same degree of sophistication, as he was used to hearing in uptown hangouts where musicians registered their responses to the latest output of Armstrong, Ellington, Lunceford, and Basie, or discussed the basis of their personal sense of identification with Art Tatum or Teddy Wilson, Lester Young, or Coleman Hawkins, and so on.

In college (majoring in mathematics) he had drawn cartoons influenced at first by E. Simms Campbell, Ollie Harrington, and Miguel Covarrubias, and then also by Daumier, Forain, and Käthe Kollwitz. His initial attempts at serious painting began with tempera. Then came watercolor and then oil. About which he has written as follows: "My temperas had been composed in closed forms, and the coloring was mostly earthy browns, blues, and greens. When I started working with watercolor, however, I found myself using bright color patterns and bold, black lines to delineate semiabstract shapes. I never worked long on a painting with this method or made many corrections. I had not yet learned that modern painting progresses through cumulative destructions and new beginnings.[13]

"When I started to paint in oil, I simply wanted to extend what I had done in watercolor. To do so, I had the initial sketch enlarged as a photostat, traced it onto a gessoed panel, and with a thinned color completed the oil as if it were indeed a watercolor."

Then he goes on: "Later I read Delacroix's *Journal* and felt that I, too, could profit by systematically copying the masters of the past and of the present. Not wanting to work in museums, I again used photostats, enlarging photographs of works by Giotto, Duccio, Veronese Grünewald, Rembrandt, de Hooch, Manet, and Matisse. I made reasonably free copies of each work by substituting my own choice of colors for those of these artists, except for those of Manet and Matisse, when I was guided by color reproductions."

Still later, after he began to play with pigments as such "in marks and patches distorting natural colors and natural objects as well," and found out that tracks of color tended to fragment his composition, he went back to the Dutch masters once more. To Vermeer and Pieter de Hooch in particular, he says, and then adds that it was then that he "came to some understanding of the way these painters controlled their big shapes, even when elements of different size and scale were included within these large shapes. I was also studying at the same time the techniques which enable the classical painters to organize their areas — for example the device of the open corner to allow the observer a starting point in encompassing the entire painting; the subtle ways of shifting balance and emphasis; and the use of voids, or negative areas, as sections of 'passivity' and also perhaps 'sections of reduced tension' and as a means of projecting the big shapes.

"As a result, I began to paint more thinly, often on natural linen, where I left sections of the canvas unpainted so that the linen itself had the function of a color. Then in a transition toward what turned out to be my present style, I painted broad areas of color on various thicknesses of rice paper and glued these papers on canvas, usually in several layers. I tore sections of the paper away, always attempting to tear upward and across on the picture plane until some motif engaged me. When this happened, I added more papers and painted additional colored areas to complete the painting."

Such in brief is Bearden's natural history as a painter; and appropriately — nay, inevitably — it reflects his personal involvement with the so-called Museum Without Walls, that imaginary collection or world anthology of art reproductions that enables a contemporary artist to proceed as if the art of all the ages in the world at large were coexistent (as indeed it is in the truly contemporary sensibility). Moreover, by the same token it reveals the specific nature of his personal dialogue or argument with the ongoing tradition of visual expression. Each statement of his own intentions as an artist coincidentally affirms some elements in the work of some painters and counterstates some elements in others, even sometimes not only in the same painter, but in a given painting.

The juxtaposition of paintings in Bearden's purely functional museum does not make any concessions to differences between historical periods. Only the aesthetic statement is relevant: "Some observers have noted that the apparent visual basis of my current (1969) work, the use of overlapping planes and of flat space, is similar to Cubism. In actual practice, however, I find myself as deeply involved with methods derived from de Hooch and Vermeer, as well as the other masters of flat painting, including the classic Japanese portrait artists and the pre-Renaissance Siennese masters, such as Duccio and Lorenzetti. What I like most about the Cubism of Picasso, Braque, and Léger is its primary emphasis on the essentials of structure. Nevertheless, I also find that for me the Cubism of these masters leads to an overcrowding of the pictorial space. This accounts for the high surface of the frontal planes, so prevalent even in some of the most successful early works of the Cubists. In fact, such exceptions as the collage drawings of Picasso in which emptier areas are emphasized only point up what is otherwise typical. Much of the agitation in Juan Gris's *Guitar and Flowers*, for instance, is the result of the violent diagonal twist of his planes away from the stabilizing rectangle of the surface. Even the early Cubism of Mondrian, who was in many ways a descendant of de Hooch and Vermeer, contains a number of small bricklike rectangular shapes, which strike me as being more a concession to the manner of the time than essential to his austere conception of space and structure."[14] Still it is the Cubists who provide the contemporary context for his work. The Cubists, far from painting cubes or cubicals, are nothing if not flat-surface painters.

Other specifics of his museum dialogue, as it were, are spelled out with textbook-like precision and classroom-type demonstration in *The Painter's Mind: A Study of the Relations of Structure and Space in Painting*,[15] which he wrote in collaboration with his longtime friend and colleague, the late Carl Holty, onetime member of the famous Creative Abstraction group in pre–World War II Paris, who also taught at the Art Students League. *The Painter's Mind* is a treatise on flat painting beyond everything else. In it, outstanding examples from the whole worldwide museum that is the heritage of all present-day painters are in effect reinterpreted in light of the twentieth-century emphasis on flat-surface painting as opposed to the lifelike representation and nineteenth-century misconceptions of the classical ideal and Renaissance perspective.

It was Bearden's early orientation to flat painting that led to his special interest in Stuart Davis. Indeed, it was in the very process of discussing decoration, ornamentation, and design as the primary objectives of contemporary painting that Davis, whose preoccupations were no less vernacular than avant-garde, began talking about Earl Hines and about how his own use of color intervals had been influenced by the way Hines used space as statement in building structures of sound on the piano. "Earl Hines' hot piano and Negro jazz in general,"[16] he once wrote, "were among the things which have made me want to paint, outside of other paintings." Remembering all the way back to the epoch-making Armory Show of 1913, in which he was represented by five watercolors, Davis also wrote, "I was enormously excited by the show, and responded particularly to

Gauguin, van Gogh, and Matisse, because broad generalization of form and the non-imitative use of color were already practices within my experience. I also sensed an objective order in these works which I felt was lacking in my own. It gave me the kind of excitement I got from the numerical precision of the Negro piano players in the Negro saloons, and I resolved that I would quite definitely have to become a 'modern' painter."[17]

At first Bearden didn't really know what to make of the fact that Davis, who had a large record collection to be sure, so often insisted on making a connection between painting and jazz. He had already had to endure more than his share of pseudo sophisticated ofays showing off how hip they were to the uptown jive, and there was always another one of those perhaps well-intentioned but boring do-gooders determined to talk about something you know about so as to make you feel comfortable in the great white world outside of Harlem. But as Davis went on to clarify his conception of the role jazz played in *predetermining an analogous dynamics in design,* Bearden was able to see just how fundamental all of Davis's points about jazz were. He was talking about how one was *disposed,* or rather predisposed, to process *any raw material* into aesthetic statement.

What Davis made him realize as never before was the workaday relationship of all of his formal training and apprenticeship, of all the abstract formulations and theoretical concerns to his basic idiomatic conditioning. "And from then on," he said, "I was on my way. I don't mean to imply that I knew where I was going. But the more I just played around with visual notions as if I were improvising like a jazz musician, the more I realized what I wanted to do as a painter, and how I wanted to do it.

"I must say I was not just impressed but also deeply moved by the fact that Stu Davis, who so far as I was concerned was one of the best American painters around, felt that it was so crucially important and worked so long and deliberately to acquire something that, as he pointed out, I had inherited from my Afro-American environment as a matter of course. I had gone to him to find out more about the avant-garde, and he kept trying to make me appreciate the fact that so far as he was concerned the aesthetic conventions of Harlem musicians to which so many of my habitual responses were geared, were just as avant-garde as Picasso, Braque, Matisse, Mondrian, and all the rest. By the way, jazz, especially boogie-woogie, was the main thing Mondrian wanted to talk to Davis about during the several times they met."

# III

*The Painter's Mind* is in a very real sense a book about how to see the aesthetic statement in pictures in spite of the subject matter, or in any case, whatever the subject matter, and also in spite of, or whatever the stylistic convention. It is a book about structure and space with primary emphasis on design, decoration, and ornamentation as the indispensable fundamentals of visual expression. It does not discuss color, which as charcoal drawings and sketches and as black-and-white reproductions show, is a *dispensable* fundamental; but the implication is that color, like form, is to be used not in imitation of nature, but for decorative, ornamental, and design values.

According to *The Painter's Mind*, perspective and illusion are not essentials, only conventions, while structure is always necessary in any work of art. "Many things are revealed to us as we look at a work of art with its multiplicity of images. Not all who look will see the same thing; some people, for instance, will be pleased by a particular image, others depressed — each according to his temperament, his imagination, and his spiritual needs. But whatever the image, the only reality present is structure. There is no face, no ship, no landscape, no real depth. These are illusions; the structure that supports them is not."

Such contentions are entirely consistent with Bearden's orientation to flat painting, the use he makes of Byzantine painting and African art, his deliberate violations of scale, and his arbitrary use of color. (Obviously, his use of jet black as a color for human beings is not meant to be naturalistic.) Perhaps not so obvious is the fact that even when black functions as a symbolic reference to so-called black people of Africa and the United States, it is not the reference that is of paramount importance but the design: how the black shape works with other shapes and colors.

Moreover, black may or may not say Afro, but inevitably says silhouette, and almost always has the effect of a cutout in a collage, perhaps the flattest of flat painting.

Everything in *The Painter's Mind* is predicated upon the definitive assumption of twentieth-century artists that the painter should dominate his subject matter rather than be dominated by it. His talent is not at the service of description. What counts is how what is said is said. It is a process of stylization. Even when the examples under discussion are such classic classical representations of religious subject matter as Duccio's *The Marys at the Sepulchre* or Giotto's *The Resurrection*, or Tintoretto's *The Baptism*, or Rembrandt's *Bathsheba*, what the authors concern themselves with are the particularities of technique that enable each master to make the painting his individual aesthetic statement beyond all else.

Only about his complete nonfigurative works, however, is Bearden likely to go so far as to say what Georges Braque, for instance, once said about the subordination of subject matter: "When you ask me whether a particular form in one of my paintings depicts a woman's head, a fish, a vase, a bird, or all four at once, I cannot give a categorical answer, for this 'metaphoric' confusion is fundamental to the poetry.... It is all the same to me whether a form represents a different thing to different people or many things at the same time, or even nothing at all; it might be no more than an accident or a 'rhyme'—a pictorial 'rhyme,' by the way, can have all sorts of unexpected consequences, can change the whole meaning of a picture—such as I sometimes like to incorporate in my compositions."[18]

Indeed, Bearden is convinced that Braque's statement is clearly an exaggeration. The subjects in a Braque painting are more denotative than his declaration would lead you to expect. Whatever else they may be, any layman can see that his still-lifes are made from tables, bottles, glasses, musical instruments, and so on. Bearden feels that Braque is closer to actual practice when he goes on to say: "Objects do not exist for me except insofar as a rapport exists between them and between them and myself. In other words it is not the objects that matter to me but what is in between them; it is this in-between that is the real subject of my pictures."[19]

In practice, Bearden's position is closer to what Stuart Davis seems to have had in mind when in reference to one of his paintings done in 1924–25 he said that they were based on "a generalization of form in which the subject matter was conceived as a series of planes, and the planes as geometrical shapes—a valid view of the structure of any subject—these geometrical shapes were arranged in direct relationship to the canvas as a flat surface."[20] In some paintings, Davis goes on to say, "the large forms were established on the flat-surface principle, but the minor features were still imitative."

It is generally accepted that twentieth-century painting does not have to tell a story and does not have to depict anything. Its figures can be shapes that mean nothing. Nevertheless, Braque's declarations seem to be somewhat modified, if not contradicted by his use of such titles as *Bottle and Glass, Man with Guitar, Bottle of Rum, Violin and Pipe, Still Life with Guitar, Painter and Model*. It is no doubt true that these are only shapes that tell no story. It is also true that no very special meaning is attached to these objects per se, that, in effect, they have been neutralized so that they exist primarily as elements in a picture not concerned with factual description. But it is likely to be less true that it would have made no difference to Braque if viewers saw cats and dogs instead of bottles and glasses and two generals instead of the painter and his model — although Braque could have made pretty much the same pictorial statement with two generals. Perhaps it is more to the point to say that bottles, glasses, guitars, violins, pipes, and even painters and models were not used to record, suggest, or symbolize anything about liquids, music, tobacco, and so on, rather only because they were ordinary, familiar three-dimensional objects, and as such could be used to emphasize the fact that the painter is working in terms of flatness and not perspective. Similarly, when letters are used in a Léger or Davis painting, whatever they may or may not spell, they function as two-dimensional ornamental shapes, and they also serve to keep the surface as flat as, say, a Mondrian.

But all the same, Bearden, who is nothing if not an exponent of the flat surface, sees no reason why his pictures should not tell a story so long as the narration and depiction do not get in the way of the painting as such. In his view, a painting does not have to say anything either literal or symbolic, but it can if it wishes. Of course, it must always avoid unintentional counterstatement or detrimental empathy. On the other hand, there can be no question of any violation of scale, perspective, or nonrealistic color destroying the illusion in a flat painting, since description is always subordinate to design.

Bearden is convinced that doctrinaire artists who would rigorously exclude all descriptive elements from all of their work are placing unnecessary restrictions on themselves. He sees no reason why aesthetic statement cannot be multidimensional. Certainly there is no inherent reason why a mural, for example, cannot be narrative without compromising its function as an ornament. Bearden, who has done both figurative and nonfigurative murals for interior as well as exterior walls, claims that he is aware of a preference only after the composition of a given project is already under way.

In any case, although the figurative shapes in his painting are almost always a matter of improvisation, and are completely subordinate to the most fundamental requirements of design, decoration, and ornament, once they come into existence as realistic objects, even as they fulfill their indispensable function as elements in the composition they acquire powers of suggestion and illusion that may be very strong indeed. Sometimes they stimulate associations with concrete objects, places, and events, and sometimes they become symbolic evocations by the same token. In other words, unlike Braque's neutralized bottles, glasses, guitars, painters, and models, Bearden's flat-surface musicians, train cutouts, his rural and urban landscapes with their farmers and apartment dwellers are not only meant to be taken as representations of very specific examples of reality, they may be deliberately symbolic at the same time, as in the case of *Carolina Shout,* for instance. What the figures suggest is an ecstatic high point in a down-home church service. At the same time, however, the title, made famous by a Harlem Stride piano composition, implies that the movements and gestures are not unrelated to the dance hall, the jook joint, the honky-tonks, and the barrelhouse. So even as the figures evoke the Sunday morning service, there are also overtones of the Saturday night function referred to in *Mecklenburg County Saturday Night.*

The evocations and associations in Bearden's works are indeed so strong, and so deliberately and specifically and idiomatically either down-home rural or up-north urban, that perhaps it is not too much to say that his preoccupation with imagery from a special American context, which he uses in much the same way as Picasso, and especially Miró, uses Spanish imagery, is surpassed only by his commitment to the aesthetic process that will give his painting the "quality of a flat surface decorated by hand" — and also gives him the option to use any raw material whatever, or no identifiable subject matter at all.

But the fact is that once his arbitrary shapes and photo cutout details become figures in paintings, what they suggest very often reflects some aspect of the idiomatic particulars of Afro-American life. In other words, in spite of the obvious fact that he does not work primarily in terms of illusion, the trains, for example, that are present in so many of his pictures are meant to be taken as real-life railroad trains. As such, however, they connote as well as denote, as do the locomotives in the old guitar and harmonica folk blues. And as do those in Ellington's "Daybreak Express," "Way Low," "Happy Go Lucky Local," "The Old Circus Train Turn Around Blues," "Loco Madi," and so on and on inbound and outbound. They are also not only the northbound limiteds and specials that down-home folks used to take or dream of taking up the country or the southbound ones bringing tidings and/or visiting relatives, or "my baby back to me," but are sometimes also symbolic of the totally imaginary vehicles in the spirituals and of the ever so metaphorical, but no less boardable, underground railroad of the fugitive slaves.

Perhaps the most distinctive, if not the definitive feature of Bearden's treatment of the figurative elements in his paintings is the pronounced emphasis that is almost always given to the ceremonial dimension of each scene and event. Even in his portraits, whether of individuals, couples, or groups, the people not only seem to pose for the occasion exactly as folks used to get themselves up to watch the birdie for the photographer of yesteryear, with his view camera on a tripod, his black cloth, and rubber-ball plunger. They also seem posed not only for the occasion, but also as if for some special occasion. There are few candid shots. Even when, as in the series of black-and-white *Projections* (1964),[21] there are unmistakable evocations of newsprint and movies, it is the choreographic movement of the old silent films that comes to mind (along with the old newspaper *stills*), not the documentary Technicolor of *National Geographic* magazine.

Nor is there any contradiction between the compelling impact and hence importance of Bearden's subject matter as such, and the assessment of what is relevant and irrelevant in visual art given in *The Painter's Mind*. For, as should be obvious enough to anyone with even a slight familiarity with Byzantine, Romanesque, and African art, it is precisely by working primarily in terms of ornamentation and decoration that he generates the strong ceremonial and ritualistic associations that some reviewers refer to as mythic overtones. The ornamental emphasis also frees the evocative dimension of his work from sentimentality and provincialism. Compared to the ceremonial dignity of Bearden's radiant still-lifes, Degas's great "snapshots" of ballet dancers, for example, look almost as genre as Millet's peasants. By contrast, not only are Bearden's North Carolina cotton pickers anything but genre, his folk and jazz musicians are depicted with a ritual formality that suggests characters in a ballet.

The ornamental and ritual emphasis also serves to counterstate the pathetic (as it does in the case of the agony in the highly stylized representations of the Crucifixion). As is to be expected of an artist who began as a political cartoonist and remains an enthusiastic admirer of Grosz, Goya, Daumier, Forain, and Kollwitz, Bearden sometimes, especially in his urbanscapes, creates configurations that may be taken as social commentary. But even so, the overall impact of *The Block*, *The Street*, *Evening Lenox Avenue*, *The Dove*, *Rocket to the Moon*, and *Black Manhattan*, for example, is, as he intended, much closer to such Ellington tone parallels and celebrations as "Uptown Downbeat," "Echoes of Harlem," "I'm Slappin' Seventh Avenue with the Sole of My Shoe," "Drop Me Off in Harlem," and "Harlem Air Shaft" than to any of the Welfare Department tear-jerk rhetoric so habitual among so many mostly cynical spokesmen (and persons!) and so readily accepted and repeated by the world's champion one-upmen (and persons!) become do-gooders.

Incidentally, having grown up in a close contact with such prominent Afro-heritage figures of the so-called Harlem Renaissance, New Negro movement as Arthur Schomburg, Langston Hughes, Countee Cullen, Claude McKay, and Aaron Douglas, Bearden has always had a special interest in African art. But it was not until he began working in terms of the assumptions underlying *The Painter's Mind* that he discovered the pragmatic aesthetic relevance of African art — along with that of Byzantine, Japanese and Chinese art — to Cubist and post-Cubist painting. Before that he, like so many other U.S. Negro artists, attempted to identify with African art racially, or in any case politically (and also in its entirety), only to have his images come out looking exactly as if they were derived from the Mexican images of Diego River and Miguel Covarrubias, and from one Winold Reiss,[22] to whom as a matter of fact they were infinitely closer in spirit, and intention as well, than to Ife, Dogon, Fon, Senufo, or Benin.

He learned to apply certain devices of stylization appropriated from African art but, needless to say, he could not use African devices as if he were an African, because, for all his ancestral bloodlines, he could not be idiomatically African, not being native to African experience. He could not be idiomatically Spanish, Dutch, or French either. He could only be idiomatically American, and most specifically, blues idiom American. And that, it just so happens, is quite enough, because as a twentieth-century American he not only can but also must synthesize everything in the world as a matter of course — and feed it back to the world at large as a matter of course.

In all events, Bearden has made it clear that his actual use of African art is based on aesthetic, not political, and certainly not racial considerations. Accordingly, the very strong African-like elements in his work are derived not nearly so directly from the African artifacts on display in the Schomburg library in his old neighborhood as from such Cubist adaptations as, say, Picasso's *Demoiselles d'Avignon*. Moreover, it is on Picasso's terms, as it were (not to mention prices), that Bearden clearly intends his own appropriations to be judged.

## IV

Of far more fundamental significance than any question of how much of the art of ancestral Africa is discernible in the work of Romare Bearden is the blues idiom. It is the aesthetics of jazz musicianship that has conditioned him to approach the creative process as a form of play and thus disposes him to trust his work to the intuitions that arise in the course of creating it, which, in turn, also enables him to make the most of the fact that the primary emphasis of contemporary painting is on design, decoration, and ornamentation.

It is also his blues idiom orientation to vamping and riffing and otherwise improvising (as classic African artists were forbidden by custom to do but as frontier Americans were required by circumstances to do) that leads him to dominate his subject matter precisely as the jazz musician does. Any musical subject matter whatsoever is only raw material to be processed into King Oliver music or Jelly Roll Morton music or Louis Armstrong music. A traditional twelve-bar blues progression becomes "Parker's Mood." A thirty-two-bar popular standard titled "Please Don't Talk About Me When I'm Gone" is transformed by Thelonious Monk into "Four in One" as if it were only a folk ditty.

Nor is such domination merely in the interest of a romantic proclamation of individuality per se. Far from being egotistical in any conventional sense, it is rather a matter of just such free enterprise as is to be expected in an open and ever-changing society, as opposed to closed ones that are rigidly restricted by tribal taboos, or by despotic rulers. But even more than that, it represents the artist's participation in an ongoing dialogue with tradition and his never-ending struggle in the void. What it is mainly concerned with is not so much the individual as with human existence as experienced by an individual. At any rate, when the blues-oriented listener hears only a few bars of music on the radio or a phonograph and says Ole Louis or says Ole Duke or says Ole Count or says That's Yardbird or That's Monk or That's Miles or says I hear you, Trane or I hear you, Ornette, he has said it all. Moreover, he has spoken with the same sophisticated awareness of art as a playful process of stylization as that which qualifies the art critic to take only a glance at a picture and say: a Picasso or say a Matisse or say a de Kooning, Motherwell, Hans Hofmann, and so on. He is identifying the essence of the musical statement not by subject matter and title but by how it is played, as the art critic does with a picture when he tells how it is put together simply by acknowledging the name of the artist.

Whatever Ellington played became Ellington, as whatever Picasso painted became a Picasso beyond all else. And the same is true — and has been for some time now — of Romare Bearden. When one looks at his paintings one sees more than the subject matter. Ultimately it is not only Bearden's North Carolina or Bearden's Harlem or Bearden's musicians or Bearden's Odysseus, but also a Bearden stylization of an attitude toward human existence, a Bearden statement/counterstatement and thus that which stands for Bearden himself, and hence a Bearden (*which, incidentally, one is probably much more likely to see in real life after rather than before seeing in a frame*).

And what finally is a Bearden if not design or ornament or decoration for a wall, where it hangs not primarily as a record but as an emblem or badge or shield or flag or banner or pennant, or even as a battle standard and existential guidon. And of what is it emblematic if not that in terms of which the fundamental rituals of the blues idiom condition one to survive (with one's humanity, including one's sense of humor, intact, to be sure). What indeed if not flexibility become elegant improvisation not only under the pressure of all tempos and not only in the response of all disjunctures, but also in the face of ever-impending nothingness. Yes, it is precisely in doing this that a Bearden wall ornament functions as a totemistic device and talisman for keeping the blues at bay, if only intermittently.

## NOTES

From *Romare Bearden: 1970–1980*, exh. cat. (Charlotte, NC: Mint Museum, 1980); reprinted in Albert Murray, *The Blue Devils of Nada: A Contemporary American Approach to Aesthetic Statement* (New York: Pantheon, 1996).

1. Romare Bearden and Albert Murray met in Paris in 1950 and became close friends after Murray moved to New York City in 1962.

2. This essay was written for the catalogue for *Romare Bearden: 1970–1980*, an exhibition organized by the Mint Museum, Charlotte, North Carolina, and on view at the Mint from October 12, 1980, to January 4, 1981.

3. Bearden's *Odysseus* exhibition was on view at Cordier & Ekstrom Gallery, New York, from April 27 to May 28, 1977. See figs. 26,27 and 43 in this volume.

4. Exhibition on view at Cordier & Ekstrom, New York, from November 8 to December 16, 1978, with "picture titles and text reviewed and edited by Albert Murray." See figs. 2 and 3, in this volume.

5. *Maudell Sleet's Magic Garden* (collage on board, 1978) was included in both the *Profiles/Part I* exhibition at Cordier & Ekstrom and the Mint Museum's exhibition. The text accompanying the picture in the *Profiles/Part I* exhibition was: "I can still smell the flowers she used to give us and still taste the blackberries."

6. Brand of pure cane syrup made by the Alabama-Georgia Syrup Co., of Montgomery, Alabama.

7. This long quotation, like most others from Bearden in this 1980 essay, is original to Murray's text. In the notes that follow, only quotes from sources published prior to 1980 are documented.

8. In a television interview with Charlayne Hunter-Gault (*The MacNeil/Lehrer Report,* June 26, 1987), Bearden said: "I listened for hours to the recordings of Earl Hines at the piano. Finally, I was able to block out the melody and concentrate on the silences between the notes. I found that this was very helpful to me in the transmutation of sound into colors and in the placement of objects in my paintings and collages. . . . Jazz has shown me the ways of achieving artistic structures that are personal to me."

9. The Columbia Amusements Co. and the Keith-Albee-Orpheum Corporation booked vaudeville and burlesque acts throughout the early twentieth century.

10. The Theater Owners' Booking Association (TOBA, 1920–circa 1935) was a vaudeville circuit for black performers working all-black venues. Among the largest of TOBA's venues were the Howard Theater (1910), in Washington, D.C., and the Lincoln (1915) and Lafayette (1912), in Harlem.

11. Black actress and entertainer known as "The Blackbird of Harlem" after her starring role in the Broadway revue *Lew Leslie's Blackbirds* (1926–27). She died in 1927, at the age of thirty-one, from tuberculosis.

12. See Romare Bearden, "Rectangular Structure in My Montage Paintings," *Leonardo* 2.1 (January 1969); see full text in this volume, pp. 121–32. Murray's quotations from this article are freely adapted from Bearden's published text.

13. Bearden, "Rectangular Structure."

14. Bearden, "Rectangular Structure."

15. Romare Bearden and Carl Holty (1900–1973), *The Painter's Mind: A Study of the Relations of Structure and Space in Painting* (New York: Crown, 1969).

16. Stuart Davis, "The Cube Root," *ARTnews* (February 1943).

17. Stuart Davis, autobiographical statement for *Stuart Davis* (New York: American Artists Group, 1945), AAG Monographs, No. 6.

18. Georges Braque, in an interview with John Richardson ("The Power of Mystery") published in the *Observer* (UK), December 1, 1957, and revised by Richardson for his book on Braque in the Penguin Modern Painters series (1959).

19. Braque, "The Power of Mystery."

20. Stuart Davis, quoted in Eugene C. Goosen, *Stuart Davis* (New York: Braziller, 1959).

21. This exhibition, which was on view at Cordier & Ekstrom from October 6 to October 24, 1964, marked a major turning point in Bearden's career.

22. German-born black graphic artist (1886–1953) who provided the decorations for Alain Locke's anthology *The New Negro.*

# THE POLITICAL BEARDEN

*Brent Hayes Edwards*

Throughout the large body of criticism on the significance of Romare Bearden as an artist, it remains uncommon to find his work or career being described as *political* in any sense of the term. Upon first glance, this reluctance may seem surprising, given that Bearden was indelibly forged as an artist in the cauldron of unrest and activism of the 1930s, and given that the "turning point" or "anchor"[1] of his development as a painter — his use of photomontage and photostat techniques in his Projections series — took place in 1963–64, in a manner that was directly related to his experience as an artist during the Civil Rights movement. The issue is all the more complex in that this shying away from the political is not just a feature of the critical treatments of Bearden's art, but also a predilection in Bearden's own comments on his career. In a 1969 essay he wrote with the help of Albert Murray for the magazine *Leonardo*, Bearden opens by discussing his education during the mid-1930s at the New York Art Students League under George Grosz: "When I first started to make pictures I was particularly interested in using art as an instrument of social change. As far as I was concerned at the time . . . art techniques were simply the means that enabled an artist to communicate a message — which, as I saw it then, was essentially a social, if not a political one."[2] But by the conclusion of the essay, he tells us that it is not his "aim to paint about the Negro in America in terms of propaganda," and warns that "in some instances commentators have tended to overemphasize what they believe to be the social elements in my work."[3] Asked in an interview about his political affiliations the year before, he had proclaimed, "I have none."[4] And up to the end of his life, his statements were consistent in their agnosticism: "If you look at one of my paintings, it does not tell you to go out and vote, but it does tell you about the eternal verities of life," he said in the 1980s, adding that political exhortation and protest "isn't, I think, the province of art anymore — if it ever has been."[5]

In the influential considerations of Bearden by his friends Ralph Ellison and Albert Murray, the word *political* is studiously avoided. Ellison, in his seminal catalogue essay from 1968, refuses to employ the term, but also might be said to indicate by implication the very horizon of its applicability. Characteristically, Ellison is above all concerned to champion the aesthetic at the expense of the "sociological." Bearden, with his extraordinary formal innovation and his keen sense of tradition, captures the complexities of the world with "the eye of a painter, not a sociologist."[6] His painting offers a "freshness of impact that employs neither sociological cliché nor raw protest." Unlike so many African American artists, Bearden has succeeded in not being "restricted by sociological notions of racial separatism." There is undeniable power in his collages, but "no preaching," Ellison says.[7] And yet, Ellison makes clear the degree to which Bearden's photographic collages of the mid-1960s arise out of the historical context of the period, and possess a relevance that might have easily been termed *political*, if that word were allowed to have some resonance beyond the narrow straits of cliché and protest: Bearden's "ability to make the unseen manifest," Ellison argues, "allows us some insight into the forces which now clash and rage as Negro Americans seek self-definition in the slums of our cities."[8]

Writing against the current, here I will suggest a few of the ways one might indeed consider Bearden's work as political: through the insights it offers into what one might term the politics of process, the politics of pedagogy, and the politics of collaboration. My point is not to seek out and identify some fixed checklist of investments or characteristics in his work, but instead to argue that his art must force us to redefine our very definitions of politics.

Such an approach to Bearden must involve a reconsideration of the photomontage works I have already mentioned. As Myron Schwartzman has written, "Bearden's Projections of the early 1960s were not only the result of his decisive turn from abstraction to representational work in collage by 1963–64 but also the articulation of his attitudes as an artist toward political and social upheaval."[9] The formal innovation, as Bearden puts it, involves the incorporation of "techniques of the camera eye and the documentary film to, in some measure, personally involve the onlooker."[10] Famously, works such as *Mysteries, Spring Way, Uptown Looking Downtown*, and *The Dove* are composed of cutouts of photos from popular magazines and books. This both relies on the "documentary" aspect of periodical print culture, and at the same time seems to disturb or threaten the naturalism — the seemingly transparency and authenticity — of that source medium, since the photos are systematically cut up, reconfigured, and recombined. As Bearden once told Mary Schmidt Campbell, "In my work, if anything I seek connections, so that my paintings can't be only what they appear to represent."[11]

First of all, this cut-up process breaks the seeming integrity, and the implied ethnographic fixity, of the original journalistic images. The collages are "documents" that shimmer and shake. As Bearden puts it, "when some photographic detail, such as a hand or eye, is taken out of its original context and is fractured and integrated into a different space and form configuration, it acquires a plastic quality it did not have in the original photograph."[12] Also, since many "disparate elements" (say, an eye from a photo of an African American in the U.S. South in *Life* magazine, and a mouth from a photo of a Benin mask from *National Geographic*) are combined in a single figure, a single face, the strategies of collage demonstrate that the complexity of black individuality and black life can only be captured using "multiple forms of representation."[13] In other words, the technique defies and explodes the dumb reductiveness of racial stereotype — the notion that the black experience can be summed up with a single adjective, dismissed with a single symbol. One is compelled instead to navigate the multiplicity that makes up any individual, any historical moment, any scene on any day on any Harlem street — to come to terms with relationality, with what Bearden comes to call the *intervals* innate in human life: "Objects do not exist for me," he has said, "except insofar as a rapport exists between them and between them and myself. In other words it is not the objects that matter to me but what is in between them; it is this in-between that is the real subject of my pictures."[14]

This effect can only be termed political, for it transforms the way we see the world around us: it requires that we learn what Bearden, in a 1975 essay called "Humility," calls "wisdom in the face of complexity."[15] On more than one occasion, Bearden describes his approach to improvisation in painting by referring to the writings on war strategy of the Prussian general Carl von Clausewitz. According to Clausewitz, "the solution to a battle is very simple. . . . The difficulty, he said, is that you have so many choices as to which one to pick as the right one. . . . You have this confusion: you must remember this confusion. How in all this confusion do you pull all these things together?"[16] If collage technique can be said to be a way to "remember the confusion" that is the condition of decision, then it is political in a sense that is eminently Ellisonian, if we recall the injunction at the end of *Invisible Man* that "the mind that has conceived a plan of living must never lose sight of the chaos against which that pattern was conceived."[17]

Cutout collage is also Ellisonian in that it cuts time; it sees around corners. I have always found it striking that the raw material of Bearden's Projections is so often photographs from weekly magazines and monthly journals. That is, the cutouts in their very form are an intervention into "the image of American society presented by the newspapers, magazines and radio," which according to Ellison "often missed much of the sheer human complexity of the life we knew."[18] Bearden's collage painting breaks up the serial time of news culture, undoing its easy generalizations and endlessly repeated formulae, with an art that reveals "that which has been concealed by time, custom and our trained incapacity to perceive the truth."[19] The same year Bearden first showed his Projections, Dr. Kenneth Clark wrote about the Harlem riots that the violence had less to do with police brutality—much less some behavioral pathology—than with the "basic and complex problems" of the neighborhood, "the pattern of violence which is Harlem," as he described it: "the chronic day-to-day quiet violence to the human spirit which exists and is accepted as normal."[20] If news coverage can be said to be one mode of that "pattern," then Bearden with his collages strives "to bring a new visual order into the world, and through his art he seeks to reset society's clock by imposing upon it his own method of defining the times."[21]

In one 1967 radio interview, Bearden himself suggested that politics in art was indeed a matter of the redefinition of values through visual means: "trying to turn somebody away from something to look at it from another way."[22] We "confuse protest" when we think of it as solely a matter of "illustration," as though political art must involve a realistic depiction of injustice, Bearden explained; "protest art doesn't always have to be about a Negro being lynched."[23] Politics in art can also be a matter of a certain brand of incisive humor, Bearden argued, citing the short films of Charlie Chaplin and the plays of Bertolt Brecht. And even a seemingly straightforward still life by Cézanne can be considered "a great protest painting," Bearden said—alluding to the 1898 *Still Life with*

*Skull* ("a sideboard, some apples, a skull, a tablecloth")—because it represents a rejection in its very form of "all of the existing values in art of the time—the Academy and all of the moribund values that it stood for."[24] In other words, even when Bearden shied away from words such as *protest* and *political*, it was less a matter of quiescence or apathy than a sign of his reluctance to reduce those terms into a hidebound aesthetics of social realism, as though there were only a limited and fixed range of ways that art could have an impact in the world. This expansive, open-ended, continually recalibrated sense of the political crops up time and again in Bearden's interviews as well as in his writings, such as this undated poetic fragment in which the speaker longs for the capacity to return to a past moment that suggested "what unknowing things know" in a way that charted "where the edge of my world can be":

What is it?
I'm trying really to remember
The clock has stopped
Now I can never know
Where the edge of my world can be
If I could only enter that old calendar
That opens to an old, old July
And learn what unknowing things know . . . [25]

Such a resetting of values through art might also be described as a form of pedagogy: we *learn* to see otherwise. Bearden was never an academic, but he was a committed teacher. We should recall that his turn to photomontage had its origins in an autodidactic approach to European art history: Bearden first used photostat enlargement when he was studying techniques of oil painting by enlarging photographs of works by Giotto, Duccio, Rembrandt, De Hooch, and others, coloring in the reproductions to gain a sense of their spacing and structure.[26] Albert Murray has said that the photo projection, for Bearden, was first and foremost "a teaching device."[27] I would go even further: the impulse to "projection" might best be described as an impulse toward the pedagogical amplification of polyphony. The Projections blow up the journalistic document in both senses of the verb.

Of course, pedagogy is very much the concern of almost all of Bearden's published writing as well, especially the books he co-wrote with Carl Holty and Harry Henderson.[28] Jacqueline Francis reminds us that *The Painter's Mind*, the book Bearden and Holty wrote over more than twenty years of correspondence and conversation, is expressly addressed to the "young artist" and the "modern student."[29] In the introduction to the monumental *A History of African-American Artists*, Henderson explains the origins of that project:

> Our attempt to create a history of African-American artists grew out of a
> request in 1965 from the Museum of Modern Art to Romare Bearden that he
> talk with a group of students about the history of development of black artists
> in America. He found that he could put together a few scanty notes on only a
> dozen artists before his own generation. His concern about this situation led to
> our discussions, our research, and to this book — a book of discovery, a chal-
> lenging effort to uncover the history of African-American artists.[30]

This longstanding and multifaceted commitment is animated by a politics
of pedagogy — an engaged sense of teaching as a crucial mode of social and
epistemological intervention — which we have not yet given the attention it de-
serves in coming to terms with Bearden's legacy.

Bearden and Henderson structure their history of African American visual
art around the lives of individual artists, "believing individual histories to be
most revealing."[31] Nonetheless their own joint project might be taken as evidence of the importance of collaboration for Bearden. Indeed, one might say
that the most remarkable characteristic of Bearden's career may be his persistent devotion to working with others. There remains much to say about this
facet of his work, since even some of his most intimate partners, like Albert
Murray, have tended to insist on his individual talent and originality — the
"consistency" of his sensibility — rather than elaborating on the processes of dialogue and mutual instigation that so clearly informed that accomplishment.[32]
It has been suggested that the origins of this sensibility lie in Bearden's first
years as a young artist in the 1930s, when he participated in the "306 Group"
and the Harlem Artists Guild, and took a studio just above the workplace of
Jacob Lawrence, and in the same building as writers such as Claude McKay,
William Attaway, and Allan Morrison.[33] But it is equally fascinating that the
epiphany of photomontage has its origins in a collective of fifteen black artists
called Spiral who met in July 1963 in Bearden's studio on Canal Street to discuss
the responsibility of the artist in the face of the Civil Rights movement.

Originally convened a month before the epochal March on Washington
"for the purpose of discussing the commitment of the Negro artist in the present struggle for civil liberties, and as a discussion group to consider common
aesthetic problems" (as Bearden himself recorded in his notes from the first

meeting),[34] the Spiral group continued to meet regularly over the next year and a half. Bearden said later that their ongoing, loose, sometimes contentious discussions about aesthetics and current events "meant a great deal to me especially in the formulation of my present ideas and way of painting."[35] The group acquired a meeting and gallery space on Christopher Street in the Village and organized a group show titled "Black and White." Bearden apparently suggested that the group work together to make a collaborative mural for the show. One member, Emma Amos, recalled that he brought "an enormous picture file, all cut out in shapes and stuffed in a bag . . . and spread it out all over the floor."[36] Only a couple of members, Richard Mayhew and Reginald Gammon, took up Bearden's suggestion, but they eventually lost interest, and Bearden ended up making by himself the photomontages that would become the Projections series. I am less concerned with the fact that the collaboration was aborted than with the way that collage for Bearden *starts* in collaboration — not just as an improvisational mode of composition, not just as an engagement with the documentary elements of photography, but also as an impulse to work together. Even later, Bearden would sign one of his earliest collages "Spiral Group."[37]

What would it mean to take seriously this collaborative impulse, not as some sort of threat to the integrity and independence of Bearden's ability as an artist, but as a political stance with profound implications for our entire understanding of art, imagination, and alliance? The point is not simply to note Bearden's "famously sociable nature,"[38] but moreover to ask whether there is a constitutive relationship between his "abundantly creative career" and the manifold "bonds and associations he made with other artists, particularly young writers, musicians, and photographers."[39] As art historian David C. Driskell has observed, "for Bearden, the making of friendships often went hand in hand with the making of art. He cherished sharing his artistry with those who sought his wise counsel, a gift that people of his genius rarely bestow."[40] If it might seem uncommon or perplexing to find such a deep collaborative ethos in an artist so often characterized as a singular "genius," it is because the very practice of collaboration — the simple fact of making things together in a manner that can make it difficult to discern where one person's contribution ends and another's starts — seems contrary to many of our expectations about individualism and authorship. But collaboration is also an issue of time. After all, the only way to share one's artistry is to *give time*, which is also to take precious time "away" from one's own practice, and to insist both that something invaluable happens when people take the time to work together, and by implication that one's own artistry cannot take precedence over the artistry of others. This is to say that to consider the importance of collaboration for Bearden must also mean to think about what one could call the politics of generosity.[41]

In the *Nicomachean Ethics*, Aristotle famously defines generosity specifically in relation to economic wealth. For Aristotle, however, generosity is not a matter of the sheer quantity of money one gives—a man who gives more money to the needy is not thereby more generous—but instead of the giver's "character" or "substance."[42] Interestingly, some translations of the *Nicomachean Ethics* employ the word *liberality* for this quality instead of *generosity* because, as one recent translator explains, *liberality* "reflects the connection of the Greek noun with *eleutheros*, free."[43] This is a quality evoked in countless descriptions of Bearden's personality: he was liberal with his time (which is not to say profligate, which is not to say undisciplined), as though he recognized that the only way to find himself as an individual artist was in the company of others, working with them, talking with them, laughing with them, studying with them.

It is possible to consider the implications of such remarkable generosity historically, as it were, in terms of the role and responsibilities of the black intellectual. From that angle, there is a striking divergence even between close colleagues and friends—between Bearden and Ralph Ellison, for example—that can only be called a political divergence.[44] It is also possible to consider the implications of generosity from an aesthetic point of view. The question then would be: is there a relationship between the freedom inherent in generosity, on the one hand, and the freedom that characterizes any artistic practice—the task, as Bearden himself puts it, of making "the right choices" in the face of a "mass of confusion"—and perhaps especially the inherently improvisational medium of collage, on the other?[45]

In *A History of African-American Artists*, the book Bearden co-wrote with Harry Henderson, there is no section devoted to Bearden's own work and career. Instead, as Jacqueline Francis has noted, Bearden shows up as a fellow traveler, an activist, a participant: "his membership in artists' circles and his interventions in the public discourse about black aesthetics and identity earn mention."[46] Even if this reticence is rooted in a characteristic "modesty," as Francis surmises, it still may also be read as a serious argument about the significance of collaboration in the history of African American visual art. It is certainly a stance that can be traced all the way back to the inception of Bearden's life as a practicing artist. In his very first published article, the 1934 "The Negro Artist and Modern Art," Bearden argued that the black artist

> must not be content with merely recording a scene as a machine. He must enter wholeheartedly into the situation he wishes to convey. The artist must be the medium through which humanity expresses itself. In this sense the greatest artists have faced the realities of life, and have been profoundly social.[47]

On one level, by writing that the greatest artists have been "profoundly social" Bearden was calling for what he termed "an intense, eager devotion to present day life": visual art that captures the ferment of social experience. But when he describes the artist himself as a "medium" of human expression, there is also the kernel of Bearden's commitment to artistic collaboration — a sense that art is unavoidably and complexly a social activity.

It is crucial to add that the fleeting model of Spiral is first of all a model of a black artistic *collective*, one that should take its place in the long and understudied history of black artistic and political collectives including — to mention only a few of Spiral's peers in the mid-1960s — the Umbra Poets' Workshop on the Lower East Side in New York, the Black Artists' Group in St. Louis, and the Association for the Advancement of Creative Musicians in Chicago.[48] Given the generational and artistic diversity of Spiral — the members of which "ranged from Abstract Expressionists to social protest painters," as Bearden noted[49] — it is worth recalling that collectivism can involve but does not necessitate collaboration, the difficult process of actually making art together. A collective is first and foremost what Andrew Ross calls "an adventure in mutuality," one organized not through some deference to hierarchy, much less by the fiction of unanimity, but instead by the premise of the "reciprocity of practice."[50] Thus the Spiral group's statement at their 1965 show emphasized the members' "mutual respect," which simultaneously made room for a "diversity" of interests and approaches.[51] The point is not to lament the failure of Spiral to "define and establish a unique aesthetic style reflecting African-American experience," as though the goal of collectivism is to discover some single proper black style — but instead to evaluate Mayhew's contention that the "basic Spiral concept" was above all a concern "with supporting one another."[52] Collective endeavor cannot simply invoke a "pluralism" of positions; one has to be willing to fight over the stakes of one's work, to push others and be pushed in return, throughout driven by what Stuart Hall has termed a "will to connect."[53]

One of the founders of the Subaltern Studies collective of historians, Ranajit Guha, has suggested that it is necessary to approach collective work

> not in a spirit of comparison and competition, but of convergence. To converge is to meet in a point as lines do in a figure, or to approximate as numbers do in a mathematical series, toward a given limit. Generally speaking, it is one thing to incline toward another in a specified direction and approach it closely enough to verge on it. There is nothing in these meanings shown for this phrase in the *Concise Oxford Dictionary* to impute to it any presupposition of similarity or to tie it to the notion of parity, as in comparison. For tendencies can be dissimilar and unequal in important respects and yet share an orientation toward some horizon each can recognize as its own. . . . There is room enough in such coalescence for all such tendencies to come alongside each other and let their borders touch in a lateral solidarity.[54]

These are useful formulations, if not necessarily easy solutions. From this perspective, collectivism must necessarily involve debate and dissent, but always in the view of a shared horizon. One might add that whether one calls the convergence a "solidarity" or not, another name for that horizon is the political. Collectivism is a struggle on the way to that limit point, carried out through what Guha calls "criticism anchored in convergence" — criticism that must go both ways, as convergence "relies on reciprocity as the very condition of its possibility."[55] In other words, collectivism means striving constantly to come together not in harmony, but in something like a productive dissonance.

Although the original group stopped meeting in the fall of 1965, Richard Mayhew has contended that as a force, Spiral never ended. As a concept, it retains a "mystique" that still compels: "like the spiral, it continues to extend, to engulf and encompass more and more black artists."[56] If so, then the formal principle of collectivism is embedded in Bearden's technique of photostat enlargement, and is implicit in all his collage paintings: like the photostats, collectivism works by *projection*, by the proliferation of relation, by what Mayhew calls "extended concept."[57] Another term for Bearden's photo-collage aesthetic, then, could have been the name of the collective itself: *spiral*, as the group statement at the first show defined it, "because, from a starting point, it moves outward embracing all directions, yet constantly upward."[58] This is to say that Bearden's collage work, his richest and most enduring mode, is itself an elaboration and exploration of the politics of collectivism: an imperative not just to improvise — putting something on top of something else — but also to play the pieces *together*.

## NOTES

1. Sarah Kennel, "Bearden's Musée Imaginaire," in *The Art of Romare Bearden*, ed. Ruth Fine (Washington, DC: National Gallery of Art/New York: Harry N. Abrams, 2003), 144.

2. Romare Bearden, "Rectangular Structure in My Montage Paintings," *Leonardo* (January 1969): 11; see full text in this volume, pp. 121–32. In writing this article, Bearden and Murray apparently drew from material in an interview Bearden had done the year before: Henri Ghent, interview with Romare Bearden, June 29, 1968, transcript, Archives of American Art, Smithsonian Institution, Washington, DC; full text in this volume, pp. 54–84.

3. Bearden, "Rectangular Structure in My Montage Paintings," 18.

4. Ghent, interview with Romare Bearden, transcript page 18.

5. Charles H. Rowell, "'Inscription at the City of Brass': An Interview with Romare Bearden," *Callaloo* 11, no. 3 (Summer 1988): 432.

6. Ralph Ellison, "Introduction" to *Romare Bearden: Paintings and Projections*, exh. cat. (Albany: Art Gallery of the State University of New York at Albany, 1968), reprinted as "The Art of Romare Bearden" in *The Collected Essays of Ralph Ellison*, ed. John F. Callahan (New York: Modern Library), 692; see full text in this volume, pp. 196–203.

7. Ellison, "The Art of Romare Bearden," 689, 692.

8. Ellison, "The Art of Romare Bearden," 692.

9. Myron Schwartzman, *Romare Bearden: His Life and Art* (New York: Harry N. Abrams, 1990), 209.

10. Bearden, "Rectangular Structure in My Montage Paintings," 14.

11. Ruth Fine, "Romare Bearden: The Spaces Between," in *The Art of Romare Bearden*, 33.

12. Bearden, "Rectangular Structure in My Montage Paintings," 17.

13. Bearden, "Rectangular Structure in My Montage Paintings," 17; Fine, "Romare Bearden: The Spaces Between," 39.

14. Albert Murray, "The Visual Equivalent of the Blues: Romare Bearden, 1970–1980," in *Romare Bearden: Finding the Rhythm*, exhibition catalogue, ed. Thomas R. Torperzer (Norman: University of Oklahoma Museum of Art, 1991), n.p.

15. Romare Bearden, "Humility," *New York Times* (January 31, 1975): 27; see full text in this volume, pp. 162–63.

16. Rowell, "'Inscription at the City of Brass': An Interview with Romare Bearden," 435.

17. Ralph Ellison, *Invisible Man* (1952; reprint New York: Vintage, 1989), 580.

18. Ralph Ellison, "Bearden," memorial address, 6 April 1988, *Callaloo* 36 (Summer 1988), 418; see full text in this volume, pp. 204–8.

19. Ellison, "The Art of Romare Bearden," 684–85.

20. Kenneth Clark, "Behind the Harlem Riots — Two Views," *New York Herald Tribune* (July 20, 1964): 1, 7.

21. Ellison, "The Art of Romare Bearden," 686.

22. Jeanne Siegel, "How Effective Is Social Protest Art? (Civil Rights)," interview with Romare Bearden, Alvin Hollingworth, and William Majors, WBAI radio broadcast, 14 December 1967, collected in Siegel, *Artwords: Discourse on the 60s and 70s* (Ann Arbor, MI: UMI Research Press, 1985), 92.

23. Siegel, "How Effective Is Social Protest Art?" 90, 88.

24. Siegel, "How Effective Is Social Protest Art?" 90.

25. "The Poetry of Romare Bearden," in *Romare Bearden in Black-and-White: Photomontage Projections 1964*, ed. Gail Gelburd (New York: Whitney Museum of American Art, 1997), 63.

26. Bearden, "Rectangular Structure in the Montage Paintings," 12.

27. Myron Schwartzman, interview with Albert Murray, September 1978, quoted in *Romare Bearden: His Life and Art*, 211.

28. Romare Bearden and Carl Holty, *The Painter's Mind: A Study of the Relations of Structure and Space in Painting* (New York: Crown, 1969; reprint New York: Garland, 1981); Romare Bearden and Harry Henderson, *Six Black Masters of American Art* (Garden City, NY: Zenith Books, Doubleday, 1972); Romare Bearden and Harry Henderson, *A History of African-American Artists from 1792 to the Present* (New York: Pantheon, 1993).

29. Jacqueline Francis, "Reading Bearden," in Fine, *The Art of Romare Bearden*, 187.

30. Harry Henderson, "Introduction," *A History of African-American Artists from 1792 to the Present*, xiii. See the chapter "The Twenties and the Black Renaissance," pp. 133–55 in this volume.

31. Henderson, "Introduction," xiii.

32. See Myron Schwartzman, "A Bearden-Murray Interplay: One Last Time," *Callaloo* 11, no. 3 (Summer 1988): 414. On the collaborations between Murray and Bearden, with titles in general (such as the *Prevalence of Ritual* series) and with the *Profiles* exhibitions in particular, see Schwartzman, *Romare Bearden: His Life and Art*, 216.

33. See Schwartzman, *Romare Bearden: His Life and Art*, 78–82; Ghent, interview with Romare Bearden, transcript page 2.

34. Bearden and Henderson, *A History of African-American Artists*, 400.

35. Ghent, interview with Romare Bearden, transcript page 9.

36. Gail Gelburd, "Romare Bearden in Black-and-White: The Photomontage Projections of 1964," in *Romare Bearden in Black-and-White*, 18. On the origins of Spiral and the plans to collaborate on a collage, see also Fine, "Romare Bearden: The Spaces Between," 28.

37. Schwartzman, *Romare Bearden: His Life and Art*, 211.

38. Francis, "Reading Bearden," 187.

39. David C. Driskell, "Foreword," in *Romare Bearden: Photographs by Frank Stewart* (San Francisco: Pomegranate, 2004), n.p.

40. Driskell, "Foreword."

41. I am grateful to Greg Tate for first asking me to reflect on the implications of Bearden's generosity at the conference at Columbia University where I first presented a shorter version of this essay.

42. Aristotle, *Nicomachean Ethics*, trans. David Ross, ed. Lesley Brown (New York: Oxford University Press, 2009), 61. It should be evident that in linking the question of generosity to giving time, I am also thinking of Jacques Derrida's *Given Time I: Counterfeit Money*, trans. Peggy Kamuf (Chicago: University of Chicago Press, 1992).

43. Translator's note, Aristotle, *Nicomachean Ethics*, 224.

44. With regard to the question of Ellison's generosity, one might consider the distressing evidence compiled in Arnold Rampersad's *Ralph Ellison: A Biography* (New York: Alfred A. Knopf, 2007).

45. Rowell, "'Inscription at The City of Brass': An Interview with Romare Bearden," 435. Myron Schwartzman describes collage as inherently an "improvisational medium" in *Romare Bearden: His Life and Art*, 217.

46. Francis, "Reading Bearden," 189.

47. Romare Bearden, "The Negro Artist and Modern Art," *Opportunity: Journal of Negro Life* 12 (December 1934): 372; see full text, pp. 87–90 in this volume.

48. See Michael Oren, "The Umbra Poets' Workshop, 1962–1965: Some Socio-Literary Puzzles," in *Studies in Black American Literature Vol. II: Belief vs. Theory in Black American Literary Criticism*, ed. Joe Weixlmann and Chester J. Fontenot (Greenwood, Fla.: Penkevill Publishing Co., 1986), 177–223; Lorenzo Thomas, "The Shadow World: New York's Umbra Workshop and Origins of the Black Arts Movement," *Callaloo* 4.1 (October 1978): 53–72; Benjamin Looker, *BAG: "Point from which creation begins": The Black Artists' Group of St. Louis* (St. Louis: Missouri Historical Society Press, 2004); George Lewis, *A Power Stronger Than Itself: The AACM and American Experimental Music* (Chicago: University of Chicago Press, 2008).

49. Bearden and Henderson, *A History of African-American Artists*, 400.

50. Andrew Ross, "Production," *Social Text* 100 (Fall 2009): 199. For the "reciprocity of practice," and on collectivism more broadly, see especially, Brent Hayes Edwards, Anna McCarthy, and Randy Martin, "Collective," *Social Text* 100 (Fall 2009): 74.

51. "Foreword," *First Group Showing (Works in Black and White)*, exhibition brochure (New York: Spiral Gallery, 1965), quoted in Fine, "Romare Bearden: The Spaces Between," 29.

52. Richard Mayhew, quoted in Romare Bearden and Harry Henderson, *A History of African-American Artists*, 403.

53. Stuart Hall, "Cultural Studies and Its Theoretical Legacies," in *Cultural Studies*, ed. Lawrence Goldberg, Cary Nelson, and Paul Treichler (New York: Routledge, 1992), 278.

54. Ranajit Guha, "Subaltern Studies: Projects for Our Time and Their Convergence," in *The Latin American Subaltern Studies Reader*, ed. Ileana Rodríguez (Durham, NC: Duke University Press, 2001), 37. See also Ranajit Guha, "On Some Aspects of the Historiography of Colonial India," in *Selected Subaltern Studies*, ed. Ranajit Guha and Gayatri Chakravorty Spivak (New York: Oxford University Press, 1988), where he writes, "we have no doubt that many other historiographical points of view and practices are likely to converge close to where we stand. Our purpose in making our own views known is to promote such a convergence" (43).

55. Guha, "Subaltern Studies," 38.

56. Mayhew, quoted in Bearden and Henderson, *A History of African-American Artists*, 403.

57. Mayhew, quoted in Bearden and Henderson, *A History of African-American Artists*, 403.

58. "Foreword," *First Group Showing (Works in Black and White)*, exhibition brochure (New York: Spiral Gallery, 1965).

# CIRCE IN BLACK
## HOMER, TONI MORRISON, ROMARE BEARDEN

*Farah Jasmine Griffin*

In 1977 two major African American artists, Romare Bearden and Toni Morrison, produced epic works inspired by African American culture and Homer's classic poem, the *Odyssey*. Bearden's *A Black Odyssey* is a series of twenty collages based on episodes from Homer. An exhibition of the works opened in April 1977 at the Cordier & Ekstrom Gallery on the East Side of Manhattan. Later that year, in September 1977, Alfred A. Knopf published Toni Morrison's third novel, *Song of Solomon* — the work that made undeniable her position as one of the world's most significant novelists. Like Bearden's *Odyssey* series, *Song of Solomon* brought together elements of Homer's work with scenes and symbols from African American history and culture. Although Morrison and Bearden were contemporaries and she visited him in his studio at least twice, she does not recall having seen the *Black Odyssey* exhibition. (Bearden would later gift her with his own highly colorful rendering of her character Pilate from *Song of Solomon*.[1]) Neither is the first African American artist to engage the *Odyssey*; Ralph Ellison's *Invisible Man* (1952), with its numerous references to the Homeric poem, precedes them by decades. With Ellison's central question of black identity in mind, let us ask: What do Morrison's and Bearden's 1977 engagements with Homer yield for modern representations of black life?

Bearden's collages are not illustrations of Homer's poem, but interpretations and elaborations of it, conversations with it. Bearden claims the *Odyssey* as a form that lets him orchestrate the epic tale of black Americans' ongoing search for home. Along the way, he places the African American blues tradition in dialogue with the Western literary tradition, and in so doing grants new insight into both; but most importantly, he reveals both the broad Western literary tradition and the deep riverbed of the blues as parts of the same ongoing human story. Morrison's work is driven by the forced movement from Africa to America, migrations from the American South to the North and back (including a mythical effort to return to Africa), a search for home and for both the father and the grandfather: the long-lost paternal ancestor and mythical flyer home to Africa. Morrison stirs a rich mix of ingredients from African American vernacular culture — folk tales of conjurers and flying Africans, blues songs, children's ring games, Afro-naming patterns — into forms and figures borrowed from Homer's *Odyssey*.

## LOCATING CIRCE

Morrison and Bearden were part of a continuum positing strong ties between the Western classics and peoples of African descent. In 1970 the classical scholar Frank M. Snowden, Jr., published *Blacks in Antiquity: Ethiopians in the Greco-Roman Experience*, followed by his co-authored *Image of the Black in Western Art I: From the Pharaohs to the Fall of the Roman Empire* (1976).[2] As early as 1948, Snowden, who joined Howard University's classics department faculty in 1940, published an important essay entitled "The Negro in Ancient Greece." The black presence in the ancient world, encounters and influences between Africans, Greeks, and Romans, as well as the ways contemporary conceptions of race departed from those of the ancient world — these were life-long topics of interest for Snowden.

Can there be any doubt that Bearden and Morrison, both serious readers and students of literature and history, were aware of Snowden's work? From 1949 to 1953, Morrison was an undergraduate classics minor at Howard, where she studied with Snowden, then chair of the classics department. Morrison did not take any class at Howard specifically on the black presence in the ancient world. She does note, however, that Snowden in particular always made clear that there was "much more" to the classical world than the Greeks and Romans,[3] and that she may have first become aware of Africans in ancient Greece through Snowden's classes. Though we may not be able to pin down the origins of her interest in this Afro/Euro-classics nexus, it has been an ongoing concern that flowered most fully in her 1988 essay, "Unspeakable Things, Unspoken." She writes:

> A large part of the satisfaction I have always received from reading Greek trag-
> edy, for example is in its similarity to Afro-American communal structures (the
> function of song and chorus, the heroic struggle between the claims of com-
> munity and individual hubris) and African Religion and philosophy. In other
> words, that is the reason it has quality for me — I feel intellectually at home
> there. . . . The point is, the form (Greek tragedy) makes available these varieties
> of provocative love because it is masterly — not because the civilization that is its
> referent was flawless or superior to all others.[4]

The novelist and the artist may also have been drawn to Homer because of the ancient Greeks' ready acknowledgement of the importance of Africa (of Egypt in particular) and Asia to the world they knew. From Homer to Herodotus, Greek writers were fully aware of the wide phenotypical and cultural variety of their world and staked their claims of superiority in their *Greekness*, not in any modern categories of race.[5] As Tessa Roynon notes, in 2006 when Morrison served as guest curator at the Musée du Louvre, "she designed three parcours or itineraries through the Antiquities collections, which were centered on her chosen overall theme . . . 'Etranger chez soi,' or 'The Foreigner's Home.'" The objects she chose "emphasized both the hybridized nature of the ancient world and the implications for modernity when the hybridity of that world is recognized." Roynon also argues that Morrison has always been interested in the Africanness of Euro-classicism as conventionally construed: the "confluence between African and Greek and Roman cultures."[6]

Consider that both Bearden and Morrison create superhuman figures modeled on Homer's Circe. Homer's creation is the enchantress from Greek oral traditions who turns humans into beasts. The daughter of the Sun god Helios and Oceanid Perse, she is also the aunt of Medea (herself an othered, foreign, priestess/maker of magic). Circe is well versed in the transformative powers of herbs and potions. Is it any wonder that both Bearden and Morrison would see her as a conjure woman? In the *Odyssey*, Circe lives in a mansion on the isle of Aeaea, far in the east. When Odysseus and his men, on their journey from Troy to Ithaca, come upon Circe's beautiful home, it is surrounded by lions, wolves, and other tail-wagging beasts. The men hear Circe singing. She welcomes them into her palace, and after drugging them she changes them to swine. Eventually Circe seduces Odysseus, who will remain her lover for a year and ultimately persuade her to reverse his men's sorry state. When their yearning for Ithaca compels Odysseus to depart she instructs him to go to Hades to consult with the spirits of the dead to find the way home. With her magic powers, and yet her inability to forestall her own abandonment, Circe has remained one of the most enduring figures in Western art, literary and otherwise: she who transforms those she encounters as she in turn is transformed by poets and painters who represent her.

Though Homer offers no evidence of her color, black Circes appear elsewhere in ancient Greek iconography — for example, on a drinking cup of the Classical era (fig. 26). Snowden describes this wine cup as follows: "In a skyphos, found in the sanctuary of the Kabeiroi near Thebes, Circe is depicted offering a cup to Odysseus. The snub nose, subnasal prognathism, and thick lips of Circe are clearly Negroid." Although we may now accuse Snowden of a kind of racial essentialism here, the profile of the Circe figure to which he alludes clearly does look like a person of African descent. Snowden makes note of black Circe's appearance on another vessel in which "Odysseus receives the magic draught from the black enchantress, one of whose victims, already a swine, stands in her loom." Both vessels date from the second half of the fifth century BCE. Snowden reads other black figures in Greek art from the fourth century BCE as devolving into "caricature and burlesque."[7] But according to Sheldon Cheek, such exaggerated "visual characterization of blacks as figures from Greek legend may have been derived from the belief that the African physiognomy could ward off the forces of evil." Cheek identifies these pieces as ritualistic objects, "associated exclusively with the Kabeirion, a sanctuary located several miles outside the Greek city of Thebes." This scholar also discusses an ancient cup featuring Odysseus's encounter with "the sorceress Circe," who offers him a potion (fig. 27). This Circe "appears unmistakably as a black woman, while Odysseus's image is in keeping with the standard type of the old man in Greek art." According to Cheek, "the underlying emphasis on powerful, occult forces in the Circe scene made it an ideal subject for use at the Kabeirion. The moment of potential metamorphosis from a rational creature into another, less comprehending form alludes to the ecstatic experience undergone by the initiates of the cult."[8]

Although she does not consider these ancient black Circes, Judith Yarnall's *Transformations of Circe: The History of an Enchantress* is nonetheless quite useful for exploring the goddess's many appearances through Western culture, from the *Odyssey* and *Aeneid* to *The Faerie Queene*, from James Joyce's *Ulysses*

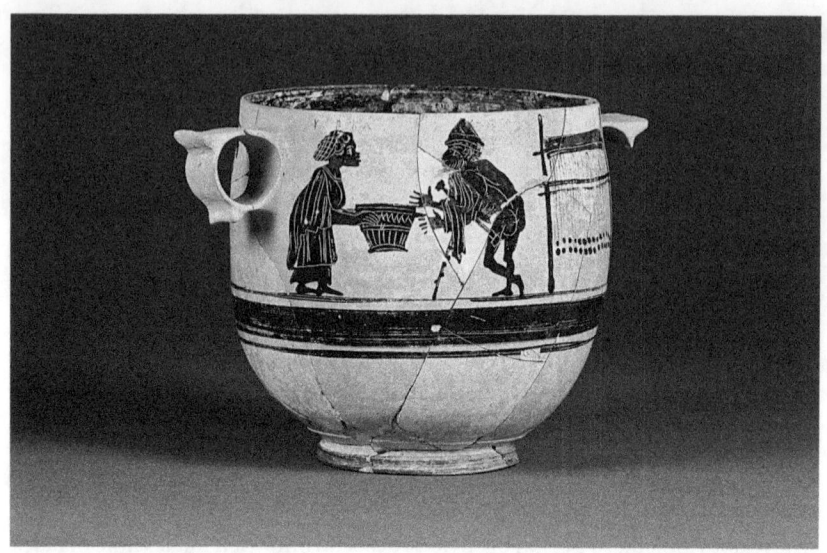

FIGURE 26  Circe and Odysseus. Black-figure skyphos from Boeotia, attributed to the
Kabeirion Sanctuary group, 450–420 BCE. British Museum, London (1893,0303.1). Courtesy
Bridgeman Images

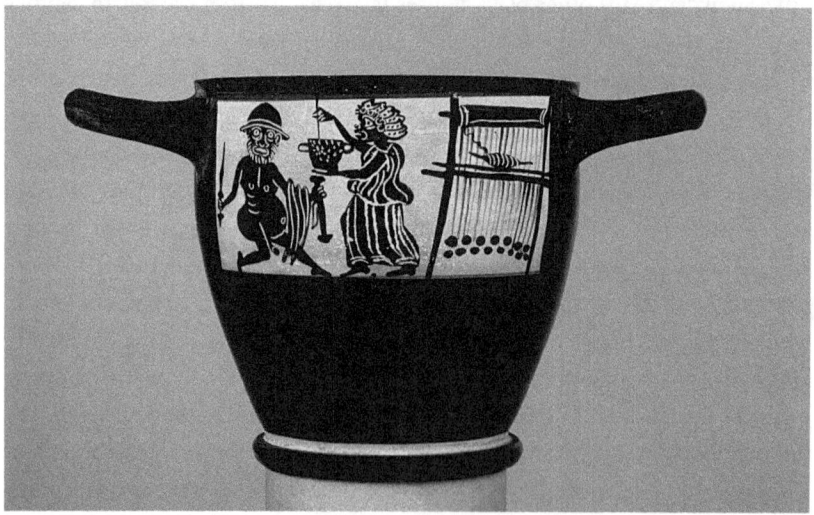

FIGURE 27  Circe and Odysseus. Black-figure skyphos from Boeotia, attributed to the
Kabeirion Sanctuary group, 4th century BCE. Ashmolean Museum, University of Oxford
(AN 1896–1908 G249). Courtesy Bridgeman Images

to Eudora Welty's eponymous short story and Margaret Atwood's "Circe/Mud Poems." For Yarnall, Circe is an archetype who serves as "an expression of a basic human experience, fear or desire." Throughout the centuries, Circe is represented as a figure of transcendence and transformation, one whose powers typically are overtly sexual in nature. Whether ancient, modern, or contemporary, myths of Circe "can be seen as mirrors, sometimes clouded and sometimes clear, of the fantasies and assumptions of the cultures that produced them."[9]

Bearden appears in one of Yarnall's footnotes as one of three twentieth-century male visual artists, including Georges Braque and Marc Chagall, who are attracted to the Circe myth. She considers his *Circe's Domain* collage the "most striking" of the series, observing, "Bearden's Circe is fiercer than Homer's; perhaps it was also inspired by legends of the warrior women of Dahomey." According to Yarnall, Morrison's Circe "is not the main focus of Morrison's attention or imagination, and so her own history and sensibility are not thoroughly explored." For this reason Yarnall does not elaborate upon *Song of Solomon*.[10]

# CIRC(E)ULATIONS

When Bearden and Morrison imagine Circe, this woman of ancient properties maintains her magical powers but possesses none of the grotesqueness of the caricatures on the Greek cups. She appears in three of the Beardens: *Circe's Domain*, *Circe Turns a Companion of Odysseus Into a Swine*, and *Odysseus Leaves Circe*. Robert O'Meally notes, "There are more images of Circe than of any other figure, including Odysseus."[11] In each of these works Circe appears with other figures. But it is important that in 1977, Bearden produced yet another Circe, a magnificent one not included in the Cordier & Ekstrom exhibit. Perhaps she was too powerful to be contained by any single series' narrative. This Circe demands her own telling.

The image I want to emphasize is Bearden's collage of various papers with foil, paint, and graphite on fiberboard: the untitled one I'm calling *Black Circe* (Plate 6). It is stunning. In this work, Circe alone dominates. As contemporary collage, she stands in bold profile, reminiscent of hieroglyphic figures on the walls of Egyptian tombs or the flattened black figures of Greek pottery. Black Circe, however, is also on the move. She is an African priestess/royal figure, attended by birds, snakes, and a miniature lion. This Circe is enchanting, seductive, powerful, and very black. Her blackness also recalls Morrison's character

Pilate's rejoinder (in *Song of Solomon)* to the idea that the color black, even "pitch black," was ever just one thing:

> You think dark is just one color, but it ain't. There're five or six kinds of black. Some silky, some woolly. Some just empty. Some like fingers. And it don't stay still. It moves and changes from one kind of black to another. Saying something is pitch black is like saying something is green. What kind of green? Green like my bottles? Green like a grasshopper? Green like a cucumber, lettuce, or green like the sky is just before it breaks loose to storm? Well, night black is the same way. May as well be a rainbow.[12]

In much of Bearden's *Odyssey* series, we are struck by the deep cobalt blue of the waters upon which Odysseus travels. But in Bearden's *Black Circe* blue is not the dominant color, though a brilliant cobalt pops from the snakes, from Circe's ribbons, and the fringes of her skirt. Instead it is the vividness of *red* that most commands attention here. Against the urgency of this work's red, Circe seems to dance. I am especially drawn by that space of red that is created between her curved torso and her graceful arm. Here is an alluring choreography of North Africa (especially Nubian and Egyptian) or of the Middle East. Black Circe's hand, positioned like a dancer's, gestures down to the elegant calf and pointed toe. It should not surprise us that Bearden's Circe uses dance as one of her tools of magic, seduction, and conjure. (Bearden's wife, Nanette, was a modern dancer/company leader.) Dancers are shape-shifters, transforming their own bodies as through their art they transform the consciousness of those observing them. Bearden's dancing Black Circe thus joins a long, international line of dancer divinities, from the dancing Hindu Shiva to the dancing Orisha of Condomble and Santeria ritual. Choreographed movement through time and space has long been attributed to divine figures, across the world.[13]

Among Circe's adornments—which include bracelets, earrings, bejeweled collar, and headdress—are a snake wrapped around her lower arm and a bird balanced in her hand. From Eve and the serpent in Eden, Damballah the snake god of Vodun, and the staff that turns into a snake as evidence of God's power in the book of Exodus, the snake frequently accompanies the spiritually powerful figure. The word *Circe* is the feminine form of *kirkos,* ancient Greek for "falcon" or "hawk." Furthermore, as Yarnall posits, "Long before Homer imagined Circe, birds had been associated with the divine."[14] Consequently, Bearden's Circe is embellished with symbols of spiritual power that link her to ancient civilizations from Africa to Asia, the Middle East, and beyond.

Morrison's character Circe is an enchantress as well, one possessing a seductive, "mellifluent" voice. But at almost one hundred years old, her appearance is witchlike. She is a midwife who lives in the ruins of a mansion, surrounded by specially bred guard dogs. After the murder of their father, Macon Dead, Sr., Circe, a servant in the former slaveholding Butler household, rescues, hides, and takes care of his two children, Macon Dead, Jr., and Pilate. Many years later, Macon's son Milkman Dead searches for the gold he and his father believe Pilate has buried near their childhood home. Milkman seeks and finds Circe, who he hopes will be able to point him toward the money. Instead she guides him to trace his family's history and pathways toward his identity. Having been his protector, Milkman now calls her "healer, deliverer, in other words she would have been the head nurse at Mercy." As with Homer's Circe, Morrison's Circe serves as Milkman's guide to the realms and spirits of the dead: she who sends him farther south and fills in the story of the first Macon and his Native American wife (Milkman's grandmother), Sing.

Homer's Circe is drastically *othered*: not Greek, not goddess, not mortal. Morrison suggests the Africanicity of Circe, dwelling as she does between the worlds of the spirit and of the mortal, a woman whose practice of the medicinal arts is magical. She is keeper of the past through which Milkman must pass to reach his ancestors, his history, himself. She charts the path. With their high-columned mansion, the white Butlers laid claim to a classical past created to serve the slaveholders, an invented classicism stripped of its polycultural depth and diversity. But Morrison assures us that it is the enslaved whose roots are more ancient than Eden and whose progeny reach into the present.

Similarly, Bearden invokes polyculture by framing Circe with a classical column on the right, but a totemic column atop an altar on the left, complete with a votive skull indicating her power over life and death.

The practice of slave masters naming their slaves after classical figures may explain how Circe acquires her name. In this way she shares a literary kinship with Faulkner's Clytemnestra, called Clytie, from *Absalom, Absalom*. Both figures ironically take on otherworldly characteristics of their classical namesakes. Clytie is the biracial daughter of the slave owner Thomas Sutpen. Throughout that novel, Clytie is an all-knowing though almost silent figure who maintains a sense of loyalty to the family of her birth until the book's end, when in a final dramatic act, she sets fire to the plantation home. Much has been written about Morrison's relationship to Faulkner, both because she wrote her MA thesis on him and because of the numerous instances of interplay between her work and his. Speaking of similarities between Clytie and Circe, critic Nancy Ellen Batty notes "the remarkable intertextual resonance between Quentin's encounter with the Sutpens' house servant, Clytie, and Milkman's encounter with the Butlers' servant Circe." For Batty, Clytie and Circe are drawn together by "their classically inspired names, their wizened appearances, their apparently extreme ages. Each guards, if for very different reasons, a former master's house."[15] Unlike Clytie, Circe has no biological relationship to the white family to whom she is enslaved. Nor is she loyal to them. Whereas Clytie's defiance of the white Rosa Caulfield is to protect the family, Circe's defiance is ultimately to protect the children of a man killed by the Butlers.

Circe is the subversive agent in the master's house, undermining it from within. Unlike Clytie, Circe doesn't burn the mansion; she outlives its owner, claims her space within it, relishes watching it rot. She tells Milkman: "They loved this place. Loved it. . . . They loved it. Stole for it, lied for it, killed for it. But I'm the one left. Me and the dogs. . . . Everything in this world they lived for will crumble and rot." What doesn't rot on its own, she will allow the dogs to destroy. She asserts, "Ha! And I want to see it all go, make sure it does go, and that nobody fixes it up."[16]

Under her watch there will be no further reproduction of the master class, but she nurtures the Native/black progeny. As Homer's Circe directs Odysseus and sends him on his way, Morrison's Circe is the gateway to a deeper South, to which she sends Milkman. She directs him to a place of origins — Shalimar, Virginia — that is closer to Africa, which holds the blood of the ancestors as well as their stories, their history, their myths, and their meanings. Circe, the immortal, lives for a patient sense of revenge and for the return of the black son. She gains pleasure not by killing but by watching her master's monument to history decay from within.

Through her Black Circe figure, Morrison questions the quest that animates the *Odyssey*: a quest defined by plundered booty, traffic in women, slavery, and plotting a return that will reestablish the order of the patriarchy. She juxtaposes this version of the quest narrative with one that uncovers a suppressed history of those victimized of the West, and that manifoldly questions the patriarchy as it insists, at quest's end, on reconstructed masculinities and femininities.

If Yarnall is correct in her assertion that versions of Circe are "mirrors . . . of the fantasies and assumptions of the cultures that produced them," then what do Morrison's and Bearden's Circes have to say about the times in which they were produced? Both artists turned to the epic as a form for casting a tale

of the African Diaspora. They were not alone: 1977 also saw the first showing of the mini-series *Roots,* which may be called an epic as well, on national
television. (Bearden did the January 22–28, 1977, cover for the *T V Guide* that
announced this new series.) All these long-form works appeared during a decade
that witnessed important strides for African Americans as well as backlash to the
progress made during the Civil Rights and especially the Black Power movements.
Instead of dealing with the urgency and immediacy of the tumultuous sixties
and early seventies, each takes a long view, insisting on a black history stretch-
ing back to ancientdom and tracing a people of world significance. They cast
figures in black that are larger than life, spanning seas and continents, and who
bring with them their own traditions and blue-fused cultures. By the late seventies the epic dimensions of Black American History were more evident than
ever: the migrations of the Middle Passage, the Civil War, Reconstruction, the
Great Migration, and the Black Freedom Struggle. All of these are fundamental
to the stories of the West, a configuration which is itself dependent upon and
shaped by peoples of African descent. The Circe figure gives place of honor to
the power and mystery of a black woman, who whether Goddess, Queen, or
Servant is both a connection to the past and navigator of the future.

From Homer to Bearden to Morrison, Circe migrates through time and
space, texts and contexts, shaping, defining, refining all with whom she comes
into contact. When her vehicle is Bearden's *Black Odyssey* or Morrison's *Song of
Solomon* — she challenges, speaks to, incorporates, deconstructs, and redirects
a tradition that can never again render itself only white and male.

## NOTES

1. See Toni Morrison, "Abrupt Stops and Unexpected Liquidity: The Aesthetics of
Romare Bearden," pp. 178–84, fig. 22, in this volume.

2. Frank M. Snowden, Jr., *Blacks in Antiquity: Ethiopians in the Greco-Roman Experience* (Cambridge, MA: The Belknap Press of Harvard University Press, 1970); Jean Ver-
coutter et al., *The Image of the Black in Western Art, Volume 1: From the Pharaohs to the
Fall of the Roman Empire* (Cambridge, MA: Harvard University Press, 1976); Frank M.
Snowden, Jr., "The Negro in Ancient Greece," *American Anthropologist* 50.1 (1948): 31–44.

3. Conversation with the author, August 22, 2016, 3:30 PM.

4. "Unspeakable Things Unspoken: The Afro-American Presence in American Literature" (The Tanner Lectures on Human Values. Delivered at the University of Michigan,
October 7, 1988), *Michigan Quarterly Review* 28.1 (Winter 1989): 2.

5. Morrison writes of the "inauguration of classical studies and Greek," which witnessed the elimination "of Egypt as the cradle of civilization and its model, and [replaced] it with Greece. The triumph of the process was that Greece lost its own origins and became itself original"; "Unspeakable Things Unspoken," 150.

6. Tessa Roynon, *Toni Morrison and the Classical Tradition: Transforming American Culture* (Oxford: Oxford University Press, 2013), 396, 381.

7. Snowden, *Blacks in Antiquity*, 27, 160.

8. Sheldon Cheek, "Why Greek Goddesses Appear as Black Women on an Ancient Ceramic Cup," *The Root*, http://www.theroot.com/articles/history/2015/05/blacksinwesternarttwhygreekgoddessesappearasblackwomen/2/.

9. Judith Yarnall, *Transformations of Circe: The History of an Enchantress* (Urbana: University of Illinois Press, 1994), 2.

10. Yarnall, *Transformations of Circe*, 221, 183.

11. Electronic exchange with the author, October 4, 2018. For context, see also Robert O'Meally, *Romare Bearden, A Black Odyssey* (New York: DC Moore Gallery, 2008), 46–54.

12. Toni Morrison, *Song of Solomon* (New York: Vintage, 2004), 41.

13. In certain traditions, Jesus Christ is regarded as Leader of the Dance. See Havelock Ellis, *The Dance of Life* (New York: Modern Library, 1929), 40–41.

14. Yarnall, *Transformations of Circe*, 29.

15. Nancy Ellen Batty, "Riff, Refrain, Reframe: Toni Morrison's Song of Absalom," in *Unflinching Gaze: Morrison and Faulkner Re-Envisioned*, ed. Carol A. Kolmerten, Stephen M. Ross, and Judith Bryant Wittenberg (Jackson: University of Mississippi Press, 1997), 84.

16. Morrison, *Song of Solomon*, 77.

# CONJURE AND COLLAPSE IN THE ART OF ROMARE BEARDEN

*Rachael DeLue*

To begin, let me say something about the first word in the title of this essay: "conjure." The verb "to conjure" is a complex one, for it includes in its standard definition a great range of possible actions or operations, not all of them equivalent, or even compatible. In its most common usage, "to conjure" means to perform an act of magic or to invoke a supernatural force, by casting a spell, say, or performing a particular ritual or rite. But "to conjure" is also to influence, to beg, to command or constrain, to charm, to bewitch, to move or convey, to imagine, to visualize, to call to mind, or to remember. "Conjure" was used in English as early as the fourteenth century; it derived from the Latin "conjurare," meaning to band together through an oath or conspire.[1] As such, "to conjure" bears a significant, resonant weight, one constituted by its tangle of meanings as well as by its long passage across continents and through history. For the twentieth-century American artist Romare Bearden, the term "conjure" had a very specific meaning. The shape of that meaning is the subject of this essay.

Born in 1911 in Charlotte, North Carolina, Bearden moved with his family to New York City in 1914, settling in Harlem by 1920. As a child and young man, Bearden attended public school in New York, but also spent long stretches of time with relatives in Pittsburgh, PA; Mecklenburg County, NC; and Lutherville, MD. As a young adult in the 1930s and, after that, in the 1940s and 1950s, Bearden juggled college; work as a cartoonist and illustrator; a job with New

York's Department of Social Services; art classes; a stint in the army; solo and group exhibitions at various New York galleries; study in Paris at the Sorbonne; travel in Italy and Spain; contact with prominent artists and philosophers, including Joan Miró, Pablo Picasso, Gaston Bachelard, and Hannah Arendt; commercial songwriting; and marriage. In 1959, he and his wife, Nanette, whom he had wed in 1954, moved into a loft on Canal Street in Manhattan, where Bearden would reside for the rest of his life.[2]

During this time, Bearden's work for the most part alternated between social realist imagery — straightforward, unstinting depictions of everyday people, especially the working class, including his *Factory Workers*, from 1942, which was chosen to illustrate an article in *Fortune* magazine entitled "The Negro's War" — and experimental, quasi-abstract pictures, often with biblical or mythical subjects, such as *The Payment of Judas* (1945–46).[3] Through the 1950s, Bearden's primary medium was paint — oil, acrylic, watercolor, or gouache — but in the late 1950s and early 1960s he began to experiment with collage, pasting paper onto canvas to create figurative or abstract compositions; he also turned out a small number of completely nonobjective works.[4]

It was not until 1964, when he was in his early 50s, that Bearden turned his full attention to the medium of collage and, also, to the medium of photomontage, a technique in which a picture is created by combining cutout parts of photographs. It was at this moment that he began producing the works for which he is now best known, including *The Dove* (1964) (fig. 28), a collage made out of cut and pasted paper affixed to board and elaborated with gouache and pencil.

In *The Dove*, Bearden presents the scene on a New York street, the sidewalk thick with people strolling, talking, leaning, looking out of windows, and sitting on stoops. The picture registers almost immediately as a snapshot of the noisy, thick hustle of urban life and it does so despite the fact that it is, as a picture, a very strange one. Scraps of paper, cutout photographs, and touches of paint and pencil form the bodies, buildings, and objects that we see. Bits of imagery from widely disparate sources — newspapers, magazines, product labels, construction paper, black-and-white or color photographs, wallpaper samples, architectural drawings — combine to create not a set of coherent forms but a series of disjointed and bizarrely scaled objects and bodies that lurch and stutter down the street as would a marionette puppet across a stage if operated by someone still learning the ropes. In the right half of the picture, a man whose head is far too large for his body, his eyes blocked or lopped off by a scrap of

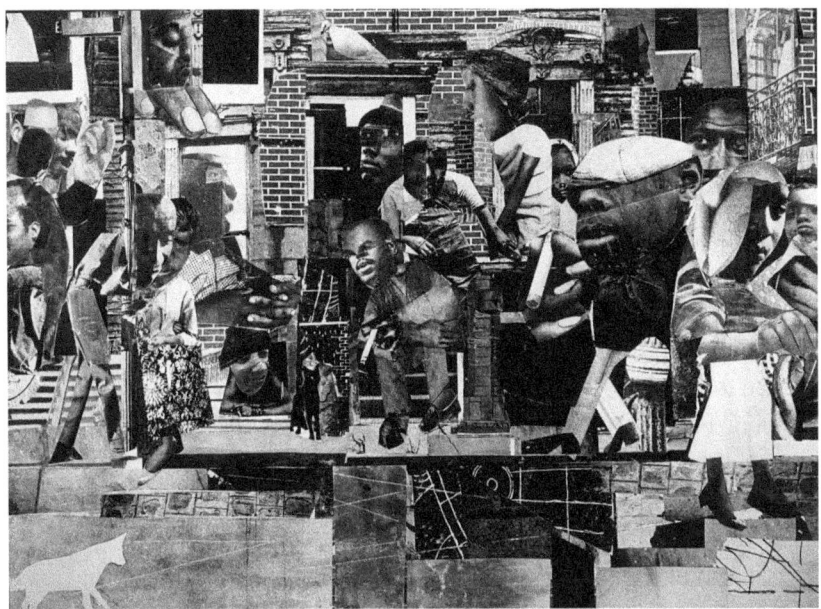

FIGURE 28 Romare Bearden, *The Dove (Projection)*, 1964. Print of montage painting, 35 × 48 in. (88.9 × 121.9 cm). Art © Romare Bearden Foundation/Licensed by VAGA, New York

paper representing a cap, leans against a fire hydrant as a massive hand proffers an even more massive cigarette. Behind him stands a woman who holds in one oversize hand a piece of red and yellow fabric bearing a child's head and in the other a length of twisted, rope-like metal; the tumult of her barely cohering body is exacerbated by the shifting and irregular patchwork quilt of colors and patterns on which she walks. To the left of the eyeless man a cluster of five figures — a child, a woman, and three men — unfolds in space, accordionlike, such that they seem to expand and contract in size, ballooning or shrinking, but not at all consistently or according to the rules of proportion or scale, so that it feels as if one sees them simultaneously from close up and far away. Their body parts spill and tumble across the small space that they occupy, seeming to come together as human wholes only by chance. A similar effect governs the left half of the picture, occupied by at least eight different figures, and here it can be even more difficult to tell which leg, arm, head, finger, or eye belongs to whom. Vivid reds, yellows, blues, and browns punctuate Bearden's view of this New York street, which is otherwise a near-colorless mélange of washed-out grays and blacks, creating a vibrant, rhythmic march from one side to the other that further disrupts the stability of the scene, sending its contents spinning and making it near impossible for the eyes to slow down and settle on a particular part, pinballing as they do from one thing to the next.

Contributing to the strangeness of the scene, despite its whirl and tumult and its effects of fragmentation and dislocation, and also despite its visual appeal — the fact that one just does not want to stop looking because Bearden offers such a fascinating and perplexing set of sights to see — is the picture's seamlessness, even slickness. To make his collages, Bearden began with a small board to which he added his cut paper and photographs as well as his paint and pencil marks; he then applied a resin emulsion adhesive to the whole and pressed the pieces to the board with a roller such that they settled into the viscous and thick adhesive and lay flat and still. While the adhesive dried, Bearden weighted the boards so that they would not warp.[5] Such a technique, in *The Dove* and in Bearden's other collages, creates the effect of a heavy varnish laid down over a painting's surface; despite the variation among the collage's many parts, the individual pieces can seem, at a material level, and against all odds, to be cut from the same cloth, their differences in texture and depth smoothed out and suppressed by the unifying, even petrifying resin. That such a smooth, fluid surface gives rise to such exuberant cacophony is part of what I would call the strange magic, and also the strange pleasure, of Bearden's collages.[6]

Almost all of the collages from this period boast similar effects. Their subject matter, as with *The Dove,* is also typical: scenes from everyday life in the African-American communities of New York, Pittsburgh, Charlotte, and other of Bearden's haunts, and Bearden's own memories of these places and their people growing up — sitting down to a meal or a game of cards, watching trains pull in and out of the yard, listening to music on a Saturday night. Typical in style and subject, also, are works such as *Prevalence of Ritual: Conjur Woman* (1964) (fig. 29) and *Conjur Woman* (1971) (fig. 30). Both feature a "Conjur Woman" ("conjur" without an "e," as Bearden spells it), and thus bring us back to that wide-ranging and slippery verb I discussed above, "to conjure." Bearden's turn to collage in 1963 was accompanied by the appearance of the character of the conjur woman in his work; the frequency with which he depicted or evoked her in the mid-1960s and beyond suggests her special significance within his artistic practice and also, I would argue, a special relationship between her and the very medium of collage. "A conjur woman," wrote Bearden in 1969, "was an important figure in a number of Southern Negro rural communities. She was called on to prepare love potions; to provide herbs to cure various illnesses; and

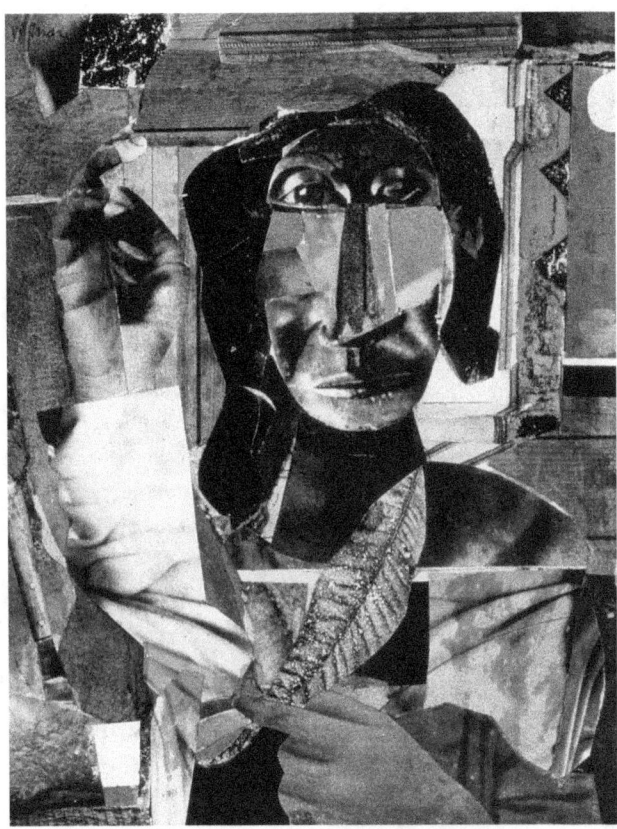

FIGURE 29 Romare Bearden, *Prevalence of Ritual: Conjur Woman*, 1964. Collage of various papers with foil, ink, and graphite on cardboard, 9 3/8 × 7 1/4 in. (23.8 × 18.4 cm). Art © Romare Bearden Foundation/Licensed by VAGA, New York

to be consulted regarding vexing personal and family problems. Much of her knowledge had been passed on through the generations from an African past, although a great deal was learned from the American Indians. A conjur woman was greatly feared and it was believed that she could change her appearance."[7] With roots in African tradition and wisdom, then, the conjur woman was an important part of many African American communities, in the Southern United States and also in the North, where the tradition had migrated along with its practitioners and believers: important as an actual, physical presence — someone whom a person could hire to cast a spell or cure an ailment — or important simply, but not insignificantly, as an idea, metaphor, or myth.[8]

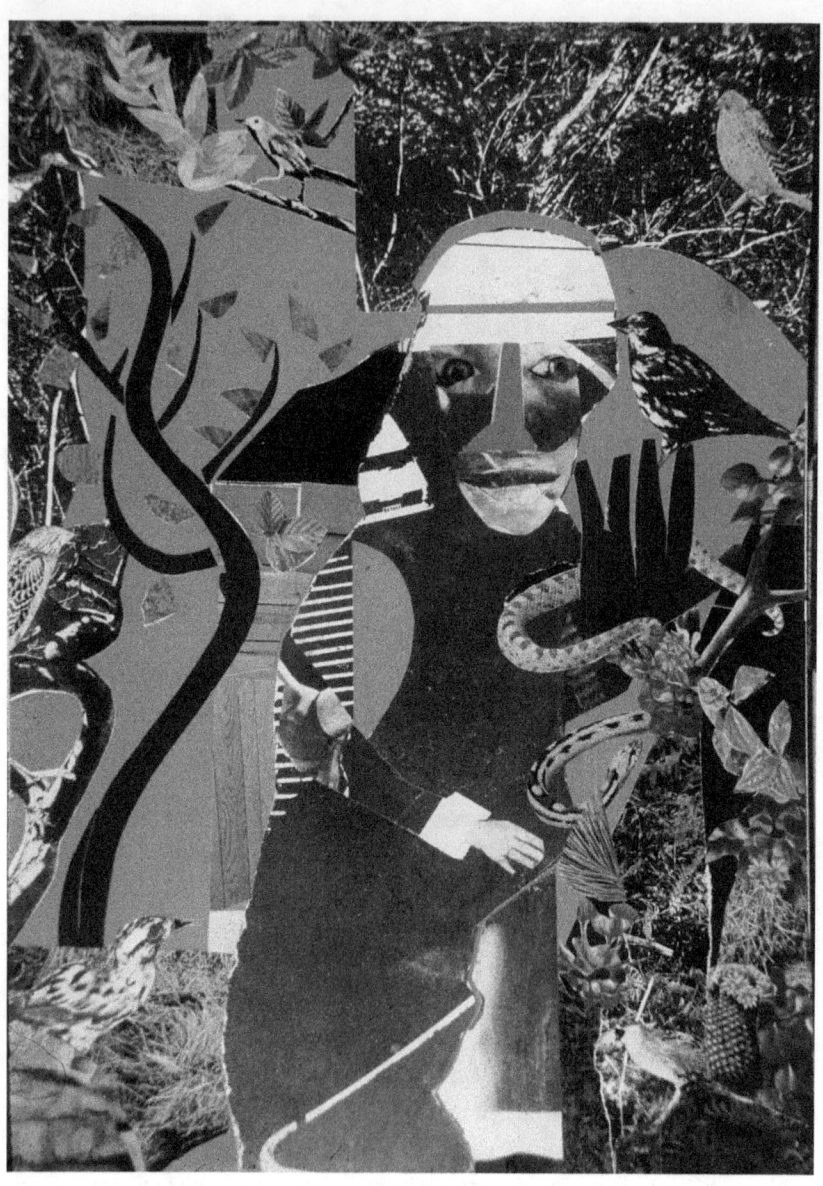

FIGURE 30 Romare Bearden, *Conjur Woman*, 1971. Art © Romare Bearden Foundation/ Licensed by VAGA, New York

Scholars tend to agree that the conjur woman, as with train yards, evening card games, and weekend music-listening, was for Bearden a subject close to home, an autobiographical evocation of the community to which he belonged and the characters, beliefs, and traditions that were a fundamental part of his life growing up in the South and in New York's Harlem. Scholars have also suggested that Bearden's conjur women called forth for him an alternate sphere, a rich and redolent zone of magic and the supernatural adjacent to but distinct from the everyday, what constituted a world apart from the prejudice, racism, and segregation regularly faced by African Americans in their normal existence, one that looked back to and drew on traditional African or African American culture for strength and solidarity as well as a way forward in the now.[9] Indeed, there can be no doubt that these works are about self, tradition, and race. How could they not be, given who made them — Bearden, an African American deeply invested in the politics of equality, an artist and activist both — and, also, given what they depict?

But what I want to suggest is that there is more to the story than this, and the "more" I wish to evoke has everything to do with what I characterized as a special relationship between conjure and the medium of collage in Bearden's practice. I have always been struck by the fact that Bearden turned to collage in the 1960s, at a moment well past the heyday of the medium. Collage was for artists like Pablo Picasso and George Braque in the early years of the twentieth century a means by which to engineer a radical transformation of painting and the pictorial surface, and collage along with photomontage offered a vehicle of social critique for artists of the European avant-garde during the interwar period, the cutting, slicing, fragmenting, and reconstituting involved in making a collage or photomontage providing apt metaphors for the trauma and violence of war and political oppression, the evisceration of the status quo, and the piecing together of new societal forms.[10] But what, decades later, was collage for Bearden? What bite could it possibly have well after the fact of its initial radicalness, when it was old news instead of new?

As it happens, Bearden turned to making collages almost by default. In 1963, a few months before Martin Luther King's historic march on Washington, he began meeting regularly with other socially and politically minded artists, all of them African American. They gathered in Bearden's Canal Street studio and called their cohort "Spiral," a term that was meant to represent expanding positive energy. Meetings were held to discuss art and brainstorm exhibition opportunities, but above all the group wished to explore collaboratively the potential role for artists in the struggle for Civil Rights. At one such meeting, in 1963, Bearden suggested that the group collaborate on an art project, and he showed his colleagues a stack of clippings from newspapers and magazines that he hoped could be used in the collective creation of a collage, an activity he believed could model the kind of collective action the group wished to pursue in the political realm.[11] The idea did not catch on, but this marks the point at which Bearden himself took up the project of collage and began making the works under discussion here. Bearden's proposal of a collective action collage, and the fact that he carried forth the project on his own, makes clear that he understood the medium to have value beyond the artistic and also that he believed that as an object, a literal *thing*, collage might do powerful, transformative work.[12]

Put another way, Bearden wanted his collages to conjure. Of course, all representational images conjure in the sense that they gather together colors and shapes to form an image of the world and in so doing call to the minds of their viewers various ideas, emotions, associations, and memories. But in making the conjur woman so prevalent in his imagery and in adopting the medium of collage, which by its very nature extracts material from the world and then transmutes it, turning so many scraps of paper into a novel physical form, Bearden suggested that he had in mind for his art an instrumentality beyond the norm, a capacity, akin to that of the conjur woman, that exceeded human limits and approximated new ways of seeing and being. Bearden did not think he could make his pictures really, in a literal sense see or act — of course not — but in them he set about fashioning a model of what it might be like to see and know the world through other than human eyes, much as a conjur woman through ritual objects, herbal mixtures, incantations, and rites harnessed the supernatural to interrupt and transform the natural, human-bound course of things. Indeed, what one sees when looking at one of Bearden's collages, including *Prevalence of Ritual: Mysteries* (1964) (fig. 31), is not what the eyes would see, or could ever see, were one looking at the actual world, at least not quite. To be sure, the viewer, in point of fact, does look at the actual — the physical, material — world when looking at one of these works, for the collages are made out of literal pieces of that world: they give that viewer the "real" in no uncertain terms. But those pieces, excerpted, rearranged, and shellacked flat to a board still seem to arise as if through a form of extra-human sight. One sees not as a human does, but as a camera lens might, zooming in and out as scale enlarges and contracts and objects balloon and shrink, or perhaps like an insect, the compound vision of which, enabled by clusters of hundreds, even thousands, of visual receptors, produces not a single coherent view but a mosaic pattern of alternating lights and darks. The fact that the viewer recognizes what he or she sees as the literal real — actual artifacts from everyday life, newspaper clippings, photographs, and so forth — and the fact that one of Bearden's resin-heavy, board-backed collages feels solid and weighty in the hand, as much brute object as it is image, make *how* that viewer sees these things, in a manner unavailable to the unaided human eye and that renders null the physical, gravitational limits of the material world, feel all the more bizarre and unexplained, *enchanted* even. The kind of attention Bearden pays to eyes through his collages suggests just such an investment in new ways of seeing.[13] In *Mysteries,* a female figure just to the right of center, the one who holds a child, boasts a face created from at least six different sources. One of her eyes, the one to our right, however, appears to hover above her face, the pasted square of paper thus calling to mind the grotesque enlargement and spatial displacement of the eye that occurs when a person looks through a magnifying glass, an optical effect that I take to be yet another emblem of other-than-human sight. In this scenario, then, Bearden reiterates the supersight he bequeaths to his viewer by compelling that viewer to come face to face with another supersighted being, a *seer,* one with a giant, outsized eye that is echoed and rearticulated in the patched-on, cyborg-like eyes of the figures at the extreme right and left edges of the scene. In the photogravure and aquatint version of this work entitled *The Train* that Bearden made several years later, in 1975, the woman's eye is again singled out, bursting emphatically as it does from a surrounding, receding wash of blue. The conjur women in Bearden's collages, themselves feature the eyes of animals or ritual masks, further underscoring the extra-human seeing Bearden seems to wish to call forth and incarnate in his collage works. And in *The Dove,* the only bodies that Bearden allows to be whole, not made up of multiple parts and thus fully in charge of their actions as well as their being, are those of animals: a cat (or is it a dog?) that watches over the street from the lower left, another cat seated at the base of the stoop, its eye shining bright against its black fur, and the dove (of the title) who surveys the scene from a perch above the door, and who calls to mind the traditional Christian symbol for the Holy Spirit. All three reinforce, as manifestly seeing *animals,* this call for extra-human perception.

In another work, *Prevalence of Ritual: Baptism* (1964) (fig. 32), which would become, along with *Prevalence of Ritual: Mysteries,* part of a series, Bearden extracts and recombines animals, humans, and inanimate objects to create a mass of simultaneously monstrous and alluring bodies, the bulk of them waist-deep

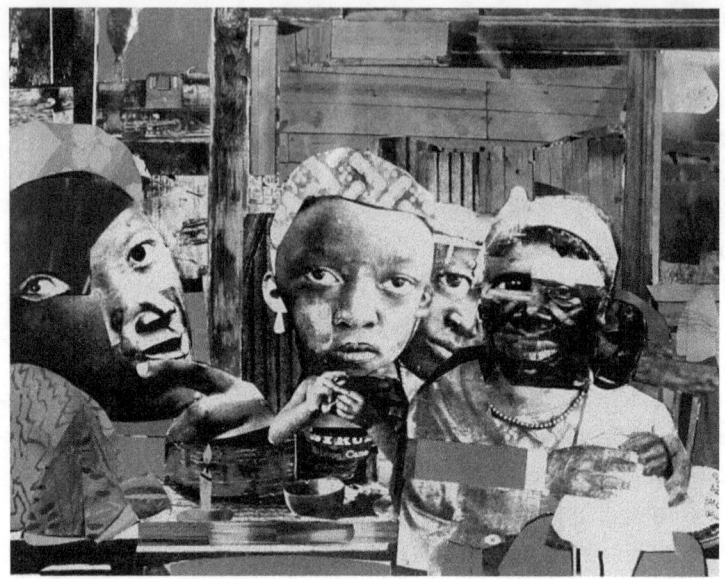

FIGURE 31 Romare Bearden, *Prevalence of Ritual: Mysteries*, 1964. Art © Romare Bearden Foundation/Licensed by VAGA, New York

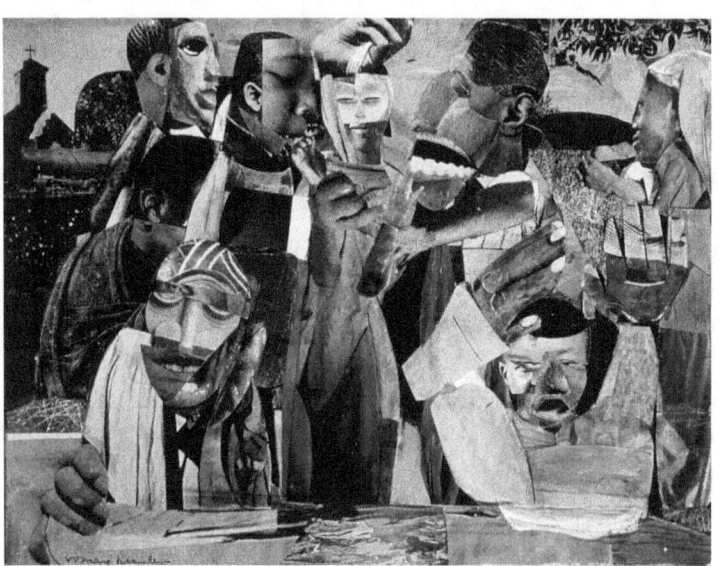

FIGURE 32 Romare Bearden, *Prevalence of Ritual: Baptism*, 1964. Collage of various papers with paint, ink, and graphite on cardboard, 9 1/8 × 12 in. (23.2 × 30.5 cm). Hirshhorn Museum and Sculpture Garden, Smithsonian Institution, Gift of Joseph H. Hirshhorn, 1966. Art © Romare Bearden Foundation/Licensed by VAGA, New York

in water. Here, the rite of river baptism evokes Bearden's childhood memories of the South but also serves as a metaphor for ritual transformation and reconstitution.[14] It is tempting to imagine the dripping resin adhesive that Bearden poured over his clippings and cutouts as akin to the water that pours over one's head in a baptism ceremony, depicted here by a hand spouting water at the top of the scene. It is equally tempting to see the immersion of the paper scraps in the viscous adhesive of the collage as akin to bodies plunged into liquid for the purpose of ritual rebirth. It is as if Bearden, already bent on using the physical material of the world in his work, rather than just pictorial representations of this world, wished for his weighted-down, solid pictures to *embody* ritual practice by approximating the literal forms and properties of the materials and instruments used in a transformative, being-reconfiguring rite: collage *as* ritual or incantatory object, one might say.

What is more, Bearden performed his own transformative ritual in the course of creating and deploying his collages, first by conjuring them from the everyday world and then by using them as instruments to conjure yet another form. Bearden created approximately two dozen collages in the mid-1960s, including the ones I discuss here; all of these he converted into photostats, which he called "Projections." Produced by using an oversize camera loaded with rolls of photographic paper rather than film, a photostat consists of an image produced directly from the original, either a negative or a positive image — in Bearden's case, a positive one — and enlarged.[15] In rendering his collages photostatically, taking the original form and calling forth from it something new, Bearden replaced his own eyes and hands with those of a machine — not to valorize or glorify machine production, but to, once again, suggest an extra-human mode of seeing and making, one analogous to the conjuring he so regularly depicted and that, through its many operations, from invocation and transformation to visualization and conveyance, embraced and instantiated the myriad meanings of the verb "to conjure." As with photography, the photostat technique used light, that "pencil of nature," as the medium by which an image was generated, and it is not hard to imagine Bearden here as a kind of conjure figure, compelling the light to do this bidding so as to make a new thing arise from the old, as with the curing of an illness, the settling of a dispute, or the shape-shifting attributed to the conjure woman herself. The fact that Bearden chose a female figure to serve as his surrogate or avatar underscores his wish to signal the displacement of natural vision through the incarnation of a form of seeing that transcended the limits of human cognition and, also, the limits of human biology.[16] It should be clear by now that Bearden would have had many reasons to wish for himself such powers: he was an ambitiously imaginative artist, but he was also deeply invested in changing the world. The group endeavor "Spiral" arose as much from political conviction as it did from artistic affinity and its one and only group show, held in 1965 in New York, took direct aim at the Museum of Modern Art, whose series of "Americans" exhibitions, initiated in 1929 and continuing into the 1960s, had as of 1965 not featured a single African American artist. The fact that Bearden's contribution to the Spiral show was a photostat enlargement of one of his collages, Conjur Woman (1964), underscores the links he made among conjuring, art making, and transformative action in the political sphere.

And what of "collapse," the term that follows on the heels of "conjure" in my title? I will spare the reader the dictionary definition, not to worry. But I do intend something specific in using the term, for by collapse I do not mean failure or breakdown; rather, I want to evoke another sort of dismantling or giving way. Ralph Ellison's Invisible Man (1952) opens with the following lines: "I am invisible, understand, simply because people refuse to see me. Like the bodiless heads you see sometimes in circus sideshows, it is as though I have been surrounded by mirrors of hard, distorting glass. . . . That invisibility to which I refer occurs because of a peculiar disposition of the eyes of those with whom I come in contact. A matter of the construction of the inner eyes, those eyes with which they look through their physical eyes upon reality."[17] In 1966, in response to a question from a journalist, Bearden declared that "Western society, and particularly that of America, is gravely ill and a major symptom is the American treatment of the Negro."[18] In a world where not just eyes, but the very mechanism of cognition — the inner perceptual apparatus by which humans come to know and to judge — was subject to dysfunction and the social body as a whole was stricken with disease, nothing but a literal collapse, a dismantling of old ways of seeing and knowing, and a piecing together of new modes of perception and being, would suffice. Such a collapse, to Bearden's mind, was something art, and collage in particular, could help to conjure.

## NOTES

From nonsite.org, no. 7 (October 11, 2012).

1. "Conjure," Oxford English Dictionary (New York: Oxford University Press), http://www.oed.com/view/Entry/39295?rskey=OyMkKa&result=43650&isAdvanced=true# (accessed October 4, 2012).

2. For biographical information, here and throughout this essay, I rely on the following sources: Kinshasha Holman Conwill, Mary Schmidt Campbell, and Sharon F. Patton, *Memory and Metaphor: The Art of Romare Bearden, 1940–1987* (New York: Studio Museum in Harlem; New York: Oxford University Press, 1991); Gail Gelburd and Thelma Golden, *Romare Bearden in Black and White: Photomontage Projections 1964* (New York: Whitney Museum of American Art, 1997); Ruth Fine, et al., *The Art of Romare Bearden* (Washington, DC: National Gallery of Art, 2003); Lee Stephens Glazer, "Signifying Identity: Art and Race in Romare Bearden's Projections," *Art Bulletin* 76.3 (Sept. 1994), 411–426; Ruth Fine and Jacqueline Francis, eds., *Romare Bearden, American Modernist*, Studies in the History of Art 71 (Washington, DC: Center for Advanced Study in the Visual Arts, National Gallery of Art, 2011); and Carla M. Hanzal, et al., *Romare Bearden: Southern Recollections* (Charlotte, NC: The Mint Museum, 2011).

3. "The Negro's War," *Fortune* 25.6 (June 1942), 76; Ruth Fine, "Romare Bearden: The Spaces Between," in Fine et al., *The Art of Romare Bearden*, 14; Herbert R. Hartel, Jr., "Bearden, Romare," *Encyclopedia of the Harlem Renaissance*, Volume 1, A–J, ed. Cary D. Wintz and Paul Finkelman (New York: Routledge, 2004), 105.

4. For examples of Bearden's work from all phases of his career, see Fine, et al., *The Art of Romare Bearden*; Fine discusses Bearden's early work, including his abstractions, in her catalog essay "Romare Bearden: The Spaces Between" (2–28).

5. Gail Gelburd, "Romare Bearden in Black and White: The Photomontage Projections of 1964," in Gelburd and Golden, *Romare Bearden in Black and White*, 20.

6. See also Raél Jero Salley's detailed analysis of the formal structure and effects of Bearden's collage technique in "Staging a Visual Circus: Bearden's Mysteries of 1964," in *Romare Bearden in the Modernist Tradition*, ed. Ellie Tweedy (New York: Romare Bearden Foundation, 2008), 77–83.

7. Romare Bearden, "Rectangular Structure in My Montage Paintings," *Leonardo* 2.1 (January 1969), 12; see full text in this volume, pp. 121–32; quoted in Gelburd, "Romare Bearden in Black and White," 33.

8. For discussion of Bearden and the tradition of the conjure woman, see Nnamdi Elleh, "Bearden's Dialogue with Africa and the Avant-Garde," in Fine et al., *The Art of Romare Bearden*, 156–171; Alicia Garcia, "Muse and Method in Romare Bearden's Obeah Watercolors," in Richard J. Powell, et al. *Conjuring Bearden* (Durham, NC: Nasher Museum of Art, Duke University, 2006), 34–47; Gelburd, "Romare Bearden in Black and White," 33–37; Leslie King-Hammond, "Bearden's Crossroads: Modernist Roots/Riffing Traditions," in Hanzal, et al., *Romare Bearden: Southern Recollections*, 86–103; Richard J. Powell, "Changing, Conjuring Reality," in Richard J. Powell, et al., *Conjuring Bearden*, 19–31 (see pp. 296–306, in this volume); Sally Price and Richard Price, *Romare Bearden: The Caribbean Dimension* (Philadelphia: University of Pennsylvania Press, 2006), 121–53.

9. See especially Glazer, "Signifying Identity"; Powell, "Changing, Conjuring Reality"; and the section entitled "Romare Bearden's Critical Modernism" in Tweedy, ed., *Romare Bearden in the Modernist Tradition* with essays by Helen Shannon, Geoffrey Jacques, Kymberly N. Pinder, and Amy Mooney as well as a conversation among Melvin Edwards, William T. Williams, and Dawoud Bey (21–66). See also Darby English, "Ralph Ellison's Romare Bearden," in Fine and Francis, ed., *Romare Bearden, American Modernist*, 11–25, for a critical look at the relationship in the scholarly literature among Bearden, history, and race, or what English calls the "confusion of aesthetics and sociality" (15).

10. For a discussion of Bearden and earlier examples of avant-garde collage, see Patricia Hills, "Cultural Legacies and the Transformation of the Cubist Collage Aesthetic by Romare Bearden, Jacob Lawrence, and Other African-American Artists," in Fine and Francis, ed., *Romare Bearden, American Modernist*, 221–47, and Helen Shannon, "African Art and Cubism, Proto-Collage, and Collage in the Work of Romare Bearden," in Tweedy, ed. *Romare Bearden in the Modernist Tradition*, 21–30. Other versions of collage emerged in the postwar period, of course, most notably those of the British pop artist Richard Hamilton and his counterparts in the United States, including Tom Wesselmann and Robert Rauschenberg, but Bearden's collages and photomontages most closely resemble their early twentieth-century European precedents. For Bearden and pop art, see Pepe Karmel, "The Negro Artist's Dilemma," in Fine and Francis, ed., *Romare Bearden, American Modernist*, 249–68.

11. Emma Amos and Courtney J. Martin, "Conversation: The Spiral Group," in Tweedy, ed., *Romare Bearden in the Modernist Tradition*, 85–92; Fine, "Romare Bearden: The Spaces Between," 28–29; Jacqueline Francis, "Bearden's Hands," in Fine and Francis, ed., *Romare Bearden, American Modernist*, 131; Gelburd, "Romare Bearden in Black and White," 18–20; Karmel, "The Negro Artist's Dilemma," 256–57; and Jennifer Wingate, "Romare Bearden," *Art Criticism* 14.1 (1999), 7–10. Spiral had just one group exhibition, in 1965, called "First Group Showing: Works in Black and White"; as I will discuss later in the essay, Bearden exhibited a photostat of his collage *Prevalence of Ritual: Conjur Woman* (1964), now in the collection of the Studio Museum in Harlem; see Fine, "Romare Bearden: The Spaces Between," 29. An exhibition on the group, entitled "Spiral: Perspectives on an African-American Art Collective," was mounted by the Birmingham Museum of Art (Alabama) in 2010 and traveled to the Studio Museum in Harlem in 2011.

12. Greg Foster-Rice is similarly interested in the generative materiality of Bearden's collage technique, which he refers to as bricolage in discussing Bearden's *The Block* (1970); Greg Foster-Rice, "Bearden's Tactical Collage," in Tweedy, ed., *Romare Bearden in the Modernist Tradition*, 103–112.

13. Gelburd discusses eyes in her "Romare Bearden in Black and White," 36. See also English, "Ralph Ellison's Romare Bearden," in which the author links the visual passage

of the beholder through the kaleidoscope of Bearden's collages to the act of seeing lucidly and complexly, as opposed to mundanely or commonly (22).

14. For discussion of the subject of baptism or the metaphor of water more generally in Bearden, see Gelburd, "Romare Bearden in Black and White," 25–33, and Kymberly N. Pinder, "Deep Waters: Rebirth, Transcendence, and Abstraction in Romare Bearden's Passion of Christ," in Fine and Francis, eds., *Romare Bearden, American Modernist*, 143–65.

15. Fine, "Nurtured and Necessary: Mothers of Invention," in Fine and Francis, ed., *Romare Bearden, American Modernist*, 187–188; Gelburd, "Romare Bearden in Black and White," 20. For detailed discussion of Bearden's technique, see Mary L. Corlett, et al., *From Process to Print: Graphic Works by Romare Bearden* (New York: Romare Bearden Foundation, 2009).

16. For a general discussion of the role of women in Bearden's art and life, see Richard A. Long, "Bearden and Women," *International Review of African American Art* 22.3 (2009), 15–19.

17. Ralph Ellison, *Invisible Man* (New York: Random House, 1982, 1952), 3. In his "Ralph Ellison's Romare Bearden," English considers the relationship between Ellison's description of the protagonist of *Invisible Man* and Bearden's collage technique (20–23), and in "Signifying Identity," Glazer characterizes the social and political meaning of Bearden's photomontages and photostats by considering their status as mechanical reproductions as well as their relationship to documentary photography and photojournalism.

18. Fine, "Romare Bearden: The Spaces Between," 28.

# CHANGING, CONJURING REALITY

*Richard Powell*

Over the course of his career Romare Bearden created at least a dozen works on the subject of the "conjur woman." She emerges in many of these pictures as specterlike, hovering among low-lying tree limbs and sharing the dense turf with wayward sparrows and black snakes. Her composite body gives next to no indication of her gender, apart from a kerchief-covered head and a calf-length "Old Mother Hubbard" dress. Her race, rather than being identifiable through the typical phenotypic markers, manifests itself in the work's external, African American context, and in Bearden's carefully selected and collaged facial features, mostly lips and noses cut from photographs of African masks. Collaged eyes and hands, intentionally mismatched and evoking the "too big" and "too small" fairy-tale modes of observation, hint at her abilities for prescient sight and root work: the attributes of a bona fide conjurer.

Works such as *Prevalence of Ritual: Conjur Woman as an Angel* (1964) (fig. 33), *Prevalence of Ritual: Conjur Woman* (1964) (see fig. 29), *Conjur Woman* (1971) (see fig. 30), *Profile/Part I, The Twenties (Mecklenburg County), Conjur Woman and the Virgin* (1978) (fig. 34), and *The Conjur Woman* (ca. 1979), all form a fascinating assemblage of distinct yet unified works. If one adds to this group those early paintings, mid-career collages and prints, and later watercolors and monotypes — that, within their broad panoply of pictorial subjects and themes, include folkloric, female characterizations that strongly resonate with

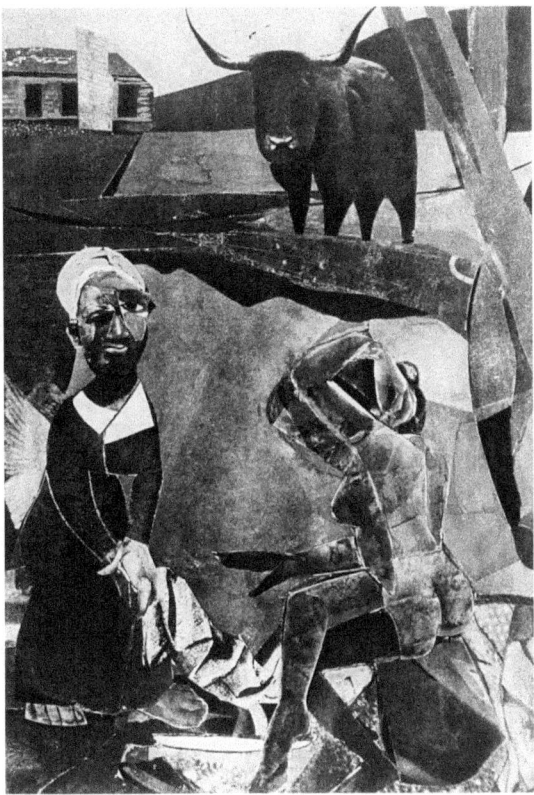

FIGURE 33 Romare Bearden, *Conjur Woman as an Angel*, 1964. Montage painting, 40 × 30 in. (101.6 × 76.2 cm). Art © Romare Bearden Foundation/Licensed by VAGA, New York

the conjur woman *proper* — then one could easily say that Bearden was smitten with this figural/visual trope.[1]

On the occasion of the conjur woman's official debut — the *Projections* exhibition at New York's Cordier & Ekstrom Gallery in October of 1964 — Bearden wrote the following about her: "Only the conjur woman, alone in the woods, seems unaffected by her solitude; therefore no train defaces her woods. A conjur woman, they say, can change reality, but for the rest of us, it is too late. The World is without her kind of mystery now."[2] Apart from his explanation about the absence within this work of yet another one of his pictorial absorptions — the train — Bearden strikes a nostalgic tone, reminding viewers that the conjur woman's mutable powers were no longer a significant feature of life. The preoccupations of the contemporary man and woman and the shift to a post-industrial, urban existence had created a world in which "her kind of mystery" was not so much a relic as entirely extinct. The conjur woman's "train,"

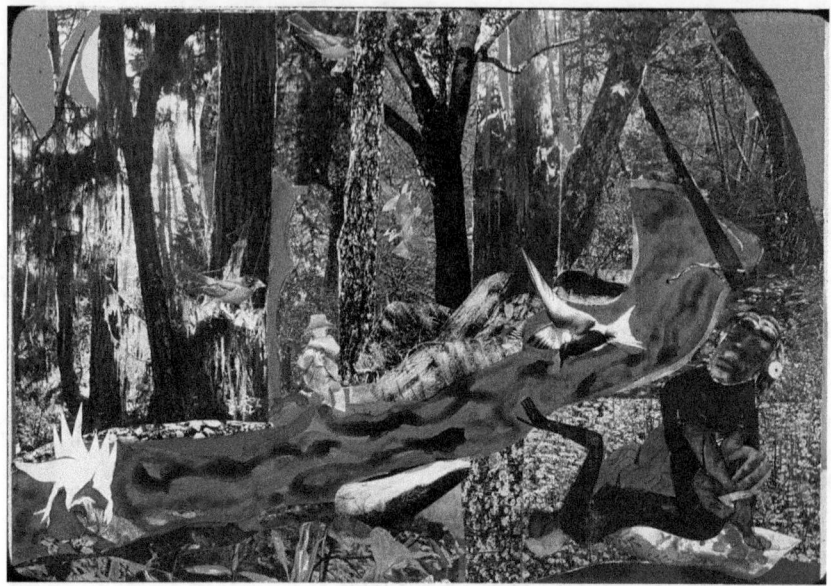

FIGURE 34 *Profile/Part I, The Twenties (Mecklenburg County): Conjur Woman and the Virgin,* 1978. Collage on board, 13 3/4 × 19 3/4 in. (34.9 × 50.2 cm). Collection of the Studio Museum in Harlem. Museum Purchase. 97.9.14. Art © Romare Bearden Foundation/Licensed by VAGA, New York

figuratively speaking, had already left the proverbial station, leaving the public to ponder other, more immediate concerns.

Yet the conjur woman and her various personae (e.g., She-ba, Salome, Circe, Maudell Sleet [a figure from Bearden's childhood], and the anonymous female blues singers) persisted, winding their way through Bearden's work like deep, ineradicable taproots. The space that Bearden allowed in his art for such sphinxlike sentinels begs the question of why they were there in the first place, and prompts an inquiry into what they signified for him beyond a transubstantiating, reality-altering embodiment of mystery.

In one of her earliest incarnations, *Prevalence of Ritual: Conjur Woman as an Angel* (1964) (fig. 33), the conjur woman is a handmaiden in charge of a lady's toilet and, as the picture's title and her wings suggest, in disguise as a divine caretaker. Whether the jagged, brown horizon above the conjur woman and the lady is sufficiently impassable to keep a mincing longhorn in the distance at bay is unclear, although the conjur woman's cockeyed and besmirched expression introduces other fears and anxieties into this scenario. In this otherworldly send-up of the classic Europa and the Bull theme, Bearden has added the conjur woman as a kind of third wheel, creating a ménage-à-trois in which seduction is shown by way of this figure's masked, hypnotic dominion, rather than through the lady's beauty or the bull's brawn. Novelist Ralph Ellison's comparison of Bearden's conjur woman "with the ubiquity of the witches who haunt the drawing[s] of Goya" aptly delineates this character, likening her to a part nurturing, part carping chaperone who, without warning, is capable of transforming herself from protector to procuress.[3]

That same year Bearden created two additional collages of this subject, one set loosely in a portrait format (see fig. 29) and the other featuring her full figure and the previously referenced forest. This latter conjur woman — a fragmented and bizarre woodland creature — carries none of the narrative baggage that these other two *Prevalence of Ritual: Conjur Woman* collages have. Rather, she is a stoic, inscrutable presence, whose cut and torn reprographic formation is an appropriate state of being given her debut during that media-conscious, Marshall McLuhanesque moment in the 1960s.

While not explicitly mentioned by name she appears in another early collage, *Illusionists at 4 PM* (fig. 35; Plate 4). Here two opposing figures — one prominently standing in front of a dog and a small inconsequential figure, and the other seated alone at a dining table — compete for the "conjur woman" title. But the robust singularity of the standing figure gives her the advantage over the seated one, as well as the former woman's wielding of a long-handled, scepterlike spoon, held by an incongruous, colossal hand. The implied rivalry here brings to mind cultural historian Marina Warner's definition of *conjuring*: "Used both for devilry and natural magic; witnesses and participants play a crucial part in establishing the shifting boundary between the entertainer's sleight of hand and the paranormal."[4]

Although Bearden often expressed his concerns about commentators overemphasizing what they believed to be the social elements in his art, the works themselves — comprising a virtual universe of black folk types and characterizations — countered his own argument, and illustrated rarely broached perspectives on racial and cultural identity.[5] "I felt that the Negro was becoming too much of an abstraction," Bearden famously stated about popular, circa-1960s representations of African Americans, "rather than the reality that art can give a subject. . . . What I've attempted to do is establish a world through art in which the validity of my Negro experience could live and make its own logic."[6] And the logic of the female conjurer in *Illusionists at 4 PM*, in charge of a domestic interior in which a late afternoon repast becomes part of an elaborate, mysterious sacrament, defies common, modern sense. "As a Negro," Bearden told art critic Dore Ashton, "I do not need to go looking for happenings, the absurd, the surreal, because I have seen things that neither Dalí, Beckett, Ionesco or any of the others could have thought possible."[7]

Singer Nina Simone, herself a musical "conjure woman" in nightclubs and concert halls at the time, made disclaimers and declarations similar to Bearden's visual and verbal overtures to the conjur woman, singing,

> Baby, you'll understand me now
> If sometimes you see that I'm mad;
> Don't you know no one alive can always be an angel
> When everything goes wrong you see some bad;
> But I'm just a soul whose intentions are good;
> Oh, lord, please don't let me be misunderstood.[8]

In these autobiographical lyrics, Simone pairs her tempestuous behavior with a prayer for indulgence. And despite the conjur woman's anachronistic appearance, supposed ferocity, and superhuman powers, she is not an altogether unsympathetic character. By presenting her in a forest abundant with medicinal herbs and plants, or in tense domestic settings, Bearden alluded to her pharmacological and prophylactic aspects (e.g., preparing love potions, providing herbs to cure various illnesses, and counseling clients in regards to vexing personal and family problems).[9] Similarly, Nina Simone reminded listeners that the heterodox belief systems and conjur women which she often sang about were also occasionally therapeutic and psychological restoratives for the community, or what literary critic Richard Brodhead (in his treatise on the conjure figure in American literature) has described as "a recourse, a form of power available to the powerless in mortally intolerable situations."[10]

By locating these evocative, spiritual currencies in the archaic figure of the conjur woman, Bearden was casting his lot with the folk romantics of his day such as anthropologist Mircea Eliade and folklorist Richard M. Dorson, intellectuals who, rather than privileging the pronouncements of the then-popular structuralists, Neo-Freudians, and Marxist theoreticians (e.g., Roland Barthes, Norman O. Brown, and Herbert Marcuse), looked toward modernism's more pedestrian counterpart — folk and popular culture — for philosophical confirmation. The conjur woman's origins in a place and time as far removed as anyone could be from the stainless steel luminosity and Day-Glo colors of the

1960s and 1970s gave Bearden's art an idiosyncratic, appreciable vantage point: an ironic version of the self-segregated theater balcony from which "the innerness of the Negro experience" could be savored by blacks without pandering to racist pigeonholing or racial propaganda.[11] As committed as Bearden was to the efforts to restore and expand civil rights, he vehemently resisted the call to place his art in service to a political agenda. Instead he chose to affect social change via a shrewd cultural strategy: artistically invoking the iconic heroes and heroines of the disenfranchised African American majority. In that era of debates, demonstrations, and riots, the prospect of changing the subject (or "changing reality") was appealing, even if such substitutions for "the Negro problem" might reside, as Bearden provocatively proposed, in an old black woman's body.

Bearden's conjur woman was neither eroticized nor made into a passive, objectified figure for ridicule or pity. Instead she jumpstarts each work of art in which she appears, and introduces cultural and spiritual variables into social discourses that were too often drowned out in the din of technological advancements and the despair of community disintegration. She was a power figure and a possessor of secrets that societal/political structures could not eliminate or buy off. In *Conjur Woman and the Virgin* (fig. 34) — arguably one of Bearden's most enigmatic renderings of her — she performs plein air "surgery" on the "Virgin," alongside a dark blue stream and under a tall canopy of pine trees. Parenthetic witnesses (or co-conspirators) to this bloodletting — a white egret attacking a snake and a tawny-complexioned fisherman sitting on the water's edge — further complicate the scene, and introduce decidedly symbolic and perhaps autobiographical dimensions to the proceedings. Is this a cold-blooded murder being shown here, or is this a Romare Bearden allegory on the loss of idealized virtue and the acquisition of true wisdom? As a folk character who historically was both knowledgeable about the past and capable of revealing horrific, yet fundamentally liberating, truths, the conjur woman was, indeed, a human razor, cutting away the psychological chastity belts of the uninitiated and educating the innocents about the often ruthless, cutthroat ways of the real world.[12]

Although feminism was not a part of Bearden's lexicon, he implicitly understood that this new/old image of his had to reside in the most appropriate personage: a figure recognizable as being a fitting vessel and vehicle for these changes to the standard racial script. And like Ralph Ellison's largely silent, but all-seeing/all-knowing, apocryphal black folk critic, Bearden's catalyst would also have to be an agency-filled representative of old. That such an entity would ultimately be a woman meant that she was drawn from Bearden's deep, deep memory reservoir of the women he knew or had known and considered elemental, powerful, and transforming in his life.[13] His great-grandmother Rosa, grandmother Cattie, mother, Bessye, and wife, Nanette, were all certainly forces of nature with which to contend, but the woman whom he repeatedly spoke of as his personal fomenter to rethinking his art was Ida, a prostitute-turned-cleaning-lady that Bearden met in 1940. After Bearden rejected Ida's suggestion to paint her, Ida's retort (which Bearden paraphrased in subsequent interviews) is telling: "'I know what I look like,' she said. 'But when you can look and find what's beautiful in me, then you're going to be able to do something on that paper of yours.' That always sort of stuck with me," Bearden acknowledged.[14]

Placing this statement with Bearden's conjur woman imagery (as well as opposite New York photographer Sam Shaw's well-known series of studio shots of a young Bearden pondering a black female model) drops Bearden's (and Ida's) words in a bubbling cauldron of ideas and possibilities: rethinking commonplace (and often racist) Western notions of beauty, the juxtaposition of desire and representation, revelations and self-discoveries as advanced from the social margins, and returning to one's originary (female) roots as a way out of the artistic routine and into a new, cultural rebirth among other thoughts. It is precisely the conjur woman's corporeal detachment from the conventional male gaze (whose alternative was deftly articulated to Bearden by Ida) that empowers her and shifts her visual allure to the natural world and, on the cultural front, to the African diasporic principles of art-as-healing, art-as-metamorphosis, and art-as-spiritual-renewal. And Bearden's methods for introducing this figure in his art — by distilling Cubist and Dadaist fracture through the deconstructive aesthetics of jazz composition and African American folk collage/assemblage — matched this new/old female subject perfectly.

Along with his claims (like those of his friends and colleagues Ralph Ellison and Albert Murray) on the universalizing principles of art, Bearden was a "race man" who presented his modernist self through assorted facets of cultural blackness and hybrid, formalist strategies of image making. Subjects like the conjur woman became the thematic substratum that anchored many of these explorations. As seen in a detail from an *Untitled* quilt (1976) (figs. 36 and 37), a black female cameo forms the core design element of the repeated silkscreen patterns in this rare example of textile art by Bearden. The paired leaves and appendage-like roots that, from top to bottom, sprout from the woman in the cameo are the telltale signs of her conceptual allegiance to the conjur

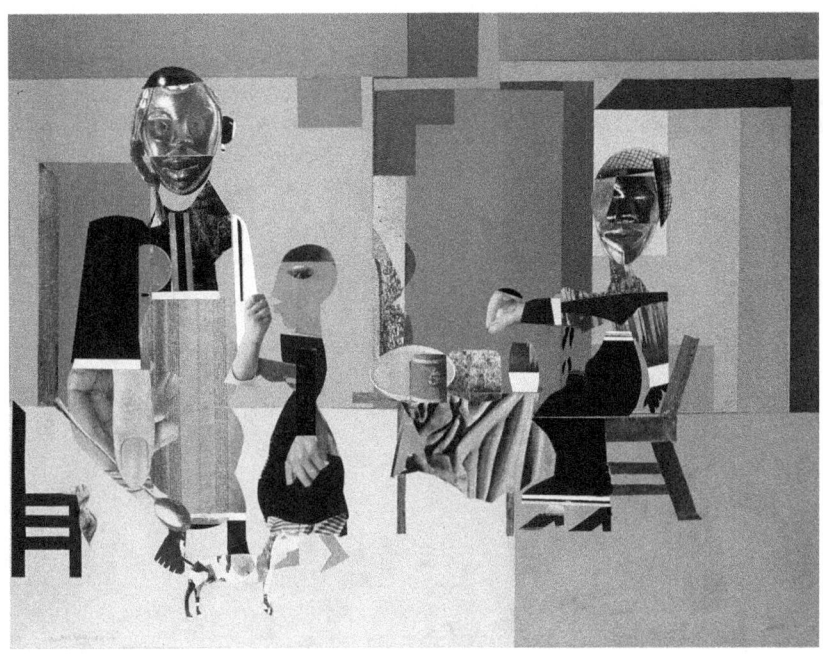

FIGURE 35  Romare Bearden, *Illusionists at 4 PM*, 1967. Montage painting, 30 × 40 in.
(76.2 × 101.6 cm). Collection of halley k harrisburg and Michael Rosenfeld. Art © Romare
Bearden Foundation/Licensed by VAGA, New York

woman: medicinal roots and herbs being the conduits through which she puts
her clients in contact with the spirit world.[15]

Indeed, the reality-altering attraction to the conjur woman was predicated
on Bearden's fervent belief in the social and political importance of traditional
black culture, especially in the face of what he perceived as an encroaching
modern amnesia.[16] The Mecklenburg County, Pittsburgh, and Harlem communities where he had grown up had all been razed, repaved, and emptied of
their picturesque "Negro-ness" by the 1960s. While the Civil Rights movement
had certainly brought about needed improvements in the economic, political,
and social lives of African Americans, what accompanied these changes was
what Bearden viewed as a declining sense of race solidarity across generations
and, more importantly, the loss of a cultural memory: the shared experiences
of blacks during the pre–Civil Rights era that, although debilitating in terms of
one's interracial dealings and broader aspirations in the world-at-large, provided
black people with a nurturing if insular sphere in which to operate. As Bearden's
art demonstrates, that world was just as much about Duke Ellington's music

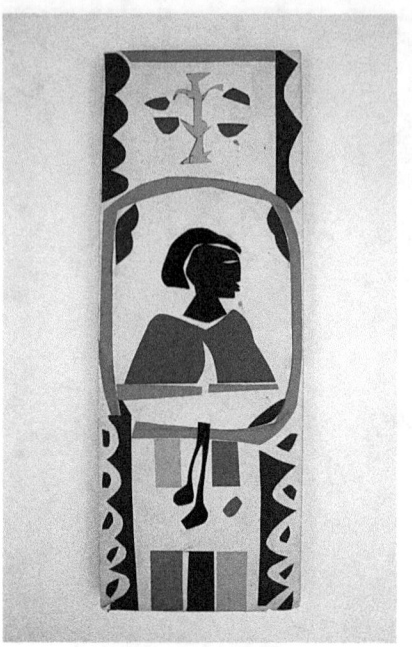

FIGURES 36 AND 37 *Untitled (Medallion Quilt)*, and detail, 1976. Silkscreen on cotton, 94×76 in. (238.8×193 cm). Collection of Susie Ruth Powell and Franklin R. Anderson. Art © Romare Bearden Foundation/Licensed by VAGA, New York

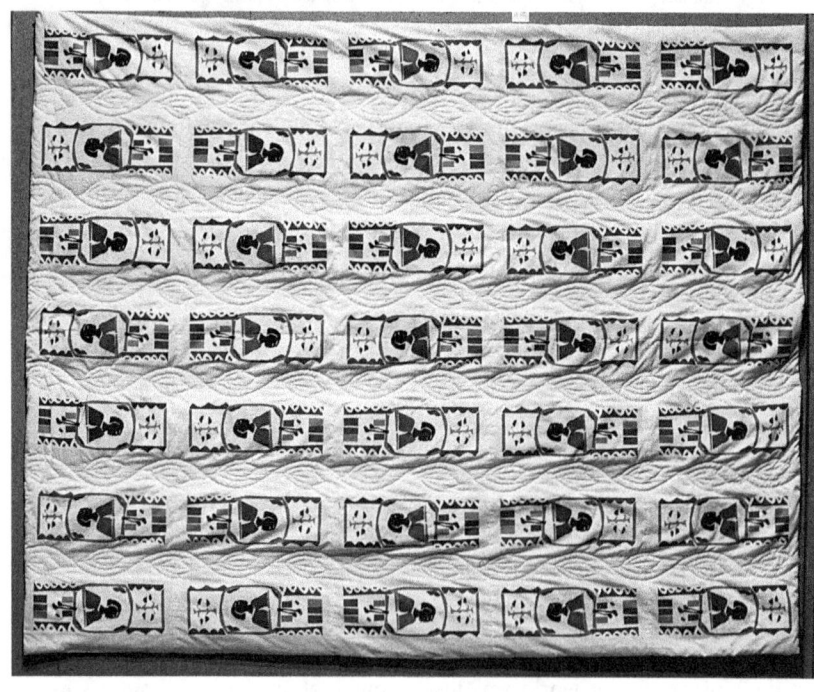

and Harlem nightlife as it was about racial epithets; as much about patchwork quilts and rousing church sermons as it was about lynching; and was as much about the wisdom of elders and sympathetic teachers as it was about blocked school entrances. For all of her rustic, superstition-filled associations, the conjur woman represented a third stream for Romare Bearden. At a time when "for the rest of us, it is too late," Bearden's conjur woman reminded audiences of the enduring, ghostlike presence of the past; redolent with the aura of the ancestors and yet endowed with enough spiritual authority to transform and breathe life into a soulless, ahistorical society.

## NOTES

From Richard J. Powell, Margaret Ellen Di Giulio, Alicia Garcia, Victoria Trout, and Christine Wang, *Conjuring Bearden*, exh. cat. (Durham, NC: Duke University Press, 2006).

1. Scholars of American modernism are eternally grateful to National Gallery of Art curator Ruth Fine for her Promethean efforts in assembling that museum's 2003 Bearden retrospective. Unless otherwise noted, all biographical references in this essay come from: Ruth Fine, *The Art of Romare Bearden* (Washington, DC: National Gallery of Art, 2003).

2. Dore Ashton, "Romare Bearden — Projections," *Quadrum* 17 (1964): 99–110.

3. Ralph Ellison, "Introduction," in *Romare Bearden, Paintings and Projections*, exh. cat. (Albany: Art Gallery of the State University of New York at Albany, 1968), n.p.; reprinted as "The Art of Romare Bearden" in Ralph Ellison, *Going to the Territory* (New York: Random House, 1986); see full text in this volume, pp. 196–203.

4. Marina Warner, *The Inner Eye: Art Beyond the Visible* (London: The South Bank Centre, 1996), 33.

5. Romare Bearden, "Rectangular Structure in My Montage Paintings," *Leonardo* 2.1 (January 1969): 19; see full text in this volume, pp. 121–32.

6. Charles Childs, "Bearden: Identification and Identity," *ARTnews* 63 (October 1964): 24–25, 54, 61–62.

7. Dore Ashton, "Bearden — Projections," 109.

8. Nina Simone, "Don't Let Me Be Misunderstood" (1964) on *Nina Simone/Jazz Masters* 17 1994 CD Reissue, PolyGram Records, Inc. 314 518 198-2.

9. For an exegesis of the African American conjurer's immersion in the world of spiritually charged plants and natural phenomena, see Theophus H. Smith, *Conjuring Culture: Biblical Formations of Black America* (New York: Oxford University Press, 1994), 5–6.

10. Richard Brodhead, "Introduction," in Charles W. Chesnutt, *The Conjure Woman and Other Conjure Tales* (Durham, NC: Duke University Press, 1993), 9.

11. Childs, "Bearden: Identification and Identity," 62.

12. I am indebted to Mary Schmidt Campbell, Dean of the Tisch School of the Arts, New York University and a leading Bearden scholar, for bringing the complexities of *Conjur Woman and the Virgin* to my attention.

13. Mary Schmidt Campbell, "Introduction," in *Mysteries: Women in the Art of Romare Bearden* (Syracuse, N.Y.: Everson Museum of Art, 1975).

14. Calvin Tomkins, "Putting Something over Something Else," *New Yorker* 53 (November 28, 1977): 58; see full text in this volume, pp. 31–53.

15. See Donald J. Waters, "The Persuasive Nature of Superstition: A Matter of Health," in Waters, *Strange Ways and Sweet Dreams: Afro-American Folklore from the Hampton Institute* (Boston: G. K. Hall & Co., 1983), 75–84.

16. Similar sentiments were shared by friends Ralph Ellison and Albert Murray, as evidenced in: Ralph Ellison, *Shadow and Act* (New York: Random House, 1964), and Albert Murray, *The Omni-Americans: New Perspectives on Black Experience & American Culture* (New York: E. P. Dutton, 1970).

# ROMARE BEARDEN'S
## *LI'L DAN THE DRUMMER BOY*
## COLORING A STORY OF THE CIVIL WAR

*Robert Burns Stepto*

*Li'l Dan the Drummer Boy* is the only children's book written and painted (I prefer that term instead of "illustrated") by Romare Bearden. He completed the artwork in 1983; twenty years later in 2003 Simon and Schuster published *Li'l Dan* in its Simon and Schuster Books for Young Readers series. Like a number of books brought out in that era, *Li'l Dan* includes a CD. In this instance, the CD is a recording of Maya Angelou reading Bearden's story. Another part of the strategy to attract readers is its foreword, written by African American Studies luminary Henry Louis Gates, Jr. Professor Gates knew Romare Bearden during the years when he was writing and painting *Li'l Dan*, and he vividly recalls the Saturdays he would spend with Bearden and Albert Murray visiting bookstores, sharing lunch, enjoying each other's company. For lunch, Bearden would invariably order a huge fruit salad. Gates offers a remarkable comment about that choice: "Although he claimed that dietary considerations informed his choice, I was convinced that he ordered the fruit salad in order to devour the colors, like an artist dipping his brush into his palette. . . . He had a master's eye, for sure, but he also had a kid's fascination with color and all of its magical qualities." Those thoughts have stayed with me and have informed my readings of *Li'l Dan*. It is a story told in colors as painted by Bearden and as seen by young Dan. Words like "Confederate" and "Union" are abstract; they are words that Dan (and many of us) cannot "see." But Dan can see "horsemen in gray uniforms . . . through clouds of brown dust." And Dan can later see "black men in blue uniforms" who are suddenly now at "the big house where the 'master' lived," and who adopt him as one of their own (Plate 7). *Li'l Dan* is indeed, magically and intentionally, a colored book!

In the discussion of *Li'l Dan* that follows, I will be attentive to how Bearden's colors tell Dan's story. I'm interested in how clothing is colored—an obvious point here being that Mr. Ned (Li'l Dan's drum master and father figure), Li'l Dan, and the black soldiers all wear the color blue. How the landscapes are textured and shaded is also something to observe: how and when is the land seemingly barren and when is it a rainbow of warm colors?

Special moments in the story are those nine instances when the first letter of a new section of the story is actually painted by Bearden, thus introducing shapes, colors, and narrative alike. The shapes and colors of the letters either initiate or repeat shapes and colors in Bearden's full-page image that is opposite the narrative.

This storytelling strategy is pursued right from the start of *Li'l Dan* in the first two pages. The prose narrative begins, "The workday was long and hard for slaves on cotton plantations," with the "T" in "The" painted an orange-tan in its cross piece and blue in its vertical member. As the narrative develops and as we begin to absorb the accompanying image on the opposite page, we realize that the cross piece in the "T" is Mr. Ned's drum, the drum that came from Africa and that links fathers to sons, especially when "fathers" like Mr. Ned take time at the end of a hard day to teach "sons" like Li'l Dan how to play the drum. The vertical blue portion of the letter "T" is the same blue and shape of Mr. Ned's pants leg in the large image. Thus, the painted "T" at the very beginning of the story begins both a verbal and visual narrative of Mr. Ned, Li'l Dan, and what they share.

In the next pages of the section, Dan borrows an axe and goes out into the woods where "he worked all day making his own drum." Chopping the wood he needs is but the beginning of Dan's use of local resources: the drumhead is created from a pig hide that is "pulled taut with the heavy twine used to bind the cotton bales." In short, the bale twine that could solely represent a slave's labor, confinement, and servitude is instead an integral part of Dan's creativity. When we see the web of twine in every forthcoming image of the drum, we cannot help but be reminded of how the twine in this story enwraps a drum, never once a cotton bale.

The section concludes with an image of Dan and Mr. Ned facing each other with the drum centered between them. Mr. Ned (note that in this "slave narrative" this colored man is always "Mr. Ned" not simply "Ned") praises Dan's workmanship and admires the drum: "You got a real fine drum there." Mr. Ned and Dan in a sense frame the drum, the drum being in turn the bond between them. This is the first image of the drum; we readily see the web of twine holding the pig hide in place. We also note that Mr. Ned, Dan, and the drum are all the same shade of brown.

In the next section of the story, Dan is again outdoors, this time playing his drum. The first sentence tells us that "Dan tried to imitate all the sounds he heard around him." The "D" in "Dan" is another initial letter in a story section that Bearden paints in multiple colors: in this instance, red, blue, a light brown or tan, and a dark brown or black. The painted "D" thus gathers many of the colors in the painting accompanying the narrative: red is the color of blossoms, fruit, and one of the birds; blue colors Dan's overalls (his "blue uniform"); Dan is a light brown, as are the gently curving trees that in a sense cradle him and his brown drum; Dan's hair is black, and so is the twine upon the drum.

Bearden is also attentive to what the shape of the "D" might contain and convey. This "D" looks at once like a tree leaf and a bird's wing; the bold, dark, angular lines within the shape even suggest a harp — the "harp" of all the sounds that Dan seeks to imitate: people singing, birds cawing, leaves clacking, the patter of rain, and crash of thunder. Knowing that Dan set himself to this task right from the beginning of his drumming makes it all the more plausible that he will convincingly create the sound of cannon fire with his drum near the end of the story.

The Civil War surges into the story when Dan hears "a loud galloping noise down the main road." It is "a long line of horsemen in gray uniforms" sweeping "down the road through clouds of brown dust." Quite significantly, the bright colors of the previous landscape are replaced by "gray uniforms"; furthermore, "clouds of brown dust" predominate over the brown of Dan and his drum, both of which lie on the ground in a far lower corner of the painting. This section of the story begins, "One day Dan noticed there was hardly anyone in the fields." The scene is soon filled with Confederate soldiers on horseback and in wagons. Bearden paints the "O" in the word "One" to resemble one of the Confederate wagon wheels and colors it the same shade as the brown dust. The painted first letter of an episode thus once again initiates new verbal and visual components of Dan's story.

Dan next runs up to "the big house where the 'master' lived." What does he find there? "[B]lack men in blue uniforms." Bearden pursues several points here, beginning with his presentation of the word "master." Offering "master" with the "m" in lower case reminds us of the several Paul Laurence Dunbar poems that make a very clear distinction between "master" and "Master" — God the Father (see, for example, Dunbar's "Antebellum Sermon"). But Bearden goes a step further: in his story "master" is not only in lower case but also in quotation marks. The word is thereby rendered as something not to be taken seriously; the diacritical markings (which are visual and verbal) make the word a joke.

There is also something quite particular in Bearden having the cotton plantation already occupied by Union soldiers — specifically, "black men in blue uniforms." In this Civil War story, the black men are soldiers, not custodians or contraband. They carry guns, not shovels; they are led by a black officer and it is they who liberate the cotton plantation.

The officer, a captain, speaks with Li'l Dan, asking him his name and the whereabouts of his parents. We learn at this point in the story that Dan's parents "were sold away when [he] was most young"; that he "belongs" to nobody, just to the plantation — to "here." The captain replies, "Well, son . . . you don't belong here anymore. You're free now." The exchange reminds us of Frederick Douglass's poignant declaration that all slaves are orphans. It also establishes right from the moment that Dan encounters the black men that he has found a semblance of family, black family, and that the captain who calls him "son" will indeed become, after Mr. Ned, one of Dan's "fathers."

The two paintings that follow are remarkable especially in how they contrast with the way Bearden previously presented the Confederates in gray fleeing in the brown dust. The first image places Dan and his drum at the beginning of a tree-bordered path that stretches forth to a distant green and golden vista, with a golden sun in view that suggests the beginning of a golden new day. The warmth and vastness of the landscape presents Possibility, Hope. Much to the point: black soldiers brought this on.

The colors of the path to the future appear as well in Bearden's painting of the letter "D" in the word "Dan" at the beginning of Dan's conversation with the captain. The colors fill the shape of the "D": it looks almost like a sail curved out by the wind from the vertical member (the mast?) of the "D." This may seem odd in a story so obviously land bound, however, the "sail" may well be a visual expression of how Dan's future might "catch a breeze" and soar.

The very next painting retains the lush greens, oranges, and golds of Dan's future path. There is even once again a gold-orange sun in the sky. Hugely different is the orderly and seemingly endless parade of black soldiers in blue that encircles the bottom and left-hand portions of Bearden's notably circular image. The circle bespeaks the world that the soldiers are creating for themselves — and for Dan, who tags along at the end of the procession. The circle may also be described as encircling the white structure in the middle of the painting. If that structure — with a mass of blue soldiers behind it as well as encircling it — is "master's" big house, then the painting is offering a quite specific statement of how the world is changing, or may change.

The orderliness of the black soldiers in blue marching through a vibrant landscape is in huge contrast to the earlier depiction of soldiers in gray scrambling through clouds of brown dust. Compared to the one, ragged, empty Confederate wagon, the Union army wagons appear orderly in transit as well as full of rations, supplies, and goods. Two of the most interesting details are in the painting's center foreground. A Union flag stands up in the center of the image, apparently hoisted by black soldiers. Also foregrounded is the one white soldier in the image: he is close to the flag and he is the only soldier in the foreground on horseback. That may well be the one touch of what Sterling Brown would have called "critical realism" in this robust celebration of black Union soldiers.

The blue of the soldiers (and of Dan's overalls) and the gold-orange of the new day become the colors with which Bearden paints the initial letters of the next two story sections. The "T" at the beginning of "The soldiers came to know Li'l Dan" stands out because it is so much like the "T" at the very beginning of the tale. The difference is that the colors of the members are reversed. Now, the horizontal member of the "T" is blue (not the tan/orange of Mr. Ned's drum) while the vertical member is orange (not blue like Mr. Ned's trousers). Moreover, the vertical orange member is marked with dark lines that make it look like a portion of the cowcatcher on the front of the locomotive in the adjoining painting. The painting has in its background two main components: a cluster of black soldiers in blue (with a Union flag) and the locomotive — something completely new in Dan's world that nonetheless happens to be familiar shades of brown and orange with touches of green. It is thus fair to say that while Dan's world has radically changed — the black soldiers and the locomotive surely represent that — the colors of his world have somehow remained the same.

All this prepares us for the principal new father in Dan's life, a black soldier named Scipio. Scipio is father to a boy the same age as Dan; he hopes one day to go back where he came from and find his son. Meanwhile, he cares for Dan, calming his fears and, the text tells us, lifting him up on his shoulders and carrying him into the train when the rest of the soldiers climb aboard (see Plate 7).

Once again, Bearden is careful in how he names and identifies the good black men who are Dan's "fathers." Mr. Ned is *Mr.* Ned, a master drummer who was taught to drum by his father. Mr. Ned's drum came from Africa, perhaps with his father. Scipio could be one of those mocking slave names like Jupiter or Plato or Napoleon, but Bearden is more likely honoring Scipio by likening him to Scipio Africanus, who earned the agnomen "Africanus" when he defeated Hannibal in the second Punic War. Scipio is thus linked to Africa and to military victory.

The train transports Li'l Dan to his new life with Scipio and the black soldiers of Company E. He now lives in what Scipio calls a "bivouac" area, a strange new name for a strange new place quite different from the cotton plantation. Bearden's first painted image of this new landscape is cold, almost desolate: the steam engine on the left and platoon of soldiers on the right cradle and define a spare space marked only by uninviting white tents and a few green trees in the distance. All this makes the burst of warm colors in the painting on the very next page all the more exceptional. It is evening at the bivouac but hardly dark, and not just because of the campfires or the golden moonlight. It is bright, warm, and festive because Li'l Dan is playing his drum for the soldiers. The soldiers are taking care of him, their "mascot," but Dan and his drum are also taking care of *them*. (Note the cap on Dan's head — hip, urban, worn backward! Dan is a *jazz* man!)

Late on one such night, the bugle blares and the men of Company E awake and hasten to march through the night to battle. The first Bearden painting in this part of the story presents Li'l Dan still asleep, covered in blue, with his drum nestled next to his head. The next painting portrays the moment at daybreak when Dan, who has followed the soldiers, sees them right when the "woods ahead of them exploded with gunfire and cannon." A striking feature of this painting is that the bright explosion of weapon fire appears in the distance just beyond the white and green of a cotton field. Li'l Dan's past and present are thus jarringly present in the landscape right before his eyes.

Suddenly, Scipio sees Dan and cries out: "Boy, you get away from here! Go back over that hill and wait until we come for you!" We hear both concern and affection: Scipio doesn't just say "go back over there," he also says "we will come for you." The image Bearden paints to portray this confrontation offers nothing more (or less) than an agitated, gesticulating Scipio and a somewhat cowering Dan with his drum near his feet. The image builds Dan's story in two key respects: it rehearses and yet revises the third image in the book in which Dan and Mr. Ned, the first father figure, stand with the drum between them, and it prepares us for the very moment when Dan climbs a tree with the drum he has had with him all along and sees the "gray horsemen heading right to where Company E was posted."

We turn the page and, for the first time in this part of the story, we come upon a Bearden painting that takes up the whole page; it is not sharing the page with verbal narrative (Plate 8). The verbal narrative is on the facing page, with the first letter being a painted "D" (in the word "Dan") filled mostly with the blue of Dan and the soldiers but also with a touch of the brown of the tree and of Dan's skin.

The painting presents Dan in the tree, bent over his drum, trying his best to create the sound of cannon that may convince the Confederates to turn away. More particularly, it presents the precise moment when Dan leaves off attempting the sound with his hands and starts to beat the drum with two sticks. That works! The narrative puts it this way: "Dan broke off two sticks and hit the drum sharply with them. *Smack! Smack!* That's better! Just a bit sharper. Crack! Crack! Yes, this was it! This was the sound of the cannon the men called 'five pounders'."

The Confederates turn back and Li'l Dan is a hero, but that is not the only reason this is a special moment in the story. It is special as well because of what it represents in Dan's evolution as a drummer, an artist. Dan's perch in the tree reminds us of the early images of his nascent musicianship wherein he goes into the woods seeking wood for building his drum and soon thereafter nestles outdoors so that he might hear and begin to imitate on his drum the myriad sounds around him. The "crack" of cannon fire is a man-made, destructive sound altogether different from the "cawing" of birds or "clacking" of leaves, but it is also a sound Dan must learn to imitate, given the world he now lives in. Imitating cannon fire turns out to be the most extraordinary way that Dan can take care of the black soldiers who have taken in him — and his drum.

The fact that this is the one moment in the entire story when Dan plays his drum with what are, in effect, drumsticks has elicited commentary. I myself prefer to admire Dan's inventiveness, his improvisation. Once again, he is successfully finding what is nearby that will work to create the "music" so essential for the moment.

Robert Williams, in his review of *Li'l Dan* in *Rooftop Reviews* (October 2011), remarks, "For me, the best part of this story is the combination of the African drum being used . . . with the European style of beating a drum with a stick . . . The combination of the two cultural methods underscores our reliance on one another, as people, in the face of the dangers that confront us all." This is a good point but it risks suggesting that Dan will never go back to playing the drum with his hands — or that he would be regressing in some way in doing so.

Bearden clearly addresses all this in the very last image of Dan playing his drum. Upon the invitation of none other than General William T. Sherman, who has learned of Dan's "heroism" and of the "good use" Dan made of his drum, Dan joins the Army's Drum Corps. The General's last words to Dan (created of course by Bearden) are: "And listen, Dan, you play your drum in your own way."

The image that follows and that concludes the story presents Dan centered and in front of the Drum Corps. He wears the same blue uniform that the other (white) drummers are wearing, but he is playing *his* drum (not a "Drum Corps" drum), and he is a brown boy playing it with his brown hands, not the drumsticks all the others are employing. He is at once an African American and an American as well as a Union soldier and a musician on his own terms. That is another aspect of his exceptional heroism, achieved even as a boy.

The pages leading up to Dan's encounter with General Sherman are full of images of the jubilant soldiers of Company E: they know what caused the "men in gray" to turn back! Twice, Dan is hugged by "Big Scipio," who at one point gets down on a knee and embraces him saying, "Dan . . . you and your drum surely saved us." As before in several other illustrations, Dan's drum is always part of the picture, and the cotton bale twine that holds the drum together is always on view.

This final part of the story is framed by Bearden's last two painted letters in the written narrative. The "T" that begins the sentence "The lead officer of the cavalry heard this sound" is colored gray and presented with touches that clearly suggest that the "T" represents the uniforms of the "men in gray" who hear Dan's cannon sound and turn away. Thereafter, we have the pages with the images of the jubilant black soldiers.

The next and final painted initial letter appears in this sentence: "When the battle was over, General William T. Sherman himself asked to see Li'l Dan." The "W" is blue and gold and that repeats, even reinforces, the blue and gold we see in the cloth and buttons and belts of the Union uniforms. But recall, blue and gold have already been established as the colors of the new day, the new life, that Dan and his drum face at the beginning of their path to the future.

Bearden's final two painted letters tell us once again that this is a Civil War story, a fight between the gray and the blue. But in between the gray and blue are black folk and a brown drum.

## NOTE

From Tapan Basu and Tasneem Shahnaaz, eds., *Crossing Borders: Essays on Literature, Culture, and Society in Honor of Amritjit Singh* (Vancouver: Farleigh Dickinson University Press, 2017).

# IMPRESSIONS AND IMPROVISATIONS
## A LOOK AT THE PRINTS OF ROMARE BEARDEN

*Mary Lee Corlett*

*Improvisation, contrary to a lot of popular thinking, must be
very exact. It is a reverberation, or an extension in another direction,
from the basic thematic material.*
— Romare Bearden

The art of Romare Bearden is an improvisational collaboration with process, in which he revisits and reshapes central themes and imagery in multiple contexts, accumulating and expanding meaning over time.[1] The recurrence of motifs in Bearden's work — the core images that appear and reappear — has been well-noted.[2] As the artist and printer Robert Blackburn remarked, Bearden "had no problem in seizing on themes, like the Mecklenburg thing, or trains. He had no compunction about reworking these images that interested him. These things were the soil from which he drew his imagery."[3] Bearden's prints explore all of the same broad themes that are at the heart of his artistic production, including memories of Mecklenburg County, North Carolina, and the Caribbean, ritual and myth, women, jazz and blues. And his iconic vocabulary — the train, the rooster, the guitar — is found here as well.

Ralph Ellison addressed the intersections of process and metaphor, technique and sensibility in Romare Bearden's art when he stated that "Bearden's meaning is identical with his method. His combination of techniques is in itself eloquent of the sharp breaks, leaps in consciousness, distortions, paradoxes, reversals, telescoping of time, and surreal blending of styles, values, hopes and dreams which characterize much of Negro American history. Through an act of creative will, he has blended strange visual harmonies out of the shrill, indigenous dichotomies of American life and in doing so reflected the irrepressible thrust of a people to endure and keep its intimate sense of its own identity."[4]

Blackburn indicated that "the themes to which Bearden confined himself allowed him a certain freedom to improvise within the limitations."[5] It could certainly be argued further that, for Bearden, his previous work functions for him as a starting place, with each composition the potential basis for the next one. Subjects, themes, motifs, and even meaning and connotation are reworked, rethought, reinvented, and then transformed. Bearden's entire oeuvre is an interweaving of this sensibility and technique. Process becomes a mechanism, a vehicle, an agent for change and variation. As Mary Schmidt Campbell wrote, "Change in technique, the process of call and recall, from Projection, to collage, to quilt, produced radical changes in the image."[6]

"You can't always do things the same way."[7] This was Bearden's response, as quoted by Carroll Greene, when asked why he had taken up collage and moved away from abstraction in his work. But this simple statement could also be cast as the guiding principle of his entire artistic practice, including his work in printmaking. Bearden was not a prolific printmaker, yet he created a significant body of work in a variety of mediums, including etching, collagraph, lithography, and screenprint.[8] He approached these techniques in a uniquely personal way, and his finest prints reveal a dynamic exploration of their processes. When working in tandem with a master printer — and in particular with Blackburn, with whom he shared a lifelong friendship, and Mohammad Khalil and Kathy Caraccio, the printers he met at Blackburn's Printmaking Workshop — Bearden's vision inspired technical innovation and invention.

Bearden's association with Blackburn dated back to the mid-1930s when they both met with the artists' group 306 and worked at the Harlem Community Art Center.[9] Thus began a near-legendary alliance, underscored by Bearden's service on the board of the Printmaking Workshop from the time that it was officially incorporated in 1971 until his death. During those two decades Bearden worked expansively at the workshop,[10] creating a remarkable body of work using a variety of processes.

Blackburn was a master lithographer, who learned the technique in his youth at the Harlem Art Center, then opened his first workshop in 1948. There, working with Will Barnet, he established his reputation for innovative color lithography. From 1957 to 1962 he served as master printer for Tatyana Grosman at her renowned Universal Limited Art Editions. But Bearden rarely chose lithography when working with Blackburn,[11] electing instead to explore mostly etching, collagraph, and monotype. These processes consistently opened up new expressive possibilities for Bearden, and thus his Printmaking Workshop prints are surely his most vibrant and daring.

Bearden did produce a significant body of work in lithography with the European-trained Joseph Kleineman and his associate Maureen Turci at JK Fine Art Editions (also known as Atelier Nouveau) from about 1978 through 1984.[12] In addition, he worked with a number of other printers, workshops, and contract shops during the 1970s and 1980s, producing screenprints and lithographs with, among others, Hugh MacKay's screenprint shop, Atelier 52 (associated with HMK Fine Arts, New York);[13] Judith Solodkin (Solo Impressions, New York);[14] Paul Narkiewicz, New York;[15] Norman Lassiter, Roni Henning, and Steve Maiorano at the New York Institute of Technology Print Workshop;[16] Sirocco Screenprinters, New Haven (under the supervision of Ives-Sillman);[17] Charles Cardinale, Fine Creations, Inc., New York;[18] and Brandywine Workshop, Philadelphia.[19] In many instances Bearden produced a single work with a printer or shop, often as a benefit, or for inclusion in a group portfolio.[20]

Bearden's earliest graphic work included a substantial body of political cartoons, published during the 1930s in journals such as New York University's *Medley* and the *Baltimore Afro-American*, among others.[21] But his first hand-pulled prints were probably linoleum cuts.[22] Records show that Bearden took a course in linoleum block printing at NYU; in 2002 the Mint Museum of Art, Charlotte, North Carolina, exhibited two linoleum cuts, which may be from that period.[23]

The twenty-one Projections first shown at Cordier & Ekstrom, New York, in 1964 could be considered the jumpstart of his core print oeuvre.[24] The Projections are enlargements made from collages using the photographic photostat process and intended to be produced in small editions.[25] Photographic processes played a significant role in Bearden's art — from the photostats to collage elements clipped from printed sources to the prints themselves. Bearden used whatever was available to him. As Ruth Fine has further noted, the "use of a range of photographic duplication methods to develop variations of an image at different sizes over many years is a central component of Bearden's creative methodology."[26]

The Projections are perhaps the ultimate embodiment of the transformative effect of process in Bearden's art, where *process* provides a new lens with which, through augmented scale, modified coloration, and altered surface texture, Bearden shifts the visual reality of the image, renews the experience of his signature vocabulary, and intensifies meaning and compositional impact.[27]

The power of Bearden's art hinges on this sort of transformation. His practice was a continuous process of revisiting vocabulary, reinventing imagery, reordering compositions, and reorganizing structure, with each new arrangement suggestive of what had come before but moving beyond to reflect new meaning, new connotations, a new subtext with new overtones and undertones. Variation and theme echo throughout Bearden's oeuvre in all media, and Bearden's most exploratory prints easily fold into and flow out of this overarching visual rhythm.

During the 1960s Bearden also explored the etching process with William Majors. Blackburn discussed this association with Fine, who wrote: "According to Blackburn, Majors' equipment was quite primitive — a wringer from a clothes-washing machine functioning as a press, perhaps the reason Bearden printed very few impressions from these experimental plates."[28] The drypoint *The Dove*, based on his collage and the related Projection, is one example from this period.[29]

The importance with which Bearden regarded printmaking even at this relatively early date is revealed in his 1966 letter to John A. Davis, editor of the *African Forum*. It was spurred by the deficient representation of African American artists in the exhibition *Twenty-Five Contemporary American Artists as Printmakers*, organized by William Lieberman for the Museum of Modern Art. Bearden wrote:

> To my knowledge he (Lieberman) made no inquiries among Negro artists to ascertain whether or not Negro painters like Norman Lewis, Alston, Woodruff, Ray Saunders, Lawrence, Hines, Hughie Lee Smith, (to mention only a few names that come immediately to mind) are actually doing prints. In this connection, Bill Majors has been instructing some of us in printmaking and a group of artists meet[s] each Saturday at his studio. He is well versed in all phases of graphic arts. Majors has a selection of his oil paintings at the Museum of Mod. Art, at present, that he had sent for Mr. Barr to see; so he certainly is both a painter and graphic artist, who, although specializing in the etching process, has worked in lithography, etc. This is also true for Emma Amos, who, incidentally, has concentrated on silk screens for the past year. But I don't think it necessary to go on. Had Mr. Lieberman been willing to look beyond the small 'in' group that dominates the current art scene, he would surely have found representative artists some of whom would have been Negro. . . .[30]

For the most part, Bearden's print images derive from collage sources, and many of them faithfully restate their origins. Yet some of his most exploratory prints did not emphasize the replication facilitated by these methodologies; instead, the artist seemed to prize the ability of printmaking to open up possibilities of variation within a repeatable structure. Exemplary are the wide variety of color effects — including rainbow roll[31] and hand-coloring — in the unique proofs Bearden executed from the matrixes for the etching *The Train*, as discussed later in this essay (see fig. 39). Conversely, in others of his editions from the mid-seventies, he seemed to be exploring methodologies for executing collage within the context of processes capable of producing exact multiples.

*Carolina Blue* (c. 1970) (fig. 38) was among his earliest screenprints and is particularly interesting in its merging of the print process with collage. Produced by Ives-Sillman, it incorporates several collaged components, including both cutouts from magazines and elements apparently hand-drawn by the artist and then printed (most likely in lithography). This print was one of the few readily available through Cordier & Ekstrom, Bearden's long-time dealer.[32]

At about the same time as *Carolina Blue*, or perhaps soon after its completion, Bearden took the concept of the collage multiple to another level with the creation of the *Ritual Bayou* series, multiple collages published by Shorewood Publishers, New York. A unique and ambitious project, the *Ritual Bayou* series was based on six of eighteen collages commissioned by Sam Shore, owner of Shorewood Atelier. Ten of the eighteen collages were shown in the 1971 Museum of Modern Art exhibition, *Romare Bearden: The Prevalence of Ritual*,[33] and eleven were on view four years later in *Mysteries: Women in the Art of Romare Bearden* at the Everson Museum of Art, Syracuse, curated by Mary Schmidt Campbell.[34] Of the original eighteen, Bearden created collage editions for *Byzantine Frieze, Carolina Interior, Memories, Mississippi Monday, Reunion,* and *Ritual Bayou* to form the *Ritual Bayou* set. These were originally intended as the first of a three-part project, advertised by Shorewood Publishers as *Trilogy*. Bearden had planned to create two additional sets of collage editions, each with six images, based on the twelve remaining collages from the Shorewood commission. Part two would have been titled *Time of the Gingham Rooster*, and part three, *Suzannah and the Bath*. Only the *Ritual Bayou* six were ever produced as multiples. Each image was to have been produced as an edition of seventy-five, mounted on finished plywood, along with a deluxe edition of twenty-five, lettered A through Y, mounted on ebony. However, it is not known

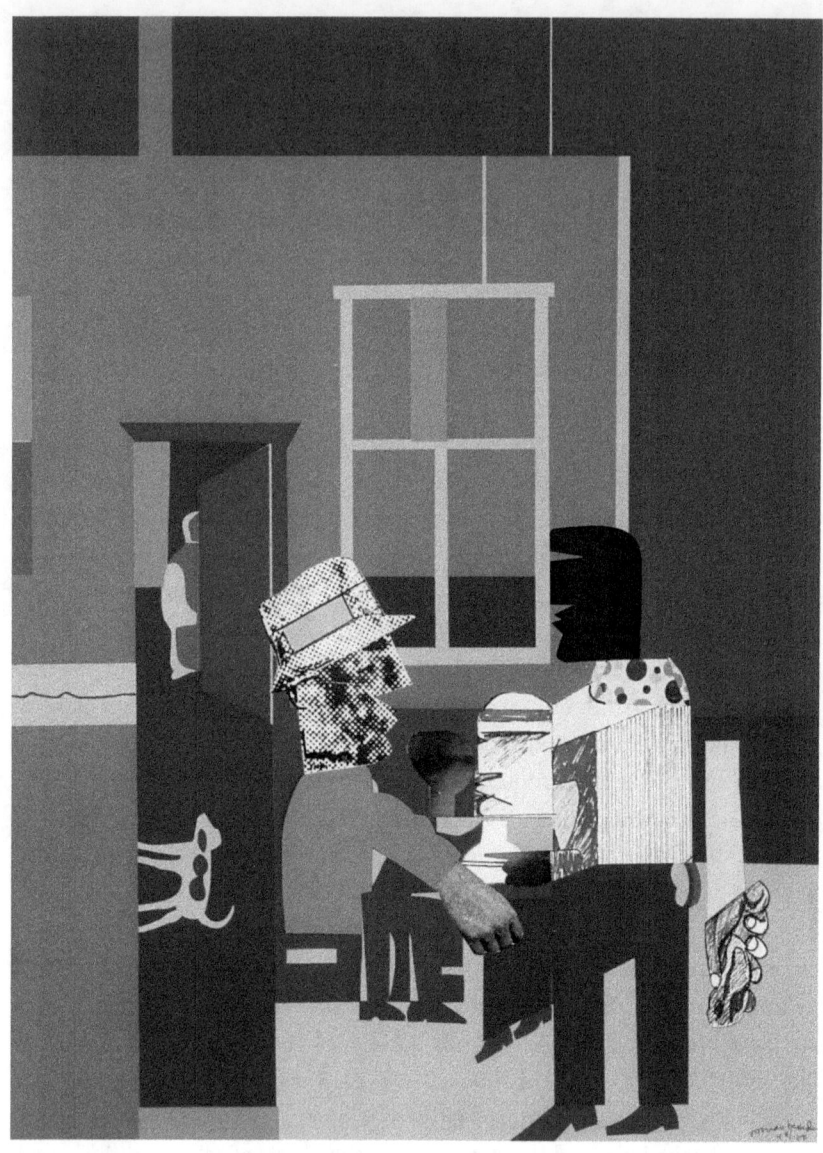

FIGURE 38 Romare Bearden, *Carolina Blue*, 1970. Screenprint with collage additions. Image: 23 7/8 × 17 7/8 in. (60.6 × 45.4 cm); sheet: 27 1/2 × 21 in. (69.8 × 53.3 cm). Printer: Sirocco Screenprinters, Ives-Sillman, Inc., New Haven, CT, Publisher: Cordier and Ekstrom Gallery, New York. Edition 100. Museum of Modern Art, Gift of Arne H. Ekstrom, New York (1051.1979). Art © Romare Bearden Foundation/Licensed by VAGA, New York

how many of each of the six subjects was actually completed, as the process of creating so many matching images became too cumbersome for the artist.[35]

Bearden's first etching at Robert Blackburn's Printmaking Workshop was *Tropical Flowers* (c. 1971–1974),[36] created with one of Blackburn's associates, artist/printer Mohammad Khalil.[37] The print was produced as a fundraiser for the Lincoln Square Neighborhood Center[38] and was one of many that Bearden would do over the years to benefit political and charitable causes.

Based on a small Caribbean-themed watercolor, the image was photographically enlarged to make the plates — a shift in scale that paralleled that of the previous decade's Projections. Unique proofs, exploring effects achieved with rainbow roll inking, for example, further indicate Bearden's approach to printmaking for its capacity to allow variety and experimentation within the parameters of an established framework.

Alex Rosenberg, of Transworld Art Corp., first spoke to Bearden about the possibility of publishing his prints shortly after they met, in about 1973.[39] *The Train* (fig. 39), published by Transworld, was printed at the Printmaking Workshop. It is based on a collage and the related 1964 Projection, *Mysteries*, but the image was transformed through the print production process.[40] Plate work, utilizing photographic techniques, was begun by Mohammad Khalil, but the edition was completed by Kathy Caraccio when Khalil had to make a trip abroad. Caraccio, who had come to the workshop in 1972 and whose expertise included viscosity printing,[41] was in the shop doing her own work when she was recruited by Blackburn to produce proofs from Bearden's plates. With Khalil unavailable, Blackburn took advantage of the "fortuitous moment" of having Caraccio in the studio, "with that palette out," as she noted, "and he [Blackburn] knew that I could plug it into that plate."[42] Caraccio created numerous and varied proofs on which Bearden adjusted the colors by expansively adding watercolor. As Caraccio recounts: "Bob Blackburn took all the proofs I did on *The Train* to Romare on Canal Street, where he [Bearden] hand-colored them. . . . Bob [later] brought [back to the workshop] a tinted proof . . . to edition. . . . I [then] chrome-faced the plate, cut the nine elements and added an aquatint plate to simulate his blue watercolor application [on] the BAT [*bon á tirer*]." Thus, in order to match the effects of the watercoloring on the proof selected as the prototype for the edition (BAT), Caraccio decided to cut the plates to create nine separate components. These could be worked individually to enhance texture and depth in specific areas, inked in isolation, and reassembled as one unit for printing in one pass through the press.[43] The technique opened

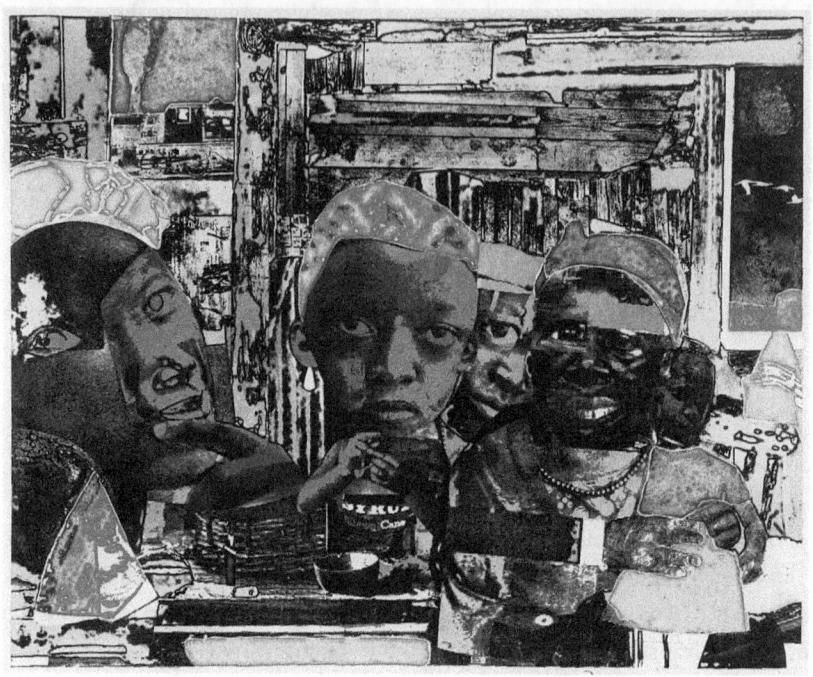

FIGURE 39  Romare Bearden, *The Train*, 1975. Photogravure and aquatint. Plate: 17 11/16 × 22 1/8 in. (44.9 × 56.2 cm); sheet: 22 1/4 × 30 1/8 in. (56.5 × 76.5 cm). Printer: The Printmaking Workshop, New York. Publisher: Transworld Art, New York. Edition 125. Museum of Modern Art, New York (250.1975). Art © Romare Bearden Foundation/Licensed by VAGA, New York

up additional possibilities for complex inking without requiring a color registration system to keep the colors perfectly aligned. As described by Caraccio: "Because the plate was deep etched, it was receptive to viscosity inking (a yellow roll was applied to the background) and viscosity rolling was done on some of the cut bits but not all and not in the same colors. In actuality, the printing took two passes because of the need to add the blue watercolor effect that Bearden added to the first color proofs presented for his approval." *The Train* was also issued in a deluxe edition printed on paper to which Bearden had added watercolor before the printing.[44]

Bearden further extended his engagement with *The Train* by reconstituting a dozen of the individual experimental proofs produced from these plates as a sequence of unique impressions, known collectively as *12 Trains*.[45] The varying and subtle nuances of light, tone, and atmosphere of these distinctively hand-tinted images are evocative of different times of day (daybreak to midnight), qualities of illumination (soft to bright, glaring to dark), and different moods (vibrant to heavy, enlivening to oppressive).

*The Train* was in production at approximately the same time as *The Family* (fig. 40), which was included in the three-volume portfolio *An American Portrait, 1776–1976*, containing works by thirty-three artists and published by Transworld Art to commemorate the American bicentennial. The process for producing the plates for *The Family*, as with *The Train*, began with the making of multiple transparencies (Kodaliths) of the collage, photographed through various halftone screens to produce different patterns and textures,[46] which Bearden then cut apart and re-collaged. The reconfigured transparency-collage was then rephotographed to make the Kodalith for the key plate. Proofs of the key plate were printed in both relief and intaglio, and supplementary plates were then made for added color.[47] Caraccio recalls that for both *The Family* and *The Train*, sepia proofs were made to test the viscosity, "to determine where the rollers would hit."[48] As Fine has pointed out, when comparing the proofs from the key plates to the final edition of *The Family*, it is clear that Bearden continued to rework the composition in the proofing stages — for example, he added drawing to the children's faces.[49] Caraccio noted that adjustments to the plate for the face of the smallest figure at the table had to be made because that part of the image wasn't printing clearly in initial proofs. The plate was thus physically ground out in that area, and the image was redrawn by Bearden so that it could be re-etched.[50]

*The Family*, along with *The Train* and *12 Trains*, represents quintessential Bearden printmaking — improvisation, variation within structure; collage practice customized for creating the matrix. Together these prints reveal the substance of Bearden's aesthetic methodology as described by Blackburn and recorded in the 1995 film, *Romare Bearden: Visual Jazz*: "I learned mostly with Romie the idea to feel very, very free. Don't fix your idea too much because if you fix your idea you've nowhere to expand to. . . . He never had something that was so tight that he couldn't alter it."[51]

*The Family* was immediately recognized as an important work in twentieth-century printmaking. In an *Arts Magazine* article about the portfolio, John Loring described Bearden's print as "among the finest of the prints [in the portfolio]." He continued, "Romare Bearden's *The Family* [is] rich in tone and feeling for the monolithic strength of love, respect, and cooperation binding together the seemingly insoluble complexities of human relations."[52] More than a year later, in an *Art in America* article, "American Prints from Fuses to Fizzles," a reflection

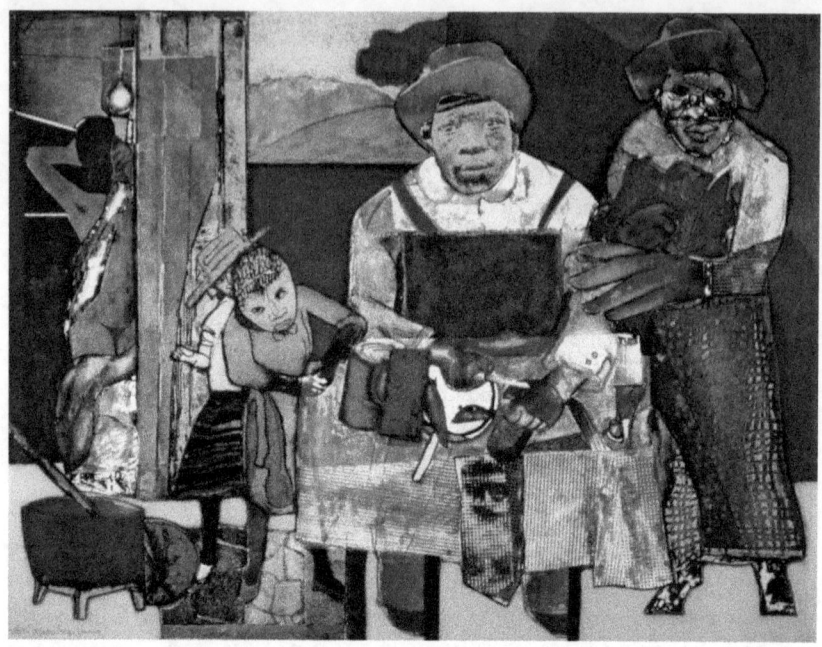

FIGURE 40 Romare Bearden, *The Family* from *An American Portrait, 1776–1976* (portfolio), 1975. Color photo-etching and aquatint on paper. Plate: 15 × 20 5/16 in. (38.1 × 51.6 cm); sheet: 21 × 28 1/8 in. (53.5 × 71.4 cm). Printer: The Printmaking Workshop, New York. Publisher: Transworld Art, New York. Sidney and Lois Eskenazi Museum of Art, Indiana University Bloomington. Art © Romare Bearden Foundation/Licensed by VAGA, New York

on the state and direction of American printmaking in general, Loring identified *The Family* as one of several notable contemporary etchings "of particular excellence," noting that it was "rich in surface and in emotional texture."[53] In 2003 Fine added, "Other dramatic and successful color photo-etchings followed, but none attempted to push the combination of photography, collage, and etching beyond what was accomplished in *The Family*."[54]

Bearden's work at the Printmaking Workshop, perhaps particularly his monotypes and monoprints (when techniques such as rainbow roll were employed), provided significant financial support for the shop.[55] The monotypes, which were generally called "oils on paper" when exhibited, constitute a body of work within Bearden's exploration of printmaking that is his most spontaneous and lyrical. Khalil remembers that Bearden and Blackburn worked closely together behind closed doors, allowing for maximum absorption in the process.[56] And Cullen noted that Bearden sometimes employed a stencil to block out certain areas, retaining the white of the paper — such as in the piano in *Ellington Sounds: Reminiscing in Tempo*[57] — a methodology that brings a collage aesthetic to the process.

Bearden supported Blackburn's efforts in other important ways, too, such as writing the introductory text for *Impressions: Our World* (1974), a Printmaking Workshop portfolio of works by African American artists. The portfolio includes work by Emma Amos, Benny Andrews, Vivian Browne, Eldzier Cortor, Norman Lewis, Mohammad Khalil, Vincent Smith, and John Wilson. He also provided a statement for the exhibition catalogue *Art in Print: A Tribute to Robert Blackburn* (Schomburg Center, November 30, 1984–January 18, 1985).

Bearden made some of his finest collagraphs at Blackburn's workshop during the mid-seventies. Exact dating is often elusive, as Bearden rarely inscribed these impressions, and at this writing few records relating to them are known. A Printmaking Workshop invoice for "printing services," dated October 17, 1972, for four "collographs [*sic*] executed on cardboard" titled *3 Women*, *The Street*, *3 Faces*, and *Mountains* is one such significant document.[58] Another is a note on Bearden's personal letterhead, written and signed by Blackburn and dated November 9, 1974, stating, "received from Romare Bearden relief blocks (cardboard) of *Iliad I* [and] *Iliad II* to be experimentally proofed —"[59]

Mohammad Khalil has said that he believes that Blackburn introduced Bearden to the collagraph process, perhaps in the early or mid-seventies. According to Khalil, Blackburn showed Bearden techniques for making the plates, which Bearden made in his studio and brought to the workshop for printing.[60] Of all of the printing techniques he employed, collagraph and monotype were the processes for which Bearden was most hands-on in making the printing matrices.

Bearden employed two basic methods for creating his collagraph plates. He would cut and layer cardboard to build an image, sometimes meticulously scoring and removing a thin layer from selected areas of the topmost pieces for further nuance. The matrix for *Untitled Woman in the Garden*[61] was composed and scored in this way. Alternatively, he would apply runnels of glue in a dense interweaving of line, as can be seen in *Mysteries*.[62] He would also combine both approaches on a single matrix, as was done to produce *Prelude to Troy (No. 2)* (fig. 41). These methodologies were standard to making collagraphs, a popular process among printmakers at the time.[63] But it is easy to see how this technique would hold particular appeal to Bearden, playing to his strengths as a

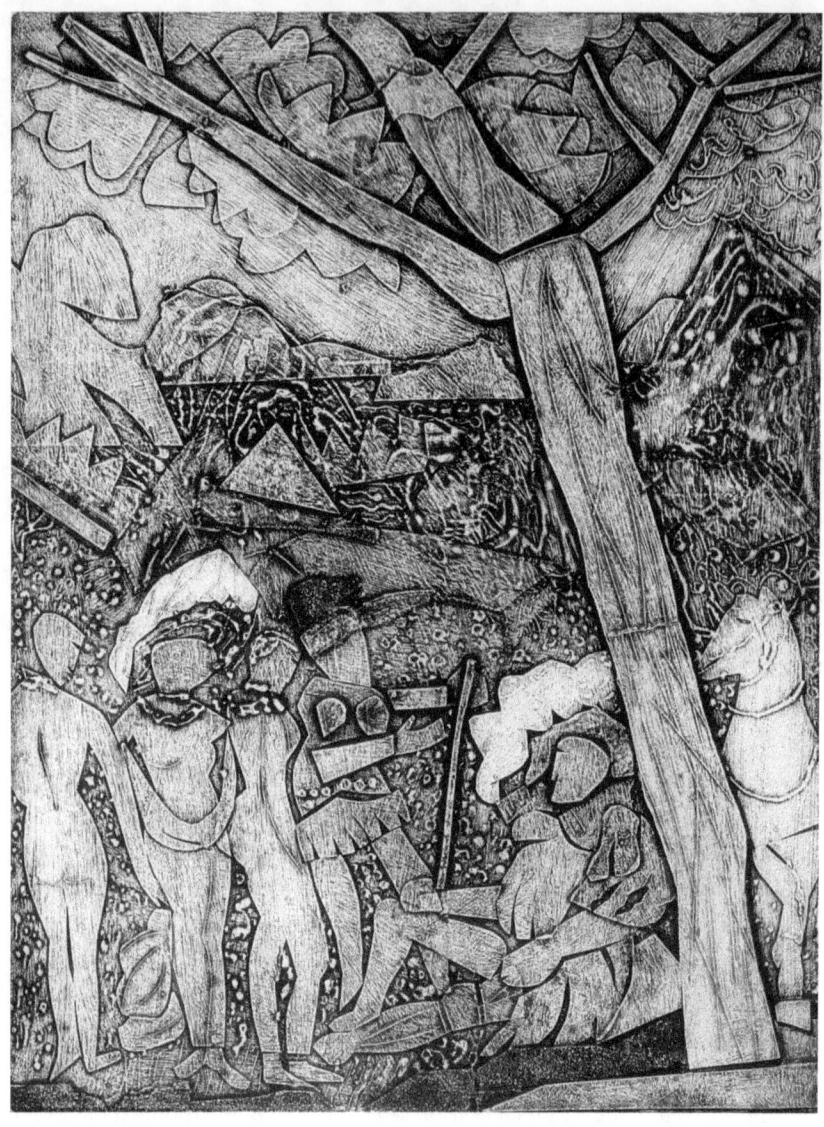

FIGURE 41 Romare Bearden, *Prelude to Troy (No. 2)*, 1974. Collagraph in blue on wove Arches paper. Plate: 60.9 × 46.8 cm (24 × 18 7/16 in.); sheet: 76.2 × 56.2 cm (30 × 22 1/8 in.). National Gallery of Art, Gift of Yvonne and Richard McCracken and Mary and Jerald Melberg, Washington, DC (2000.58.1). Art © Romare Bearden Foundation/Licensed by VAGA, New York

draftsman and collagist extraordinaire and enabling him to make a distinctive contribution to the history of the process.

The matrices themselves are beautiful objects, finely crafted works of art in their own right. The impressions pulled from them are varied and experimental. For example, the individuality of impressions of *Iliad*[64] highlights this key aspect of Bearden's printmaking: as with his art in other mediums he uses process as a means to revisit compositions, reinvent vocabulary, change context, and redefine meaning. His most inventive prints, including these collagraphs, celebrate the capacity of the medium to facilitate reiteration and recurrence, while avoiding duplication or repetition. Although multiple prints were made from these plates, only one collagraph is known to have been published as an edition, in addition to a few varied proofs; that is *Prelude to Troy*.[65]

*Mysteries* is among the most archetypal Bearden images. Quintessentially transformative, the subject was brought to life over a span of years, beginning in the sixties as collage and as a photostat, and again in the seventies as an etching *(The Train)* and a collagraph.[66] Keeping the basic forms, Bearden nonetheless altered the collagraph composition in myriad nuanced ways. The matrix is beautifully drawn, its strong forms and textures setting up a decidedly distinctive rhythm from the variants in other media. The collagraph print is the reverse of the variants in other media, because the image on the plate, obviously, was drawn in the same direction as the other images. Several impressions of the collagraph are known, each inked and wiped with subtle differences.

A reworking of the printed surface of the collagraph *The Guitar Player (Saturday Night)*[67] using pencil and possibly an eraser (producing soft abrasions) can be seen on some impressions of this print in the collection of the Bearden Estate. Bearden also altered the surface of some of the impressions of the collagraph *The Street*[68] by working back over selected areas with dense pencil lines. *The Street* replays figurative components from the 1964 collage *The Street* and its companion *Projection*[69] — the figure climbing the stairs in the middle-ground, the guitar player with the fedora, among others — redrawn and reinvented out of the emphatic, viscous glue lines that Bearden used to create the plate. The pulled impression was, of course, a mirror image, providing another means for a compositional variation on a theme.[70]

Bearden often began a new work in any medium by revisiting a previous composition, using this process of re-exploration to create new contexts and new meanings out of past history. His prints are indeed a seamless part of this approach to artmaking. A photograph of Bearden in his studio in 1979[71] is particularly revealing: Bearden is seen working on what might be the collage, or a perhaps a proof, related to the print *Jazz II*,[72] spread out flat before him on a table top. Propped against the wall in front of him is what appears to be a reproduction of another work, the collage *Jazz — Kansas City* (1977),[73] which clearly bears a structural relationship in its compositional arrangement to the print. Not in the photograph, yet predating both of these compositions, are a related collage and its companion Projection titled *Jazz: (Chicago) Grand Terrace — 1930s* (from 1964).[74]

Another jazz-themed lithograph, *Le Jazz (Out Chorus II)*,[75] reveals a similar set of contrapuntal relationships. It is related in subject and structure to the Projection *Jazz: (N.Y.) Savoy–1930s* (1964),[76] and numerous other compositional reinventions exist as well, including the collages *Improvisations* (1968–69)[77] and *One Night Stand* (1974).[78] *Le Jazz (Out Chorus II)* also finds a reprise in one of Bearden's final works, the collage *Opening at the Savoy* (1987) (see fig. 47). The oversized musical notes on the music stand in the foreground of the collage are among the elements that relate specifically to the lithograph. A photograph of Bearden working on this collage was taken by *New York Newsday* photographer Bill Davis and appeared in *Newsday Magazine*, January 17, 1988.[79]

Jazz subjects recurred frequently in Bearden's art, but as has been frequently noted, even more important than the theme itself is the abstract way in which jazz-style thinking and the concept of improvisation influenced his artmaking. Through multiple related compositions, he continuously reinvented his visual vocabulary, always keeping something of what came before, remaking without replacing. A composer writes a piece of music so that it will be performed, repeated, even reinterpreted (as in variations). Music is ritual; it provides a sense of history, connection, and continuity, all of which also define Bearden's artistic practice.

In 1971 Bearden told Carroll Greene, "I try to show that when some things are taken out of the usual context and put in the new, they are given an entirely new character."[80] At the time he was describing the interrelationships and associations created by the juxtaposition of elements within a single collage, but the characterization certainly can be applied more broadly to his compositional sequences as well.

Bearden explored music and myth, ritual and continuity in three suites of prints, all produced during the 1970s. The last of these is the *Jazz* series of lithographs, printed in Joseph Kleineman's atelier and published in 1979.[81] The other two came earlier in the decade. The first was *Prevalence of Ritual*, Bearden's only series housed in a portfolio, issued in a gray, cloth-covered folder — five bold and beautifully executed screenprints, printed by Sirocco Screenprinters and published by Cordier & Ekstrom and Ives-Sillman in 1974.[82]

Hilton Kramer praised the set when it was exhibited at Cordier & Ekstrom, writing in the *New York Times* in 1974:

> This small exhibition consists of only five works — a portfolio of screen-prints entitled "Prevalence of Ritual," in which Mr. Bearden has applied the imagery familiar to us in his recent paintings to the print medium. What is remarkable here is the technical perfection of the results. The original designs employed certain elements of collage, including fabric, corrugated paper and materials of diverse texture and color. All of these differences in the visual "weight" of each constituent form are beautifully realized in these printed versions. A good deal of credit must go to the printers — Ives-Sillman of New Haven — but the work is Mr. Bearden's, of course, and the characteristic vitality of his art is once again confirmed.[83]

His second suite, also screenprints, was a set of six, based on his Odysseus series of collages[84] — *Cattle of the Sun God, Circe Turns a Companion of Odysseus into a Swine, Home to Ithaca, Odysseus Leaves, Siren's Song, Troy (The Burning of Troy)* — published by Hugh MacKay (HMK Fine Arts Inc.) and printed at MacKay's screenprint shop, Atelier 52. Debra Rhodes Smith, who worked for MacKay from 1977 to 1981, and who assisted Bearden at the time he signed the suite, remembers that during production "every step was supervised by him and he had a watchful eye."[85]

During the mid to late seventies Bearden produced at least four prints with the New York Institute of Technology Print Workshop. Frances Lassiter, who was chair of the art department at NYIT, founded this screenprinter's workshop with the goal of engaging professional artists with printmaking in an academic environment, for the benefit of both artist and student. Norman Lassiter, her husband at the time, was the workshop's first director.[86] *Baptism* (c. 1975), screenprinted by Lassiter, may have been among the first works produced at the shop.[87] He has said that he believes that Frances Lassiter, having received funding for the project from the New York State Council on the Arts, initially approached Bearden about making *Baptism* for the benefit of the Alvin Ailey Dance Company. (A poster edition, smaller in scale, was also produced.)[88] Lassiter's memory is that the collage model was smaller than the edition print, and that he, Lassiter, did color separations, bringing the image up to final scale.[89]

He then worked with Bearden through the proofing stages, going to the artist's studio to discuss progressive proofs and making modifications until Bearden was satisfied with the result.[90]

Printer Roni Henning succeeded Lassiter to become the workshop's second director, and she worked with Bearden on three other prints executed during the mid- to late seventies:[91] *Sorcerer's Village*, or *Sorcerer (African Fantasy)*, and *Two Women* both combined lithography and screenprint; *Blue Carolina Morning* (c. 1977), or *Untitled (Southern Interior)*,[92] was screenprint only.

Both *Sorcerer's Village* and *Two Women* were based on previously executed collages;[93] the plates were most likely created using photographic processes and the screens utilized both hand-cut film stencils and photo separations that Henning produced using a copy camera. Frances Lassiter arranged for the lithography portion to be executed elsewhere,[94] and Henning then received the lithographed edition to complete with the addition of screenprinting in the NYIT workshop.

Henning remembers working much more closely with the artist on *Blue Carolina Morning* than the other two. As with the others, the process began with photo separations, but as the work on this print progressed Bearden eventually eliminated all of the photo work. *Blue Carolina Morning*, along with an example of one of the annotated proofs, is reproduced in Henning's book *Water-Based Screenprinting Today*, where she describes the importance of the proofing process to Bearden in a brief essay, "Creating a New Original with Romare Bearden." Henning writes: "Each time I visited his studio, he quietly reviewed the new proof, then drew all over it and instructed me on the new color changes. The piece went from a white photo collage to a graphic gray, red, and blue print. He even changed the figures. At each stage, he seemed to know exactly what he was aiming for, but every time I returned, he changed it again. On the fourth and last proof, he drew his final changes. He even added the mop from the original back in. The final proof that satisfied him no longer resembled the original collage."[95]

In fact, the proofing process was critical to Bearden in the development of many of his printed images: with the proofs before him, Bearden began the real work of transforming the image from source to print. The variants of *Tropical Flowers*, the multitude of annotations on working proofs such as those for *Blue Carolina Morning* are only two instances among the many examples of Bearden's approach to printmaking — of creating variation upon an underlying structure, as jazz improvisation. Khalil noted that when working with Bearden on an etching, Khalil "would proof different things for Romy to show him different things that I could do with the plate. . . . I used to go to his studio in Queens or downtown to his place on Canal Street and show him what I had done. I would talk to him directly and/or I would leave it for him to think about and see what he wanted. Then I would go back and look at the notes and sometimes give him something else."[96]

Nanette Bearden also noted the importance of the proof in her husband's approach to printmaking: "Whenever he was working on a print, he would come home in the evening with the latest proofs from the plate and he would fret over them and ask me what I thought and make his own notes in the margins. He did not want to forget the changes he would suggest the next morning to the printmaker."[97]

By the mid-seventies printmaking was taking an increasingly important place in Bearden's artistic practice. This is evident not only from the virtuosity of *The Train* and *Family*, but also from the increasing number of prints he produced during the last half of the decade and into the 1980s. This activity no doubt was made easier for Bearden by the organizational role June Kelly played as his manager, beginning in 1975.[98] At this time Bearden also joined with Bill E. Caldwell, Willem de Kooning, and Jacob Lawrence to create the Rainbow Art Foundation to provide assistance to struggling young artist-printmakers.[99]

*Come Sunday*, underway in December 1974 and published in 1976 in the portfolio *1776 USA* by Contemporary Artists in celebration of the American bicentennial, is among Bearden's early lithographs.[100] A number of photographs taken by Lucia Woods Lindley document the production and Bearden's work in creating the plate.[101] The printer was Paul Narkiewicz[102] and the photographs show Bearden working closely with him in Narkiewicz's studio, drawing in marker on mylar to create the key plate and using the collage as a source. A comparison of the print to the related collage[103] shows the myriad subtle ways in which Bearden altered the drawing. Tusche was employed in spatters and washes, creating a rich surface with a variety of textures that further differentiated the print from the collage, while keeping essential forms and structure.

Bearden continued to expand his engagement with the process of lithography in Kleineman's atelier on Van Dam Street and later (1984) on Watts Street in New York, where he began working in 1978.[104] As Myron Schwartzman has noted,[105] it was Kelly, Bearden's manager, who introduced the artist to the printer, ushering in a particularly productive period for Bearden's printmaking.

The *Jazz* series, printed in Kleineman's shop and published by London Arts in 1979, is closely related to Bearden's monotypes/oils on paper.[106] Unlike other prints produced with Kleineman, continuous-tone photographic work was used to create the plates for this series. But working on Mylar, Bearden enhanced the photo-based images with hand-drawn tusche washes. Kleineman recalled, "It was an evolving process — improvising as we went along, the artist responded according to the colors printed. After a few colors were printed the composition takes shape, the artist sees what needs to be adjusted. Step by step the print is built to completion."[107]

Schwartzman has written that Bearden and Kleineman "were at ease working together, and each man's thorough craftsmanship and spontaneous, jazz-like creativity made for a good synthesis of master artist and master printmaker."[108] Bearden produced more than twenty prints with Kleineman and his long-time associate, Maureen Turci, who joined the shop in 1980.[109] In addition to the *Jazz* series, he made lithographs for two group portfolios: *In the Garden* (1979), for *American Portfolio*, published in 1980 (with Lester Johnson, Alice Neel, Will Barnet, Henry Pearson, Sharon Sutton; London Arts) and *Pepper Jelly Lady*, for the *Presidential Portfolio*, published in 1980 by the Democratic Service Corporation, Washington, DC.[110] Bearden also worked with Kleineman and Turci to produce several commemorative/benefit prints, such as *Morning of the Rooster* (1980),[111] published in celebration of the opening of the exhibition *Romare Bearden: 1970–1980*, at the Mint Museum, Charlotte, North Carolina; *Autumn of the Rooster* (1983), executed for the hundredth anniversary of the Brooklyn Bridge;[112] *The Lamp* (1984), for the NAACP Legal Defense and Educational Fund on the thirtieth anniversary of the Supreme Court's *Brown v. Board of Education* decision; and *Homage to Mary Lou* (1984) (Plate 9), which was one of several works Bearden did to support his wife's dance company.[113]

Kleineman has stated that Bearden would often work on several print images simultaneously. Their subjects often related to collages Bearden had begun producing about 1978,[114] recalling childhood memories of Mecklenburg County, North Carolina, and thus providing the theme for what could be considered an informal series.

Using a drawing or a collage source, Bearden employed transfer paper to put the image onto the metal lithography plate. Whereas Kleineman laid down large color areas using tusche, the artist himself drew in the details, using both lithographic crayon and liquid tusche — sometimes as washes, sometimes with a crow-quill pen to get a particularly fine line.[115] According to Kleineman, proofing records no longer exist, but the printer believes there would have been a small set of progressive proofs, with three or four colors at first, then with more added, as well as artist's proofs and printers' proofs for most editions.[116]

Bearden's work with Kleineman underscored Bearden's consummate skills as a draftsman, accentuating both the delicacy and the powerful simplicity of his lines: from the intricate pattern of the quilt in *Mecklenburg Autumn* (1979) to the delicate floral design on the bedspread in *Falling Star* (1979) to the Matissean elegance of the drawing of the rooster or the patterning on the woman's headscarf in *Morning of the Rooster* (1980).[117] Bearden also used tusche washes to great effect, for example, to create the vibrant, pulsing color in the dress of the woman in *Falling Star*, or to interact with the simple, expressive line work of the images that seem to emerge from and fade into the mist of the enlivened border of *Pepper Jelly Lady* (1980).

When a selection of Bearden's lithographs, etchings, and screenprints was exhibited in 1985 at Lehman College Art Gallery in the Bronx, critic Vivien Raynor wrote:

> So seductive is his color that it is easy to overlook his equally skillful draftsman-ship. Note the Matissean contours of Circe, who has just turned one of Odysseus's companions into a marvelous black hog with white tusks; the expressive hands of the pupil in "Piano Lesson" and the sinuous marriage of man and musical instrument in "Walking Bass."
>
> Mr. Bearden is a master of all three mediums, but lithography does his gifts for color, pattern, texture and detail the most justice.[118]

A comparison of a collage of *The Piano Lesson*[119] to the related edition print *Homage to Mary Lou* highlights the dynamic nature of Bearden's imagery as he reinvented it in another medium, subtly reworking the structure and adjusting internal relationships between forms while maintaining the overall composition. Bearden simplified some elements — such as the table ensemble in the lower left corner — while making others more complex. The sheet music, for example, which is blank in the collage, carries a full complement of music notes in the print. *Homage to Mary Lou* is one of Bearden's most complex lithographs, employing eighteen colors from eighteen plates, and adding elements such as the fabric textures of the green foreground rug, offering a direct correlation to his collage aesthetic.

The nature of Bearden's involvement in the production of the print matrix varied widely — from the collagraphs, where he entirely handcrafted the matrices, to screenprints such as *Blue Carolina Morning*, where, as printer Henning indicated, his focus was not on the screens themselves, but on working with the proofs. Bearden seems to have chosen a middle ground with much of his work in lithography. For most of the prints he did with Kleineman he used transfer paper and worked directly on plates with tusche or lithographic pencil. *Morning of the Rooster* is completely hand-drawn; the border for *Pepper Jelly Lady* was drawn by Bearden on Mylar, then transferred to the plate. Fabric textures, such as those found in *Homage to Mary Lou*, were either drawn on the plate or transferred directly. Even in the *Jazz* series, where photographic processes were used in the making of the plates, Bearden would add tusche work on Mylar to achieve the effects he desired.

Bearden's use of photographic processes in his print production was generally in step with what other artists were doing during the same years. With the advent of what is often called the print renaissance of the 1960s, and the growth of the collaborative workshops, such as Universal Limited Art Editions and Gemini GEL, some artists were producing prints in both "fine art" and "commercial" environments, using whatever means were available to them to get to the desired result and to reach the desired audience.[120] As Fine has further noted, "[Bearden] would have understood that edition prints could introduce his (and other artists') imagery to a wider public than unique works and that they enabled people of limited means to own an original work, something that his friends recall as being exceedingly important to Bearden."[121]

In an extension of that spirit, Bearden, like many artists, produced prints in support of political or social causes, or to honor, commemorate, or celebrate an event. In addition to those already mentioned, another example is *Sunday Morning at Avila*,[122] an etching edition printed by Mohammed Khalil. It was commissioned in 1981 to mark the honorary performance at Carnegie Hall of *Four Saints in Three Acts*, conducted by Joel Thome in celebration of the eighty-fifth birthday of Virgil Thomson, co-author (with Gertrude Stein) of that 1934 opera.

Bearden also designed images for publication as posters, book or magazine covers and illustrations, and album covers.[123] There are also many cases in which preexisting collages or paintings were selected for reproduction in this new context.

Aside from the exhibition of his photostat Projections in 1964, Bearden's prints occasionally appeared in exhibitions beginning in 1970. Early that year,

Cordier & Ekstrom included the collaged screenprint *Carolina Blue* in a solo exhibition of Bearden's collages, and Tirca Karlis Gallery, in Provincetown, followed suit in August. Another of Bearden's prints may have been on view in the 1970 group exhibition *Contemporary Graphic Art on Contemporary Law and Justice, 1870–1970* at the Pratt Graphics Center, New York.[124]

In the summer of 1974 Cordier & Ekstrom featured the *Prevalence of Ritual* screenprint portfolio in an exhibition and the next year *Baptism* was introduced in Paris at Albert Loeb Gallery in *Romare Bearden: Collages*.[125] In 1976 thirty-seven Bearden monotypes (called oils on paper) were on view at Cordier & Ekstrom in *Romare Bearden: Of the Blues (Second Chorus)*.[126] Almost simultaneously, eleven prints were included in a solo exhibition at the Firehouse Gallery, Nassau Community College.[127]

In 1982 the Birmingham Museum of Art, Alabama, was among the first museums to feature Bearden's prints in *Romare Bearden "Jazz."*[128] Several of the *Jazz* series lithographs were included. Later that year the Hickory Museum of Art showed two lithographs — *In the Garden* (1976) and *Morning of the Rooster: Mecklenburg County* (1980) — in *The Afro-American Presence in the Arts, Past and Present from North Carolina Collections*.[129]

Wesleyan University in Middletown, Connecticut, seems to have been the first institution to focus an exhibition solely on Bearden's prints, opening *Romare Bearden: Prints* in February 1981.[130] It was followed later that year by *Prints and Watercolors by Romare Bearden*, held at the Museum of the National Center of Afro-American Artists in Roxbury, Massachusetts, and a contemporaneous solo exhibition at Morgan State University, in Baltimore, which featured screenprints, lithographs, and watercolors.

Bearden's prints were generally well received by the critics, as exemplified by John Loring's early praise of *The Family* and Vivien Raynor's 1985 exhibition review, quoted above. Writing in *Newsday* in 1986 about Bearden's edition prints — which were on view along with his monotypes and watercolors in a solo exhibition at the Flushing Gallery in Queens[131] — Karin Lipson noted:

> By contrast to Bearden's paintings, his prints have been executed with tightly controlled precision. These lithographs and silkscreens have a flat, decorative element that can make them look from afar like richly colored textiles. (In their design quality, they bring to mind Bearden's famed collages, none of which appear in this show.) While some of the prints, too, have an island setting, the most stunning are three silk screens on mythological themes, from Bearden's

six-part "Odysseus Suite." This is the *Odyssey* acted out to an African beat. The city of Troy, seen in flames in one piece, is a North African place of mosques and minarets. Figures are black, knife-wielding, African warriors. Despite their bellicose subject matter, though, these works are so precisely patterned, so geometric, that they have the calming look of an ancient frieze. Two etchings, called *The Family* and *Mysteries*, especially, show Bearden in a different mode, delving into a side of Caribbean life that is private and secretive. *Mysteries*, especially communicates a sense of repressed violence, or at least of guarded hostility. A series of faces stares out at us with a look that means "don't trespass." Always an artist of depth, Bearden has here created the antithesis of the grinning "come on down" island travel poster.[132]

In 1987, when Bearden's health was failing, *Romare Bearden: Collages and Prints* was on view at St. John's Museum of Art in Wilmington, North Carolina.[133] This solo show was among the final exhibitions featuring his prints before his death in March 1988.

The relationship of Bearden's print imagery to its source (usually collage), and in fact its place within his entire oeuvre, is marked by a tenacious, yet agile, flow from one composition to the next. The whole of his pictorial vocabulary coalesces, diverges, and coalesces again, over time, thereby accumulating context and reference within the history of his imagery and enriching an ever-evolving meaning. Recurring objects, recurring themes and subjects, and recurring rituals are the substance of human existence and at the heart of Bearden's art. In this sense, Bearden's printmaking, as a component of his larger artistic practice, is an embodiment of quest — the search for revelation in repetition, extension (as in series), and reinvention. Like the art of the storyteller — the griot — with each retelling comes a new richness, nuances, and accumulated context. This story, this journey, and the capacity and opportunity to reinvent oneself, are intrinsic components of the American psyche.

As evidenced in a sequence of works such as *12 Trains* — printed impressions made unique with hand-coloring — or the many printed variations of his collagraphs, with proofs intermittently reworked with pencil, print processes offered Bearden the specialized means of bringing variation out of repetition. The print matrix presented the artist with the opportunity for endless variety while using a repetitive substructure; it provided another way of coming back, then, to take the work to a new place, of making something new out of the known.

Ritual is by definition repetitive, and it is at the core of Bearden's aesthetic. Ritual connects past to present. Ritual in Bearden's art is the combining of tradition and repetition with new meaning and invention, speaking to the universality of human experience. Printmaking, a ritual in itself, offered Bearden an additional means for reinvention, for revisiting themes and images, and at its best in Bearden's hands, it became a tool for improvisation.

## NOTES

From "Impressions & Improvisations: A Look at the Prints of Romare Bearden," in Mary Lee Corlett, *From Process to Print: Graphic Works by Romare Bearden* (Petaluma, CA: Pomegranate Communications, 2009).

1. Epigraph quoted in Edward F. Weeks, "Introduction," *Romare Bearden: Jazz*, exh. brochure (Birmingham, AL: Birmingham Museum of Art, 1982), n.p.

2. See Ruth E. Fine, *The Art of Romare Bearden*, exh. cat. (Washington, DC: National Gallery of Art, 2003), and Myron Schwartzman, *Romare Bearden: His Life and Art* (New York: Harry N. Abrams, 1990), two major monographs on the artist.

3. Deborah Cullen interview with Robert Blackburn, in *Finding the Tone: Romare Bearden's Monotypes and Robert Blackburn's Printmaking Workshop*, exh. brochure (New York: Lori Bookstein Fine Art, 2000), n.p.

4. Ralph Ellison, "Introduction," in *Romare Bearden: Paintings and Projections*, exh. cat. (Albany: Art Gallery of the State University of New York at Albany, 1968), n.p.; reprinted as "The Art of Romare Bearden" in Ralph Ellison, *Going to the Territory* (New York: Random House, 1986); see full text in this volume, pp. 196–203.

5. As paraphrased by Cullen, *Finding the Tone*.

6. Mary Schmidt Campbell, "Romare Bearden: A Creative Mythology." PhD diss. (New York: Syracuse University, 1982), 267.

7. Bearden, quoted in Carroll Greene, "Romare Bearden: The Prevalence of Ritual," in *Romare Bearden: The Prevalence of Ritual*, exh. cat. (New York: Museum of Modern Art, 1971), 4.

8. The most substantial catalogue focusing on Bearden's prints to date is *A Graphic Odyssey: Romare Bearden as Printmaker* (Philadelphia: University of Pennsylvania Press, 1992), for an exhibition organized and circulated in 1992 to 1997 by the Council for Creative Projects, Inc., New York. Texts are by: Nanette Rohan Bearden, Gail Gelburd, June Kelly, and Alex Rosenberg. Hereafter cited as *Graphic Odyssey*, 1992. The catalogue checklist included 114 prints.

9. For information on Blackburn, see Cullen, *Finding the Tone*; Hildreth York, "Bob Blackburn and the Printmaking Workshop," *Black American Literature Forum* 20, no. 1/2

(Spring–Summer, 1986): 81–95; and *Will Barnet/Bob Blackburn: An Artistic Friendship in Relief*, exh. cat. (La Grange, GA: Cochran Collection, 1997).

10. In *Finding the Tone*, Cullen notes that Bearden first worked at Blackburn's Printmaking Workshop in 1974. An invoice in the Romare Bearden Papers, 1945–1981, in the Archives of American Art, Smithsonian Institution, however, indicates that Bearden collagraphs were printed at the workshop as early as 1972. See Romare Bearden Papers, Series 2: Correspondence; Correspondence, October, 1972–1981; (Box 2, Folder 1), Collections Online, image 17.

11. Blackburn printed the lithographs that accompanied the Bearden collaboration with Derek Walcott: *The Caribbean Poetry of Derek Walcott & the Art of Romare Bearden* (Colophon title: *Poems of the Caribbean*), published by the Limited Editions Club, New York, 1983. Two prints identified as lithographs from the collection of the Printmaking Workshop were included in the 1984–85 exhibition and catalogue, for which Bearden also wrote a brief appreciation: *Art in Print: A Tribute to Robert Blackburn* (New York: Schomburg Center for Research in Black Culture, 1984), nos. 7 and 14. One of these, *Tidings* (lithograph, 1977), may be a screenprint and may have been printed earlier in the decade.

12. Background about Joseph Kleineman can be found on the workshop's website: http://mojoportfolio.com/About.cfm (accessed April 16, 2017).

13. Odysseus series; see reproductions in *Graphic Odyssey*, 1992: *Odysseus Leaves*, 59; *Troy (The Burning of Troy, The Fall of Troy)*, 60; *Cattle of the Sun God*, 61; *Circe into Swine*, 62; *Siren's Song*, 63; *Home to Ithaca*, 64.

14. *Island Dream*; see *Graphic Odyssey*, 1992: reproduced as *Caribbean Landscape*, 88.

15. *Come Sunday*, from *1776 USA* group portfolio; see reproduction in *Graphic Odyssey*, 1992, 107.

16. See reproductions in *Graphic Odyssey*, 1992: *Baptism*, 73; *Sorcerer's Village*, as *Sorcerer (African Fantasy)*, 65; *Two Women*, 102; *Blue Carolina Morning*, listed as *Untitled (Southern Interior)*, 115; see also Roni Henning, *Waterbased Screenprinting Today: From Hands-On Techniques to Digital Technology.* (New York: Watson-Guptill Publications, 2006), 18.

17. *Prevalence of Ritual*, solo portfolio; see *Graphic Odyssey*, 1992: *Delilah (Sampson and Delilah)*, repr., 74; *In the Garden*, checklist, 109; *Noah, The Third Day*, repr., 71; *Prologue to Troy (Before Troy)*, repr., 75; *Salome (John The Baptist)*, checklist, 112. The Ives-Sillman blindstamp also appears on the print *Carolina Blue*, repr., 43.

18. *Processional*; see *Graphic Odyssey*, 1992, repr., 93; Fine Creations, Inc. has also been recorded as the printer for *Slave Ship*; see *Graphic Odyssey*, 1992, repr., 67.

19. *Return of Ulysses*; see *Graphic Odyssey*, 1992, repr., 66.

20. Publishers of Bearden's work include: J. K. Fine Arts (June Kelly), New York; London Arts, Inc., Detroit, Michigan; Transworld Arts, Inc. (Alex Rosenberg), New York; HMK Fine Arts (Hugh MacKay), New York (*Odysseus* suite, *Roots*); as well as Cordier

& Ekstrom, New York, and Ives-Sillman, New Haven, Connecticut (*Prevalence of Ritual* portfolio); and Shorewood Publishers, Inc., New York (*Ritual Bayou*).

21. For a listing of Bearden's political cartoons, see Corlett bibliography, in Fine, *Art of Romare Bearden*, 278–80.

22. If the fulcrum of Bearden's artistic practice is theme and variation, it takes on a new dimension in the artist's lack of concern for consistency in dating, titling, and even completing editions to their purported number. The unintended consequence of these practices has been the generation of confusion and misinformation about his prints over the years. Also, the existence of unrecorded states and proofs has made Bearden's print oeuvre difficult to catalogue and study. Another factor is the inconsistent nature of printmaking documentation prior to the evolution of more standardized records developed in the printer/publisher workshops of the 1960s and later. See, for example, Fine's comments in Fine, *Art of Romare Bearden*, fn. 127, 258.

23. These two prints were among works from the estate of Jack Schindler, a commercial designer (his company was *Today's Displays* in Long Island City in Queens, New York) from whom Bearden had rented studio space, and who may have been instrumental in introducing Bearden to the photostat process. See Fine, *Art of Romare Bearden*, 59, and fn. 142, 259; and *Recollections of Charlotte's Own Romare Bearden*, exh. cat. (Charlotte, NC: Mint Museum, 2002), checklist, 60.

24. *Romare Bearden: Projections*, exh. cat. (New York: Cordier & Ekstrom, 1964).

25. See Fine, *Art of Romare Bearden*, 30 and fn. 110, 257; Dore Ashton, "Romare Bearden: Projections" (with French summary), *Quadrum 17* (1964): 99–110, 185; *Romare Bearden in Black-and-White: Photomontage Projections 1964*, exh. cat. (New York: Whitney Museum of American Art/Philip Morris, 1997) with texts by Gail Gelburd, Thelma Golden, Albert Murray (interview), and Romare Bearden (poetry).

26. Fine, *Art of Romare Bearden*, 99, following her discussion of the interrelationship among the collages *Carolina Interior* (1970), *Mecklenburg Morning* (c. 1978), and *Mecklenburg Morning* (c. 1979) and their respective bases in photostat and photocopy.

27. This effect was noted by critics such as Frank Getlein, who wrote that the photostat "pulls all the disparate elements together into a single continuing surface. This is what Bearden's projection contributes to the original collage." Frank Getlein, "Confrontation at the Corcoran," *Evening Star*, October 3, 1965, F6.

28. Fine, *Art of Romare Bearden*, 59.

29. Reproduced in Mary Lee Corlett, *From Process to Print: Graphic Works by Romare Bearden*, exh. cat. (Petaluma, CA: Pomegranate Communications, 2009), 40. The related exhibit was organized and circulated by the Romare Bearden Foundation, New York.

30. Bearden letter (undated) to John A. Davis, with cover letter (dated December 2, 1966) from Davis to Alston (and others), in Archives of American Art, Smithsonian Institution, Charles Henry Alston Papers, Correspondence: undated, 1931–1977, reel 4222.

31. "Rainbow roll" is the term used to describe the process by which several colors of ink are applied adjacent to each other on an inking slab and then rolled onto a matrix, creating a rainbow effect.

32. The print consistently appears on Cordier & Ekstrom inventory lists (private archive). Bearden was with the gallery from 1961, when it was Daniel Cordier & Michel Warren, Inc., until his death in 1988.

33. See *Romare Bearden: The Prevalence of Ritual*.

34. See *Mysteries: Women in the Art of Romare Bearden*, exh. cat. (Syracuse, NY: Everson Museum of Art of Syracuse and Onondaga County, 1975).

35. See *Romare Bearden: 1970–1980*, exh. cat. (Charlotte, NC: Mint Museum, 1980), 119; *Mysteries*; *Romare Bearden: Prevalence of Ritual*; Schwartzman, *Romare Bearden: His Life and Art*, fn. 17 (for ch. 6), 310. It is possible these collages may have been included in the exhibition *Romare Bearden/Richard Lindner*, held May–June 1973 at Shorewood Atelier Gallery, New York, and were the subject of the article by Louis Chapin, "The Medium Is the Message," *Christian Science Monitor*, July 28, 1973, 15. The collages listed in the *Mysteries* catalogue, all dated 1970, are collage on board: *Reunion*, 16 1/8 × 11 7/8; *Orange Morning*, 14 × 18; *Dressing Up*, 16 1/2 × 12; *Before the First Whistle*, 15 × 19 3/4; *April Green*, 19 × 14 3/8; *Time of the Gingham Rooster*, 16 × 12; *Sunrise Coffee*, 17 3/8 × 21 1/4; *Cypress Moon Pond*, 11 3/8 × 15 1/2; *Mississippi Monday*, 11 × 14 1/2; *The Unforgotten*, 25 × 22 3/4; *Hometime*, 27 × 45 7/8. Others, presumably in the series, named by Campbell, "Romare Bearden: A Creative Mythology," 272–73, are: *Flight of the Pink Bird, Ritual Bayou*, 13 1/2 × 15 3/4; *Memories*, 14 × 19 3/4; *Green Times Remembered (The Wishing Pond)*. The catalogue for *Bearden: Prevalence*, Museum of Modern Art, 1971, also includes: *Carolina Interior*, 13 × 15 3/4; *Dream Time*, 17 1/8 × 22; *Flights and Fantasy*, 8 3/4 × 11 5/8.

36. Reproduced in Corlett, *From Process to Print*, 43.

37. As he stated in a recorded interview with Diedra Harris-Kelley and Pamela Ford of the Romare Bearden Foundation, May 23, 2007, published in Corlett, *From Process to Print*, Khalil worked as a printer for Robert Blackburn from about 1967.

38. Khalil identified the beneficiary as the Lincoln tenement buildings in a recorded, unpublished interview with Diedra Harris-Kelley (Romare Bearden Foundation) and Jerald Melberg, April 12, 2007. For information about the Lincoln Square Neighborhood Center and its community-based programs, see their website: www.lsncny.org. *Tropical Flowers* may be slighter later in date than the date recorded (c. 1971–1972) in *Graphic Odyssey*, 1992, 114. Bearden's house in St. Martin, Antilles, was built in 1973, the same year he executed a number of collages based on island themes and exhibited at Cordier & Ekstrom in *Romare Bearden: Prevalence of Ritual, Martinique and Rain Forest*, March 28–April 28, 1974. In addition, correspondence in the Archives of American Art, Smithsonian Institution, seems to be related to this print and would indicate a later date: in a letter to Bearden dated May 21, 1974, the center's president Harry S. Mur-

phy, Jr., wrote: "I should long since have written to thank you for your efforts on behalf of our Neighborhood Center. Unfortunately, I have been on something of a treadmill since the 10th of March, and many things have been postponed longer than I would wish. Your etching was extremely well regarded. It was sufficiently different from the prints of our previous years to provide a very welcome change of pace in content. I am not sure that you know what came before your print, so I will tell you that the first was an abstraction by Paul Jenkins, the second an Alan d'Arcangelo abstract, the third an op work by Richard Anuszkiewicz, and the fourth a representational work by Raphael Soyer. . . . I especially want you to know that, as a graphic designer, I understand the creative process, and the magnitude of the effort involved in the creation of a work like the one you did for us." Romare Howard Bearden Papers, 1945–1981; Series 2: Correspondence; Correspondence, October, 1972–1981; (Box 2, Folder 9), Collections Online, image 9.

39. Alex Rosenberg, transcript of unpublished interview with Jerald Melberg, 14 April 2007, provided to the author by Jerald Melberg Gallery.

40. See *Romare Bearden: Visual Jazz*, African American Artists series (video recording), Chappaqua, New York: L & S Video, 1995; 28 min. color, VHS; narrated by Wynton Marsalis; directed by David Irving. The film includes footage of Bearden, comments by Robert Blackburn, and some discussion of *The Train*. See also Deborah Wye, *Artist & Prints: Masterworks from The Museum of Modern Art* (New York: Museum of Modern Art, 2004), 221. The collage is in the collection of the Boston Museum of Fine Arts; repr. in Fine, *Art of Romare Bearden*, 35. The Projection, *Mysteries I*, is reproduced at http://www.dcmooregallery.com/artists/romare-bearden/featured-works/projections?view=thumbnails (accessed March 5, 2017).

41. Caraccio worked at the Printmaking Workshop from mid-1972 through 1976. Viscosity printing utilizes inks of differing consistencies or viscosities (the term describing the rate of flow of an ink) adjusted with linseed oil and applied to the same plate; the inks remain naturally separated due to differing rates of flow. Ink with a flow quality of peanut butter is applied with a soft roller over a deep etched plate to which a layer of ink with the flow quality of honey has already been rolled with a hard roller over the top. Thus a plate can be printed in multiple colors with a single pass through the press. With thanks to Kathy Caraccio for her assistance with this definition and for providing the peanut butter/honey analogy in email to author, September 5, 2008.

42. Caraccio, unpublished (recorded) interview with Diedra Harris-Kelley, Pamela Ford, and Janet Wall, February 8, 2008.

43. In an email to the author, August 28, 2008, Caraccio noted: "During my time at the Printmaking Workshop many artists cut their plates. I also think like a sculptor and cut my plates while studying with Arun Bose at Hunter, now Lehman College." Unless otherwise noted, Caraccio quotes in this essay are taken from this email.

44. Reproduced in Corlett, *From Process to Print*, 15. The regular edition was 125, the deluxe edition was 25. As described in the Transworld Art Corp. promotional materials (Library, Mint Museum): "The collage effect of the print was achieved by employing a variety of techniques, notably color viscosity with the edition of aquatint and stencils. . . . The artist watercolored 25 sheets of 500 lb. Fabriano Classico paper. The two plates were then printed on the watercolored paper creating a very special deluxe edition of unique prints."

45. Reproduced in Corlett, *From Process to Print*, 2009, 44–46. Caraccio suggested that these twelve impressions probably included proofs that were among the initial plate proofs pulled by Caraccio, or single-color intaglios pulled by another printer, which were then hand-colored by Bearden.

46. Cullen, *Finding the Tone*, n.p., identifies Herb Wheeler, of Fish, Wheeler Co., Inc., as the maker of the halftone screens in line and dot patterns used in Bearden's photo-etchings. See also Fine, *Art of Romare Bearden*, 61, for a brief discussion of the making of the plate for *The Family*.

47. Fine, *Art of Romare Bearden*, 61, also discusses this process. Caraccio was the printer for this edition, with Emily Trevor (email to author, August 28, 2008).

48. Caraccio, unpublished (recorded) interview, February 8, 2008.

49. Fine, *Art of Romare Bearden*, 61. The publisher, Alex Rosenberg, donated seventeen proofs for *The Family*, some with hand-colored additions, to the Freedman Gallery at Albright College, Reading, Pennsylvania, one of which was included in their exhibition, *Alex Rosenberg: Collector and Patron*, October 30, 2008–January 14, 2009.

50. Caraccio, unpublished (recorded) interview, February 8, 2008. See also interview with Caraccio, in Corlett, *From Process to Print*, 119.

51. Quoted in *Romare Bearden: Visual Jazz* (video recording), 1995.

52. John Loring, "American Portrait," *Arts Magazine* 50 (November 1975): 59.

53. John Loring, "Special Section: Reproducibles: American Prints from Fuses to Fizzles," *Art in America*, 65 (January–February 1977), 34.

54. Fine, *Art of Romare Bearden*, 61.

55. Per Khalil in unpublished interviews, April 12, 2007, and May 23, 2007. See Corlett, *From Process to Print*, 113.

56. Khalil interview, May 23, 2007, in Corlett, *From Process to Print*, 113. Caraccio also remembers working on at least one monoprint with Bearden: *Jazz Musicians of Storyville*, possibly with another assistant (email to the author, August 28, 2008).

57. Reproduced in Cullen, *Finding the Tone*.

58. Archives of American Art, Smithsonian Institution, Romare Bearden Papers, Series 2: Correspondence; Correspondence, October 1972–1981; (Box 2, Folder 1), Collections Online, image 17. The invoice was for six impressions of each, with the exception of *3 Women*, for which there were eight. The printer was also noted on the invoice: Michael Felber, with proofing by Bob Blackburn and Harriet Corey.

59. Archives of American Art, Smithsonian Institution, Romare Bearden Papers, Series 3: Writings By and About Bearden; Miscellaneous Notes, c. 1950s–1980s; (Box 3, Folder 4), Collections Online, image 22.

60. Khalil interview, May 23, 2007, in Corlett, *From Process to Print*, 111–12.

61. Reproduced in Corlett, *From Process to Print*, 18.

62. Reproduced in Corlett, *From Process to Print*, 68.

63. See John Ross, Clare Romano, and Tim Ross, *The Complete Printmaker: Techniques, Traditions, Innovations* (New York: Free Press, 1990).

64. Reproduced in Corlett, *From Process to Print*, 66–67; see also: http://www.nga.gov/content/ngaweb/Collection/art-object-page.117694.html (accessed March 5, 2017).

65. Per Khalil interview, May 23, 2007, in Corlett, *From Process to Print*, 111: 1974, ed: 10, printed by Mohammed Khalil.

66. *Graphic Odyssey*, 1992, 110, gives the date of the collagraph as 1970–74, but the later end of that timeframe is more likely. The work was also erroneously identified on the *Graphic Odyssey* checklist as a sugarlift. Reproduced in Corlett, *From Process to Print*, 68.

67. Reproduced in Corlett, *From Process to Print*, 61.

68. Reproduced in *Graphic Odyssey*, 1992, as *Saturday Night*, no. 68, p. 86 (the matrix is reproduced in Corlett, *From Process to Print*, 62). The print in *Graphic Odyssey* looks to have been produced after the plate apparently broke and was repaired; there is also an impression in the Bearden Estate that looks to have been pulled before the break occurred. It is interesting to note that the 1972 Printmaking Workshop invoice cited above, which listed four collagraphs including *The Street*, also indicates that a "repair" was made by Bob Blackburn, but no specifics are given to connect that repair to a specific work.

69. Milwaukee Art Museum; both reproduced in Fine, *Art of Romare Bearden*, 36; see fig. 7, in this volume.

70. For other related images, see: *Untitled (Urban Landscape)*, etching, c. 1970 (repr. in Corlett, *From Process to Print*, 42; listed in *Graphic Odyssey*, 1992, 115); *The Street*, watercolor and collage on board, 1985, 20 × 28 (repr. in *Something All Our Own: The Grant Hill Collection of African American Art*, Alvia J. Wardlaw, ed. [Durham, NC: Duke University Press, 2004], 102, 103).

71. Reproduced in *Romare Bearden in Black-and-White*, 76; Corlett, *From Process to Print*, 19.

72. Reproduced in Corlett, *From Process to Print*, 107.

73. See Christie's, New York, Contemporary Art, Part II, sale 8170, May 4, 1995, lot 190.

74. Reproduced in *Romare Bearden in Black-and-White*, 78–79.

75. The impression in the Bearden Estate is titled *Out Chorus* and is signed and inscribed: AP 1/2 (repr. In Corlett, *From Process to Print*, 89); an alternate title has also

been used, *Le Jazz (Out Chorus II)*, with the date recorded as 1966–67 (*Graphic Odyssey*, 1992, 110, repr. 111).

76. Reproduced in *Romare Bearden in Black-and-White*, 48.

77. Reproduced in *Romare Bearden & Sheldon Ross: Artist & Dealer*, exh. cat. (New York: Franklin Riehlman Fine Art and Megan Moynihan Fine Art, 2004), n.p.

78. Reproduced in Schwartzman, *Romare Bearden: His Life and Art*, 236.

79. The photograph accompanied the article by Les Payne, "America's Greatest (Overlooked) Artist," *Newsday Magazine*, January 17, 1988, 6–11, 18–20, where the title of the collage is given as *Blues Singers from the Delta*. The photograph is also reprinted in Schwartzman, *Romare Bearden: His Life and Art*, 300.

80. Greene, "Romare Bearden: The Prevalence of Ritual," 4.

81. See *Introduction for a Blues Queen*, 1979, reproduced in Corlett, *From Process to Print*, 78.

82. Reproduced in Corlett, *From Process to Print*, 95–99. Related large-scale drawings in colored marker and paint are in the collection of the Bearden Estate.

83. Hilton Kramer, "Art: Intimacy and the 'Infinite,'" *New York Times*, June 22, 1974, 18.

84. The collages of this series were exhibited at Cordier & Ekstrom; see *Romare Bearden: Odysseus Collages*, exh. cat. (New York: Cordier & Ekstrom, 1977) with essay by Calvin Tomkins. For a discussion of these works, see Robert G. O'Meally, "Romare Bearden's Black Odyssey: A Search for Home," in *Romare Bearden's Black Odyssey*, exh. cat. (New York: DC Moore Gallery, 2007). Fine, *Art of Romare Bearden*, 88, has noted the existence of related works, done as carbon paper tracings, with added collage elements and watercolor.

85. Per email correspondence with Debra Rhodes Smith, May 17–19, 2008. *Homage to Ithaca* and *The Fall of Troy* from the suite are reproduced in Corlett, *From Process to Print*, 104–5 and 106, respectively. Bearden's association with Hugh MacKay seems to have begun with the *Roots* projects, produced in conjunction with the eponymous, highly acclaimed television mini-series based on the book by Alex Haley. Bearden had created the image for the January 22–28, 1977, cover of *TV Guide* magazine, and MacKay was involved in the subsequent production of the *Homage to Roots* lithograph based on the cover image. Bearden would later exhibit prints along with collages and watercolors at MacKay's HMK Fine Arts Pacific Design Center (May 1980). MacKay was also affiliated with Editions Lahumière in Paris, which also showed prints. Bearden deemed his affiliation with MacKay as productive enough that he recommended that a good friend and fellow artist, Herbert Gentry, seek him out: "On Friday morning, I went to see Hugh McKay [*sic*], who is doing the 'Roots' print. . . . If you do go to Basel, Hugh will be there — his European Gallery (prints) is Lahumière — they will have a stall. Also, it is at 88, Blvd. de Courcelles in Paris. But Hugh will not stay in Europe too long. . . . See Hugh by yourself if possible. He is very fond of me & can be helpful. You must make it

there. He's a good contact." Undated letter, Bearden to Herbert Gentry (attached envelope postmarked May 31, 1977). Private archive.

86. Unless otherwise noted, information about the NYIT Print Workshop comes from conversations with Norman Lassiter (August 14, 2008); Roni Henning, who directed the shop after Lassiter (August 4, 2008; with follow-up emails, September 24–25, 2008); and Steve Maiorano (August 13, 2008), who was a printer at the shop. With many thanks to Peter Voci, Chair, Fine Arts Department, New York Institute of Technology, for assisting me in initiating these contacts.

87. Reproduced in Corlett, *From Process to Print*, 100.

88. Printer Steve Maiorano, who was a student at the New York Institute of Technology at the time and worked as Lassiter's assistant, also worked on both the edition print and the poster edition. A document in the Archives of American Art, Smithsonian Institution, is most likely related to the production of this print, however, no title is referenced in the record. In part, the document, dated December 13, 1974, and signed by Frances Lassiter, states: "This correspondence shall act as a confirmation of the receipt of one original collage, one large Photostat collage, and the negative image employed in the making of the Photostat. . . . These pieces have been loaned by you to the NYIT Print Workshop for use in the production of work under a grant from the New York State Council on the Arts. This work shall consist of: 1) a limited edition of screen prints accordingly — 50 prints to be signed and numbered by you, for your perusal[,] 5 artists's proof [*sic*] to be signed and numbered by you for your perusal[,] 6 H.C. copies to be signed and numbered by you for the NYIT Print Workshop[.] 2) A Poster edition of 400 to be produced for the Alvin Ailey Dance Group's Sprin[g] '75 season under this grant. You will receive 25 posters for your perusal"; Romare Bearden Papers, Series 2: Correspondence; Correspondence, October 1972–1981; (Box 2, Folder 10), Collections Online, image 40. A second NYIT document in the archive, dated February 14, 1975, titled "Edition Release for 'The Baptism'" and signed by both Lassiter and Bearden, marks the completion of the project, identifying the edition as a fourteen-color screenprint consisting of fifty impressions numbered 1/50–50/50; and six HC numbered with roman numerals, the first four of these designated for NYIT and the last two for the artist; Archives of American Art, Romare Bearden Papers, Series 2: Correspondence; Correspondence, October 1972–1981; (Box 2, Folder 11), Collections Online, image 17. Correspondence also included in the Archives of American Art, addressed to the Alvin Ailey Dance Theatre from Frances Lassiter, dated March 11, 1975, indicates a smaller-scale edition of 400 posters was to be completed by April 15, 1975; Romare Bearden papers Series 2: Correspondence; Correspondence, October, 1972–1981; (Box 2, Folder 11), Collections Online, image 41.

89. Any required camera work was most likely done by E & A Screen Graphics, in Glendale, Queens; suggested by Maiorano in telephone interview, August 13, 2008, and affirmed by Henning, email to author, September 25, 2008.

90. Norman Lassiter, from a telephone conversation with the author, August 14, 2008.

91. Steve Maiorano dates the works between 1975 and 1977, while Henning thought they may have been produced a little closer to the end of the decade. A document produced by the Business Committee for the Arts, New York, featured a reproduction of *Blue Carolina Morning* and provides a basis for dating this work with the following caption: "Cover of 1977 'Business in the Arts' Award entitled BLUE CAROLINA MORNING, by Romare Bearden. Limited edition commissioned by *Forbes Magazine* and the Business Committee for the Arts and presented to 41 corporations for outstanding programs in support of the arts in calendar year 1977." Romare Bearden Papers, Archives of American Art, Series 7: Printed Material; Examples of Artwork for Publications, c. 1970s; (Box 3, Folder 15), Collections Online, images 6 and 7.

92. Possibly listed twice in *Graphic Odyssey*, 1992, as *Untitled (Southern Interior)*, 115, and as *Blue Carolina Morning*, 116. Henning's impression is inscribed with the title *Blue Carolina Morning*.

93. *Sorcerer's Village* is reproduced in Corlett, *From Process to Print*, 102. For a reproduction of *Village of Yo*, a related collage, see Fine, *Art of Romare Bearden*, 43.

94. The lithography may have been done by Joe Petruzzelli, unconfirmed at this writing.

95. Henning, *Water-Based Screenprinting Today*, 18. For a reproduction of related collage, see *Blue Interior, Morning* (1968), collage of paper and synthetic polymer paint on composition board, 44 × 56 in., The Chase Manhattan Bank, New York, cat. no. 31, in *Romare Bearden: Prevalence of Ritual*, 15 (repr.), 16 (checklist). There is also a collagraph matrix in the collection of the Bearden Estate that is compositionally related to these works.

96. Khalil, unpublished interview, April 12, 2007; see also, Khalil interview in Corlett, *From Process to Print*, 114.

97. Preface, dated June 1991, in *Graphic Odyssey*, 1992, 7.

98. Kelly also published Bearden's *Jamming at the Savoy*, a photoetching printed by Mohammad Khalil and produced for the Brooklyn Museum showing of the exhibition *Romare Bearden: 1970–1980*, organized by the Mint Museum, Charlotte, North Carolina.

99. See Peter Nesbett, *Jacob Lawrence: Thirty Years of Prints (1963–1993): A Catalogue Raisonné* (Seattle: Francine Seders Gallery in association with University of Washington Press, 1994), 33. Correspondence in the Archives of American Art, Smithsonian Institution, Romare Bearden Papers indicates that Bearden was involved with the Bicentennial Rainbow Print Scholarship Fund in 1975; see Series 2: Correspondence; Correspondence, October 1972–1981; (Box 2, Folder 12), Collections Online, image 11.

100. Reproduced in Corlett, *From Process to Print*, 76. *Le Jazz (Out Chorus II)* was dated 1966–1967; see *Graphic Odyssey*, 1992, 110. *Carolina Memories (Tidings)*, reproduced in Corlett, *From Process to Print*, 92, is another early lithographic print; dating from about 1970–1972, it combines a four-color halftone photolithograph with screen-

printed additions. Another lithograph from the early 1970s is *Dreams of Exile*, c. 1973; published by Harry N. Abrams, Inc., New York, in conjunction with the book *The Art of Romare Bearden: The Prevalence of Ritual*. Danielle Fox, "Multiple Originals: Art Publishing in the 1960s US" (PhD diss., Northwestern University, Evanston, Illinois, 1996, 267, 269–70) notes that Harry Abrams was an enthusiastic print collector and supporter of Universal Limited Art Editions.

101. See *Romare Bearden: Southern Recollections*, exh. cat. (Charlotte, NC: Mint Museum of Art, 2011), 122–23. Lindley generously provided a record of these photographs to curator Ruth Fine, in August 2003, at the time of the opening of the Bearden retrospective Fine was organizing for the National Gallery of Art.

102. Narkiewicz, an artist as well as printer, also did lithography for Jack Beal, Alex Katz, and Catherine Murphy.

103. *Carolina Morning*, 1974, collage and mixed media on board; reproduced in *Romare Bearden: Southern Recollections*, 125.

104. The first of Bearden's publications from the shop date from 1979.

105. See Schwartzman, "Joseph Kleineman and Romare Bearden," http://www.akama .com/company/Mojo_Portfolio_a44303287631.html (accessed October 26, 2018). Confirmed by Kleineman, email from Maureen Turci to the author, August 13, 2008.

106. *Introduction for a Blues Queen*, 1979, from the *Jazz* series, is reproduced in Corlett, *From Process to Print*, 78. For further information about Bearden's oils on paper, see reviews of the exhibition *Of the Blues (Second Chorus)*, Cordier & Ekstrom: Michael André, "New York Reviews: Romare Bearden," ARTnews 75 (March 1976): 131–32, 134; Susan Howe, "Romare Bearden at Cordier & Ekstrom," *Art in America* 64 (November–December 1976): 122; John Russell, "Art: Alex Katz's Idyllic and Simplified World," *New York Times*, February 28, 1976, 22L (embedded review); Schwartzman, *Romare Bearden: His Life and Art*, 230; Fine, *Art of Romare Bearden*, 101–4; Cullen, *Finding the Tone*.

107. Email from Kleineman/Turci to the author, August 13, 2008. A number of color separation plates for works in the *Jazz* series exist, along with "black lines" — black outline proofs that were, as described by Kleineman in the August 13th email, "the 'skeleton' of the image, indicating composition and placement for the color separation areas." With thanks to Adam Schuster for supplying information about and sharing images of some of the plates and proofs for works in this series (email/telephone conversation with the author, March 24, 2008).

108. Schwartzman, "Joseph Kleineman and Romare Bearden."

109. *Jazz* series: *Bopping at Birdland (Stomp Time)*; *Brass Section (Jamming at Minton's)*; *Introduction for a Blues Queen*; *Louisiana Serenade*; *Out Chorus (Rhythm Section)*; *Tenor Sermon*; *Walking Bass*; *Conversation*; *Falling Star*; *Lantern (The)*; *Mecklenburg Autumn*; *Morning (Carolina Morning)*; *Open Door (The)*; *In the Garden*; *Pepper Jelly Lady* (publ. in *Presidential Portfolio*, Democratic Committee Service Corp., 1980); *Two Worlds*

(1980); *Morning of the Rooster* (1980; in conjunction with Mint Museum exh.); *Quilting Time* (1981); *Autumn of the Rooster* (1983; Brooklyn Bridge); *Homage to Mary Lou* (1984); *The Lamp* (1984; NAACP).

110. Reproduced in *Graphic Odyssey*, 1992, 79, and Corlett, *From Process to Print*, 83, respectively. Bearden contributed lithographs to a several group portfolios to support political or social causes in the 1970s. Earlier contributions included: *Mother and Child*, in *Conspiracy: The Artist as Witness* (Boston: David G. Godine and the Center for Constitutional Rights, 1972); *Come Sunday (Mother and Child)*, in *1776 USA* (Contemporary Artists, Inc., 1976); *The Family*, an etching, in the portfolio *An American Portrait, 1776–1976* (New York: Transworld Art) was also published during this period.

111. Reproduced in Corlett, *From Process to Print*, 82.

112. Per email from Kleineman/Turci, August 13, 2008. *Autumn of the Rooster* (1983) is reproduced at http://www.mojoportfolio.com/Artwork-Detail.cfm?ArtistsID =1175&NewID=10625 (accessed March 19, 2017).

113. For a reproduction of *The Lamp*, see Corlett, *From Process to Print*, 88. Other work for the dance company included the image *The Dancer* (lithograph, c. 1982, repr. in *Graphic Odyssey*, 1992, 20, 21), which may not have been produced as an edition, but related program/logo/poster designs do exist. Alex Rosenberg indicated in an unpublished interview with Jerald Melberg, April 14, 2007, that four Bearden lithographs printed by Atelier Ettinger, New York, and published in 1979 raised funds for the dance company: *Conjunction, Firebirds, Pilate*, and *Three Women (Easter Sunday)*. Nanette Bearden founded the company in 1976 as the Nanette Bearden Contemporary Chamber Dance Group. It later became the Nanette Bearden Contemporary Dance Theater.

114. Schwartzman, *Romare Bearden: His Life and Art*, 283, noted: "The almost gravitational pull toward early memories of Mecklenburg had focused much of Bearden's collage work since 1978." Mecklenberg imagery was showcased in the 1983 exhibition, *Mecklenburg Autumn*, at Cordier & Ekstrom (exh. cat., November 12–December 17, 1983), which included twelve oils with collage. Among the collages exhibited was *The Piano Lesson*, which was to be revisited in the 1984 print *Homage to Mary Lou*. It is also interesting to note that the collage entitled *China Lamp* (1983), reproduced in the catalogue, incorporates an element (the cloth on the sewing machine) related in its striation to the imagery created with halftone screens such as in *Out Chorus* (1979–80; repr. in Corlett, *From Process to Print*, 53).

115. For a more in-depth discussion of one of these lithographs, see Corlett, *Falling Star*, cat. no. 88, in *Collection Highlights: Telfair Museum of Art*, Hollis Koons McCullough, ed. (Savannah, GA: Telfair Museum of Art, 2005), 246–47.

116. Author's telephone conversation with Joseph Kleineman, March 22, 2004.

117. Reproduced in Corlett, *From Process to Print*, 80, 81 and 82, respectively.

118. *Romare Bearden: Selected Prints: ["Black Roots, Jazz Music, Universal Myth"]*, Lehman College Art Gallery, Bronx, New York, 29 January–3 March 1985. Reviewed by

Vivien Raynor, "Constructive Art at Purchase, Bearden's Fantasy at Lehman," *New York Times*, February 10, 1985, 24 WC.

119. Reproduced in Schwartzman, *Romare Bearden: His Life and Art*, 37. On the same page is an ink drawing on tracing paper that Schwartzman identifies as the maquette for the print. Kleineman (email, Kleineman/Turci, August 13, 2008) has characterized it as "study drawing." There are significant, if often subtle, differences in the imagery as rendered in each of several variations, including the "study drawing," the collage under discussion (40×31 in.), the collage most closely related to the print (29×22 in.; repr. in Fine, *Art of Romare Bearden*, 136), and the edition print itself. At least one other collage variant is known (27 1/4×19 3/4 in.; private collection).

120. Roy Lichtenstein, for example, produced prints at Gemini GEL and Tyler Graphics, Ltd., and other printer/publisher workshops, but also worked with contract printers, for example, Charles Cardinale or Sirocco Screenprinters, two shops also utilized by Bearden, and produced work intended for wider publication—such as posters, book jacket images, etc. For a contemporary account of print production and the market through the 1970s, see Theodore B. Donson, *Prints and the Print Market: A Handbook for Buyers, Collectors, and Connoisseurs* (New York: Crowell, 1977). Donson includes a brief discussion of London Arts, as well as Hugh MacKay and HMK Fine Arts, two publishers of Bearden's prints. Other resources include: Danielle Fox, "Multiple Originals: Art Publishing in the 1960s US"; Deborah Wye, *Artists & Prints: Masterworks from the Museum of Modern Art* (New York: Museum of Modern Art, 2004); *Printmaking in America: Collaborative Prints and Presses, 1960–1990*, exh. cat. (New York: Harry N. Abrams, in association with Mary and Leigh Block Gallery, Northwestern University, Evanston, Illinois, 1995), with essays by Trudy V. Hansen, David Mickenberg, Joann Moser, and Barry Walker.

121. Fine, *Art of Romare Bearden*, 60.

122. Reproduced in Corlett, *From Process to Print*, 56.

123. Examples include the 1976 Olympics poster (repr. Swann Auction Galleries, Sale 2136, lot 180); the *Jazz Rhapsody* collage for the cover of Kamau Kenyatta's album *Strong Men* (1982); as well as album covers for Donald Byrd's *Thank You . . . For F.U.M.L (Funking Up My Life)* (1978) and Wynton Marsalis's *J Mood* (c. 1985). For additional information about jazz album covers, see Robert G. O'Meally, "Jazz Albums as Art: Some Reflections," *The International Review of African American Art* 14, no. 3 (1997): 38–47. Bearden's journal covers include *Crisis 77* (March 1970) and those executed for *Time* ("John Lindsay," November 1, 1968) and *TV Guide* ("Roots," January 22, 1977; football cover, September 17, 1977). Other illustrations include: *The Street (Composition for Richard Wright)*, illustration for Richard Wright, "What Sets Storms to Rolling in His Soul," *New York Times*, April 8, 1977, A27; *The Caribbean Poetry of Derek Walcott and the Art of Romare Bearden* (New York: Limited Editions Club, 1983). Bearden also wrote and illustrated a children's book, published posthumously: *Li'l Dan, the Drummer Boy: A*

*Civil War Story* (New York: Simon and Schuster, 2003). See Corlett bibliography in Fine, *Art of Romare Bearden*, 278–81 for citations for these and other covers and illustrations.

124. The Pratt exhibit ran 7–30 April. A work entitled *Saturday Night* was listed on the loan receipt (Cordier & Ekstrom files; private archive), and there is a collagraph with that title, but no medium was given on the receipt.

125. Cordier & Ekstrom, June 4–July 12, 1974; see Kramer, "Art: Intimacy and the 'Infinite,'" 18. Loeb, May 21–June 7, 1975; see Fine, *Art of Romare Bearden*, 233.

126. February 11–March 13.

127. February 22–March 14.

128. February 14–March 28, 1982 (traveled).

129. October 3–November 3, 1982.

130. Center for the Arts, Wesleyan University, February 3–22.

131. February 6–March 22, 1986.

132. Karin Lipson, "From Uptown to the Islands," *New York Newsday*, February 24, 1986, 2:17. *Two Women* (lithograph) was reproduced.

133. The exhibition, held February 6–March 28, was organized by the Jerald Melberg Gallery, Charlotte, and included 17 collages and 10 prints. See Ben Steelman, "Visual Magic and Music on View," Wilmington (N.C.) *Morning Star*, February 6, 1987, 1D.

# BEARDEN'S CARIBBEAN DIMENSION

*Sally Price and Richard Price*

In the three decades since his death, a great deal has been written about Romare Bearden. With few exceptions, this literature has adopted a North American perspective, focusing almost exclusively on his life in the United States and the artwork that depicts his experiences in North Carolina, Harlem, and the bayous of Louisiana, with only scattered allusions to the role of the Caribbean islands in his life and in his art. But Bearden himself was insistent that, for him, the Caribbean was vital: "Art will go where energy is," he said on more than one occasion. "I find a great deal of energy in the Caribbean. . . . It's like a volcano there; there's something underneath that still smolders."[1] Throughout the final fifteen years of his life, when he was dividing his time between New York and the French/Dutch island of St. Martin, all of Bearden's art was imbued with the colors and rhythms of the Caribbean.[2]

His personal ties with the region began in the early 1950s, when he met Nanette Rohan, daughter of immigrants from the island of St. Martin, at a benefit for victims of a Caribbean hurricane. They were soon married, and with her help, he pulled himself out of an emotionally and artistically stagnant period that he'd been living through for several years. They moved into a fifth-floor walkup on the edge of New York's Chinatown that doubled as studio and living quarters. They did some traveling. And in 1960 they took their first trip to the Caribbean.

By 1970, as Bearden's reputation grew, the Caribbean had become a cruise-ship escape from the pressures of life in New York, and plans were made for a house in St. Martin, to be built on land owned by Nanette's family. They began spending several months each year on the island, where Bearden turned most of his new-felt energy to watercolor. Back in the United States, he was receiving increasing recognition — a Guggenheim Fellowship in 1970, a one-man retrospective at the Museum of Modern Art in 1971, election to the National Institute of Arts and Letters in 1972, and an honorary degree at the Pratt Institute in 1973. The late 1970s brought more awards, more honorary degrees, commissions from the *New York Times* and the Alvin Ailey American Dance Theater, and a long profile in the *New Yorker*.[3]

But the Caribbean was also becoming an important site for his artwork. And while he continued his artistic output on a range of North American themes from New Orleans and jazz to conjur women and southern gardens, the aqueous forms and luminous colors that captured his tropical sunsets and seascapes and market scenes from the Caribbean began to carry over into his New York studio. By the late 1970s, childhood memories of the U.S. South and images of Harlem jazz clubs had become saturated with the rich chromatics of the islands. And his ties with a whole range of people in the Caribbean, from artists and intellectuals to taxi drivers and restaurant owners, became an important part of his life and art. He produced a collage series on the travels of Odysseus in 1977 that drew on Caribbean settings. And he collaborated on important multimedia projects with his St. Lucian friend Derek Walcott, providing both the illustrations and the overall design for their 1981 book, *The Caribbean Poetry of Derek Walcott and the Art of Romare Bearden*, which had an introduction by Nobel laureate Joseph Brodsky.[4]

Anyone engaging Bearden's reputation as the collagist chronicler of Harlem and the U.S. South, as the artistic ethnographer of the world of jazz, and as a modern-day narrator of Odyssean voyages, must inevitably confront the relative roles — and the delicate interaction — of form and content. How did his exceptionally insistent focus on structure, spatial relations, and the visual dynamics of a flat surface play into his gift for capturing the heartbeat of urban scenes, the complex fragrances of a southern garden, the mellow tones and percussive heat of a jazz session, or the sultry air of the Louisiana bayous that have so indelibly marked his reputation as an American artist? His Caribbean artworks raise questions about the same tension. How did his concerns with the formal properties of a canvas work together with his ability to capture the exuberance of a

Carnival dancer, the otherworldliness of an Obeah in trance, the lush moisture of a tropical garden, or the magic of a flame-red Caribbean sunset?

Bearden's imbrication in the Caribbean was gradual. At the beginning, he looked at the region with an external, American gaze. It's true that he had had some relation with the Caribbean while he was growing up. He'd played baseball in Negro leagues that included Puerto Ricans and Cubans, hung out with Jamaican writer Claude McKay, and lived through Garvey's rise and fall in a Harlem that included many Caribbean immigrants. But as late as the 1960s, he viewed the Caribbean mainly as a cruise-ship destination, a vacationland, and an escape from the pressures of New York.

Beginning in the 1970s, aqueous tropical colors saturate Bearden's Caribbean paintings, and they also seep into his portrayals of Harlem and the U.S. South, imbuing them with a new luminosity. Diaphanous faces mark a state of deep trance, and the roosters of Mecklenburg County farmyards give way to fighting cocks on the island of St. Martin.

During their first few years in St. Martin, the Beardens engaged in very little social activity, but eventually they began stepping out in the community, going to local cultural events, and getting to know others on the island. Their circle was decidedly eclectic. Josianne Fleming was a cultural organizer and wife of the mayor of St. Martin. Nanette's father's cousin "Moti" played the concertina, Brooksie the taxi driver was the proud father of several dozen island children, "Uncle Oswald" raised goats, Louis Richardson owned a magnificent estate, Jeanne ("Ma") Chance ran a creole restaurant, Bobo Claxton played the saxophone, and Fabian Badejo was a Hausa from Nigeria who directed the Council of the Arts. As for the artists in their circle: Gloria and Marty Lynn had left a fast-lane life in New York to recapture the idealism of their student days in the 1960s, Ruby Bute dreamed of opening an art school, Roland Richardson made etchings of historic buildings, Cynric Griffith was from St. Kitts, Lucia Trifan was from Romania, and Mosera was a Rasta from St. Lucia. In interviews with us, each one spoke of Bearden with affection, and each one had stories, and usually a painting or two, to back up these memories. Lasana Sekou, for example, told us how, a few days after he returned to the island during his undergraduate years at Howard University and gave a "Black Power" poetry reading, Bearden appeared at his door with a watercolor for him—a fluid work incorporating fragments of one of the poems he'd read that evening.[5]

Color was the first obvious change in Bearden's work more generally, once he moved to the Caribbean, and the critics were quick to pick up on the difference. In 1980 Avis Berman remarked in *ARTnews* that "Vibrant, opulent color [has become] a constant, which Bearden attributes to sojourns in the West Indies."[6] Even in his jazz works, such as *At Connie's Inn* (now in the Brooklyn Museum of Art), iridescent greens strongly recall paintings in a Caribbean series that he was calling "Martinique/Rain Forest."[7] And his North American paintings, with American birds and plants, locomotives, and houses in the rural South, were gradually complemented by scenes from the Caribbean, with lush rain forest vegetation, egrets, and other tropical animals.

Especially in the 1970s, much of Bearden's Caribbean work was landscape inspired — beaches, mountains, sunsets, flowers, fishing boats. *In a Green Shade*, while created in 1984, exemplifies this focus on island scenery (fig. 42). As the 1980s progressed, however, Bearden increasingly engaged with Caribbean social realities, from carnival parades to magic and trance, as if he were gradually coming to grips in his work with the human element in the island.

It is instructive to look at Bearden's late Caribbean experience through the eyes of Derek Walcott, who chose one of Bearden's Odysseus series collages, *The Sea Nymph* (fig. 43), for the dust jacket of *The Star-Apple Kingdom*, a collection of his poems on Caribbean themes.[8] Walcott, not only a Nobel laureate in literature, but also a serious amateur painter, had come to have tremendous respect for Bearden both as an artist and as an intellectual. In speaking with us at his home in St. Lucia, he seconded something that many others had already told us — that Bearden's knowledge of literature was wide and deep and solid, ranging from detective novels to Greek classics and nineteenth-century British poetry. He also emphasized the ways he thought Bearden's work was under-appreciated in the U.S. art world — and why:

> Let's consider any establishment or orthodoxy that says, "Yeah, but it's so special — it has to do with black people catching hell in the South, or still being happy in a certain kind of a way." So you have this absurdity of an empire pronouncing its benediction on the very fucking suffering it caused! So it says, "Oh yes, Jacob Lawrence is fantastic." Why is he fantastic? Because he shows all these niggers tryin' to get to heaven, you know, material heaven. And that's why *he's* fantastic. . . . So he's fine. "Horace Pippin is fantastic," because he's a humble nigger who really couldn't paint very well, but he had that charm that is really a quality of the primitive. . . . But Romare . . . was genuinely erudite.[9]

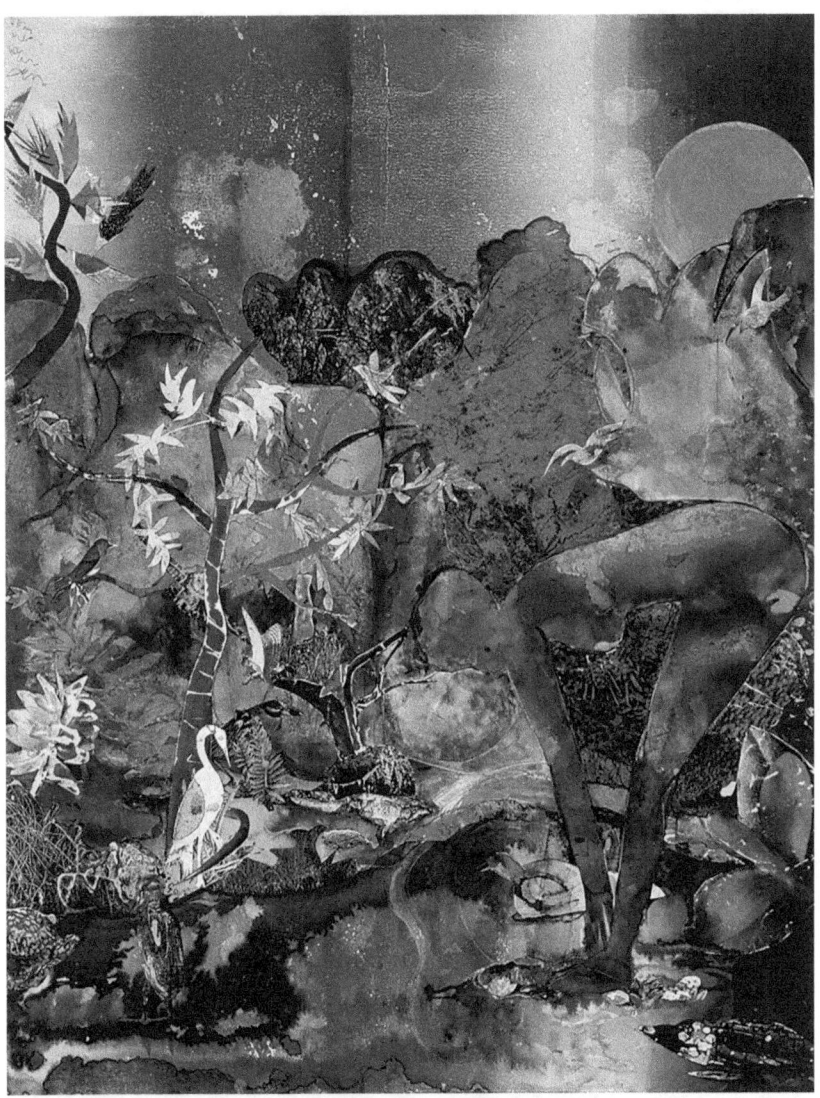

FIGURE 42 Romare Bearden, *In a Green Shade (Hommage [sic] to Marvell)*, 1984. Collage of various papers with paint, ink, and graphite on fiberboard, 39 1/4 × 30 1/4 in. (99.7 × 76.8 cm). Collection of Yvonne and Richard McCracken. Art © Romare Bearden Foundation/Licensed by VAGA, New York

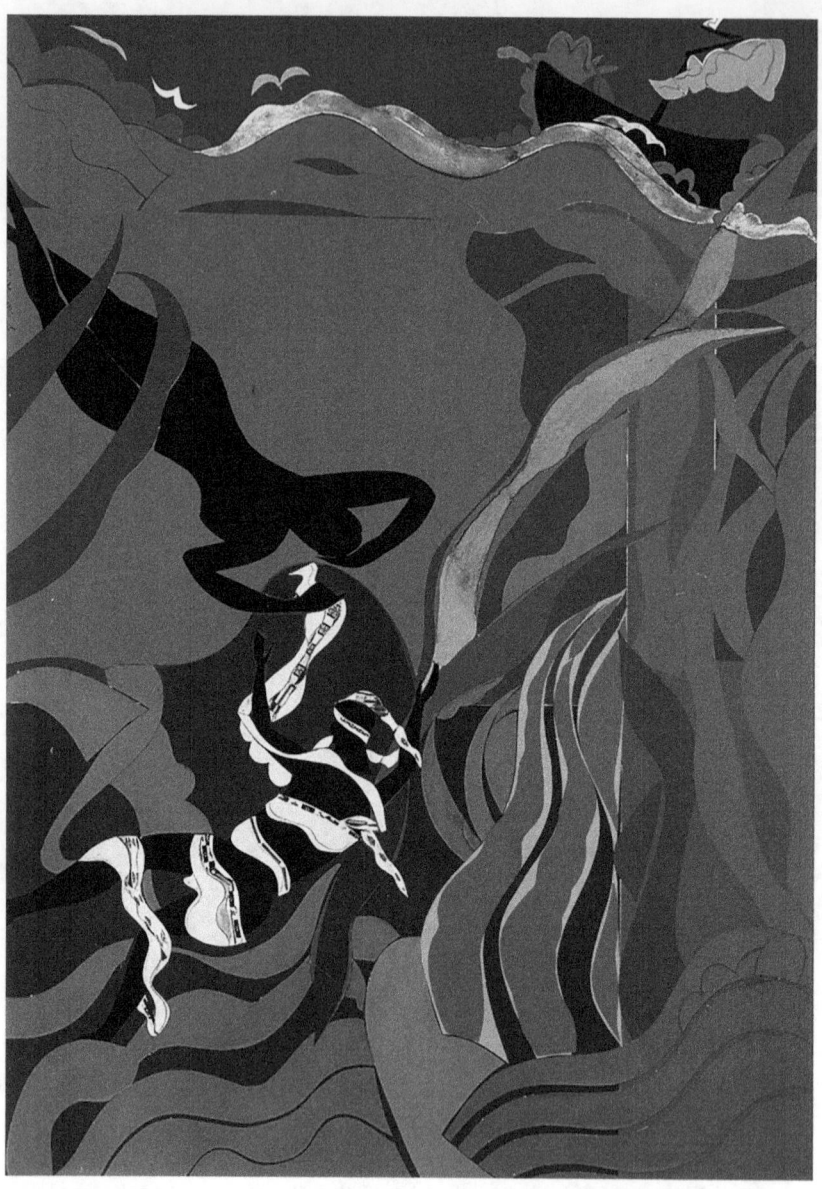

FIGURE 43 Romare Bearden, *The Sea Nymph* (Odysseus Series), 1977. Collage of various papers with paint and graphite on fiberboard; 44 × 32 in. (111.8 × 81.3 cm). Collection of Glen and Lynn Tobias. Art © Romare Bearden Foundation/Licensed by VAGA, New York

Walcott also stressed Bearden's gift as a raconteur who was bursting with stories that could go on as long as there was someone listening. He told us:

> Romare telling a story was fantastic. I know the great one he told about being on a schooner sailing the islands. He told of how the boat went adrift, and then he described the cargo, the pigs, the sailors, the people on board. . . . Oh God, if that had been taken down verbatim — I mean the sentence structure of the narration! Romare's genius had as much to do with his verbal ability to tell a story as his "scissors" ability to tell a story.

But Walcott was equally excited by his friend's art:

> The paintings have such fantastic dignity. . . . They are *moving* and you say to yourself, "Jesus Christ, I'm being moved by paper, not by paint!" That's beyond Matisse. It's even beyond Picasso. You can look at a Picasso painting and say, "This is about that." You can work it out in terms of the paint. But once you look at a Bearden, you *assume* the history that's there in the painting. And the movement inside you of looking at the painting is a profound experience. People have no idea of the depth of it — and because it's black, it's more poignant, it's more tragic. You're talking about Whitman here, you know!

When Walcott, who had crafted the great Caribbean epic *Omeros* (1990), spoke to us about Bearden, whose series of collages based on Homer's *Odyssey* portrays a black Odysseus, he located their common ground in a relationship to the coral sea of the Caribbean, a sea as worthy of epic poetry and truly great art as that other one on the shores of the Greek islands. But he also located their common ground in Obeah, the special Caribbean brand of belief and healing, trance and sacrifice, drama and ritual that Bearden eventually took on in what is arguably his greatest Caribbean-based work.

In St. Martin, Bearden had heard countless stories about the ways Obeah intervened in people's daily lives, helping them deal with illness, affairs of love, political scandals, and domestic frictions. In the 1980s, the island's population of ritual practitioners included many Haitian immigrants as well as a few people from the Dominican Republic. The practitioner would sit in front of a table, conduct divination, and go into trance — often with the aid of a tape cassette playing ceremonial music from back home. And once the problem was identified, a solution would be prescribed, most commonly a ritual bath composed of herbs, roots, and perfumes. Native St. Martin practitioners also read tarot cards and gazed into magical mirrors. The recourse to Obeah was never

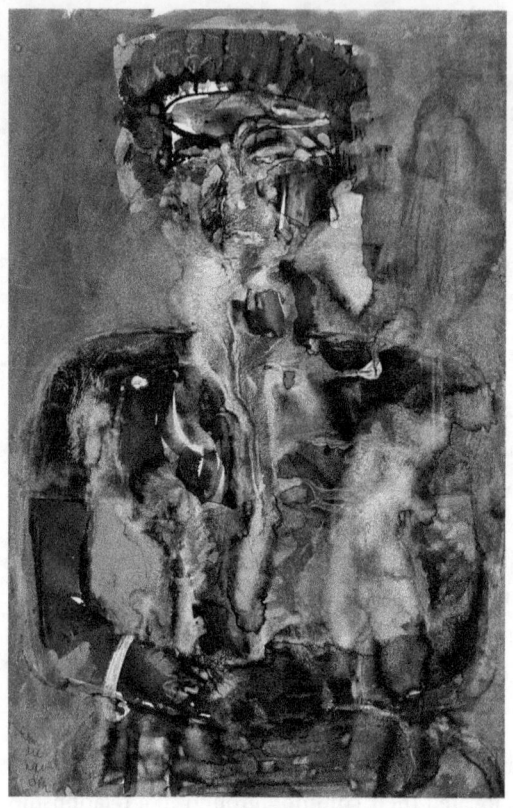

FIGURE 44  Romare Bearden, *Obeah in a Trance (Possession de la Sorcière, Manmbo-A Procédé)*, 1984. Watercolor and gouache on paper, 29 5/8 × 19 3/8 in. (75.2 × 49.2 cm). Art © Romare Bearden Foundation/Licensed by VAGA, New York

considered entirely "respectable," but it was very commonly used to explain why particular relationships, commercial dealings, or political affairs were developing as they were.

In 1984, for a few intense weeks, Bearden became wrapped up in some of the deepest of Caribbean mysteries, exploring the smoky, shadowy, often-invisible spirit-world of Obeah. For the first time in his Caribbean work, he dared to follow the approach he had developed during the past two decades in the Mecklenburg and Harlem collages, choosing, as Mary Schmidt Campbell has written, "to penetrate the interior of the lives he portrayed and, having pierced the skin of those day-to-day lives, connect his people and events to larger more universal themes."[10] In October 1984, he exhibited *Rituals of the Obeah*, a striking series of eighteen watercolors, in New York (see fig. 44, *Obeah in a Trance*).[11]

Critics picked up on Bearden's exploration of this smoky, shadowy, often-invisible spirit-world. Michael Brenson, writing for the *New York Times*, noticed how "Bearden's stains ... run over the figures, enveloping them in hypnotic fumes. In 'Obeah in a Trance,' the watery murk that eats into the figure like acid tells us that her personality has been dissolved by her trance."[12] Eric Gibson observed in the New Criterion that Bearden had abandoned "the calm, ordered world of retrospection [characteristic of his Mecklenburg work] and the Cubist-derived syntax of the collage form, for an expressionism that addresses itself to subjectivism of another sort, namely the magical, otherworldly realm of the imagination." For Gibson, the shift from the sharp edges and clearly defined form of collage to the "overlaid washes of pigments within which figures and images are loosely drawn ... and emerge from and sink back into a lurid, hallucinatory world, a dreamlike space" helped Bearden to depict a world that is not "ordered, rational, and physical."[13]

Much of the power of the Obeah series stemmed from its resonances, for Bearden, with ancient and universal themes. But there were also other echoes, for example from his long-time fascination with the conjur woman of southern Negro rural communities who prepared love potions, provided herbal cures for illnesses, and was consulted about vexing personal and family problems.

Bearden's main man, Al Murray, placed both the conjur woman and the Obeah figures within the overarching theme in Bearden's work that he had named "The Prevalence of Ritual," intending this as a tag that would embrace Bearden's entire philosophy of art. Ritual and ceremony had, in fact, always been part of Bearden's life. As Murray wrote in 1980,

> He spent his early years in the bosom of the church, as the old folks in the pews used to say ... [where he] absorbed the spirituals, the traditional hymns, gospel songs and amen-corner moans in context and conjunction with the prayers, sermons, shouts, testifying shuffles and struts that made up the services and the rituals that gave rise to them in the first place.[14]

By 1987, death had become been an insistent, stalking presence for Bearden. The year before, as the cancer eating away at his bones made climbing the stairs to their fifth-floor apartment impossible, the Beardens had moved to the second floor and for the first time canceled their summer stay in St. Martin. Murray told us that "he [said that he] had these devils and so forth — menacing things in the bushes, and he said 'there are thorns.' He was having trouble with his back, and he was talking about his mortality — serious stuff."[15]

On his two final visits to St. Martin in 1987, Bearden worked, as one critic put it, "as if he were trying to outpaint death,"[16] producing a series of several dozen

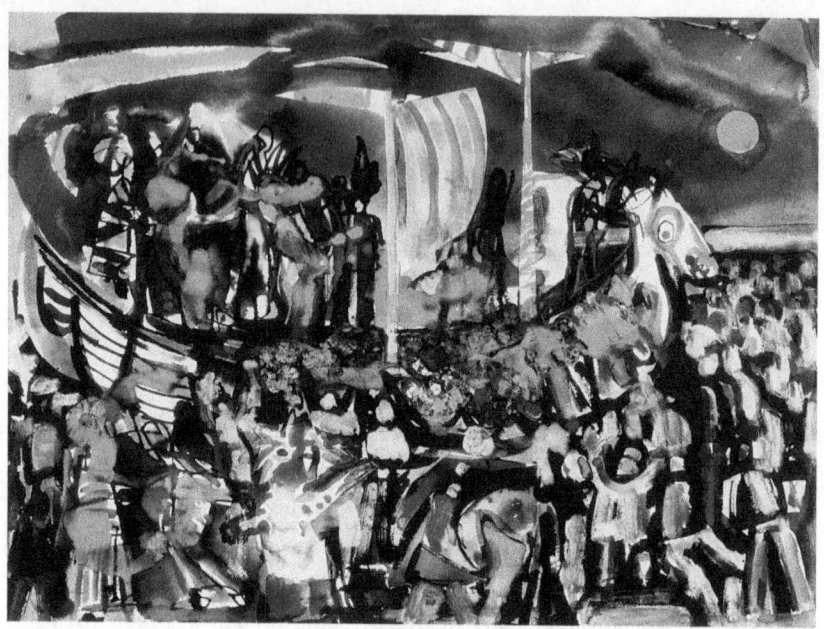

FIGURE 45 Romare Bearden, *The Carnival Begins* (1987 or 1984). Watercolor with collage, 21 1/2 × 30 in. (54.6 × 76.2 cm). Art © Romare Bearden Foundation/Licensed by VAGA, New York

Carnival images — exuberant celebrations of life, but with the grinning figure of Death lurking in the shadows. *The Carnival Begins* (fig. 45), for example, with a ship at center, emphasizes departure to another place. He also revisited a number of favorite Caribbean themes. *Lady and the God of the River*, for example, is a playful image in which a profoundly Afro-American figure, a river god, conveys all the mystery and translucence of the earlier Obeah figures.[17]

Back in New York, in the weeks before he died, Bearden had the collaboration of his studio assistant in producing two collages with watercolor — *Eden Noon* (first called *The Hundred Animal Piece*), centered, as Myron Schwartzman has written, on "a nude bathing in a pool surrounded by a playful, fantasy-landscape composed of egrets, a blue dove, a gigantic bullfrog, and various fish," and *Eden Midnight* (first called *Enchanted Places*), in which the bathing nude is under a starry sky, in a landscape filled with "mythological, perhaps prehistoric creatures — a gigantic butterfly, an alligator, and a dinosaur."[18] But he worked by himself to create his very last Caribbean painting, *At Low Tide*, where a nude, half immersed in the sea, is standing at the edge of what looks very much like St. Martin's Orient Bay.[19]

Walcott, viewing Bearden's art from his perspective in the Caribbean, argued that it was a supremely universalizing project. When he spoke with us about what the Caribbean meant to him artistically, in terms of the particulars of the relationship between the local and the universal (what Al Murray referred to as "processing the idiomatic particulars of Afro-American experience into aesthetic statements of universal relevance and appeal"[20]), Walcott could, with only slight adjustment, have been speaking for Bearden:

> In terms of Omeros, I felt totally natural, without making it an academic exercise or a justification or an elevation of St. Lucians into Greeks, or some such nonsense — because of the harbors of the Caribbean, the work of the people in the Caribbean, the light in the Caribbean. That sense of elation you get in the morning, of a possibility that is always there, and of the width of the ocean — that, to me, is Caribbean first of all.[21]

That "sense of elation you get in the morning . . . the width of the ocean" echoes powerfully with the "renewed energy" Bearden said that he felt whenever he was in the Caribbean — an energy that spilled over into all of his work, whatever its subject, during the final decades of his life.

## NOTES

1. Myron Schwartzman, *Romare Bearden: His Life and Art* (New York: Harry N. Abrams, 1990), 243.

2. This essay draws on Sally Price and Richard Price, *Romare Bearden: The Caribbean Dimension* (Philadelphia: University of Pennsylvania Press, 2006), which includes more than one hundred color images of Bearden's Caribbean paintings.

3. In April 1977 the *New York Times* commissioned a line drawing to accompany its publication of an excerpt from Richard Wright's *American Hunger*, and the next month Bearden's front curtain, "Ancestral Voices," for an Alvin Ailey premiere received rave reviews; see Schwartzman, *Bearden: His Life and Art*, 252–53, 263. For Calvin Tomkins's "Putting Something over Something Else," *New Yorker* (November 29, 1977): 53–77, see pp. 31–53 in this volume.

4. Derek Walcott and Romare Bearden, *The Caribbean Poetry of Derek Walcott and the Art of Romare Bearden* (New York: The Limited Editions Club, 1983). For images from this collaboration, see Price and Price, *Bearden: The Caribbean Dimension*, 72–78.

5. For images, stories, and paintings regarding Bearden's St. Martin friends, see Price and Price, *Bearden: The Caribbean Dimension*, 52–72.

6. Avis Berman, "Romare Bearden: 'I Paint Out of the Tradition of the Blues,'" *ARTnews* (December 1980): 60–67.

7. For the paintings inspired by visits to Martinique, see Price and Price, *Bearden: The Caribbean Dimension*, 97–107.

8. Derek Walcott, *The Star-Apple Kingdom* (New York: Farrar, Straus and Giroux, 1979). For the Sea Nymph paintings, see Price and Price, *Bearden: The Caribbean Dimension*, 96–97.

9. Our interview with Walcott took place at his home in St. Lucia, August 17, 2000.

10. Mary Schmidt Campbell, "History and the Art of Romare Bearden," in *Memory and Metaphor: The Art of Romare Bearden 1940–1987* (New York: The Studio Museum in Harlem and Oxford University Press, 1991), 9.

11. On the Obeah series, including reproductions of twenty-four paintings, see Price and Price, *Bearden: The Caribbean Dimension*, 121–53.

12. Michael Brenson, "Romare Bearden: 'Rituals of the Obeah,'" *New York Times* (November 30, 1984): C23.

13. Eric Gibson, "The Minimal and the Magical," *New Criterion* 3.5 (1985): 42–44.

14. Albert Murray, "The Visual Equivalent of the Blues," in Jerald L. Melberg and Milton J. Bloch, *Romare Bearden: 1970–1980* (Charlotte, NC: Mint Museum, 1980), 18.

15. Authors' interview with Albert Murray, Harlem, August 24, 2000.

16. Schwartzman, *Bearden: His Life and Art*, 304.

17. For *Lady and the God of the River*, see Price and Price, *Bearden: The Caribbean Dimension*, 175.

18. Schwartzman, *Bearden, His Life and Art*, 303–4.

19. For *Eden Midnight, Eden Noon,* and *At Low Tide*, see Price and Price, *Bearden: The Caribbean Dimension*, 80, 81, and 176.

20. Authors' interview with Murray, August 24, 2000.

21. Derek Walcott, "Reflections on *Omeros,*" *South Atlantic Quarterly* 96 (1997): 235.

# SHEER MASTERY
## ROMARE BEARDEN'S FINAL YEAR

*Myron Schwartzman*

## OPENING STATEMENT

Romare Bearden's interplay with the writer Albert Murray had flowered for over three decades by the time I had the good fortune to see it take place before my eyes in Bearden's final year. It had been in evidence in the 1971 Museum of Modern Art exhibition "Romare Bearden: The Prevalence of Ritual," the 1975 Cordier & Ekstrom exhibition "Of the Blues," and the two Cordier & Ekstrom "Profile" exhibitions: "Profile/Part I: The Twenties" in 1978 and "Profile/Part II: The Thirties" in 1981. In the earlier Profile exhibition, Bearden's memories of North Carolina's Mecklenburg County (his birthplace), Pittsburgh, and Harlem — as told to Murray — had been compressed into a series of single-sentence narratives handwritten by Bearden on the gallery wall beneath the collages (see figs. 2, 3). Under a collage entitled *Sunset Limited*, for instance, with a locomotive steaming through a field where a woman holds a baby while a horse and chicken feed lazily, was the memory: *The last time I saw Liza was down at the station when I left for Pittsburgh on the 5:13*. Taken in its entirety, the series, composed of about twenty collages, was like a twenty-stanza poem for me.

In late May 1987 I accompanied Murray on a visit to his longtime friend's Long Island City studio, where Romy was in the midst of creating a series of large jazz collages with Andre Thibault (known as "Teabo"), a young Canadian painter who had learned from the master over some years. Teabo was now assisting Bearden with such virtuosity that very few words passed between them; it seemed they could read each other's minds. Some eight collages had been completed, another two were in progress, and the wooden backings had been prepared for several more. What ensued was an extended conversation between Murray and Bearden in the course of which a number of collages were named, then placed in groups starting with jazz soloists and moving to duos, ensembles, and finally a large New Orleans Storyville scene that framed the musicians in a mirror (and also reflected an odalisque, a "demoiselle d'Orleans"), focusing the pattern of the whole series. Each collage's title was discovered much as jazz musicians would explore all the nuances of a piece in the course of an extended improvisation. (Though neither man actually played a musical instrument, I could picture Murray's magic fingers weaving a bass line around Bearden's spare, Basie-like piano chords, pushing, pulling back, and filling the tune with oh-so-hip embroidery.)

The first collage we saw was nearly completed: it depicted a pianist in profile at an upright piano, his large left hand displaying a wristwatch. A derby cocked down over his head, a cigar in his mouth, a bow tie, and an ornate vest completed the man's calling card (fig. 46). There was nothing "nice" about his bearing. Indeed, this virtuoso's double glissandos and other pyrotechnics would probably run other ticklers off the premises at cutting sessions. At the same time, as the legendary pianist James P. Johnson put it, "With the music he played, the tickler's manners would put the question in the ladies' minds: 'Can he do it like he can play it?'"[1] To Murray, he recalled the early masters of the stride piano, Willie "The Lion" Smith and Johnson himself, whose "Carolina Shout" had suggested the title of one of the greatest of Bearden's collages, now in the permanent collection of the Mint Museum, Charlotte. In 1955 Johnson remembered Jelly Roll Morton's attitude and bearing as he approached the piano:

> He'd take a big silk handkerchief, shake it out to show it off properly, and dust off the stool. He'd sit down then, hit his special chord (every tickler had his special trade-mark chord, like a signal) and he'd be gone![2]

Murray then pointed out that one of the greatest influences of the stridemen on a second-generation master like Duke Ellington was the emphasis Duke placed on that signature opening chord: "Then what we have, was Duke hitting that goddamn first chord, one that nobody ever heard before!"[3]

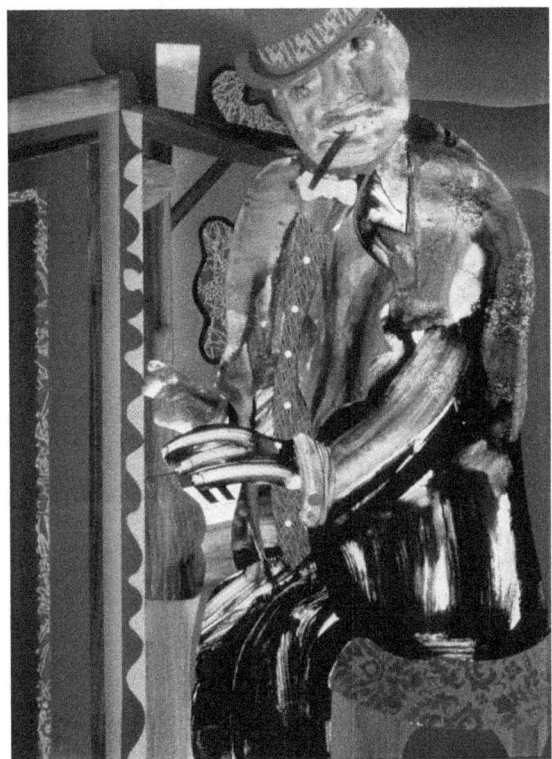

FIGURE 46
Romare Bearden, *Opening Statement,* 1987, watercolor with collage, 36 × 23 7/8 in. (91.4 × 60.6 cm). Art © Romare Bearden Foundation/Licensed by VAGA, New York

By then Murray and Bearden were improvising on these variations, moving toward a title. As he further studied the collage, especially the prominent left hand and skin tone, Murray was reminded of a left-handed piano and guitar player named Seminole, whom Count Basie recalled meeting, according to Murray's *Good Morning Blues* (Count Basie's as-told-to autobiography). Seminole, Basie remembered, was not only a dandy but quite intimidating, since he had a left hand like everyone else's right hand. "I didn't know anything about him," Basie had told Murray, "but I met him out there in Tulsa, and that was enough."[4] Now thinking about names, Murray said, "Yeah, okay, maybe you get variations like *Seminole Comes to Town, Seminole Opens,* or *Arrives in Harlem,* you know?"

"Yeah," Bearden agreed.

"Or you could have a completely ambiguous title like *The Statement!*" Both laugh. "That's visual, auditory, and everything else, right? *The Statement* [savoring it for its appeal]. Then put on a subtitle like *Uptown Manhattan, 1924.*" They laugh again.

"That's good," Bearden says.

"You know what I mean?" continued Murray. "He makes a total statement. It's real subtle, given its plastic elegance." By then they had the title, a synthesis of "opening chord" from their riffing on James P. and Duke, and the idea of that opening as a statement. Hence, *Opening Statement*. Murray summed it up:

"I think what Romy's captured in that collage is a significant moment in the tradition of the Harlem stride piano player. . . . There's an emphasis on playful elegance that Romy's got in the dress, which already suggests the elegance of his movements. And there's no question about the fact that the sounds which came out of the piano were consistent with everything about him. There's something about that which recalls James P. Johnson's description of the care with which these piano players selected their wardrobes, how they made their entrances, and how they took the time to pull their very fancy silk-lined overcoats off, and, instead of folding them, lay them lengthwise along the top of the upright piano in prominent display. Then they sat down at the piano, dusted the stool off with a silk handkerchief — sporting a fancy hat which cost a lot of money, cocked at a certain angle, took out a very fine cigar, and a gadget to clip it with, took a light, put it down, made a few runs on the piano to see if it were in tune, showing off their diamonds, rings, as well as their cufflinks. At that time, I don't think that wristwatches were very prominent. But if they had been, they would have come into play too, as Romy has chosen to depict him here. They probably had these fancy vest pocket watches, studded with a fancy chain through a button-hole. Because you see, he is wearing a waistcoat! . . . So this is a statement that he makes: a soloist coming into town *made a statement,* and that statement was in his bearing, in his being, his style, as well as his sound."

"Yeah," Bearden agreed.[5]

## OPENING AT THE SAVOY

*Opening at the Savoy* (1987) is a large collage with watercolor shown at the Thomas Segal Gallery in Boston, Massachusetts, in November of Bearden's final year (fig. 47). The piece is masterful, done on a herculean scale that would have been impossible for Romy without his colleagues Thibault/Teabo and Bob Blackburn.

For those familiar with Bearden's oeuvre in the high decade of his life beginning in 1975 with the "Of the Blues" series, *Opening at the Savoy* is a tip of the hat

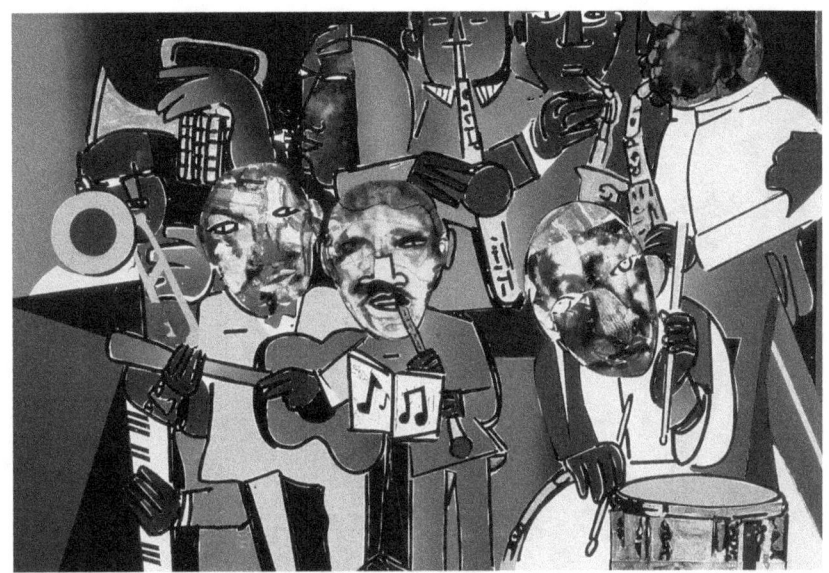

FIGURE 47  Romare Bearden, *Opening at the Savoy* 1987, watercolor and collage, 36 × 24 in. (91.4 × 61 cm). Art © Romare Bearden Foundation/Licensed by VAGA, New York

back toward his *One Night Stand* (fig. 48). In fact, the instrumentation is nearly the same, with two additional players in the 1987 work, which features drums, clarinet, guitar, piano, trombone, trumpet, and three saxophones — a nonet. *One Night Stand* has a septet, and, reading from left to right, the reverse order of the imagery of the later work. In both collages the odd, nearly-out-of-place key is the piano player, looking out from underneath the guitarist, straight at the viewer. He *knows* that he's being heard, at least by his fellow musicians, but he wants to make sure that you know it too!

In point of fact, Bearden traced *One Night Stand* and then had it enlarged from the original 8½ × 11–inch tracing paper many times larger, to what became the relatively enormous dimensions of *Opening at the Savoy*.[6] This technique looks back decades to Bearden's methodology in assembling his 1960s black-and-white Projections from their 8½ × 11–inch collage originals to 3 × 4 feet or 6 × 8 feet.

In Bearden's 1987 jazz series, individual soloists are depicted in *Trombone Solo*; *All the Things You Are*, a stunning collage with watercolor of an alto saxophonist in semiprofile; *Jackie at the Five Spot*, a trumpet player in profile, swinging hard; *Solo*, an alto sax player with his head silhouetted, his torso rendered in

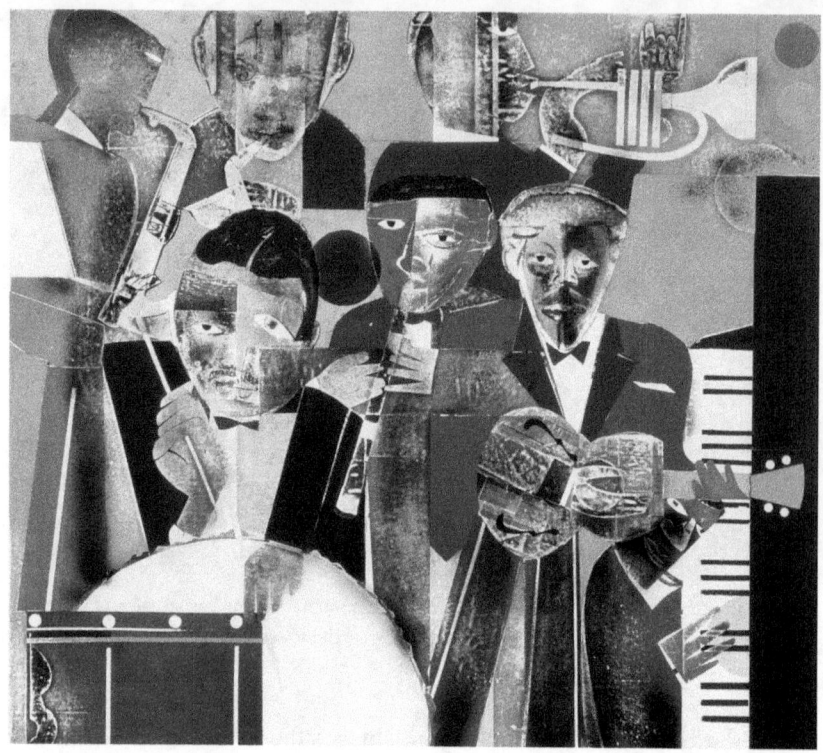

FIGURE 48 Romare Bearden, *One Night Stand* ("Of the Blues" series), 1974. Collage with acrylic and lacquer on board, 49 × 50 in. (124.5 × 127 cm). Art © Romare Bearden Foundation/ Licensed by VAGA, New York

flowing watercolor; and two individual musicians playing drums, one, entitled *Rhythm*, a study in stasis, and the other, *Fancy Sticks* (fig. 49), a study in kinesis with the drummer in flight, his sticks moving so fast that they seem to blur. Along with *All the Things You Are*, *Fancy Sticks* stands out from the rest. Both have a stunning impact, their music carried by Bearden's masterful handling of color.

Two collages on Mecklenburg themes, both measuring 20 × 24 inches, round out the show. They are entitled *Evening Guitar* and *Gospel Morning*. By far the more forceful, *Gospel Morning* derives its impact from Bearden's handling of the matriarch's face: an African mask, it confronts the viewer head on. Elsewhere in the collage, on the other side of a morning rooster, a young girl holding a tambourine is seen in profile, walking with an older sister or mother in Sunday dress, clearly on their way to church.

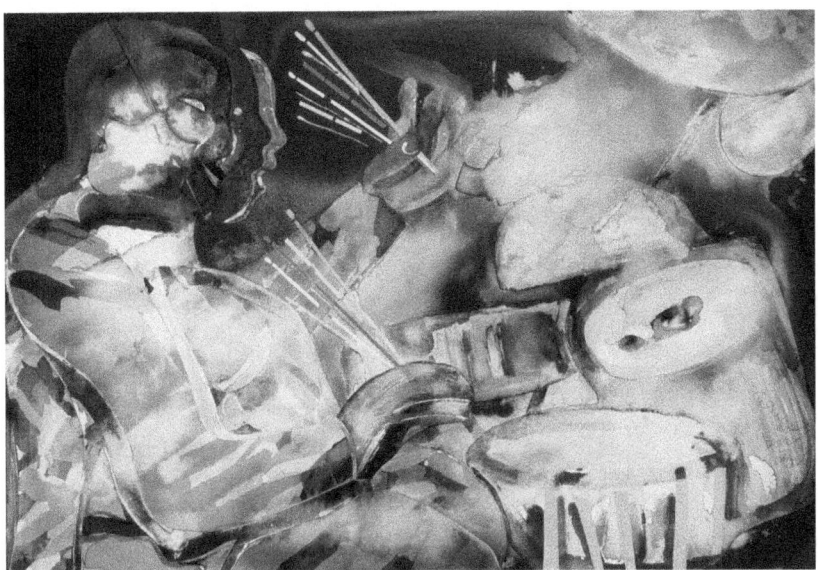

FIGURE 49  Romare Bearden, *Fancy Sticks*, 1987, watercolor and paper collage on paper laid on board, 24×36 in. (61×91.4 cm). Art © Romare Bearden Foundation/Licensed by VAGA, New York

## *"THE ARTIST WITH HIS COLORS LIGHTS HIS WORLD"*

I rarely saw Bearden struggle with a work of art, but *Autumn Lamp* (fig. 50), with its country guitarist, guitar, and lamp, did not come easily. I saw the piece develop over a three-week period, and by the time Romare had finished work, it was another thing altogether. Bearden likened the struggle to jazz improvisation: "You do something, and then you improvise." According to Bearden, Édouard Manet had said that a painting isn't ever finished: sometimes you get on the surface. By this he meant that you've got it under control. And Bearden had applied his study of Manet to his own working method: "Maybe sometimes a third of the way through, I'll say, 'I know this is coming out.' You get that feeling that the thing is going to be all right."

As Claude Monet observed of Manet, Manet always wanted his canvases to have the air of being painted at a single sitting, but when morning came, he would often scrape down what he had executed during the previous day. He kept only the lowest layer, which had great charm and finesse. And on this layer, he would again begin improvising. In this sense, for Manet, a painting was never absolutely finished; at some point, he relinquished it.[7]

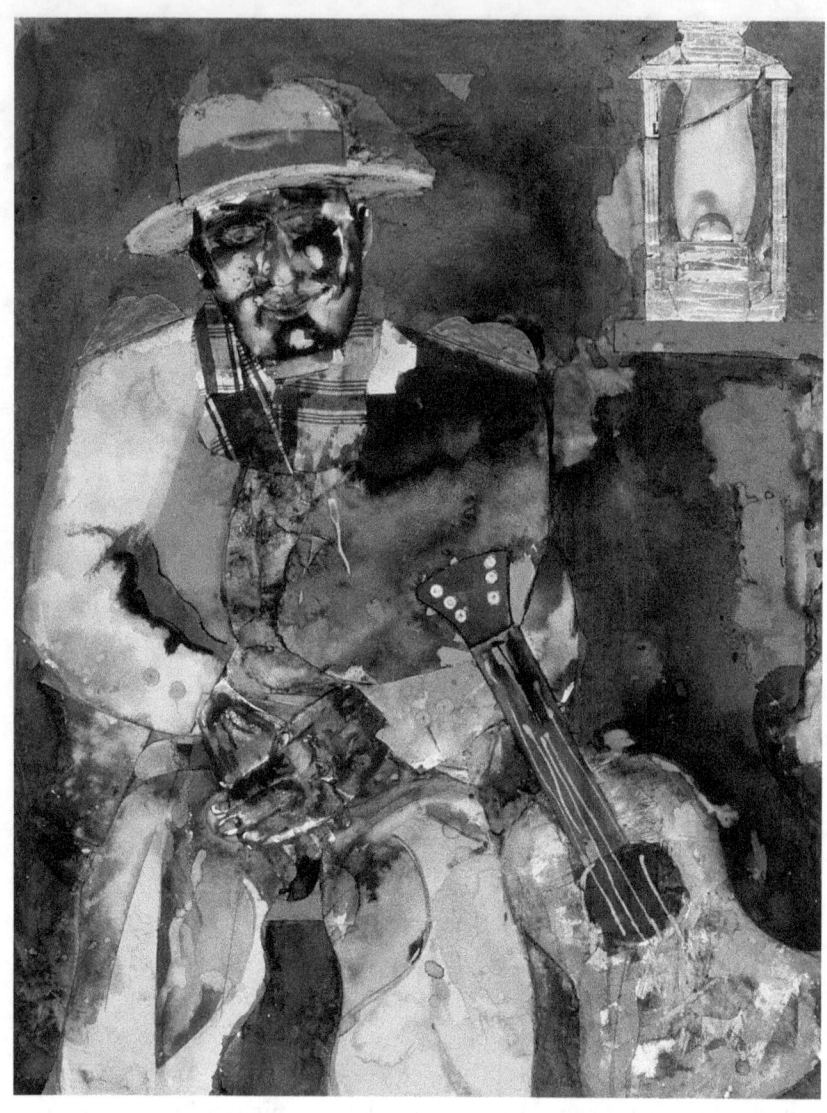

FIGURE 50  Romare Bearden, *Autumn Lamp (Guitar Player)* 1983, oil with collage, 40 × 30 in. (101.6 × 76.2 cm). Art © Romare Bearden Foundation/Licensed by VAGA, New York

That was the way Bearden struggled with *Autumn Lamp*, an oil painting with collage (40 × 31 inches). At a certain point in the process of composition, he placed a denim shirt, using actual denim, on the guitarist, "and then I knew, when I put these denim sections in, that it had a kind of set to it." But by the time Bearden relinquished *Autumn Lamp*, the only fabric remaining was a small section at the upper part of the guitarist's shirt, adorning his neck like a scarf surrounding his square chin. His guitar is at rest alongside his thigh and beneath his left arm; his long hands are at rest, one on top of the other. There is a wise smile on his lips and in his knowing eyes. He, like Romare, has played.

In 1983, the same year as *Autumn Lamp*, Bearden invited Thibault/Teabo to visit the studio more often as he executed four pure landscapes, one for each of the autumn months: *September: Sky and Morning, October: Toward Paw Creek, November: Early Frost: Cherokee Lands,* and *December: Time of the Marsh Hawk* (all oil with collage, 30 × 40 inches). A St. Martin light transfuses the lush, mythic forest of Bearden's Mecklenburg County in the series, titled "Mecklenburg Autumn," reflecting Bearden's later years in the Caribbean. And the landscapes also reflect Bearden's mastery of color as form. Indeed, as early as 1949, Bearden had written of the possibility of abstracting light. "I think of some light source that moves across the canvas, pausing to become yellow, blue, pink, or what have you during its passage; and always yellow, blue, or pink according to the painter's desire, so that the effect would have nothing to do with illumination or atmospheric effects," Bearden wrote his friend Carl Holty. "I rather envision large planes of light that spell out the form; with the philosophic intent that in a world of darkness we could hardly conceive of form except in a tactile sense. And in a sense, the artist with his colors lights his world."[8]

Although Bearden was in considerable pain by October 1987, he did some of his best work from November of that year to his last hospitalization in March 1988. At 357 Canal Street, the Beardens had acquired and furnished a second-floor apartment in the walk-up they had called home since the 1950s. It had its own bedroom, kitchen, and living room area. He was no longer obligated to climb three additional flights of stairs to the fifth floor, but with back and leg trouble, even the single flight of stairs to and from street level could be difficult to negotiate. With great apprehension, he sought to restore his health through visits to a chiropractor and gave serious thought to acupuncture.

His friend Russell Goings, who had played football for the Buffalo Bills in the early 1960s, brought over small barbells and started Bearden on exercises to strengthen his arms. And before driving him to Long Island City, Goings would massage Bearden's back and legs, which had become too thin and frail for the weight they had to support. When Bearden had completed his day's work at the studio, Goings would drive him back home to Canal Street and, if necessary, all but carry Romare up the long flight of stairs.

An August 1986 letter from Bearden to Thibault lays out the medical situation: "One can't, or shouldn't, look back, but I did wait too long before going to the Real doctors. But the neurological team at NY hospital, I think, did a good job." At the same time, Bearden adhered to his role as Thibault's teacher: "No need to tell you to keep on with your work — you have made enormous improvement. Just keep trying, as we've discussed, not to paint the objects — but the relations between them. Not this: [sketch]; this: [sketch]."[9]

Bearden's illness attacked his limbs slowly enough to allow his mastery of collage to compensate for a diminished capacity to work either on a large scale or in intricate detail. Reviewing a 1985 exhibit Richard Maschal remarked in the *Charlotte Observer*, "Bearden is leaving things out . . . his work has gotten leaner, and, paradox of art, richer. He seems less interested in the architecture of his collages and more interested in communicating his feelings." I had seen *Evening Church* (a procession led by a young girl, followed by two women and a man holding a lantern that echoes the setting sun) evolve over a period of weeks in Bearden's studio. The collage has the expressive quality of the 1983 "Mecklenburg Autumn" series; indeed, for Maschal, "the most remarkable difference [between these and past works] is these works are more painterly."[10]

Throughout an early 1987 exhibition, the last Bearden would give at Cordier & Ekstrom, Nancy Princenthal noted in *Art in America* that "the agility with which Bearden handles collage is undiminished; like his dauntless approach to sentimentality, his control of cut and torn paper recalls Matisse."[11]

Bearden's "control of cut and torn paper" no less than his "dauntless approach to sentimentality" traces a crucial affinity between him and Henri Matisse. The defining word in Princenthal's observation is "dauntless": it sums up a Hemingwayesque stance, one that Bearden's longtime friend Murray venerated, whether he found Hemingway writing about the bullfight (*Death in the Afternoon*), deep-sea fishing (*The Old Man and the Sea*), or big-game hunting (*The Snows of Kilimanjaro*). Here were two master artists who, very late in life, their bodies failing, summoned the stern will to impose order and love on their artistic worlds.

Edward W. Said wrote in his last book, *On Late Style*, of artists whose late works "crown a lifetime of aesthetic endeavor. Rembrandt and Matisse, Bach and Wagner. Said continues, "But what of artistic lateness not as harmony and resolution but as intransigence, difficulty, unresolved contradiction?"[12] Matisse, at least partially, belonged to the second camp. And Bearden's late style put him squarely in the ranks of the intransigent.

Both Matisse and Bearden were unyielding with respect to their aesthetic values. These values were centered in the primacy of relationship and love.

In 1952, for instance, near the end of his life, Matisse told an interviewer, "It's not enough to place colors, however beautiful, one beside the other. Colors must also react on one another. Otherwise, you have cacophony. Jazz is rhythm and meaning. One doesn't find any expression in what is supposed to be the relationship of their colors. If they can't create relationships, they can use all the colors in vain. Rapport is the affinity between things, the common language. Rapport is love, yes, love."[13]

And as for Bearden, I always saw a quote from the preface to Wordsworth's *Lyrical Ballads* pinned over his work table. It was an artist's manifesto: "He is the rock of defense of human nature, an upholder and preserver, bringing everywhere with him relationship and love."

By the second week of October 1987, Bearden and Thibault/Teabo were at work at the studio. Romare was in pain, and work was going much more slowly than they had anticipated. On October 16, a day on which the work had seemed particularly difficult, Bearden told Thibault that he had back cancer. Against all odds, the work continued. Bearden laid down the design of two new collages, *Blue Morning Rain* and *Moonlite Prelude*. The following Monday, alone at the studio, Thibault got a call from Russell Goings, who told him that Bearden would be returning to hospital for three or four days. Thibault picked up work on *Blue Morning Rain* from Bearden's initial design. When he called Bearden later on in the day, Romare was happy: he had just learned that Bob Blackburn had prepared new Arches papers for them, using a ground of vibrant watercolors in rainbowlike sequence rather than oils. According to Thibault, "Bob had printed wonderful patterns that, like those in a rainbow, softly melded into one another."

Bearden entered hospital on October 20, and Thibault took a week's break.

By the beginning of November, Bearden and Thibault met again at the studio and resumed work on *Blue Morning Rain*, a large collage (30 × 40 inches), using much of the iconography of Bearden's Mecklenburg. A woman stands in profile at the breakfast table opposite a seated man dressed in coveralls, hat on his head, drinking his morning coffee. The embers of a potbellied stove glow behind him. The ubiquitous rooster stands before an open door, through which the rays of the rising sun shine through the morning rain, flooding the floorboards with sunlight. Outside, a nude stands in a basin holding a towel, her back to the viewer, set against a landscape of hills, rich foliage, and a field across which a train steams in the distance. The piece was completed on November 3.

Energized, the two resumed work on *Moonlite Prelude,* a striking collage (20 × 28 inches) depicting a locomotive steaming across a long, high trestle, its engine's floodlight piercing the night sky. At the bottom of the collage, a guitar player, cigarette in his mouth, plays alongside a nude lying on a blanket, her back to the viewer.

According to Thibault, Bearden remained dissatisfied with the placement of the trestle until the fourth attempt; it had to be sanded back down to the board each time. At one point, dismayed by Bearden's request that he sand down the trestle yet again, Thibault told Bearden he felt defeated by the piece. Bearden's response was that the piece "needed to get whipped, instead of whipping us." After that, as Thibault remembers it, "we beat *it.*" Now they suspended work on *Moonlite Prelude,* for the opening of the Boston show at the Thomas Segal Gallery was upon them.

The exhibition contained seventeen works in all, six jazz collages by Bearden alone, and eleven collages with watercolor that Bearden and Thibault worked on together. Three of the collages — *Mecklenburg Gospel Morning, Evening Guitar,* and *Gospel Morning* — were on Mecklenburg themes. The others concerned jazz and Storyville. Reviews of the Segal show in the *Boston Globe* and *Boston Phoenix* praised the watercolors highly at the expense of the collages. The *Phoenix* reviewer went so far as to write, "the hit of the show is not the collages at all but a suite of watercolors on jazz themes . . . In these pieces Bearden lays his ordinarily high-keyed and dynamic colors on clean white paper, and the colors sing."

Of the collages with watercolor, neither reviewer cared for *Storyville Mirror.* Considering Bearden and Thibault's preference for *Storyville Mirror* as the centerpiece of the jazz works, reflecting the various combinations of musicians in the mirror, this is difficult to understand. But *Fancy Sticks* stood out, according to the *Globe* reviewer: "Both paint and image are generally on the move," the critic wrote. "A drummer's two sticks multiply in red, yellow, and green to suggest a blur of quick movement."

It is important to note that Bearden and Thibault had very different collage techniques. Bearden used scissors to cut the paper, for instance, while Thibault used an X-Acto knife. And whereas Bearden had always used a roller to press down the cut and glued papers, Thibault had developed the technique of using a small blue scraper for adhering the elements to the board. The dissimilar techniques decidedly affected the overall look of the finished collage work. Now, for example, if Bearden were dissatisfied with a particular part of a collage which had already been adhered to the board, he could no longer simply pull it up as he had always done in the past; as was the case with *Moonlite Prelude,* Thibault had to use a sander to take that portion of the work back down to the bare board.

Considering the vast differences in artistic sensibility, experience, and technique, how successful was the finished product in any given instance? It seems fair to say that as Bearden and Thibault continued to create over a period of months, the cohesiveness of their work together evolved, especially when they were not racing to meet an exhibition deadline. Indeed, their best collages seem to have been created in November and December 1987, and in early January 1988, well after the work for the Segal exhibition was ready. Bearden's capacity to create in no way simply deteriorated as his body failed him. To judge by his *work,* he seems to have rallied with continued treatment and to have sustained hope. This element was crucial to his creative energy. Like Henri Matisse, Romare Bearden literally lived for his art.

On December 1, the finishing touches were made on *Moonlite Prelude.* The following day, Bearden and Thibault began a collage and watercolor entitled *Autumn* (36 × 24 inches) depicting a seated, masked conjur woman whose ornate, flowered hat echoed the flowered ornamentation on her sleeves. Work was going very well, but that Friday Bearden developed a cold and was unable to leave his bed. It took him five or six days to recover. When he returned to the studio on December 10, they completed *Autumn.* The following day, Bearden signed the work, front and back, "Romare Bearden & T."

On December 14, Bearden and Thibault began work on the first of two complementary collages with watercolor. *Eden Noon* (which they first called "The hundred-animal piece") depicts a nude bathing in a pool surrounded by a playful, fantasy landscape composed of egrets, a blue dove, a gigantic bullfrog, and various fish. "In a matter of thirty seconds," Thibault remembered, "Romare had cut out the only human shape in that piece; a bathing female figure that was approximately six inches in height."[14]

From one day to the next, Bearden's health was up and down: he was under sedation for the pain. Christmastime was replete with old friends visiting the studio. Just after the holiday, on December 28, as they were putting the finishing touches on *Eden Noon,* Dr. Katarina Winnekes, curator for Kunst-Station Sankt Peter Köln, in Cologne, Germany, paid a call to discuss the idea of a European show. This buoyed Bearden's spirits tremendously. In the days following, Bearden talked with Thibault about work they could exhibit in Europe, leaning toward Storyville portraits and collages on jazz themes. In addition, they could include *Eden Noon* and its companion piece, on which they began work immediately.

*Eden Midnight,* like *Eden Noon,* has a nude bathing in a stream for its centerpiece, with a waterfall, a twinkling star in the night sky, and a fantastic landscape: it is filled with mythological, perhaps prehistoric creatures — a gigantic butterfly, an alligator, even a dinosaur. Bearden worked on this piece (which had first been called "Enchanted Places") through the first two weeks of January, despite increasing pain and sporadic inability to get to the studio. But by January 13, *Eden Midnight* was complete. Nanette, Bearden's wife, who had been coming to the studio regularly since mid-October, accompanied Romare. Thibault took a picture of the Beardens seated behind the completed work.

Taken together, *Eden Noon* and *Eden Midnight* are extraordinary work, especially *Eden Midnight.* Bearden's subject matter here combines elements found in many previous Beardens (the nude bathing, the stream, the waterfall), but with a mythological, fantastic vision that had never appeared in his work before.

Bearden continued to surprise; it was as if he were trying to outpaint death. On January 14, he arrived at the studio very early and began work on the collage of a guitar player on $30 \times 22$-inch Masonite board. That Sunday, the *Newsday* magazine section appeared, with *All the Things You Are* on its cover. Bearden was deluged by congratulatory phone calls. The following day, in incessant pain, Bearden continued work on the guitar player. The day after that, with Thibault continuing work on the guitarist, Bearden began a collage on his own. With great concentration, he undertook work on *At Low Tide,* a $20 \times 16$-inch collage with watercolor depicting a white nude in a bay surrounded by birds and tropical foliage. He completed work on it two days later, on January 21, signed it front and back and gave it to Thibault. Then he went back to work on the guitar player. The next day, Thibault saw Bearden for the last time. Bearden left early that day, concerned that Thibault might miss his train.

The last time I saw Romy at the studio, he remarked, "Great poets always write poems about the spring, because each year, people forget how beautiful spring is." The comment had been made as we looked at *Opening Statement* in spring 1987. Romare's last year had been extraordinary, sounding the deep ground-bass of his late-autumn music, the key to his "late style." From the 1983 *September: Sky and Morning* to *October: Toward Paw Creek* to *November: Early Frost — Cherokee Lands*, and finally to *December: Time of the Marsh Hawk*, Bearden's evolution showed rigorous determination. From *All the Things You Are* to *Eden Noon* and finally to *Eden Midnight*, Bearden's sheer artistic mastery, against all odds, had carried him through.

## NOTES

1. Tom Davin, "Conversation with James P. Johnson," in *Jazz Panorama: From the Pages of The Jazz Review*, ed. Martin Williams (New York: Collier-MacMillan, 1964), 61.

2. Davin, "Conversation," 60.

3. All quotations by Albert Murray are from the author's notes made during a visit to Romare Bearden's studio on May 27, 1987, in preparation for Bearden's biography. See Myron Schwartzman, *Romare Bearden: His Life and Art* (New York: Harry N. Abrams, 1990), 300.

4. *Good Morning Blues: The Autobiography of Count Basie as Told to Albert Murray* (New York: Random House, 1985). In this interview, recapitulated by Schwartzman in "A Bearden-Murray Interplay: One Last Time," *Callaloo* 36 (1988), Murray remembers Seminole, "who was also a guitar player — same thing left-handed. Left-handed guitar player. When he hit town, boy, those people at the Rhythm Club took notice." Murray goes on to recall an episode in *Good Morning Blues* wherein Basie remembers the impact of running into Seminole in Tulsa, Oklahoma.

5. Schwartzman, *Romare Bearden*, 300.

6. Telephone conversation with Andre Thibault/Teabo, early 2017. For an account of Thibault's enormous importance in Bearden's later years, see Schwartzman, *Romare Bearden*, 200–203, based on the author's interview with Thibault on April 16, 1988, about a month after Bearden's death.

7. Bearden's study of the Impressionists clearly had an enormous influence on his working method, as illustrated by his struggle with *Autumn Lamp*. For me, the key phrase is "getting on the surface"; at this point, Bearden knew he would be able to cease the work for the moment.

8. Bearden to Carl Holty, ca. mid-November 1952, headed "Sunday" and opening with the words "[Harry] Salpeter asked me to do an oil for his Xmas show," Holty Papers, Smithsonian, Archives of American Art, roll 670, frames 434 ff. Also in holograph manuscript in Bearden Papers, Smithsonian, Archives of American Art. For an extensive account of the Bearden-Holty correspondence (1948–52), see Schwartzman, *Romare Bearden*, 152–58, 172–87.

9. Letter from Bearden to Andre Thibault/Teabo, postmarked August 31, 1986. Courtesy of Andre Thibault.

10. Richard Maschal, "New Bearden Works Leaner, Richer," *Charlotte Observer* (June 2, 1985).

11. Nancy Princenthal, "Romare Bearden at the Cordier & Ekstrom," *Art in America* (Feb. 1987).

12. Edward Said, *On Late Style: Music and Literature Against the Grain* (New York: Vintage, 2007), 7.

13. Henri Matisse, interview with Andre Verdet, April and May 1952, in Jack D. Flam, *Matisse on Art* (London: Phaidon, 1973), 147.

14. Author's telephone conversation with Andre Thibault/Teabo, early 2017.

# ROMARE BEARDEN, AN INDELIBLE IMPRINT

*David C. Driskell*

Romare Bearden left an indelible imprint on artists around the nation through his friendship, his mentorship, and his contributions to the practice of art over five decades. When one surveys Bearden's background in the workplace as a social scientist, and later as a composer and lyricist, clearly revealed are an active mind, a humanitarian posture, and — most of all — a personal soul-centeredness that allowed him dexterity of mind and hand combined with an unusual energy. His oeuvre was eclectic in the early years of his development as an artist, showing influences ranging from the Dutch Masters to the cubists, Henri Matisse, and his teacher George Grosz. But it was the active mind of the artist that propelled him beyond an eclectic position and caused him to search for his own voice in the discipline of painting, one destined to become unique in the revival of interest in the medium and technique of collage. Along the way to an accomplished artistry, Bearden influenced many of his own colleagues as well as young up-and-coming artists of several generations. They saw him as mentor, teacher, and friend even in the busiest times of his career.

By recounting my own experience and interactions with Bearden, the giant among us and what some have called an artist's painter, I hope to share a personal point of view on how Bearden made such an imprint on the minds of many artists who availed themselves of his general counsel.

Few painters of the past century have achieved a more distinctive expression with regard to technique, stylistic principles, or innovative use of materials. A true heir of an all-but-forgotten strain of the Southern mystique, Bearden grew up in a family in which artistic interests were manifested through the love of music, literature, and religion, all of which were destined to make a lasting impression on his young and sensitive mind. Indeed, Bearden's sensitivity was noted from childhood to the last days he worked at his craft in his New York studio. His ability to excite the imagination by telling a story in a visual vocabulary of colors, shapes, textures, media, and form was unsurpassed. He was equally adept at telling stories aloud, thus enhancing his special status as a Southerner up north who answered the call to express the dramatic and colorful things in life by painting them and by creating a narrative within the African diaspora.

From an early age, Bearden seemed destined to make his mark as an artist in the realm of innovation, where his influence would be unmatched in his lifetime. An experimentalist of sorts seeking to be an artist with an insightful view of the world, Bearden grew intellectually as his artistry developed and defined itself along the lines of secular and religious modes of expression. Even as an adult, Bearden continued to dream of the south — of Mecklenburg County, North Carolina, where he was born — reinventing in dramatic ways his childhood and the impressions of visits he made with his parents to Charlotte. Although Charlotte was the locus of numerous works that gave his artistry a Southern folk flavor in midcareer, it was to the North, to Harlem, the city within the city, the cultural capital of black America, that Bearden turned later in life to find, without boundaries, the passion, the empathy, and the Geist with which he approached the black urban theme. Bearden's depiction of the city, with its multiplicity of goings–on, revealed his compassionate imagination, illuminated with clarity and defined and interpreted in a cinematic way. Bits and pieces of reality connected and at times were disjoined. They made their way into the parlor scenes, the juke joints, the bathing scenes, and the baptisms side by side with a fleeting way of life peculiar to the South.

Systematically and poetically perceived, Bearden's art shifted in due course from an inventive play with forms of realism to a kind of figural abstraction that was informed by synthetic cubism. The move to simplify form and embrace a modernist formula in painting, closer to formal abstraction, enables Bearden to articulate his own personal expression in a variety of painterly media, collage being the most notable.

Here I wish to recount some of the experiences that singled Bearden out as an artist's painter, a raconteur of art stories, with emphasis on his indelible imprint on numerous artists, among whom I count myself as a beneficiary of his enduring legacy. Another is Emma Amos, who, with Bearden and her teacher, Hale Woodruff, was a member of Spiral, a group of African-American artists formed in the early 1960s.[1]

I was a student of art at Howard University in 1954 when I first encountered Bearden.[2] He had stopped in briefly to greet Alonzo Aden, the director of the Barnett Aden Gallery at 127 Randolph Place NW, in Washington. Aden was arranging an exhibition of the work of several Washington and New York artists, including Lois Jones, Elizabeth Catlett, Theodoros Stamos, Richmond Barthé, Irene Rice Pereira, Charles White, Jacob Lawrence, Eldzier Cortor, Hale Woodruff, and Bearden. Aden highly respected Bearden's work, and he and James V. Herring, co-owner of the Barnett Aden Gallery, made frequent trips by car to New York to collect works they exhibited on consignment, some of which were loaned by Antoinette M. Kraushaar of the Kraushaar Galleries and Sidney Bergen of ACA Galleries. Aden and Herring paid an occasional visit to Edith Gregor Halpert at the Downtown Gallery, where they borrowed work by Jacob Lawrence, Samuel Halpert, and others. The work of these artists was exhibited without regard for race, although the principal mission of the gallery was to showcase the work of African-American artists.

I worked as an assistant or student curator at the gallery for three years, from 1952 to 1955, the last being the year of my graduation from Howard University. During these years, in addition to my work at the gallery an important experience was my summer at the Skowhegan School of Painting and Sculpture in Maine, in a community of serious artists. My major duty at the Barnett Aden Gallery was running errands, taking letters to the post office and depositing (at several nearby cleaners and hand laundries) the clothing of Aden and Herring. I drove an Imperial taxi as a means of employment between classes at Howard, and Professor Herring seemed to think I was his private chauffeur. When there were no solo exhibitions hanging at the gallery, most often a group show was arranged. And the work of Romare Bearden frequently occupied a prominent position over the mantelpiece in the main gallery, which also functioned as the living room. (I later had my first solo exhibition there, in 1957.)

It was at the Barnett Aden Gallery that I first saw Bearden's watercolor titled *War*. *War* is a loosely painted composition in which line serves to define the action as well as the figures engaged in combat with a mounted soldier. While observing certain elementary rules learned from his ongoing experimental relationship with synthetic cubism, Bearden layered and folded one formal space against another to create movement and active relief within the spatial relations of both the negative and positive spaces in *War.* The same can be said of *Poor Thirsty Souls,* executed in 1946, an oil on fiberboard that was often exhibited at the Barnett Aden Gallery. Clearly articulated in these two works and in numerous others of the same period, and seen in both the photostats and collages in subsequent years, is an interest in segmenting form in a manner that allows the shapes, contentwise, to be separated by line in the same manner as the cutout figural elements.

This formal and painstakingly reasoned development of Bearden's process in collage and painting was a well-planned and mathematically perceived concept that became indurated in his artistry. The meshing, in the photostats and collages, of numerous faces, hands, feet, and limbs compiled from an endless archive of torn magazine images, recounted in many ways Bearden's struggle during the 1940s and 1950s to stabilize and formally claim (using paint) an impressionable style that brought together all of the fragmented elements of his artistry.

I was not to have a chance to interact with Bearden the artist for several years, until the mid-1960s, but I maintained close contact with his art. I had taken a teaching post at Talladega College, in Alabama, where two of Bearden's cityscape watercolors were on loan from the Harmon Foundation (which retrieved them on my departure from the college). I left Talladega in 1962, when I join the faculty of the department of art at Howard University (through 1966). In 1967, the same two paintings were sent on indefinite loan to Fisk University, where I began teaching after leaving Howard. The two works, *Anderson Materials* and *Untitled (Cityscape),* are now in the collection of the Amistad Research Center in New Orleans.

My friendship with Bearden was renewed in the late 1960s as I revised the art curriculum at Fisk University, where the distinguished artist and teacher Aaron Douglas had taught since 1939. On visits to New York, I stopped in at Bearden's studio at 357 Canal Street on numerous occasions to chat about my own art and share with him what I was doing as the gallery director at Fisk.

In 1973, I was instrumental in inviting Bearden to be the principal speaker in the Southeastern College Art Conference, which convened at Fisk University that fall. Numerous communications ensued between us. My wife and I invited friends to our home at 1601 Phillips Street, on the Fisk University campus, to meet Nanette and Romy when they visited, after a dinner that also included

Aaron Douglas. That evening, both Douglas and Bearden vividly recounted memories of the days of the Harlem Renaissance, a conversation that still reverberates in my mind.

In the summer of 1974 I was invited by the Los Angeles County Museum of Art to serve as guest curator for its 1976 bicentennial exhibition, which I titled *Two Centuries of Black American Art, 1750–1950.* Immediately on my return from Los Angeles, I called Romy to inform him of my decision to curate the exhibition and to pass on best wishes from our mutual friend Charles White, who resided in Altadena, California. On October 19, 1974, I visited Bearden on Canal Street where he lived and continued to work on occasion, even after setting up a studio in Long Island City. I shared my plan for the exhibition and solicited information from him about the direction in which to move it. He initiated his discourse at the historical beginning, with the slave–art tradition in the United States, and all but specified the periods of production he felt pertinent to my catalog essay and to the exhibition's display of crafts, painting, and sculpture. Here, Bearden's mentorship, along with his friendship, was invaluable as I undertook to produce the most comprehensive exhibition to date on the significant contributions of African-American artists to visual culture in the nation.

We were joined in conversation late that afternoon by James Mayo, an exhibition designer for the Anacostia Museum in Washington. Our conversation lasted into the evening, concluding with a sumptuous meal in a nearby restaurant in Chinatown. This engaging conversation, with Bearden reciting an accurate and enlightening history of African-American art without notes of any kind, is only one example of how he conversed freely with me over the years, giving valuable advice whenever I called on him. And I think he was pleased with the result. The format of *Two Centuries of Black American Art* and the documentation in the catalog make it abundantly clear that I followed Bearden's suggestions when pursuing the exhibition research and presentation. In principle, this was the same plan and historical narrative that Bearden and Harry Henderson followed in writing *A History of African-American Artists: From 1792 to the Present,* published in 1993 and counted among the most comprehensive books on African-American art history.

On numerous visits to New York, I met Romy and Nanette at one of their favorite eating places. Bearden enjoyed Chinese food, and we often met at a Chinese restaurant in midtown Manhattan when I was unable to visit them downtown. There was no elevator at 357 Canal Street; one had to climb five flights of winding stairs to reach the Beardens' residence. The gray cat would

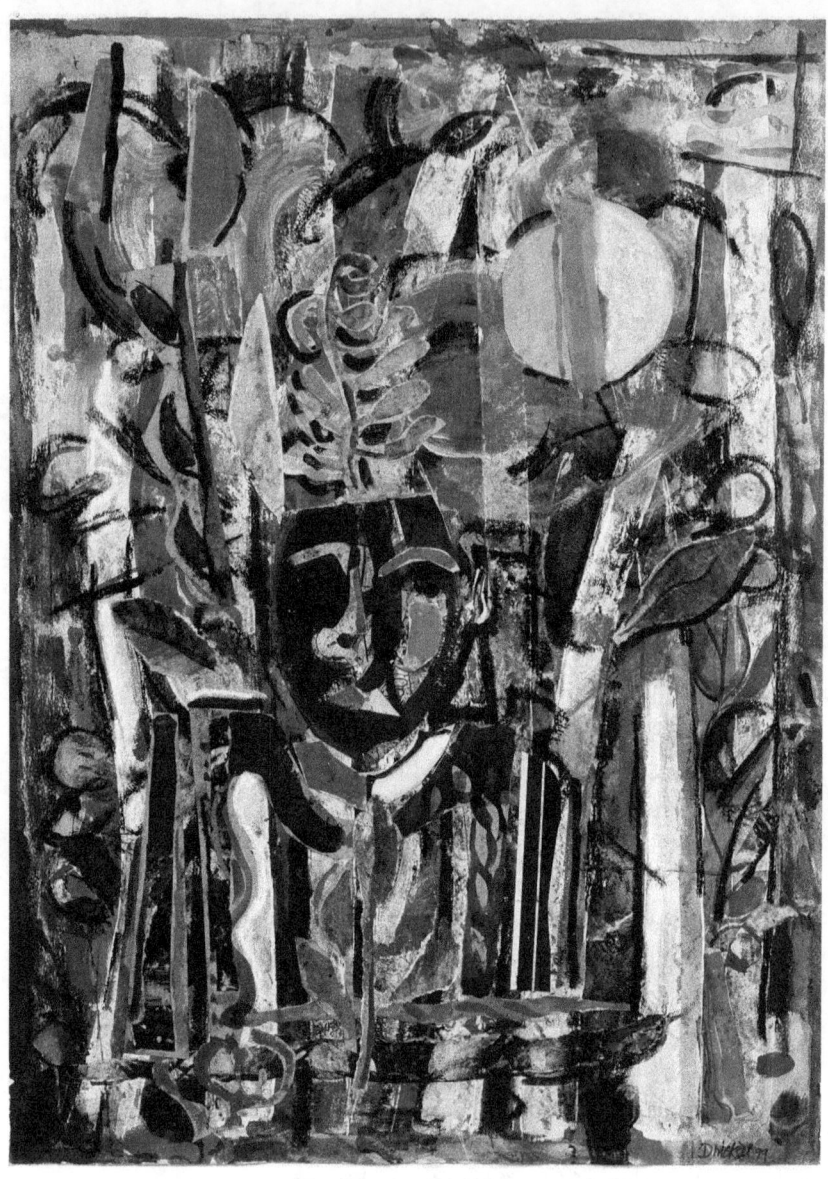

FIGURE 51 David C. Driskell, *The Jester*, 1999, collage and mixed media on paper. Courtesy of the artist and DC Moore Gallery, New York.

join us, sitting comfortably on Romy's lap during most of my visits. In addition to offering advice, Bearden also gave me works of art to add to my personal collection, including *Morning*.

On May 10, 1980, Bearden was one among some fifteen or more African-American artists who came to the opening of my first solo exhibition in New York City. He purchased a small watercolor but later graciously gave it up and allowed Norma Darden, a former model and current restaurateur, to buy the work after she expressed interest in owning it. In that exhibition, I displayed a collage titled *Homage to Romare Bearden* (ca. 1974). Bearden took me aside and expressed his delight at my facility with collage and the respect I had for him as an artist. But he said to me with ease, "David, this is not you; your strength lies in these colorful works," one of which was the small watercolor he had chosen to purchase. He continued by saying, "Yes, do pursue collage as a medium, but search for your own voice in it." This was an important lesson, instructing me, a fifty-year-old artist, with respect and humility, to seek my own vision with collage. And with that advice I began pursuing another way of working with collage as a medium, painting abstract images over a canvas or sheet of paper and tearing it into strips before forming the various shapes horizontally or vertically. In the summer of 1980 I spent two months as a fellow at Yaddo in Saratoga Springs, New York, working on the strip collage, a technique I still use in my work (fig. 51). When I reported my direction with the medium to Bearden, he was highly congratulatory.

Although we saw each other on several occasions thereafter before his death in 1988, my final visit to his studio in Astoria, Queens, was on May 12, 1984. I took the portrait painter Simmie Knox along to meet Romy. We visited for about two and a half hours. Simmie took several photographs of the two of us both inside and outside the studio. When I left, Romy presented me with a gift: *Woman and Child Reading* (Plate 10).

I have only briefly touched on the richness of the influence Bearden had on my career as an artist and writer. Bearden's creative journey was filled with extraordinary discoveries. He became well known as a young writer in the 1930s through voicing his concerns about the racial agenda he thought was imposed on black artists by the Harmon Foundation. While admitting that the patronage these artists received from the foundation was a major catalyst in bringing black artists from around the nation together in exhibitions sponsored by the foundation in the late 1920s and early 1930s, Bearden questioned the organization's motives in racializing art.

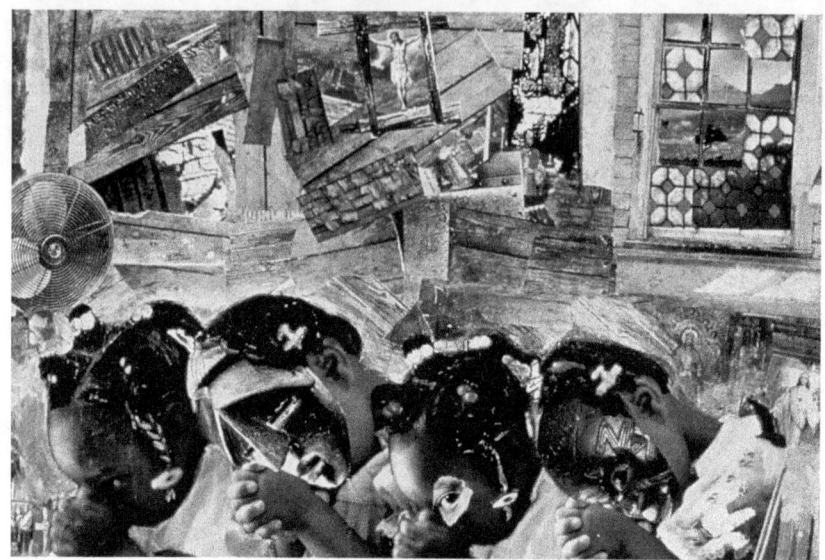

FIGURE 52 Jefferson Pinder, *Four Girls/White Jesus*, 2000, mixed media.
Courtesy of Jefferson Pinder

In the 1940s and 1950s, Bearden moved in and out of critical circles while developing his own creative voice, primarily as an artist who had an interest in both the figural and the abstract traditions and painting. He gained independence in the 1960s and 1970s by advancing a renewed interest in collage as a limitless medium of expression. By selecting collage as his principal medium, Bearden forged ahead with new methods of painterly activity. His introduction of the composite photostat image, collaged with painted elements, helped provide the crossover Bearden needed to establish unique visual aesthetic.

The originality and power of these works in collage and related media, from the hand of an individual who was both an artist and a humanist, helped make Romare Bearden one of the nation's most acclaimed African-American artists in the last quarter of the twentieth century. Bearden's lasting influence across racial and generational lines is evident both among artists who worked during his lifetime and among a new generation of artists at the opening of the twenty-first century, such as Jefferson Pinder (fig. 52). Bearden's critical and creative expression meshed memorably into a personal style that created an indelible imprint in American art.

# NOTES

From Ruth Fine and Jacqueline Francis, eds., *Romare Bearden: American Modernist* (Washington, DC: National Gallery of Art, 2011).

1. On the Spiral Group, see Jeanne Siegel, "Why Spiral?" *ARTnews 65* (September 1966): 48–51, 67–68; Romare Bearden and Henry Henderson, *A History of African-American Artists: From 1792 to the Present* (New York: Pantheon Books, 1993), 400–403; Floyd Coleman, "The Changing Same: Spiral, the Sixties. And African-American Art," in William E. Taylor et al., *A Shared Heritage: Art by Four African Americans* (Indianapolis, IN: Indianapolis Museum of Art, 1966), 148–58.

2. All dates are based on personal diaries and calendars.

# SELECTED REFERENCES

Arabindan-Kesson, Anna. "Rewriting the Modern: New Perspectives on Romare Bearden and Archibald Motley." *Journal of American Studies* 50, no. 1 (February 2016): E1. doi: 10.1017/S0021875815001954.

Bearden, Romare, and Carl Holty. *The Painter's Mind: A Study of the Relations of Structure and Space in Painting.* New York: Crown, 1969.

Bearden, Romare, and Harry Henderson. *A History of African-American Artists, from 1792 to the Present.* New York: Pantheon, 1993.

Bearden, Romare, Sam Gilliam, Richard Hunt, Jacob Lawrence, Tom Lloyd, William Williams, and Hale Woodruff. "The Black Artist in America: A Symposium." *The Metropolitan Museum of Art Bulletin* 27, no. 5 (1969): 245–61.

*Bearden Plays Bearden.* Dir. Nelson E. Breen. St. Petersburg, FL: Third World Cinema, 1981.

Bergen, Jonathan, and Diana Dimodica Sweet. *Romare Bearden, 1911–1988: A Memorial Exhibition.* New York: ACA Galleries, 1989.

Berman, Avis. "Oral History Interview with Romare Bearden, 1980 July 31." Archives of American Art. Smithsonian Institution, Washington, DC.

Breen, Nelson E. "To Hear Another Language: A Conversation with Alvin Ailey, James Baldwin, Romare Bearden and Albert Murray." *Callaloo* 12, no. 3 (Summer 1989): 431–52.

Calvin Tomkins Papers. The Museum of Modern Art Archives, New York.

Campbell, Mary Schmidt. *An American Odyssey: The Life and Work of Romare Bearden.* New York: Oxford University Press, 2018.

Cinque Gallery Records, 1959–2010, bulk 1976–2004. Archives of American Art. Smithsonian Institution, Washington, DC.

Corlett, Mary Lee. *From Process to Print: Graphic Works by Romare Bearden*. Petaluma: Pomegranate, 2009.

Dawes, Kwame Senu Neville, Matthew Shenoda, and Derek Walcott, eds. *Bearden's Odyssey: Poets Respond to the Art of Romare Bearden*. Evanston, IL: TriQuarterly Books/ Northwestern University Press, 2017.

English, Darby. "Ralph Ellison's Romare Bearden." *Studies in the History of Art* 71 (2011): 11–25.

Fine, Ruth. *The Art of Romare Bearden*. Washington, DC: National Gallery of Art in association with Harry H. Abrams, New York, 2003.

Fine, Ruth, and Jacqueline Francis, eds. *Romare Bearden, American Modernist*. Washington, DC: National Gallery of Art in association with Yale University Press, New Haven, 2011.

Fitzpatrick, Tracy, with Lowery Stokes Sims. *Romare Bearden: Abstraction*. Purchase, NY: Neuberger Museum of Art, 2017.

Gelburd, Gail, and Alex Rosenberg. *A Graphic Odyssey: Romare Bearden as Printmaker*. Philadelphia: University of Pennsylvania Press, 1992.

Glazer, Lee Stephens. "Signifying Identity: Art and Race in Romare Bearden's Projections." *The Art Bulletin* 76, no. 3 (1994): 411–26.

Greene, Carroll, ed. *Romare Bearden: The Prevalence of Ritual*. New York: Museum of Modern Art, 1971.

Greene, Nikki A. "Riffing the Index: Romare Bearden and the Hand of Jazz." In *Music, Art and Performance from Liszt to Riot Grrrl: The Musicalization of Art*, edited by Diane V. Silverthorne, 183–202. London: Bloomsbury, 2018.

Hage, Emily. "Reconfiguring Race, Recontextualizing the Media: Romare Bearden's 1968 *Fortune* and *Time* Covers." *Art Journal* 75, no. 3 (2016): 37–51.

Hanzal, Carla M. et al., *Romare Bearden: Southern Recollections*. Charlotte, NC: Mint Museum, 2011.

Harris-Kelley, Diedra. "Revisiting Romare Bearden's Art of Improvisation." In *Uptown Conversation: The New Jazz Studies*, edited by Robert G. O'Meally, Brent Hayes Edwards, and Farah Jasmine Griffin, 249–55. New York: Columbia University Press, 2004.

Hatch, James, and Camille Billops. "A Conversation with Mr. Romare Bearden." The Hatch-Billops Oral History Collection of Black Culture. New York, (recording) no. 16, December 6, 1972.

Haynes, Lauren, Jessica Lott, Samir S. Patel, Romare Bearden, and Studio Museum in Harlem, eds. *The Bearden Project*. New York: The Studio Museum in Harlem, 2012.

Hills, Patricia. "Cultural Legacies and the Transformation of the Cubist Collage Aesthetic by Romare Bearden, Jacob Lawrence, and Other African-American Artists." *Studies in the History of Art* 71 (2011): 221–47.

Howe, Susan. "Romare Bearden at Cordier & Ekstrom." *Art in America* 64 (November–December 1976): 122.

Kelly, June. "Romare Bearden." *International Review of African-American Art* 9 (1991): 19–27.

Kroiz, Lauren. "Relocating Romare Bearden's Berkeley: Capturing Berkeley's Colorful Diversity." *Boom: A Journal of California* 6, no. 3 (September 1, 2016): 50–57.

Lamm, Kimberly. "Visuality and Black Masculinity in Ralph Ellison's 'Invisible Man' and Romare Bearden's Photomontages." *Callaloo* 26, no. 3 (2003): 813–35.

Levy, Aidan. "The Quilt of Romare Bearden's Life." *The Nation*, July 13, 2018. https://www.thenation.com/article/the-quilt-of-romare-bearden-life/.

Marsalis, Branford. *Romare Bearden Revealed.* Cambridge: Marsalis Music/Rounder Records, 2003. With liner notes by Robert G. O'Meally.

O'Meally, Robert G. *Romare Bearden: A Black Odyssey.* New York: DC Moore Gallery, 2007.

Patton, Sharon F. *Memory and Metaphor: Romare Bearden, 1940–1987.* New York: Studio Museum in Harlem in association with Oxford University Press, 1991.

Payne, Les. "America's Greatest (Overlooked) Artist." *New York Newsday,* January 17, 1981, 6–11, 18–20.

Pinder, Kymberly N. "Deep Waters: Rebirth, Transcendence, and Abstraction in Romare Bearden's Passion of Christ." *Studies in the History of Art* 71 (2011): 143–65.

Powell, Richard, ed. *Conjuring Bearden.* Durham, NC: Nasher Museum of Art at Duke University. Distributed by Duke University Press, 2006.

Price, Richard, and Sally Price. *Romare Bearden: The Caribbean Dimension.* Philadelphia: University of Pennsylvania Press, 2006.

Romare Bearden Foundation. *Romare Bearden in the Modernist Tradition: Essays from the Romare Bearden Foundation.* New York: Romare Bearden Foundation. Distributed by Distributed Art Publishers, 2008.

Romare Bearden Papers. Romare Bearden Foundation, New York.

Romare Bearden Papers, 1933–79. Archives of American Art, Smithsonian Institution, Washington, DC.

*Romare Bearden: Visual Jazz.* Directed by David Irving. New York, 1996.

Rowell, Charles H. "Inscription at the City of Brass: An Interview with Romare Bearden." *Callaloo* 11, no. 3 (Summer 1988): 428–46.

Rowell, Charles H., ed. "In Memoriam: Romare Bearden" [Special section]. *Callaloo* 11, no. 3 (Summer 1988): 401–46.

Schwartzman, Myron. *Romare Bearden: His Life and Art.* New York: Abrams, 1990.

Shange, Ntozake, and Romare Bearden. *I Live in Music.* New York: Stewart, Tabori & Chang, 1994.

Sheldon Ross Gallery records, 1970–2007, bulk 1976–1995. Archives of American Art. Smithsonian Institution, Washington, DC.

Siegel, Jeanne. "How Effective Is Social Protest Art (Civil Rights)." In *Artwords: Discourse on the '60s and '70s*. Ann Arbor: UMI Research Press, 1985.

Siegel, Jeanne. "Romare Bearden: The Unknown American Negro Artist." In *Artwords: Discourse on the '60s and '70s*. Ann Arbor: UMI Research Press, 1985.

Stewart, Frank. *Romare Bearden*. San Francisco: Pomegranate, 2004.

Walcott, Derek, Romare Bearden, Michael Bixler, and Winifred Bixler. *The Caribbean Poetry of Derek Walcott and the Art of Romare Bearden*. New York: Limited Editions Club, 1983.

Washington, M. Bunch. *The Art of Romare Bearden: The Prevalence of Ritual*. New York: Abrams, 1973.

Young, Kevin. "Watching the Good Trains Go By: A Suite of Poems to Accompany Collages by Romare Bearden." *The Virginia Quarterly Review* 80, no. 1 (2004): 58–79.

# INDEX

*Italic* page numbers refer to illustrations; numbers such as *p1* refer to the color plates.

African art (continued)
on, 141–42; masking and, 5, 13, 39,
165–68; myth and, 164–65, 168–69;
"primitivism" and, 148–49; ritual and,
96. *See also* Dogon mother and child;
Igbo Ikenga figure; Luba-Shankadi
figure; Mbagani mask; Senufo female
figure; Senufo rhythm pounder
*African Forum* (magazine), 318
Africobra, 232
*Afro-American* (newspaper). *See*
*Baltimore Afro-American*
Afro-American Presence in the Arts,
Past and Present from North Carolina
Collections (exhibition, 1982), 335
Albert Loeb Gallery, Paris, 335
album covers (Bearden), 334, 349n123
Ali, Muhammad, 11
Allen, Sam, 42, 57–58
*All the Things You Are* (Bearden), 367, 376
Alston, Charles, 19, 37, 38–39, 63, 64, 83,
95, 157, 220, 226; *Blues Singer*, 225;
*Walking*, 227
Alvin Ailey American Dance Theater,
329, 345n88, 352, 361n3
American Academy and Institute of Arts
and Letters, 32
American Artists Congress, 220
American Dream, 11
American identity, 46–47, 133–34
*American Mercury* (magazine), 145
Amos, Emma, 227, 262, 318, 381
Ancient Greece, race and, 271–75
*Anderson Materials* (Bearden), 382
Andrews, Benny, 232
Angelou, Maya, 307
Apollo Theater, 14, 40–41, 43, 206, 220,
225
*Approaching Storm, The* (Bearden), 127,
128

Archives of American Art, Smithsonian
Institution, Washington, D.C., 5,
345n88
Arendt, Hannah, 16, 43–44, 58
Aristotle, *Nicomachean Ethics*, 263
Armstrong, Louis, 7, 31, 53, 166, 239, 253
art activism, 121–23
*Art in America*, 372
Art Institute of Chicago, 137
*ARTnews*, 354
Art Nouveau, 80
Art of the American Negro (exhibition,
1966), 51–52, 81–82
Arts and Letters Society of Chicago, 153n6
*Arts Magazine*, 323
Art Students League, New York, 3, 19, 36,
60–61, 117n11, 220–21, 256–57
Ashton, Dore, 66
Asian art, 21
Association for the Advancement of
Creative Musicians, 264
Astoria. *See* Long Island City studio
*At Connie's Inn* (Bearden), 354
athletics, 46; baseball, 9, 35–36; boxing,
10–11; football, 9, 371; identity and,
9–11; jazz and, 10; race and, 9–11, 74
Atlanta University, 72, 77, 93
*At Low Tide* (Bearden), 360, 376
Attaway, William "Bill," 55–56
*At the Savoy* (Bearden), 31
*Autumn* (Bearden and Thibault), 375
*Autumn Lamp* (Bearden), 369–71, 377n7
*Autumn of the Rooster* (Bearden), 332
avant-garde: art, 224, 242, 245–46;
publications, 140, 204, 221; and
collage, 287, 294n10

Bachelard, Gaston, 282
Baegert, Derick, 118n15
Bailey, Eugene, 2

Carnegie-Mellon University, 162

*Carnival Begins, The* (Bearden), 359–60, 360

carnivals, 45, 103

*Carolina Blue* (Bearden), 319–21, 320, 334–35

*Carolina Shout* (Bearden), 31, 250

cartooning, 2–3, 5, 18, 25n6, 54–55, 122; for the *Baltimore Afro-American*, 35–36, 121, 317; for New York University's *Medley*, 35, 317; printmaking and, 317. *See also* Campbell, Elmer Simms

Catlett, Elizabeth, 95, 220–21

Cato, Minta, 35, 42

Cervantes, Miguel de, 60

Cézanne, Paul, 53, 109; *Still Life with Skull*, 259–60

Chagall, Marc, 275

chaos, as redeemed by art, 165–66, 188, 207, 259

charisma, of Bearden's figures, 8–9

Charlotte, North Carolina: in Bearden's art 15, 59–60, 166, 284, 380; in Bearden's childhood, 2, 33, 54 59–60, 165, 281, 380; Mint Museum in, 254n5, 317, 364. *See also* Mecklenburg County

*Charlotte Observer*, 372

Cheek, Sheldon, 273

Chicago, Illinois: African American population of, 134, 153n3; Africobra in, 232; Association for the Advancement of Creative Musicians in, 264; the twenties in, 135, 137, 142, 148. *See also* Art Institute of Chicago; Arts and Letters Society of Chicago

*Chicago Defender*, 34–35

Chicago Women's Club, 137, 153n7

Childs, Charles, 66

Chinese art, 252; landscape painting, 45, 49, 80, 123, 232

Chinese calligraphy, 3, 21, 45

Chirico, Giorgio de, 107, 119n19

Christopher Street, New York, 47, 64, 226, 227, 262

Cincinnati Museum, 83

Cinque Gallery, New York, 52

Circe, 13; adornments of, 276; in Bearden's *A Black Odyssey* series, 270–79; on drinking cups (skyphoi), 273, 274; in Morrison's *Song of Solomon*, 270–75, 277–79; names of, 276, 277–78; Odysseus and, 270–79; in *Smoke of Circe*, 120n33; voice of, 277; Yarnall on, 273–75. *See also* black Circe; *Untitled* ("Black Circe")

City College of New York, 51, 81–82

Civil Rights movement, 50, 256–57; art history and, 18–19; black freedom movement and, 9–10, 279; Black Power movement and, 179, 279; Harlem Renaissance and, 143–44; NAACP and, 97–98, 153n6, 332; New Negro Movement and, 94–98; in sixties, 178–79, 226; Spiral group and, 47, 226, 261, 287–88, 292; as weakening cultural memory, 303, 305

Civil War, 307–14

Clark, Kenneth, 259

Clausewitz, Carl von, 258–59

Cloisters, The, New York, 117

collaboration, 3, 18–19, 25n2; politics and, 257, 261–64; in printmaking, 315; in Spiral group, 47–48, 262. *See also* Henderson, Harry; Holty, Carl; Murray, Albert; Thibault, Andre; Walcott, Derek

collage, 1–2, 4–6; African American identity and, 23–24, 50–51, 187–88, 191, 192–94, 287; in art history, 188–91, 287, 294n10; avant-garde use of, 287,

Lincoln Theatre, 240
Lindley, Lucia Woods, 331
Lindsay, Vachel, 145
linen, 123
linoleum block prints, 317
Lipson, Karin, 335–36
liquidity, 178–84
literary culture, 11–12
literary influence, 4–5, 12–13, 40, 199
literature, 204; on art history, 73–74; classical Greek, 270–79; music and, 8; naturalism in, 148; portrayal of blacks in, 147–48; reading habits and, 60; Russian, 21
lithographs, 91, 316–17, 331–34, 338n10, 346n100. *See also* printmaking
Locke, Alain L., 140–43, 146, 150, 221, 230–31; *The Negro in Art*, 222
Long Island City studio, 78–79, 331 ("Queens"), 339n23, 363–64, 371–72, 383, 385 ("Astoria")
Lorca, García, 37, 204, 223; "Lament for Ignacio Sánchez Mejías," 40, 199
Lorenzetti, Ambrogio, 124, 244
Loring, John, 323–24, 335
Los Angeles County Museum of Art, 383
Luba-Shankadi figure, 167–68, *167*
Luks, George, 94
Lutherville, Maryland, 2, 50, 281

Mack, Connie, 9
MacKay, Hugh, 329, 344n85
*Magpie, The* (magazine), 121
Maiorano, Steve, 345n88, 346n91
Majors, William, 318
Malraux, André, 60, 196
Manet, Édouard, 369
Mann, Thomas, 162–63
Maran, René, *Batouala*, 148

marriage, 44, 47, 282; for gypsies, 68. *See also* Bearden, Nanette Rohan
Marshall, Kerry James, 11
Martinique, 69–70
Maschal, Richard, 372
mask: in African art, 165–67; Ellison on, 230; identity and, 13
masking, 5, 13, 39, 165–66
Masonite, 48–49, 125, 127, 228, 376
masquerade, 11
mastery, 197, 200, 205, 371–72, 377
Matisse, Henri, 3, 42, 101, 372–73
*Maudell Sleet's Magic Garden* (Bearden), 237, 254n5
Mayhew, Richard, 81–82, 83, 262, 265
Mayo, James, 383
Mbagani mask, 166–67, *167*
McKay, Claude, 13–14, 19, 36–39, 55–56, 94
McLuhan, Marshall, 299
*Mecklenburg Autumn* (Bearden), 333
Mecklenburg County, 250, 281, 348n114, 368, 373–74, 380
Melville, Herman, 60
Menashe, Samuel, 42
Mencken, H. L., 145–46, 154n24
*Messenger, The* (magazine), 138
Metropolitan Museum of Art, New York, 32, 48, 117n10
Mexican muralism, 3, 38, 222–23
migrations, 33, 50, 134–35, 188, 271, 279. *See also* Great Migration
military, 381–82; Bearden in, 40, 56, 57–58, 72, 91, 122, 134; black Americans in, 135; in *Li'l Dan the Drummer Boy: A Civil War Story*, 308–14
Miller, Flournoy, 240
minstrel shows, 92–93, 145
Mint Museum, Charlotte, 254n5, 317, 364
Miró, Joan, 99–100, 101, 106, 107–9, 117n3

"primitivism," 103, 116, 142, 147–50, 154n30

Princenthal, Nancy, 372

printmaking, 4, 6; with Blackburn, 316–17, 318, 321–25, 338n11; collage and, 319–36; collagraphs and, 316–17, 325–27, 336, 338n10, 343n68, 346n95; Cordier & Ekstrom gallery and, 319, 335; critics on, 335–36; etching and, 318–19, 321–24; with Henning, 330, 346n95; inconsistency in prints, 339n22; with Khalil, 321, 324–25, 330–31, 334, 340nn37–38, 346n98; with Kleineman, 317, 328–29, 331–34, 347n107, 349n119; linoleum block prints, 317; lithographs, 91, 316–17, 331–34, 338n10, 346n100; monotypes, 324–25, 335; music and, 327–31; myth and, 328–29; with New York Institute of Technology Print Workshop, 329–30; photography and, 317, 331; political cartoons, 317; producers and workshops for, 317; Projections and, 317–18; proofing process in, 330–31; ritual and, 328–29, 336–37; Romare Bearden: Collages and Prints (exhibition, 1987), 336; techniques, 316; Twenty-Five Contemporary American Artists as Printmakers (exhibition, 1966), 318

Printmaking Workshop, 321–25, 341n41, 341n43, 345n88

Prints and Watercolors by Romare Bearden (exhibition, 1981), 335

process: for collage, 284, 382; creative, 14–19, 252–53; deciding what to paint, 14–16; finishing art, 104–5; having trouble with, 105; metaphor and, 315–16; proofing, 330–31; transformation and, 317–18; when and where to paint, 78–79

Profile/Part I, The Twenties (Mecklenburg County), Conjur Woman and the Virgin (Bearden), 296, 298, 301

Profile/Part I, The Twenties (Mecklenburg County): The Daybreak Express (Bearden), 15, 16

Profile/Part I, The Twenties (Pittsburgh Memories): Farewell Eugene (Bearden), 215, 215–16, 237

Profile/Part I, The Twenties (Pittsburgh Memories): The Mill Hand's Lunch Bucket (Bearden), 176, 176

Profile/Part II, The Thirties: Artist with Painting and Model (Bearden), 5, p1

Profile/Part II, The Thirties: I'm Slapping Seventh Avenue with the Sole of My Shoe (Bearden), 12, 12

Projections, 49, 125–26; black Americans on, 65–66; conjure in, 291–92, 297–98; Cordier & Ekstrom gallery and, 32, 48, 65–66, 317; critics on, 65–66; politics and, 257–58, 260–61; printmaking and, 317–18; reactions to, 65–66; social activism and, 256–57; Spiral group and, 65–66, 217, 227–30

proofing process, 330–31

prostitution, 14–15, 33–34, 38, 43, 212, 213–14

protest, 50–51, 259–60

Providence Art Club, 84

public art, 2–3

pulses, 5, 166, 172. See also rhythm

Purdy, Claude, 175–76

Queens studio. See Long Island City studio

quilting, 22, 186, 188–90, 194, 316, 333; conjur woman and, 302–5; women and, 194, 302–5

Quirt, Walter, 37, 119n26

Ter Borch, Gerard, 64, 130
theater, 138, 158, 301, 334; Alvin Ailey
    American Dance Theater, 345n88,
    352; Apollo Theater, 14, 40–41, 206;
    Broadway, 240; Lafayette Theatre, 240;
    Lincoln Theatre, 240; Savoy Ballroom,
    37, 240–41
Theater Owners' Booking Association,
    255n10
Thibault, Andre ("Teabo"), 363–64,
    371–76, 377n6
Thomas Segal Gallery, Boston, 374–75
Thome, Joel, 334
Thompson, Robert Farris, 195n6
Thompson, W. O., 153n6
Thomson, Virgil, 334
Thorpe, Carleton, 136
Threadgill, Henry, 8
306 studio (306 W. 141st St., New York),
    37, 157, 158, 220, 226; artists' group
    at, 37, 157, 261, 316. *See also* Alston,
    Charles; Bannarn, Henry
Thurman, Wallace, 138
"Time for the Bass" (Bearden), 185–86
Tintoretto, Jacopo, 209, 247–48
Tirca Karlis Gallery, Provincetown, 335
Tomkins, Calvin, 4–5, 17–18
Toulouse-Lautrec, Henri de, 2
Toynbee, Arnold, 96
tradition, 62–63, 189, 194; breaking
    conventions, 64–65; literary and blues,
    270–71
*Train, The* (Bearden), 289, 319, 322, 322–23
train imagery, 49–50, 125, 177, 186, 201–2,
    228, 287, 297–98, 374; blues and, 250
Transworld Art Corporation, 321, 323,
    342n44
travel, 69–71, 72, 179–80, 282, 351–52;
    living abroad, 76–77. *See also* Carib-
    bean; Paris, France

*Trojan War* (Bearden), 107, *108*
*Trombone Solo* (Bearden), 367
*Tropical Flowers* (Bearden), 321, 330
Turci, Maureen, 317, 332
turtles, 15
Twenty-Five Contemporary American
    Artists as Printmakers (exhibition,
    1966), 318
Two Centuries of Black American Art,
    1750–1950 (exhibition, 1976), 383
two-ness trope, 186–87. *See also* Du Bois,
    W. E. B.
291 gallery, New York, 118n13
*Two Women in a Harlem Courtyard*
    (Bearden), 22, 130, *131*, 330

Ulmer, Gregory, 190
Umbra Poets' Workshop, 264
Unicorn tapestries, 52, 102, 117n10
Universal Limited Art Editions, 316, 334
*Untitled* ("Black Circe") (Bearden),
    275–78, *p6*
*Untitled (Cityscape)* (Bearden), 382
*Untitled (Medallion Quilt)* (Bearden),
    302–3, *304*, 305
*Untitled (Southern Interior)* (Bearden),
    330
*Untitled: Duke and Billy* (Bearden),
    192–93
*Untitled Woman in the Garden* (Bearden),
    325

van Gogh, Vincent, 110
Van Vechten, Carl, 37
vaudeville, 241, 255nn9–10
Vermeer, Johannes, 7, 31, 47, 49, 64, 80,
    123, 124, 130, 244, 245
"vernacular imperative," 18
vision, artist's, 116, 200, 288–89
Vytlacil, Vaclav, 104, 118n14

Walcott, Derek, 4, 338n11, 352, 354–57, 361; *Omeros*, 357, 361
Waller, Fats, 31, 35, 53, 240
Walrond, Eric, 94
war: Civil War, 307–14; collage and, 287; World War I, 97, 122, 133, 134; World War II, 56
*War* (Bearden), 381–82
Waring, Laura Wheeler, 136
Warner, Marina, 299
watercolor, 32, 55, 121–22, 183, 184, 359–61; cityscape, 382
watermelon cakes, 50, 75
Webb, Chick, 158, 240; "Stomping at the Savoy" and, 238
Wescher, Herta, 190
Wesleyan University art gallery, 335
Wesselmann, Tom, 294n10
Western art, 163, 196, 271–73; beauty in, 302; racism of, 200; themes of, 49
White, Charles, 95, 97, 383
White, Stanford, 37, 138
Whitehead, Alfred North, 162
Whitney Museum, New York, 120n30, 194, 223
Williams, Robert, 313
Williams, William Carlos, 103–4, 118n12, 226
Williams, William T., 4
Wilson, August, 6, 7, 8, 209; *Joe Turner's Come and Gone*, 176–77; *The Piano Lesson*, 177
Wilson, Ellis, 83, 95
Winnekes, Katharina, 376
Wolfram, Eddie, 190
*Woman and Child Reading* (Bearden), 385, *p10*

*Woman in a Harlem Courtyard* (Bearden), 49
women: Bearden's identification with, 226; Chicago Women's Club, 137; conjur woman, as subject in Bearden's art, 284–87, 289–92, 296–305; Dogon Mother and Child and, 169–70; feminism and, 301–2; in Mysteries: Women in the Art of Romare Bearden (exhibition, 1975), 319, 325, 327; power women, 168–69, 301; quilting and, 194, 302–5; Senufo female figure, 168–69
Women: A Collaboration of Artists and Writers (exhibition, 1947; publication 1948), 103–4, 114, 118n12, 120n33, 226
wood panels, 48–49
Woodruff, Hale, 64, 83, 93, 139–40, 143, 225, 226, 381
"woodshed, the," 18–19
Wordsworth, William, *Lyrical Ballads*, 373
Works Progress Administration (WPA), 36–37, 95, 220
World War I, 97, 122, 133, 134
World War II, 56
WPA. See Works Progress Administration
Wright, Richard, 12, 41, 361n3
Wu, Mr. (scholar), 45

Yale Art School, 156
Yarnall, Judith, *Transformations of Circe*, 273, 275, 278
YMCA, 158; in Brooklyn, 153n6; in Chicago, 136–37; in Harlem: 36, 157

Zervos, Christian, 119n27

www.ingramcontent.com/pod-product-compliance
Lightning Source LLC
Chambersburg PA
CBHW051209170526
45166CB00005B/1813